Africa in the New Trade Environment

Africa in the New Trade Environment

Market Access in Troubled Times

Souleymane Coulibaly, Woubet Kassa,
and Albert G. Zeufack, Editors

WORLD BANK GROUP

Contents

Figures

Maps

Tables

Foreword

Africa faces a global trade environment that is continuously changing, bringing new challenges and opportunities for increasing growth and reducing poverty. Some of these developments include the increased fragmentation of production across borders; the proliferation of regional trade agreements; the relative rise of Asia (East and South Asia) as the new economic frontier; the Fourth Industrial Revolution and subsequent rise of labor-saving technologies; and most recently the COVID-19 (coronavirus) pandemic. Given the relatively small size of their economies, African countries' effective participation in the ever-evolving international trade environment remains central to boosting the region's growth and development.

Africa's exports and imports of goods and services have achieved their fastest growth in the past decade but remain low in overall volume relative to other regions. To reduce poverty on a large scale and transform their economies, African countries must scale up and diversify their participation in international markets and global value chains (GVCs). The global economy is a source of growth that African economies cannot afford to ignore. To catch up with the rest of the world, there is no alternative: the continent must link its production and trade to the global economy to take advantage of the unlimited demand and innovation along the supply chain.

This effort calls for a comprehensive and dynamic approach that requires reexamination of existing trade to expand the region's export market access and diversify its markets to new regions and new products while also strengthening regional trade. Such an approach is exactly what this book presents. It is the outcome of a journey started with an expert panel discussion on the future of global trade and its impact on Africa during the World Bank Africa Knowledge Fest on February 22, 2017. During that event, Albert G. Zeufack, chief economist, Africa Region; Aaditya Mattoo, World Bank research manager, Trade and Integration; Maria Kiwanuka, senior advisor to the president of Uganda; Annabel González, World Bank senior director, Trade and Competitiveness; Liu Yong, chief economist, Chinese Development Bank; and Lemma Senbet, executive director, African Economic Research Consortium, discussed the following questions:

- What are the trade and investment patterns in Africa over the past 20 years?
- What role has China played in these trends?
- Why is intra-African trade so low? What must be done to expand it?
- Why is African trade still dominated by raw material trade? Can regional integration initiatives promote export diversification? Or should we focus on preferential agreements with advanced economies such as the EU and the US?
- Are African countries benefiting from preferential trade access, such as under the US African Growth and Opportunity Act (AGOA) and the EU's Everything but Arms (EBA) initiative? Is the heterogeneity of growth sources among Sub-Saharan African high-growth performers related to their divergence in benefiting from these preferential schemes?
- Are we seeing a sectoral shift in Africa? Is there a changing role between agriculture and manufacturing? Which service sectors are increasingly exported by Sub-Saharan African countries? What are the constraints to unleash the potential of trade in services?

Taking on these difficult questions, a team of renowned trade economists analyzed comprehensive trade data, using state-of-the-art techniques, to develop this book's proposed strategy to bolster Africa's market access within the current global environment. It explores three key areas: (a) evaluation of the impact of trade agreements (unilateral, regional, and multilateral) with traditional partners (the EU and the US), suggesting a way forward; (b) the role of new market frontiers in Asia from the perspective of both restructuring African economies and understanding the changes in GVCs and their implications for Africa; and (c) the promise and challenges of regional trade and regional value chains. The book meticulously explores ways to maximize Africa's access to the two leading world markets—the EU and the US—while at the same time diversifying its access to the emerging Asian market. It also calls for an anchoring of the continent's market access strategy in deeper regional integration during these troubled times.

Recent initiatives in the World Bank Central, Eastern, Southern, and Western Africa subregions that we have the honor to lead are aiming to improve the business environment, build infrastructure, and promote effective regulations and institutions to reduce the cost of trading within Africa and between Africa and its key trading partners. They are in line with this comprehensive approach to positioning Africa in the new trade environment, and we look forward to seeing other international financial institutions rally around this strategy to boost Africa's development prospects in the current global trade environment.

Ousmane Diagana
Vice President for Western
and Central Africa
The World Bank Group

Hafez Ghanem
Vice President for Eastern
and Southern Africa
The World Bank Group

Acknowledgments

This project was undertaken by a team led by Albert G. Zeufack, Souleymane Coulibaly, and Woubet Kassa. The editors are thankful to Hafez Ghanem and Ousmane Diagana for their guidance. Special thanks go to Caroline Freund (formerly the World Bank's Global Director of Trade, Investment and Competitiveness) and to Albert Muchanga (commissioner for trade and industry of the African Union Commission) for their support in the launch of the research project and for their participation in the initial seminar that influenced the direction of the project. The team is grateful for the management, guidance, and support provided by Aaditya Mattoo, who cochaired a series of technical meetings to review chapters of the report. The team is also grateful for the valuable contribution of the reviewers of the book: Bernard Hoekman, professor and director, Global Economics, at the Robert Schuman Centre for Advanced Studies, European University Institute in Florence, Italy; and Michele Ruta, lead economist in the Trade and Regional Integration unit of the Bank's Macroeconomics, Trade and Investment (MTI) Global Practice.

The book has benefited from a comprehensive analysis of trade data conducted by a team of renowned trade experts using state-of-the-art techniques. Contributors include Souleymane Coulibaly, Habtamu T. Edjigu, Ana M. Fernandes, Alejandro Forero Rojas, Woubet Kassa, Hiau Looi Kee, Hibret Maemir, Aaditya Mattoo, Daniel Mirza, Nama Ouattara, Heiwai Tang, Douglas Zhihua Zeng, and Albert G. Zeufack. Conversations with César Calderón are appreciated. We are grateful for the excellent work of the publishing team—Patricia Katayama, Steve Pazdan, Deborah Appel-Barker, and copy editor Mary Anderson—for their help with the publication and dissemination process, and Sandra Gain for the initial editing of the book.

About the Contributors

Editors

Souleymane Coulibaly is the lead economist and program leader in the Equitable Growth, Finance and Institutions (EFI) Practice Group for Brunei Darussalam, Malaysia, the Philippines, and Thailand. Before moving to Manila to serve in that role, he was the EFI lead economist and program leader for Central Africa, covering a diverse set of countries: Angola, Cameroon, the Central African Republic, the Democratic Republic of Congo, the Republic of Congo, Equatorial Guinea, Gabon, Nigeria, and São Tomé and Príncipe. His publications and ongoing research focus on the impact of geography on firms' location, trade flows, and regional integration. He was a coauthor of *World Development Report 2009: Reshaping Economic Geography*; contributed to *Global Economic Prospects 2005: Trade, Regionalism, and Development*; and has published many papers in peer-reviewed journals as well as coauthoring or coediting three other World Bank books: *Diversified Urbanization: The Case of Côte d'Ivoire* (2016); *Eurasian Cities: New Realities along the Silk Road* (2012); and *Trade Expansion through Market Connection: The Central Asian Markets of Kazakhstan, Kyrgyz Republic, and Tajikistan* (2011). Souleymane, from Côte d'Ivoire, holds a double doctoral degree in international trade and economic geography from Panthéon-Sorbonne University in Paris and the University of Lausanne.

Woubet Kassa is a research economist in the World Bank's Office of the Chief Economist for the Africa Region. Before serving in that role, he worked with the Trade and International Integration unit of the World Bank's Development Research Group. He is currently working on topics including international trade, global value chains, regional integration, and industrialization. He has authored or edited several recent

World Bank works: *Industrialization in Sub-Saharan Africa: Seizing Opportunities in Global Value Chains* (2021); "Mobile Access Expansion and Price Information Diffusion: Firm Performance after Ethiopia's Transition to 3G in 2008" (2021); "Trade Creation and Trade Diversion in African RECs: Drawing Lessons for AfCFTA" (2021); and "COVID-19 and Trade in Africa: Impacts and Policy Response" (2020). Woubet holds a doctorate in economics from American University, where he is currently an adjunct professorial lecturer.

Albert G. Zeufack, a Cameroonian national, is the World Bank's chief economist for the Africa Region. Before his appointment in 2016, he was the practice manager in the World Bank's Macroeconomics and Fiscal Management Global Practice and leader of the Bank-wide community of practice for the Management of Natural Resources Rents. His main research interest is in the microfoundations of macroeconomics. He joined the World Bank in 1997 as a Young Professional and started his career as a research economist in the Macroeconomics and Growth unit of the Development Research Group. Since then, he has held several positions in the Africa, East Asia and Pacific, and Europe and Central Asia Regions. Between 2008 and 2012, on leave from the World Bank, he was the director of research and investment strategy and chief economist for Khazanah Nasional Berhad, a Malaysian sovereign wealth fund. He serves on the Technical Advisory Committee of the Natural Resource Charter at the University of Oxford, the Advisory Board of the Natural Resource Governance Institute, the United Nations Sustainable Development Solutions Network, and the board of the African Economic Research Consortium. Albert received his doctorate in economics from CERDI, the University of Clermont-Ferrand in France, where he taught before joining the World Bank. He holds a master's degree in economic analysis and policy from the University of Yaoundé, Cameroon, and has undertaken executive education at Harvard University and Stanford University.

Authors

Habtamu T. Edjigu is a consultant with the Macroeconomics, Trade and Investment Global Practice of the World Bank Group. He currently works on trade and global value chains in Central Africa. His research focuses on a range of issues related to trade and development, including firm productivity, deindustrialization, foreign direct investment, and regional integration. He holds a doctorate in economics from the University of Adelaide in Australia and a master's degree from the University of Copenhagen.

Ana M. Fernandes is a lead economist in the Trade and International Integration unit of the World Bank's Development Research Group. She joined the World Bank as a Young Professional in 2002. Her research examines the consequences of openness to trade and foreign direct investment for firm-level outcomes such as productivity, innovation, quality upgrading, and more broadly the determinants of firm performance, including the role of the business environment. She has also worked on professional services in Africa and on agglomeration of manufacturing industries in India. Recently her work has focused on the impact evaluation of trade-related policy interventions (such as export promotion and customs reforms) as well as on exporter growth and dynamics and how it is linked to development and affected by policies. Since 2011, she has managed the World Bank's Exporter Dynamics Database, the first public database to provide detailed comparable information on the microstructure of trade flows between countries. She holds a doctorate in economics and two master's degrees from Yale University and a bachelor's degree from Universidade Nova de Lisboa, Portugal.

Alejandro Forero Rojas is a researcher in the Trade and International Integration unit of the World Bank's Development Research Group. Previously, he worked in the Research Department of the Inter-American Development Bank and as a consultant on trade, competitiveness, and education research projects in Colombia. He holds a master's degree and a bachelor's degree, both in economics, from the Universidad de los Andes, Bogotá, Colombia.

Hiau Looi Kee is a lead economist with the Trade and International Integration unit of the World Bank's Development Research Group. Her research focuses on trade, productivity, and growth at the firm and aggregate levels. Her current projects include studying the domestic value added in exports; the shared-supplier spillovers of foreign direct investment; rules of origin and firm productivity in Bangladesh's garment sector; and large-scale estimations of import demand elasticities, ad valorem equivalents of nontariff measures, and trade restrictiveness indexes. Her work has been published in many general interest economics journals and top field journals, including *American Economic Review*, *Journal of International Economics*, *Review of Economics and Statistics*, *Economic Journal*, and *European Economic Review*. She holds a doctorate in economics from the University of California, Davis.

Hibret Maemir is an economist in the Enterprise Analysis unit of the World Bank's Global Indicators Group. His areas of specialization are development economics and international trade, and specific research interests include the sources of productivity differences at the firm, industry, and country level; the sources and effects of business regulatory reforms; and the effects of trade and investment liberalization on various firm-level and macroeconomic outcomes. He holds a doctorate in economics from Maastricht University.

Aaditya Mattoo is chief economist of the World Bank's East Asia and Pacific Region. He specializes in development, trade, and international cooperation and provides policy advice to governments. He was also codirector of the Bank's *World Development Report 2020: Trading for Development in the Age of Global Value Chains*. Previously he was research manager of the Trade and Integration unit of the Bank's Development Research Group. Before he joined the Bank, Aaditya was economic counselor at the World Trade Organization and taught economics at the University of Sussex and Churchill College, Cambridge University. He has published on development, trade, trade in services, and international trade agreements in academic and other journals; and his work has been cited in *The Economist*, *Financial Times*, *The New York Times*, and *Time* magazine. He holds a doctorate in economics from the University of Cambridge and a master's degree in economics from the University of Oxford.

Daniel Mirza is a professor of economics at the University of Tours, France. He specializes in international trade and more broadly in globalization issues. He is also the codirector of the International Trade and Sustainable Development (EI2D) department at the Orléans Economics Laboratory (LÉO), a National Center for Scientific Research (CNRS) University of Orléans lab. Previously, he served as the director of the Economics Department of the University of Tours (2012–16) and as president of the Research in International Economics and Finance (RIEF) network (2009–14). He is currently a research associate at the Institute for Research on the International Economy (CEPII), a research associate at the Center for Economic Research and Its Applications (CEPREMAP), and a Globalisation and Economic Policy (GEP) associate at Nottingham University.

Nama Ouattara is a field research coordinator consultant for the World Bank Group's office in Guinea and a research associate for the China Africa Research Initiative of the Johns Hopkins School of Advanced International Studies. She is an expert in development economics with a concentration in South-South cooperation. Her research focuses on how African countries can capitalize on their partnerships with China, with the aim of evaluating policies. She has 10 years of experience teaching macroeconomics, sustainable development, and international trade at the graduate and undergraduate levels. Nama has worked for national and international institutions including Mali's Ministry of Foreign Affairs, France's Agence Française de Développement, and the International Monetary Fund. She holds a doctorate in economics from Paris Sud University and a master's degree from Panthéon-Sorbonne University in Paris.

Heiwai Tang is professor of economics and associate director of the Institute for China and Global Development at the University of Hong Kong (HKU). Previously, he was tenured associate professor of international economics at the Johns Hopkins School of Advanced International Studies. He is also affiliated with the Federal Reserve Bank of Dallas and the Center of Economic Studies and Ifo Institute (CESIfo) in Munich, and is a research fellow of the Nottingham (UK) Centre for Research on Globalisation and Economic Policy. He has been a consultant to the World Bank, International Finance Corporation, United Nations, and Asian Development Bank and has held visiting positions at the International Monetary Fund, Stanford University, MIT Sloan School of Management, Harvard University, and the Research Institute of Economy, Trade and Industry (RIETI). He is currently on the editorial boards of the *Journal of International Economics*, *Journal of Comparative Economics*, and *China Economic Review*.

Douglas Zhihua Zeng is a senior economist at the World Bank and a global expert on spatial economy, technology innovation, and industrial competitiveness. Since joining the World Bank in 1998, his work has spanned numerous countries in the East Asia and Pacific, Africa, Latin America and the Caribbean, and Europe and Central Asia regions. His peer-reviewed papers and books (including coauthored or edited titles) include *Promoting Dynamic and Innovative Growth in Asia: The Cases of Special Economic Zones and Business Hubs* (2016); "Special Economic Zones: Lessons from the Global Experience" (2016); *Building Engines for Growth and Competitiveness in China: Experiences with SEZs and Industrial Clusters* (2010); *Promoting Enterprise-Led Innovation in China* (2009); and *Knowledge, Technology, and Cluster-Based Growth in Africa* (2008), among others. Before joining the World Bank, he was an economist at the Chinese Academy of Social Sciences and a Ford Foundation Scholar at Stanford University.

Abbreviations

ACP	Organisation of African, Caribbean, and Pacific Group of States
AfCFTA	African Continental Free Trade Area
Africa-5	Ethiopia, Ghana, Kenya, Nigeria, and Tanzania
AGOA	African Growth and Opportunity Act (US)
Asia-5	Bangladesh, Cambodia, China, India, and Vietnam
AVE	ad valorem equivalent
BACI	Database for International Trade Analysis
CAFTA	Central American Free Trade Agreement
CEN-SAD	Community of Sahel-Saharan States
CGE	computable general equilibrium
COMESA	Common Market for Eastern and Southern Africa
DFTP	Duty-Free Tariff Preference (India)
DVA	domestic value added
EBA	Everything but Arms (EU)
ECCAS	Economic Community of Central African States
ECOWAS	Economic Community of West African States
EPA	economic partnership agreement
EU	European Union
FATS	Foreign Affiliates Trade in Services (OECD database)
FDI	foreign direct investment
FTA	free trade area
GDP	gross domestic product
GNP	gross national product
GSP	Generalized System of Preferences (EU and US)
G-20	Group of Twenty
GVC	global value chain
HS	Harmonized System

ICT	information and communication technology
ISIC	International Standard Industrial Classification
LDCs	least developed countries
LMICs	low- and middle-income countries
MFA	Multifiber Arrangement
MFN	most favored nation
NAFTA	North American Free Trade Agreement
NTB	nontariff barrier
NTM	nontariff measure
OECD	Organisation for Economic Co-operation and Development
OLS	ordinary least squares
PTA	preferential trade agreement
R&D	research and development
REC	regional economic community
RPM	relative preference margin
SADC	Southern African Development Community
SCM	synthetic control method
SPS	sanitary and phytosanitary (measures)
STR	Services Trade Restrictions (World Bank database)
STRI	Services Trade Restrictiveness Index
3-D	three-dimensional
TBT	technical barrier to trade
TFP	total factor productivity
UN	United Nations
UNCTAD	United Nations Conference on Trade and Development
UNIDO	United Nations Industrial Development Organization
UNWTO	World Tourism Organization (United Nations)
USITC	US International Trade Commission
WAEMU	West African Economic and Monetary Union
WTO	World Trade Organization

All dollar amounts are US dollars (US$) unless otherwise indicated.

Market Access Strategy in a New Trade Environment

Souleymane Coulibaly, Woubet Kassa, and Albert G. Zeufack

Introduction

Sub-Saharan Africa faces an international trade environment that is ever changing, bringing new challenges and opportunities for increasing growth and reducing poverty. Among the latest developments, the COVID-19 (coronavirus) pandemic since January 2020 has crippled economies around the world—including in Africa—through the direct health shock, the effects of pandemic containment measures on domestic economies, and the consequent disruption of global trade in goods and services.

Even before COVID-19 struck, however, a steady string of developments had been affecting the trade environment faced by African economies. These included the resurgence of protectionist rhetoric, a global economic slowdown, proliferation of regional trade agreements at the expense of the global trading system (as represented by the World Trade Organization), increased global fragmentation of production across borders, and the Fourth Industrial Revolution (whose disruptive, labor-saving technologies include the Internet of Things, artificial intelligence, and advanced robotics).

The effective participation of Sub-Saharan African countries in this ever-evolving global trade environment remains central to boosting growth and development in the region. Indeed, the economic growth success stories of the recent past (including China, the Republic of Korea, and Malaysia) are largely attributed to their participation in international trade. Participation of firms in global trade is effective in spreading the benefits of new technology to improve overall welfare (Melitz 2003; Segerstrom 2013). Increased access to foreign markets yields increases in productivity and is central to industrialization prospects and job creation.

Because of these gains from trade as well as the special economic challenges that low- and middle-income countries (LMICs) face, preferential treatment has been considered as the most strategic instrument to promote export-led development in such economies. In 2000, the United States launched the African Growth and Opportunity Act (AGOA), specifically aimed at Sub-Saharan African countries. A year later, the European Union (EU) put into effect the Everything but Arms (EBA) preference, focusing on all least developed economies.[1] By the sheer size of these two global markets, there were heightened expectations of the AGOA's and EBA's impact on trade and growth. Yet rigorous evaluations of these preference schemes at the aggregate and product levels (using synthetic control methods and difference-in-differences analysis) show mixed results. The utilization rates for these preferences are also found to be systematically low.

This book suggests a strategic shift: while trying to maximize gains from these preferential schemes, Sub-Saharan African economies should undertake bold domestic structural reforms to scale up their supply capacity while also pursuing new market opportunities to secure market access. Indeed, with the rise of Asia as a solid third global market, exploring export opportunities in China, India, and the Association of Southeast Asian Nations (ASEAN) countries would seem to be a sound strategic move. However, given the generally small size of Sub-Saharan African economies, deeper regional integration, anchored around the continent's largest middle-income countries, is a prerequisite. To that end, Africa has embarked on the world's largest free trade project—the African Continental Free Trade Area (AfCFTA).

Recent Trade Dynamics in Sub-Saharan Africa

Sub-Saharan Africa's exports and imports of goods and services have grown rapidly over the past decade, but the volumes are still low. Though Africa accounts for a small share of global trade, the share of trade in the national income of most economies in the region is large relative to other regions. In 2019 the share of total exports in gross domestic product (GDP) was 30 percent in North America, 39 percent in South Asia, 53 percent in Sub-Saharan Africa, and 58 percent in East Asia and Pacific.[2] From 2000 to 2017, Africa's share of exports to the rest of the world made up 80–90 percent of its total exports, higher than any other region.

These data suggest the high dependence of the region's economy on international trade, making the region more vulnerable to external shocks. In the earlier phases of the COVID-19 pandemic, despite having a relatively low percentage of the world's confirmed cases, the region felt its severest economic shocks mainly through the channel of trade—pandemic-related demand and supply shocks in the region's major trading partners. Overall, Sub-Saharan Africa accounts for about 2 percent of global production and

3 percent of global trade in goods and for about 3 percent of the world's trade in services. These numbers put Sub-Saharan African trade into perspective within the global economy.

The trade dynamics of some of Sub-Saharan Africa's subregions since 2010 tell a more encouraging story about the region (figure O.1). Except for exports of goods from 2015 through 2019, Sub-Saharan Africa's trade has, by and large, grown faster than that of the world (figure O.1, panels c and d). The breakdown of exports by broad classification indicates the growth in exports of capital goods is much higher than the growth in either consumer or intermediate goods exports (figure O.1, panel e). When focusing on subregions and after 2009, East Africa's exports and imports of goods and services have grown systematically faster than those of Sub-Saharan Africa *or* the world (figure O.1, panels a and b). By contrast, Southern Africa's exports of goods have been performing on a par with the world average.

Over the past decade, Sub-Saharan Africa has diversified its major export destination markets. Although the region's share of exports of goods to Europe and North America represented 31 percent and 25 percent of its total goods exports, respectively, in 2005, those shares contracted to 25 percent and 20 percent in 2010 (figure O.2). Meanwhile, its share of goods exports to East Asian economies was steadily increasing. In addition, there was a continuous rise in intraregional trade, with a sharp rise just after 2009. Just after the peak of Sub-Saharan Africa's exports of goods in 2011, the top export destination for the region was Europe and Central Asia, followed by East Asia and Pacific, Sub-Saharan Africa, and North America.

However, these aggregate trends hide some idiosyncrasies. For instance, the sharp increase in Sub-Saharan Africa's exports to East Asia during 2010–14 was led by exports of fuels and lubricants. Conversely, the sharp decline in the region's exports to North America during 2011–14 resulted from a decline in the exports of fuels and lubricants.

A product group that is worth examining closely is the category of intermediate goods. Intraindustry trade in intermediate goods gives a rough indication of Sub-Saharan Africa's participation in global value chains (GVCs)—which, by design, is a source of productivity because the firms that are competitive at the global level tend to be the more productive ones (Melitz 2008).

Focusing on industrial supplies, Sub-Saharan Africa appears to be increasingly trading intraindustry intermediate goods with East Asia, as its exports and imports of industrial supplies to and from that region have significantly increased and been in sync since 2005 (figure O.3, panels c and d). Sub-Saharan Africa's exports of industrial supplies to the EU were more affected by the 2009 and 2014 commodity price crises and less in sync with the import flows, indicating that this trade was more tilted toward metal and mineral products.

Figure O.1   Changes in Regional and Global Trade Trends, Relative to 2005, in Sub-Saharan Africa

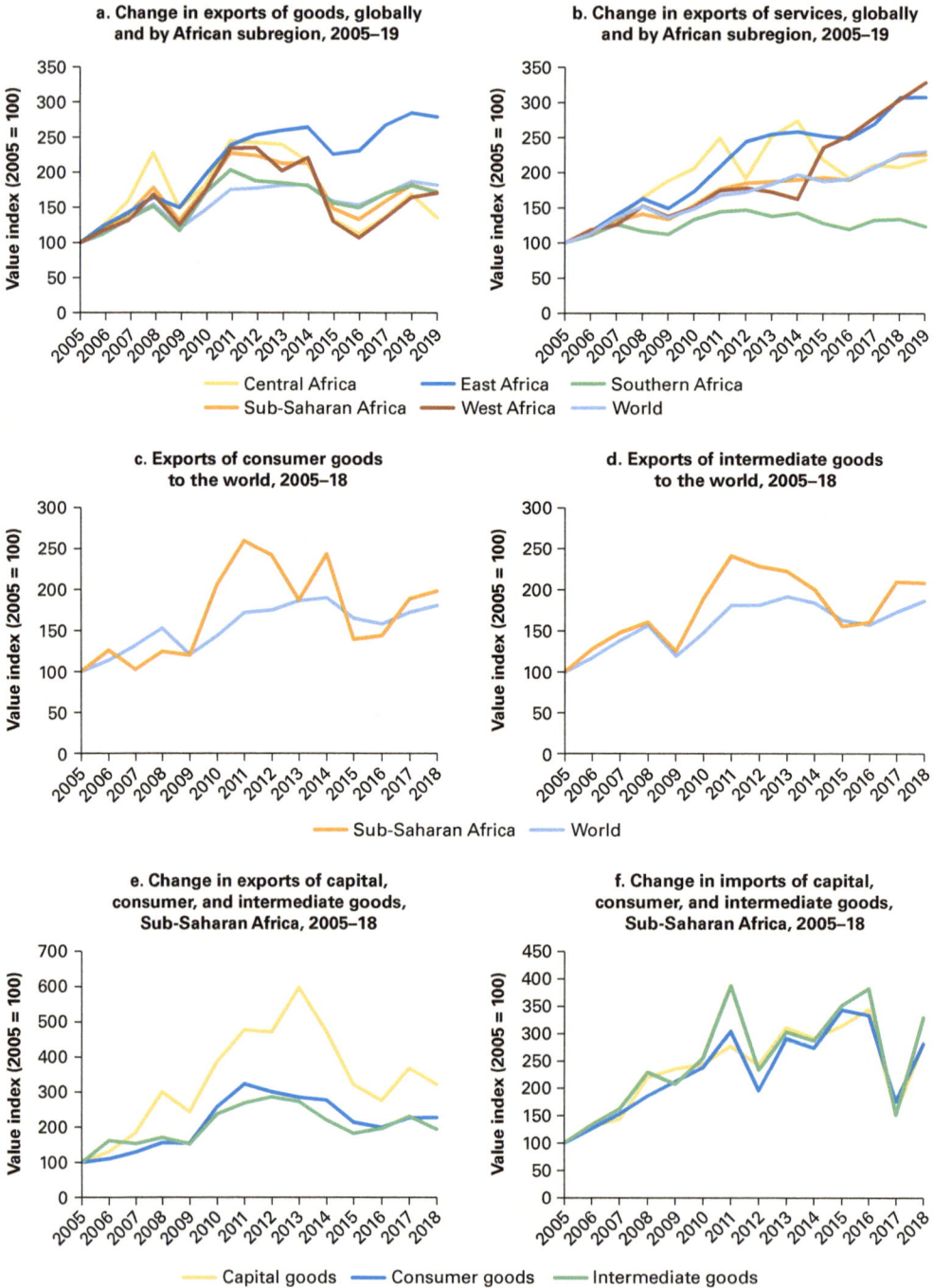

a. Change in exports of goods, globally and by African subregion, 2005–19

b. Change in exports of services, globally and by African subregion, 2005–19

Central Africa   East Africa   Southern Africa
Sub-Saharan Africa   West Africa   World

c. Exports of consumer goods to the world, 2005–18

d. Exports of intermediate goods to the world, 2005–18

Sub-Saharan Africa   World

e. Change in exports of capital, consumer, and intermediate goods, Sub-Saharan Africa, 2005–18

f. Change in imports of capital, consumer, and intermediate goods, Sub-Saharan Africa, 2005–18

Capital goods   Consumer goods   Intermediate goods

Sources: Calculations based on World Integrated Trade Solution (WITS) data (https://wits.worldbank.org/).
Note: All values are indexed setting 2005 as a common starting point (=100) to allow comparison of changes in values of varying magnitudes.

Figure O.2 Trends in Sub-Saharan Africa's Exports of Goods to Regional Markets, 2005–17

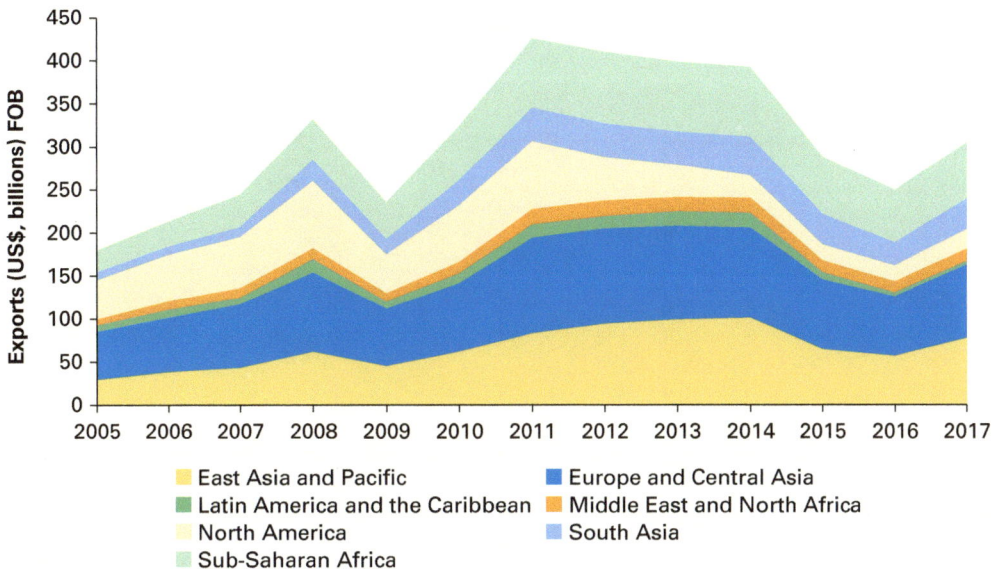

Source: Calculations based on International Monetary Fund's Direction of Trade Statistics (DOTS) database.
Note: North America is defined in this figure as Bermuda, Canada, and the United States. Mexico is included in Latin America and the Caribbean. FOB = free on board.

A closer look at disaggregated trade with the region's trading partners from 2005 through 2018 supports the observation above about the rising share of East Asia in Africa's exports and imports. Europe and North America continue to be the dominant export destinations of consumer goods from Sub-Saharan Africa, while the role of East Asia has been growing faster than that of North America as a key source of imports of consumer goods (figure O.3, panels a and b). East Asia is rapidly replacing North America and Europe as Sub-Saharan Africa's key trading partner in both intermediate and capital goods trade, particularly after 2010 (figure O.3, panels c, d, e, and f). As trade with East Asia increases with intermediate and capital goods, this has also been accompanied by rising intraregional trade.

Key Changes in the Trade Environment

The trade dynamics for Sub-Saharan Africa are happening in a changing environment. Among the many changes globally, two could significantly affect Sub-Saharan Africa in its efforts to expand trade and secure greater market access: the resurgence of protectionism (alongside rising trade tensions, particularly between China and the United States) and the rise of the Fourth Industrial Revolution. The latter is characterized by

Figure O.3   Trends in Sub-Saharan Africa's Trade in Goods, by Type and by Trade Partner Region, 2005–18

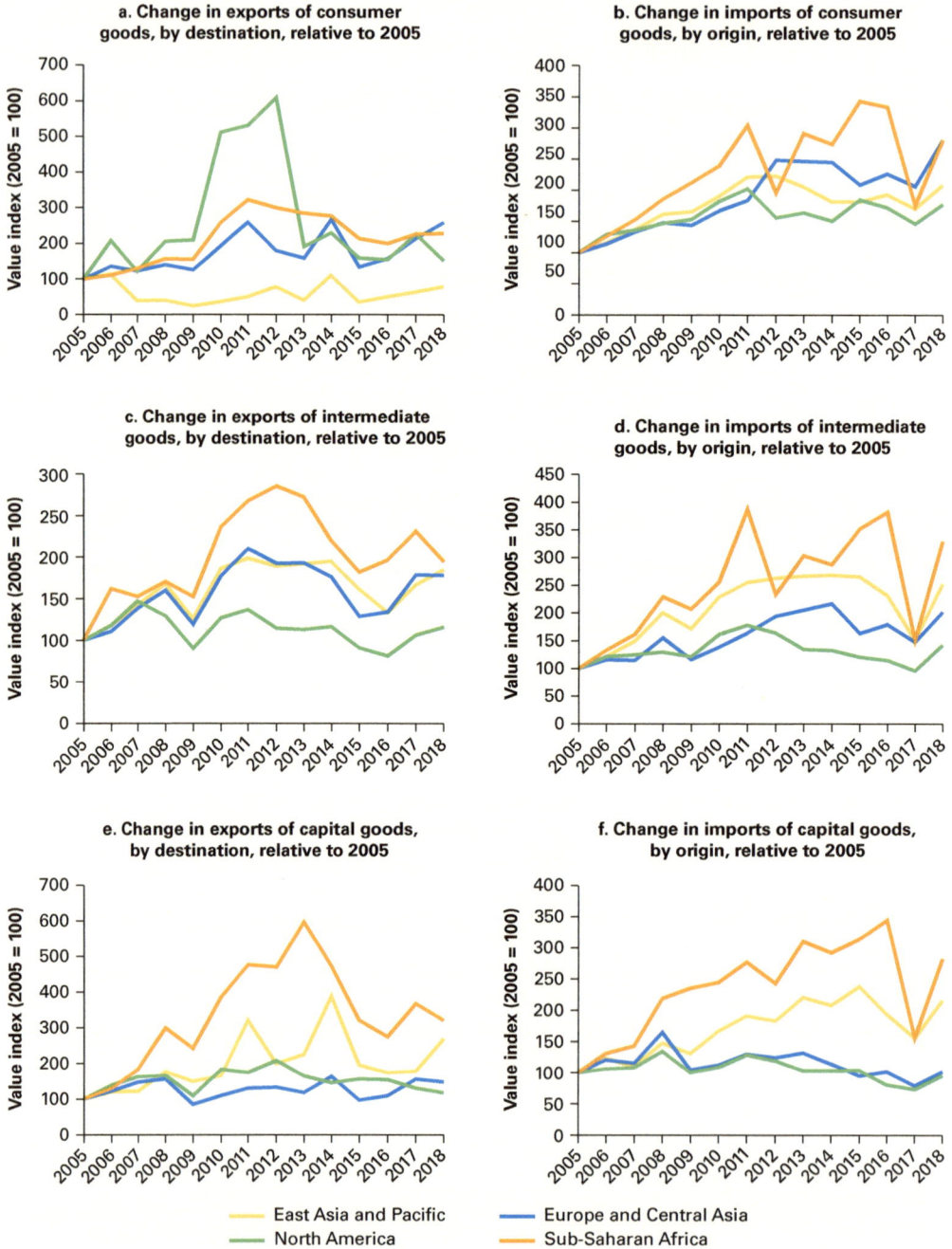

a. Change in exports of consumer goods, by destination, relative to 2005

b. Change in imports of consumer goods, by origin, relative to 2005

c. Change in exports of intermediate goods, by destination, relative to 2005

d. Change in imports of intermediate goods, by origin, relative to 2005

e. Change in exports of capital goods, by destination, relative to 2005

f. Change in imports of capital goods, by origin, relative to 2005

East Asia and Pacific   Europe and Central Asia
North America   Sub-Saharan Africa

Sources: Calculations based on United Nations Comtrade database.
Note: North America is defined in this figure as Bermuda, Canada, and the United States.

emerging technological breakthroughs in several fields, including robotics, artificial intelligence, nanotechnology, biotechnology, the Internet of Things, three-dimensional (3-D) printing, and autonomous vehicles as well as the wide penetration of social media networks, which increases the potential of trading goods and services that were long considered nontradable.

In the escalating trade war between China and the United States, Sub-Saharan Africa is not a direct target. But it might be affected by second-round effects, especially given the increasing regional presence of Chinese firms that are progressively integrating Chinese and African production networks. Other developments threatening multilateralism include the United Kingdom's exit from the EU and the rise of antitrade and antiglobalization sentiments in many high-income economies. It is to be seen how these new developments will unfold and how they could constrain Sub-Saharan Africa's new trade environment.

As for the Fourth Industrial Revolution, will it pass by Sub-Saharan Africa and marginalize the region further on the global stage, or will it level the playing field with opportunities for leapfrogging? Will it foster or deter the structural transformation the region dearly needs? In particular, 3-D printing—also known as "additive manufacturing"—is emerging as a world-shattering technology. It allows the creation of objects by printing successive layers of different materials, mostly plastic or metal, instead of subtracting or cutting material from a large piece or block (which is called "subtractive manufacturing").

Pushed to an extreme and in sectors that are labor intensive, these emerging technologies might pose a threat to the prospects of industrialization in Sub-Saharan Africa. They could also present an opportunity if services trade liberalization deepens to complement tariff liberalization and thus allow Sub-Saharan Africa to acquire the skills needed to be better connected to the global economy. At the same time, these new technologies also improve efficiency, which allows production to expand, in turn driving up trade and employment in other sectors. In fact, the available evidence shows that 3-D printing is associated with an increase, rather than a decline, in trade (Freund, Mulabdic, and Ruta 2019).

These developments confirm that the global economy is a source of growth that Sub-Saharan African countries cannot afford to ignore despite the persisting trade tensions between China and the United States. Countries in the region need to (a) optimize their access to leading world markets (such as the EU and the United States) and increase utilization rates for preference schemes; and (b) strategically diversify their market access. To succeed in such a dual approach, one more step—regional integration—must play a central role to scale up Sub-Saharan Africa's supply capacity. Before exploring these three courses of action, we start by reviewing the key ingredients needed for a successful market access strategy.

Ingredients for Sub-Saharan Africa's Market Access Strategy

Four topics are relevant to exploring ways to expand Sub-Saharan Africa's market access in the current global environment:

1. *The impact of trade agreements* (unilateral, regional, and multilateral trade agreements with the rest of the world) on Sub-Saharan Africa's trade (addressed in chapters 1–4)
2. *The role of GVCs and offshoring* in Sub-Saharan Africa's trade expansion and structural transformation (chapters 5 and 7)
3. *The prospects of regional integration* in Africa to exploit substantial economies of scale (chapter 6)
4. *The challenges to boosting trade in services* in Sub-Saharan Africa and reducing nontariff trade barriers (chapter 7).

On unilateral, regional, and multilateral trade agreements, it is worth assessing whether the EU's stated objective—to use economic partnership agreements to foster development in its low- and middle-income trading partners—would hold in a protectionist world. Would "regional integration to scale up supply capacity, and global integration to scale up demand" still be a valid proposition, as suggested in *World Development Report 2009: Reshaping Economic Geography* (World Bank 2009)? Will Sub-Saharan Africa's preferential access to the EU and the United States hold in a protectionist world? Will the rising Africa–Asia trade hold in the new global environment?

Regarding GVCs, offshoring, and structural transformation, it is worth assessing whether nontariff measures such as standards requirements and other nontariff barriers are a catalyst or a barrier to Sub-Saharan African firms' participation in food GVCs. Furthermore, with the Fourth Industrial Revolution, what will it take for Sub-Saharan Africa to continue to attract offshoring and outsourcing of manufacturing?

As for the challenges to expanding trade in services, it is worth assessing whether the services liberalization momentum will continue in a protectionist world. Would services trade liberalization still be a driver of aggregate productivity? What could happen to services preferences? The role of countries' own policies is of course the main driver of trade performance for both goods and services, and Sub-Saharan African countries will be best advised to continue their trade reform momentum.

Impact of Trade Agreements on Sub-Saharan Africa's Share in Global Trade

Unilateral trade preferences are policies enacted by high-income economies aimed at lowering trade barriers to LMICs, hence facilitating increased export earnings through larger volumes of exports and more diversified exports. Two preeminent examples are the US AGOA (extended to many Sub-Saharan African countries in 2000), followed in 2001 by the EU's EBA initiative targeting all least developed countries (LDCs) across the world.

Current Evidence on the AGOA's and EBA's Effects

The AGOA and EBA are nonreciprocal trade preference systems that have been implemented as extensions of the EU and US Generalized System of Preferences (GSP). The GSP has its roots in the second United Nations Conference on Trade and Development (UNCTAD) in 1968, Resolution 21 (II), which called for the establishment of a "generalized, nonreciprocal, nondiscriminatory system of preferences in favor of developing countries, including special measures in favor of the least advanced among the developing countries."[3]

Evidence on the ex post trade impacts of the AGOA and EBA has been mixed. Using a partial equilibrium framework, Mattoo, Roy, and Subramanian (2003) estimate that the AGOA would raise a country's non-oil exports by 8–11 percent, depending on the restrictiveness of the rules of origin in the non-apparel sectors. Most of this increase would be accounted for by the apparel sector, wherein exports would increase by an estimated average of about 8.3 percent in beneficiary countries.

Another estimate uses a model expressing EU and US imports from AGOA and EBA beneficiaries as a function of supplier countries' characteristics, importers' characteristics, and some bilateral characteristics, in conjunction with countries' exports to the United States relative to their exports to the EU, to assess the relative trade impacts of the AGOA and EBA (Collier and Venables 2007). It shows that the AGOA's apparel provision had a significant and large impact on apparel exports, whereas the EBA had a significant and positive impact only when it was treated as an innovation within the Cotonou Agreement signed between the EU and all African, Caribbean, and Pacific countries for 2000–20.[4]

In addition, Frazer and Van Biesebroeck (2010) use a triple difference-in-differences approach on US disaggregated imports from Sub-Saharan African countries to estimate the AGOA's impact on beneficiaries' trade. Their results show that the AGOA's apparel provision was associated with a 42 percent increase in US apparel imports over 2001–06.

Finally, De Melo and Portugal-Perez (2014) delve into the specific AGOA and EBA rules of origin to assess their respective impacts on African apparel trade. To benefit from these preferences, proof of the extent of local transformation is required. These rules of origin are complicated and burdensome for exporters in LDCs. Since 2001, when the US enacted a "Special Rule for Apparel" under the AGOA initiative, 22 Sub-Saharan African countries that export apparel to the United States have been able to use fabric of any origin or single transformation and still meet the criterion for preferential access. In contrast, the EU has continued to require yarn to be woven into fabric and then made into apparel in the same country (that is, double transformation).

The authors exploit this quasi-experimental change in the design of preferences to estimate the trade impacts of the AGOA and EBA from 1996 to 2004. Their estimates show that AGOA simplification contributed to an increase in export volume of approximately 168 percent for the top seven beneficiaries combined—almost quadrupling the 44 percent growth effect from the AGOA's initial preferential access (that is, without the special rule allowing for single transformation). This change in design was also important for diversity in apparel exports: the number of export varieties grew more rapidly under the AGOA special regime.

A more recent study further explores the central role of the AGOA's liberalized rules of origin. Kassa and Owusu (2019) show that they expand exports—as indicated by the experience of countries with access to the AGOA's Special Rule for Apparel—but may also limit the integration of local industries to large multinationals.

The Need for Broader, and Counterfactual, Assessments

The AGOA and EBA have been in force for nearly two decades. They are expected to boost the exports of eligible products from eligible countries. However, the bulk of the empirical assessments of their trade impacts have so far narrowly focused on apparel. There has been no counterfactual assessment of what could have been expected in boosting exports from LMICs if product and country eligibility were broadened to increase support of regional economic communities (RECs) that are committed to regional and global integration.

Indeed, the existence of many overlapping RECs in Africa has added to the "spaghetti bowl effect" of numerous crisscrossing trade alliances and agreements (figure O.4). In response, the EU has grouped the continent's countries into five regional entities to streamline the EU's Economic Partnership Agreement (EPA) negotiations with them while at the same time fostering a more effective regional integration process:

1. The Economic Community of West African States (ECOWAS)–EU EPA
2. The Central African Economic and Monetary Community (CEMAC)–EU EPA
3. The Eastern and Southern Africa (ESA)–EU EPA
4. The East African Community (EAC)–EU EPA
5. The Southern African Development Community (SADC)–EU EPA.

The members of these groupings do not fully coincide with the members of the leading RECs (figure O.4).

Counterfactual analysis. One way to expand the literature on the trade impact of the AGOA and EBA preferential schemes is through a careful assessment of each of the Sub-Saharan African RECs to determine what the trade creation impact would have been if all members were eligible and all the products for which they have a comparative advantage were covered by these two preferential agreements. Such a counterfactual analysis would highlight the potential development impact of these trade policies, particularly for the RECs that show strong commitment to deepening regional integration to scale up their supply capacity while pursuing global integration to scale up the demand they face (World Bank 2009). Chapter 3 presents such a framework to analyze the differential and complementary impacts of the AGOA and EBA.

Figure O.4   Spaghetti Bowl of African Regional and Subregional Economic Communities, 2010

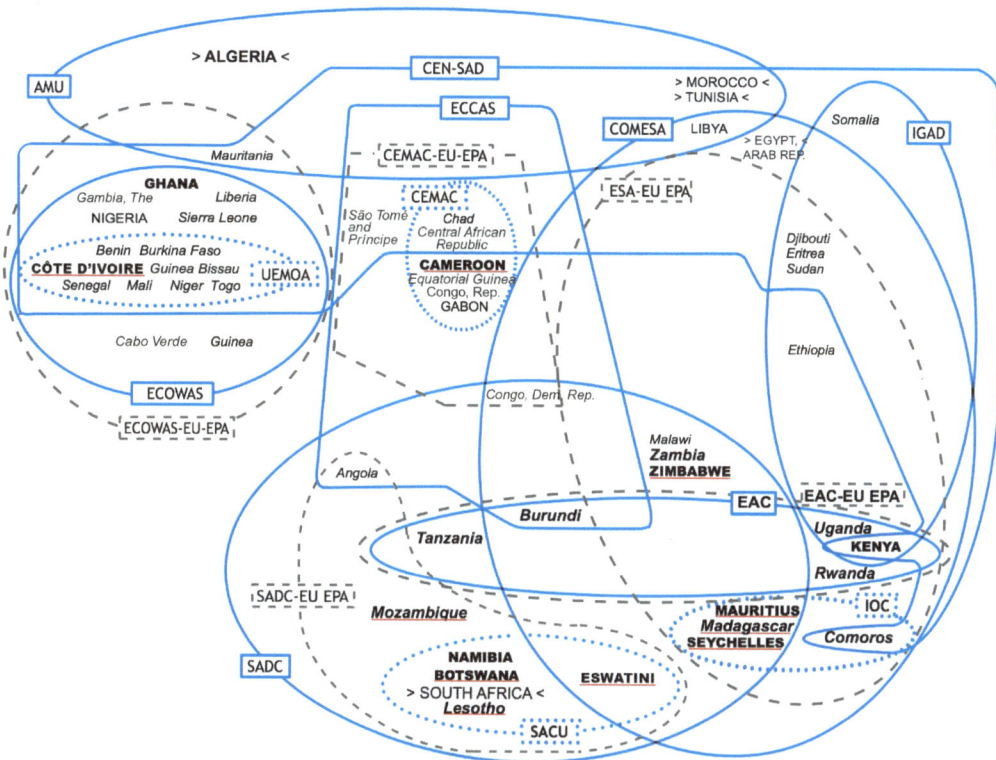

Source: ECDPM 2010. © European Centre for Development Policy Management (ECDPM). Reproduced with permission from ECDPM; further permission required for reuse.

Note: The diagram shows the overlapping memberships of African regional and subregional economic integration agreements, including the configurations of countries (in bold) that had initialed or signed an Economic Partnership Agreement (EPA) with the European Union (EU) as of 2010. Solid lines surround the regional economic communities (RECs): AMU (Arab Maghreb Union), CEN-SAD (Community of Central African States), COMESA (Common Market for Eastern and Southern Africa), EAC (East African Community), ECOWAS (Economic Community of West African States), IGAD (Inter-Governmental Authority on Development), and SADC (Southern African Development Community. Dotted lines encircle other subregional groupings: CEMAC (Central African Economic and Monetary Community), IOC (Indian Ocean Commission), SACU (Southern African Customs Union), and UEMOA (West African Economic and Monetary Union). Discontinuous (dashed) lines surround five groupings of countries in EU EPAs: CEMAC–EU EPA, EAC–EU EPA, ECOWAS–EU EPA, ESA–EU EPA, and SADC–EU EPA. "Least developed countries" (as defined by the UN) are designated by italics and small letters; countries that have concluded an EPA are in bold; countries that have signed an EPA are underlined; and countries shown between carets (for example, > SOUTH AFRICA <) have a free-trade agreement with the EU.

An updated focus on Asia. The EU continues to be Sub-Saharan Africa's major trading partner, given the historical relations and long-standing trading arrangements between the two regions. But Africa's trade with Asia has been growing much faster. Mutambara (2013) examines how intensively Africa trades with Europe and Asia, focusing on the factor intensity of the products being traded. This approach provides interesting insights into the region's product sophistication (skill and technology intensity) as well as target destinations for Africa's exports at various levels of factor intensity from 2001 to 2012. This volume complements in scope and time the coverage by Broadman (2007), who examines the performance and patterns of Africa–Asia trade and investment flows from 1980 to 2005.

Broadened analysis of key export markets. Sub-Saharan Africa's trade with Asia is increasing without formal trade arrangements between the two regions. Furthermore, this trade seems to be increasingly dominated by industrial supplies. But "industrial supplies," as described by its 1-digit Broad Economic Category (BEC-2), encompasses light manufacturing as well as roughly transformed metal products. It is therefore important to carefully assess the trends in Sub-Saharan Africa's manufacturing exports to its key markets (the EU, the United States, Asia, and Sub-Saharan Africa) and whether a structural transformation from agriculture to manufacturing is under way.

Some of these ways of expanding the literature are explored in chapters 1–3 to inform policy actions encompassing the design of preferential agreements as well as regional and global integration initiatives that could put a subset of Sub-Saharan African countries closer to the global competitiveness threshold.

GVCs and Sub-Saharan Africa's Structural Transformation

The Promise of GVC Participation

The most significant development in modern international trade is the increased fragmentation of production across international borders, giving rise to what are referred to as global value chains (GVCs). Higher GVC participation, associated with increased imports and exports of intermediate goods, provides positive spillovers to the economy. There is already a consensus on the long-term effects of GVC participation on industrialization and economic transformation. The positive impacts are found to be stronger for countries that are further from the productivity frontier.

Participation in GVCs may boost the productive capacity of local firms through several channels: increased inflows of technology and information in the production process; firms' exposure to stringent international quality standards, requirements, and competition; increased innovation; and other externalities associated with locating operations in a global production hub (Constantinescu, Mattoo, and Ruta 2017; Formai and Vergara Caffarelli 2016; Humphrey and Schmitz 2002; Tajoli and Felice 2018). Promotion of GVC participation is therefore a policy that Sub-Saharan African countries' policy makers should consider to increase the chance of success of any export-led growth strategy.

The current GVC participation of Sub-Saharan African countries is low, on average, compared with regions like East Asia or Latin America. Figure O.5 presents a summary of the region's GVC participation, by country, based on the Eora database.[5]

Figure O.5 **GVC Participation of Sub-Saharan African Countries, as Measured by Their Shares of Total Exports from Foreign and Domestic Value Added, 2015**

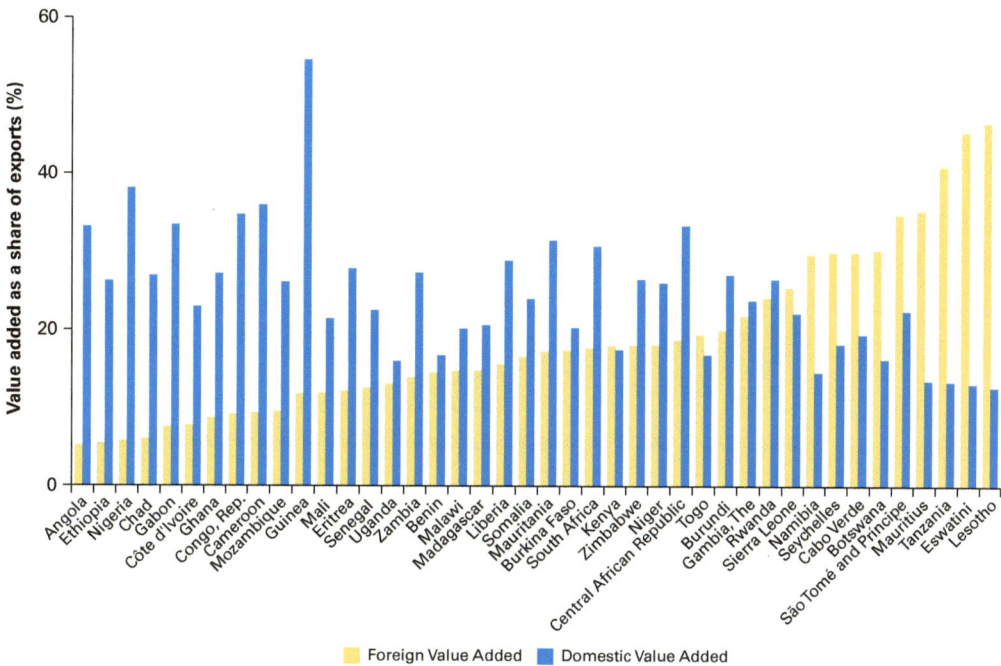

Sources: World Bank calculations based on the Eora database (https://worldmrio.com/).
Note: "Foreign value added" refers to the share of goods and services that a country imports as inputs for production of intermediate or final goods for export. "Domestic value added" refers to the share of domestically produced goods and services used as inputs for production of goods and services for export.

Several countries—Lesotho, Eswatini (formerly Swaziland), Tanzania, and Mauritius (in that order)—have the region's largest shares of foreign value added (imported goods used to produce intermediate or final goods for export) in light of their relatively large shares of imports for exporting textile and apparel products. These and several other countries have succeeded in joining textile manufacturing GVCs because of the preferential trade access that is exclusive to Sub-Saharan African countries. More recently, several East African economies (including Ethiopia, Kenya, and Tanzania) have raised their GVC participation in agroindustries and manufacturing exports—signaling the potential of GVCs for other economies in the region.

Looking at the indirect value added—countries' exports that go into the production of exports in other countries—Guinea, Nigeria, Angola, Cameroon, Republic of Congo, Gabon, and the Central African Republic (in that order)—have the highest GVC participation. Mostly, these results represent exports of petroleum, other minerals, and raw materials that are used to produce other countries' exports (World Bank 2020b). Other countries participating effectively in GVCs through indirect value added include South Africa and Mauritania.

Prospects for Increased Offshoring: The Roles of Demand, Standard Requirements, and Technology

Recent advances in information and communication technology (ICT) and falling trade barriers have led firms to retain only a subset of production stages within their boundaries and domestic economies. Consequently, a key decision facing firms worldwide is the extent of their control over the different segments of their production processes.

Alfaro et al. (2019) constructed firm-level measures of the "upstreamness" of integrated and nonintegrated inputs,[6] using input-output tables combining information on the production activities of firms operating in more than 100 countries. In line with their model's predictions, they find that a firm tends to integrate downstream stages and contract out upstream inputs to ensure quality when the demand for its final product is elastic. Conversely, a firm tends to integrate upstream stages and contract out downstream stages when the demand for the final product is inelastic. Moreover, a firm's propensity to integrate at a given stage of the value chain is shaped by the relative contractibility of the stages located upstream versus downstream from that stage, as well as by the firm's productivity.

Along these lines, Ehrich, Brümmer, and Martínez-Zarzoso (2015) examine the impact of food standard requirements on bilateral trade flows. Especially in LMICs, the required standards might exclude farmers from high-value chains because of the high investment costs associated with implementing a specific standard. The authors show that violation of the food standard requirements is the primary reason for border rejections of third countries' exports to the EU. However, such requirements also reduce information asymmetries and address the changing preferences of modern consumers. Using descriptive evidence for highly concentrated food export markets as their point of departure, they also find that the effects of food standard requirements differ for leading exporting countries compared with those that export relatively low volumes of food products. This heterogeneity of the impact of standard requirements is confirmed for 39 countries importing 12 food products from 2005 to 2012.

These findings suggest that for firms to participate in the final stage of a GVC—production—they need to be highly productive, operate in a country that can credibly enforce contracts to fulfill stringent quality expectations, and operate in a sector in which the demand for the final product is inelastic. Given the relatively weak institutions in Sub-Saharan Africa and the generally low productivity of firms, participation in the end stages of GVCs is constrained. Participation in the upstream stages of products facing a very elastic demand is still possible, but profit margins are limited. Thus, it is relevant to assess what it will take for small and medium enterprises in Sub-Saharan Africa to enter food GVCs, for instance, and to access at scale the distribution networks in leading world markets such as China, the EU, and the United States.

Furthermore, the Fourth Industrial Revolution is increasingly affecting firms' location and production fragmentation decisions (Abeliansky, Martínez-Zarzoso, and Prettner 2015). What it will take for Sub-Saharan Africa to continue to attract offshoring or outsourcing of manufacturing in the new technology environment is a topic to be explored. Part of the discussion in chapter 7 examines the important role of nontariff measures in agriculture and other sectors in Africa's participation in global and regional value chains.

Deepening Intraregional Trade and Integration in a Highly Fragmented Continent

The classical theoretical framework for analyzing the impact of a free trade area (FTA) or customs union suggests that the welfare impact is ambiguous because of the contrasting impacts of trade creation and trade diversion (Viner 1950). By allowing competition between its members due to reduced trade barriers, an FTA may promote a more efficient (re)allocation of resources within the FTA. This result is associated with what is often referred to as *trade creation*—that is, a shift in the locus of production from a high-cost producer to a low-cost, relatively more efficient producer within the FTA. Such a shift does not preclude the possibility that *nonmember* producers would still have a lower cost of production.

There is also the possibility of *trade diversion*—that is, a shift in the locus of production from more efficient production by nonmembers of the FTA to inefficient producers within the FTA, depending on the extent of the external tariffs. The impact of trade diversion could be stronger if members raise external tariffs following the FTA. Within the traditional theoretical framework, this is harmful because of the global efficiency losses and subsequent high prices in the FTA countries.

In the context of the low productivity, very high unemployment, and low-investment regimes that most Africans face, the classical theory is very restrictive for evaluating the impacts of regional integration initiatives such as the AfCFTA. A more suitable framework for analyzing the impact of regional integration is to examine the impact on welfare arising from the increased employment, productivity, incomes, investment, and overall structural transformation of developing economies to middle- and high-income economies. Arguably, the most important gains of an FTA are the dynamic gains associated with the benefits from increased competition, foreign direct investment (FDI) inflows, economies of scale, transfer of knowledge and technology, productivity, and economic diversification.

Deepening intraregional trade and integration provide the groundwork for increasing the region's trade and investment flows with the rest of the world by expanding economies of scale, which provides opportunities to attract large-scale investments and supports the creation and development of regional production networks or GVCs. Regional integration in Africa should serve as the springboard for successful integration with the rest of the world. Given that Africa is the most fragmented continent, with thick borders—a complex of both tariff and nontariff restrictions that slow down trade—there is a paramount role for national, regional, and international policy makers to adopt aggressive strategies that facilitate the integration of economies. Chapter 6 discusses developments associated with the AfCFTA and the key challenges and policy implications.

Challenges for Sub-Saharan Africa in Boosting Trade in Services

The cost and quality of services affect an economy's growth performance through their important roles in trade facilitation and impacts on aggregate productivity. The role of services in a country's engagement in international trade has gained even greater prominence with the rise of GVCs.

Why Trade in Services Matters

Services are essential intermediaries in facilitating transactions and businesses (Francois 1990) in addition to serving as inputs in the production process. Services such as finance, transportation, energy, telecommunications, legal counsel, and distribution also foster productivity in manufacturing and the overall economy—and, in doing so, improve a country's competitiveness and economic status relative to the rest of the world. There is increasing evidence that services sector liberalization is a major potential source of gains in economic performance, including productivity in manufacturing and the coordination of activities between and within firms (Francois and Hoekman 2010).

Services also provide a mechanism for diffusing production innovations and technology spillovers (Burgess and Venables 2004). For example, low-cost, efficient services in communications and transportation enhance the positive spillovers of agglomeration economies in manufacturing and other sectors (Robert-Nicoud 2008). And an efficient and productive financial sector is essential for ensuring efficient allocation of capital. The competitiveness of manufacturing firms relies in part on access to low-cost, high-quality producer services—telecommunications, transportation, and distribution services—as well as on financial intermediation (Francois and Hoekman 2010). Moreover, such services support the overall economy in several ways:

- *Lower-cost, higher-quality telecommunications* generate economy-wide benefits, serving both as an intermediate input and as a "transport" mechanism for information services and other products that can be digitalized.
- *Transportation services* contribute to the efficient distribution of goods within and between countries and are the means through which service providers move to the locations of clients (and vice versa).
- *Business services, such as accounting and legal services,* reduce the transaction costs associated with the operation of financial markets and enforcement of contracts.

- *Retail and wholesale distribution services* are a vital link between producers and consumers, with the margins that apply in the provision of such services influencing the competitiveness of firms in local and international markets.

In sum, the ability of firms to compete and grow depends on their access to telecommunications, transportation, financial services, and other business services such as accounting and legal services. Not to mention that, conversely, *high-cost, low-quality* services act as a tax on exporters. Services are thus a vital input into goods trade.

Impacts of Services Trade Liberalization

Reducing the barriers to services trade boosts the productivity of manufacturing firms. Arnold, Javorcik, and Mattoo (2011) show that allowing foreign firms to enter the services industries was the key channel through which services liberalization helped improve the performance of manufacturing sectors in the Czech Republic. In a related study, Arnold et al. (2016) examine the link between India's reforms in the services sectors and the productivity of manufacturing firms, using panel data for about 4,000 Indian firms from 1993 to 2005. They find that banking, telecommunications, insurance, and transportation reforms significantly increased manufacturing productivity.

Services reforms benefited foreign and locally owned manufacturing firms, but the effects on foreign firms tended to be stronger. An increase by 1 standard deviation in the aggregate index of services liberalization resulted in a productivity increase of 11.7 percent for domestic firms and 13.2 percent for foreign enterprises (Arnold et al. 2016). Similar results were obtained for Indonesia (Duggan, Rahardja, and Varela 2013).

To examine whether this effect is observed more generally across countries and how it is affected by differences in economic governance, Beverelli, Fiorini, and Hoekman (2017) look at the effect of services trade restrictions on manufacturing productivity for a broad cross-section of countries at different stages of economic development. They find that decreasing services trade restrictiveness had a positive impact on the manufacturing sectors that used services as intermediate inputs in production. They also find that countries with high institutional quality benefited the most from lower services trade restrictions in terms of increased productivity in downstream industries. Echoing the findings of previous studies, their analysis shows that the conditioning effect of institutions operates through services trade that involves foreign establishments (FDI) as opposed to cross-border, arms-length trade in services.

A Hard Look at Services Trade Restrictiveness

As noted earlier, trade is an important channel through which firms can improve their access to services inputs, resulting in lower prices or greater input variety. The extent to which policies restrict access to foreign services inputs is therefore likely to be relevant for downstream productivity performance. Yet the barriers to trade in services are substantial, even in high-income countries (Borchert, Gootiiz, and Mattoo 2014; OECD 2021).

Using World Bank Enterprise Surveys data, Hoekman and Shepherd (2015) examine how services productivity affects the productivity of manufacturing firms and the relationship between the manufacturers' productivity and firm-level export performance. They find a strong link between services and manufacturing performance, with the link being stronger for firms that use services inputs more intensively. At the average rate of services input intensity, they estimate that a 10 percent improvement in services productivity was associated with a 0.3 percent increase in manufacturing productivity and a resulting 0.2 percent increase in exports. At the sectoral level, they find that restrictions on transportation and retail distribution services had the largest negative impact on goods export performance.

A developing region such as Sub-Saharan Africa cannot afford to constrain its growth because of poorly performing services trade. It is therefore important to assess thoroughly the state of services liberalization in the region and estimate the productivity forgone by restricted services sectors, determining more specifically which dimensions of the economic governance and institutional frameworks are relevant in shaping the effects of services trade policies. Analysis to better understand the regulatory and trading institutions affecting the quality of services trade is therefore necessary to be able to identify specific policy implications and recommendations.

Such an exercise cannot be performed with only country-level variables. Instead, data on sector-specific governance institutions must be collected and matched with services-specific trade policy measures to assess how the services restrictiveness measures interact with different country characteristics and institutional variables—both horizontal (such as those related to competition policy) and sector-specific (such as those related to regulatory regimes). Chapter 7 of this book provides some preliminary results.

How Can Sub-Saharan African Countries Boost Exports through Preferential Access to the EU and US Markets?

Develop Institutions and Infrastructure

The first response comes from research conducted by the World Bank's Office of the Chief Economist of the Africa Region and the Macroeconomics, Trade, and Investment Global Practice (Kassa and Coulibaly 2019). This study examines the AGOA's trade creation impact using the synthetic control method—a quasi-experimental approach (see chapter 1). The novelty in the approach is that it addresses problems of estimation that are prevalent in the nonexperimental methods used to analyze the impact of preferential trade agreements.

The findings show that most of the eligible countries registered gains in exports owing to the AGOA, which compels all beneficiary countries to fully use the preferences offered by the agreement. The positive trade impacts were largely associated with improvements in ICT infrastructure; integrity in the legal and property rights institutions; ease of labor market regulations; and sound macroeconomic environments, including stable exchange rates and low inflation. By developing such institutions and infrastructure, Sub-Saharan African countries can also minimize undue exposure to a single market or few export commodities and can maximize the gains from trade.

Implement Tariff Liberalization and Other Domestic Reforms

The second answer comes from research conducted by the World Bank's Trade and Integration Research Group. Preferential access to foreign markets has been used as a mechanism to stimulate export growth in Africa, but there is little evidence on whether it durably boosts exports of manufactured goods. To address this question, Fernandes et al. (2019) exploit significant policy changes in the United States around the turn of the twenty-first century—the GSP product expansion for LDCs in 1997 and the AGOA's implementation in 2001—to assess whether preferential access increased exports of all eligible products in general and of apparel specifically. This study also examines the Multifiber Arrangement (MFA) phaseout in 2005, to assess whether any expansion in apparel exports survived the erosion of preferences.[7]

To find a causal impact of these changes on exports to the United States by a given Sub-Saharan African country, the study uses a triple-differences regression and 26 years of newly constructed data on exports to the United States at the country Harmonized System 6-digit level (1992–2017). It finds that the biggest boost from the AGOA to African countries' exports was for apparel products. However, although the marginal impacts on African apparel exports grew sharply in the first years of the AGOA, they leveled off after 2005, when the end of the MFA quotas unleashed competition from Asian countries.

Furthermore, the AGOA's impact on apparel varied across subregions. Some countries, mostly in Central and West Africa, never took meaningful advantage of the AGOA. Countries in Southern Africa displayed a boom-bust pattern with strong growth in the first years, followed by a decline in the post-MFA years. Eastern Africa saw late success but eventually sustained growth in apparel exports.

Understanding the heterogeneous responses to preferences remains a challenge (as further discussed in chapter 2). However, preliminary evidence suggests that preferential access per se is not sufficient. It needs to be complemented by three types of domestic reforms:

1. Improved access to imported inputs through tariff liberalization
2. Reduced regulatory burdens and enhanced access to infrastructure through the creation of special economic zones
3. Competitive exchange rates through flexible exchange rate regimes.

Prepare for a Post-AGOA Period by Joining Regional Integration Aspirations with Trade Agreements with the Rest of the World

The third answer comes from research conducted by the World Bank's Macroeconomics, Trade, and Investment Global Practice (Coulibaly 2017). The AGOA and the EU's EBA have helped somewhat to boost Sub-Saharan Africa's exports since 2001 (see chapter 3). However, not all African countries have benefited from the two preferential agreements, including countries in West Africa. Paradoxically, these countries host two of the most advanced RECs in Sub-Saharan Africa: the West African Economic and Monetary Union (WAEMU) and ECOWAS. WAEMU shares a common monetary policy that has consistently maintained low and stable inflation and established a customs union with a compensation mechanism to uphold the common external tariff. ECOWAS maintains a regional military force (the ECOWAS Monitoring Group) and peer pressure, which have rooted out military coups in its member countries.

Simulations derived from a Poisson pseudo-maximum likelihood gravity model estimation show that West Africa could be exporting 2.5 to 4 times more to the EU and the US if the AGOA and EBA were not implemented in a differentiated manner in terms of country eligibility, product coverage, and rules of origin (Coulibaly 2017). Given such trade creation potential for a group of countries committed to deep regional integration, a revision of the AGOA and EBA, or a special ECOWAS/WAEMU provision, would make these preferential trade agreements driving forces behind the success of regional integration in Sub-Saharan Africa.

The rising protectionist policies of high-income economies signal the rise of uncertainty in trade agreements associated with preferential access for Sub-Saharan Africa's exports. These economies are expressing interest in transitioning from nonreciprocal to more-reciprocal trade agreements in their trade dealings with LMICs, including those in Africa. The EU is negotiating EPAs with African countries, as a sign of a shift to reciprocity. The United States is considering a similar path by developing the African Free Trade Act, which plans to enter free trade agreements with selected African countries.

These developments underscore the need to prepare for a post-AGOA period with more reciprocity. African countries need to marry their regional integration aspirations with their trade agreement negotiations with Asia, the EU, and the US. (For more on trade with Asia, see chapter 4.) The region's countries need to negotiate as a group, by establishing "African Economic Areas"—neighborhood-like blocs of countries with higher potential for integration—that reinforce regional access to export markets in high-income economies.

In sum, trade agreements with individual African countries tend to reinforce the economic and political fragmentation that has long choked the region's prospects for increased integration. Changes in the relative size of export markets—and the often-low use of preferences in trading with traditional markets such as the EU and the US—suggest that Africa may need to explore new frontiers, including effective African Economic Areas, to diversify its markets as well as its exports to these markets.

How Can Sub-Saharan African Countries Diversify Their Market Access?

Tap into Growing Trade Potential with Asia

The first response comes from research conducted by the World Bank's Office of the Chief Economist for the Africa Region (Ouattara and Zeufack 2019). With the growing interdependence within the global economy, integration into GVCs can ease the industrialization process in Sub-Saharan African countries. Over the past two decades, trade flows have rapidly increased between Sub-Saharan Africa and Asia. Exporting has been an important channel through which Asian countries have accelerated their pace of growth and emerged as major international competitors. But Sub-Saharan African countries are still lagging. Chapter 4 investigates the extent to which Sub-Saharan African countries can tap into trade potential with their partners in Asia.

Asia, especially East Asia and South Asia, has been the global growth engine in the past few decades. China's economy is now larger than the US economy (in purchasing power parity). India is the world's third-largest economy, and Indonesia is on track to become the world's seventh-largest economy. In 2017, Asia made the largest contribution to world trade volume growth, accounting for 51 percent of the increase in merchandise exports and 60 percent of the growth in merchandise imports (WTO 2018).

For Africa, this indicates a significant shift from the traditional sources of market opportunities and FDI (the EU and the US) to newer sources—in Asia. The share of Sub-Saharan African countries in Asian trade has increased rapidly, and for some African countries their key trading partners are increasingly becoming China, India, and Indonesia (although the traditional export destinations still account for a significant share). Furthermore, the growing middle class and increasing demand from East Asia (accompanied by rising relative wages there), along with the shifting structure of GVCs, may offer new economic opportunities for Africa. The findings from Ouattara and Zeufack (2019) suggest that there is indeed potential for Sub-Saharan Africa's exports, given the rising middle-class consumption patterns in Asia.

Focus on Export Growth, Targeting Asia's Growing Middle Class

The second response comes from a collaborative study by the World Bank's Office of the Chief Economist for the Africa Region and the Finance, Competitiveness, and Innovation Global Practice (chapter 5). The study examines the effects of Asia's economic expansion and the subsequent upsurge in trading partnerships with Sub-Saharan Africa on investment and trade prospects for the region. It also investigates the composition of the export sector, destinations, factor intensity, and various value chain measures (for example, length of production, upstreamness, and domestic value added) of exports in trading with Asia. Although overall exports from Africa to Asia are still highly concentrated in resource-intensive sectors, a few countries have leveraged export booms to Asia to diversify their export portfolios. For instance, Ethiopia and Tanzania have been diversifying into light manufacturing GVCs. In addition to China, India has emerged as a leading trading partner of many African nations.

Chapter 5 identifies the key export sectors driving the GVC participation of African countries with Asia. It evaluates the effects of participating in Asian value chains on the factor content of exports. The study also sheds some light on the policy implications for African nations of moving up the value chains by participating in Asian GVCs. It shows that Asian economic engagement on the continent is associated with an increase in upstreamness, a measure proposed by Antràs et al. (2012). As a result, proportionally more exports to, but not imports from, Asia would help African nations move up the value chains. The effects are particularly strong among African countries that have access to the sea but are relatively poorer than their African peers. The study also shows that increasing engagement with Asia complements rather than crowds out African countries' exports to the rest of the world, suggesting no evidence of trade diversion due to participation in Asian GVCs.

To tap this rising potential, policy makers in Sub-Saharan Africa must further strengthen their countries' trade ties with Asia (chapters 4 and 5) in several ways:

- Building on achievements of recent years, countries should take steps to increase their participation in this "hub-and-spoke" pattern of trade with select Asian countries.
- A careful assessment of the changing demand patterns of Asia's growing middle class is required to inform export diversification options for the countries in Sub-Saharan Africa.
- Countries that invest in reforming their institutions—including strengthening the rule of law and contract enforcement mechanisms, reducing rent-seeking activities in specific markets, and reducing the risks of political instability—would see increasing trade with Asia and the benefits from such trade.

Overall, a policy of export orientation toward Asia can support faster growth and economic transformation and poverty reduction. The prospects for gains in structural transformation will be enhanced by the ongoing restructuring of economies in East Asia and committed leadership for reform and building up firm and state capabilities in African countries. The heterogeneities in the extent of gains from these changes are evidence that the improving external prospects and dormant comparative advantages alone will not by themselves guarantee gains—unless they are accompanied by significant efforts in focused industrial, trade, and competition policies to take advantage of such opportunities.

How Could Regional Integration Initiatives Help This Dual Strategy to Succeed?

To succeed in the proposed dual strategy—boosting exports through preferential access to the EU and US markets and diversifying their market access to Asia—Sub-Saharan African countries would need to be better integrated and deepen trade with each other. Despite some progress in recent years, African countries still have thick trade barriers around their borders, which exacerbates the fragmentation inherited from colonization and makes Africa the continent most prone to ethnic-based conflicts. The region's countries also have some of the smallest domestic markets in the world, except for the three resource-rich middle-income countries—Angola, Nigeria, and South Africa—and a few less-resource-endowed countries, such as Ethiopia.

Prospects for Africa's Access to Global Markets: Policies and Challenges

Which policies can help overcome the triple disadvantage of low economic density, long distance to world and regional markets, and thick borders? The development experiences of the East Asia and Pacific region and, recently, South Asia make the answer clear: (a) use the advantage of low labor costs and a large domestic labor force that is perhaps just moving out of agriculture in search of employment; (b) provide political and macroeconomic stability; and (c) work closely with foreign investors to arrange for better local infrastructure and access to export routes. These policy lessons are actionable recommendations for national governments in many areas, such as the emphasis on bolstering investment in infrastructure and human capital and improving market and government institutions.

But various circumstances make it difficult for countries in Sub-Saharan African to replicate East Asia's success by integrating globally:

- *Relative size of populations, markets, workforces, and economies.* Most African countries are smaller than those in East Asia in population, size of the domestic consumer market, percentage of the labor force with a minimum primary education, and economic proximity to global markets or neighbors. For example, Sub-Saharan African countries have a median population of about 12 million, compared with 50 million in emerging Asia (excluding China and India).
- *Lagging competitiveness, scale, and connectivity.* Global trade integration has advanced considerably since the 1960s, when the East Asian Tigers began their dramatic rise. And global markets have become considerably more contested and production much more

segregated into tasks that require substantial economies of scale and excellent connectivity with trading partners.

- *Technological advances that weaken demand for low-cost labor.* The relentless march of technology has reduced manufacturing employment and dampened the advantage of low-cost labor relative to capital. Policies to improve the endowment of capital thus need to be supplemented by regional efforts to create larger markets that cross borders and make Sub-Saharan African countries more attractive to foreign and domestic investors.

Efforts to Regionally Integrate Sub-Saharan African Economies

Establishing, and Deepening, the AfCFTA

An initiative that can speed integration of the countries in Sub-Saharan Africa is the framework agreement establishing the AfCFTA, which was signed by 44 countries in Rwanda on March 21, 2018.[8] As of October 2019, 54 countries had signed the AfCFTA Agreement, 40 had complied with their domestic requirements for ratification, and 34 of the 40 have ratified the agreement and deposited their instruments of ratification[9]—more than the number of ratifications required to put the FTA into effect. For the countries that deposited their instruments of ratification, the AfCFTA became operational in January 2021.

This means that Africa has put into operation the largest FTA in the world, in terms of membership, and it is expected to change the trade and investment framework of countries in the region going forward. The AfCFTA will help boost intraregional trade, strengthen the complementarities of production and exports, create employment, and limit the impact of commodity price volatility on the participants. Further negotiations are planned to cover investment, competition, and intellectual property rights.

Deepening the AfCFTA will be important. It will also be important for the countries that have not yet ratified the agreement and deposited their instruments thus far to join, to hasten the implementation for the whole region. Although the AfCFTA is a great recent development, Nigeria's delayed signing of the agreement signals reservations in the political commitment of the region's largest economy, which could constrain further integration efforts that require a high level of political commitment. Furthermore, member countries must avoid creating a trade area that provides a larger captive market without making their firms more competitive and readier to take on global markets. The approach to strengthening integration that is required for a successful AfCFTA should have three parts: improving physical integration, strengthening political cooperation, and facilitating business integration. The costs of distance and fragmentation can be reduced through intensive investment in these areas.

Leveraging RECs to Strengthen African Neighborhoods

Another way to help rekindle growth is to make Africa's neighborhoods more vibrant, especially those that include the largest resource-rich countries. This could be done by granting all the countries in regional groupings—such as ECOWAS, the SADC, and the Common Market for Eastern and Southern Africa (COMESA)—preferential access to leading world markets with attractive rules of origin, conditional on their taking the lead in promoting regional integration in West, Southern, and East Africa. This might require revisiting the US AGOA and the EU EBA programs.

In the spirit of the Group of Twenty (G-20) Compact with Africa,[10] a complementary activity under the World Trade Organization (WTO) Aid for Trade initiative could help bolster investment in sectors other than natural resources, helping to build up non-resource exports from countries within neighborhoods (or RECs).

Coulibaly (2017) proposes pursuing a three-pronged strategy—(a) pick a model REC and help it succeed, (b) enroll the REC's neighboring countries, and (c) stimulate competition with other RECs—that would trigger at least three channels of regional spillovers:

1. A *distribution effect* from the three resource-rich middle-income countries—Angola, Nigeria, and South Africa—to their regional economic partners would occur through trade in goods and services and cross-border movement of labor and capital searching for better opportunities.
2. A *domino effect*, helping countries close to the neighborhoods of these three middle-income countries to join the integration process, would enable those countries to take full advantage of the new economic opportunities generated by the coordination of foreign aid.
3. A *demonstration effect* would encourage other subgroups of countries to deepen their regional integration to take advantage of the coordinated G-20 Compact with Africa and WTO Aid-for-Trade initiatives.

Adopting New Models for International Commitments

The international community could also shift from bilateral trade agreements to contracts with African *neighborhoods* (natural trading partners that are close historically, sociologically and geographically)—specifically involving countries by neighborhood and development partner(s)—as an incentive for closer regional cooperation (Coulibaly 2017). For instance, the governments of the East, Central, Southern, and West African subregions could commit to the following:

- *Establishing African Economic Areas* that would tie together the economic interests of leading and lagging countries in each regional neighborhood
- *Encouraging the free movement* of labor, capital, goods, and services within these areas
- *Maintaining and protecting access routes* between landlocked countries and outlets for trade as well as providing the political space to support investment in the regional infrastructure that is essential for the neighborhood.

In exchange for these cross-country actions, bilateral and multilateral development partners could commit to the following:

- *Significantly increasing international financial assistance for improved social services* and other life-sustaining infrastructure designed to raise living standards and create portable human capital in lagging countries
- *Increasing financial support for growth-sustaining infrastructure*— such as ports, transportation links, and ICT—in countries where economic takeoff is most likely as well as for infrastructure to link the markets of leading countries with labor, capital, goods, and ideas from their lagging neighbors
- *Providing preferential access for Sub-Saharan African exports* to the markets of high-income countries, without strict rules of origin or eligibility criteria, so that the rules of origin do not impede rapid growth of trade in intermediate inputs with other LMICs.

Fostering Regional Cooperation on Multiple Fronts

By deepening regional collaborations—including through the timely and effective implementation of the AfCFTA—Sub-Saharan African countries can minimize the distortions of tariffs and nontariff measures and provide more opportunities for their firms to participate in regional and global value chains. Addressing these challenges requires (a) strengthening cooperation between neighboring countries to enlarge the size of the market, so that it is attractive to foreign investors; and (b) securing access to critical intermediate goods, to make the leap to a new product less costly and risky.

By looking at which sectors offer the most promise for further development, countries in natural neighborhoods can focus cooperation on sector-specific infrastructure (such as common standards, compliance, and metrology systems) and specific curricula to build a skilled labor force and adapt new technologies.

Special economic zones can also be a successful addition when they address specific market failures. However, even in a restricted area, getting the conditions right requires careful planning and implementation to ensure that the needed resources—such as labor, land, water, electricity, and telecommunications—are readily available, regulatory barriers are minimized, and connectivity is seamless. Communication with businesses in the targeted sectors is critical for ensuring that the zone meets their needs.

Contributions of This Volume

The chapters in this volume provide a range of perspectives on market access opportunities for Africa in the new trade environment. In addition to examining the role of nonreciprocal trade agreements in traditional markets—the EU and the US—studies in this volume suggest the importance of new frontier markets in East and South Asia. In addition, efforts to expand and diversify market access would be bolstered by deepening intraregional trade and integration.

In 2015, Sub-Saharan Africa was home to 27 of the 28 poorest countries in the world. By 2030, the World Bank predicts, nearly 9 of every 10 people in extreme poverty will be living in Sub-Saharan Africa (World Bank 2020a). There is now an almost universal consensus that trade can drive poverty reduction by boosting economic growth and increasing employment. Hence, to turn the tide in our goal to eradicate poverty in Sub-Saharan Africa, this volume contributes to the call for a sustained effort in the region to integrate African economies into GVCs and to deepen trade and integration within the region. Recent changes in global trade and production systems, studies in this volume show, suggest the need to rethink traditional approaches and traditional markets in fostering the region's engagement in international trade.

Notes

1. "Least developed economies" refers to countries, as defined by the United Nations, that exhibit the world's lowest indicators of socioeconomic development using specified criteria regarding poverty, human resource weakness, and economic vulnerability.
2. Data on regional shares of global trade, exports as a share of GDP, and sectoral composition of regional exports are from the World Bank's World Development Indicators database unless otherwise indicated.
3. For more information, see "Generalized System of Preferences" on UNCTAD's Trade Agreements website: https://unctad.org/topic/trade-agreements/generalized-system-of-preferences.
4. The Cotonou Agreement is a treaty between the EU and the Organisation of African, Caribbean and Pacific Group of States (ACP). Under the agreement, a new scheme of Economic Partnership Agreements took effect in 2008. This new arrangement provides for reciprocal trade agreements, meaning not only that the EU provides duty-free access to its markets for ACP exports but also that ACP countries provide duty-free access to their own markets for EU exports.
5. The Eora database is a set of intercountry, multiregional input-output tables covering 25 sectors in 189 countries from 1990 to 2015. The database has the largest coverage of countries in Sub-Saharan Africa, including 42 of 45 total countries. The data tables provide a breakdown of product use in groups based on their origin: domestically produced or imported, intermediate or final use, and the origin of imported products. The GVC indicators are constructed at the country level and decomposed into the foreign and domestic value-added components of exports, following Koopman et al. (2010) and Lenzen et al. (2012).
6. "Upstreamness," a measure developed by Antràs et al. (2012), is an input's average distance from final use. A relatively upstream sector is one that supplies a disproportionately large share of its output to other sectors that sell very little if any directly to final consumers.

7. The MFA governed world trade in textiles and apparel from 1974 through 2004, with quotas imposed on the totals that certain LMICs could export to high-income countries.
8. Chapter 6 provides a discussion of the impacts, challenges, and opportunities of the AfCFTA and the policy implications of the success of this ambitious continental project.
9. As of July 2021, of the 40 countries that have complied with their domestic requirements for ratification, 34 countries have deposited their instruments of ratification with the depositary (Chair of the African Union Commission).
10. The G-20 Compact with Africa was launched in 2017 to promote private investment in Africa, including in infrastructure. Its primary objective is to increase attractiveness of private investment through substantial improvements of the macro, business, and financing frameworks. ("About the Compact with Africa," G-20 Compact with Africa website: https://www.compactwithafrica.org/content/compact withafrica/home.html).

References

Abeliansky, A. L., I. Martínez-Zarzoso, and K. Prettner. 2015. "The Impact of 3D Printing on Trade and FDI." Discussion Paper No. 262, Center for European, Governance and Economic Development Research, University of Göttingen, Germany.

Alfaro, Laura, Davin Chor, Pol Antràs, and Paola Conconi. 2019. "Internalizing Global Value Chains: A Firm-Level Analysis." *Journal of Political Economy* 127 (2): 508–59.

Antràs, P., D. Chor, T. Fally, and R. Hillberry. 2012. "Measuring the Upstreamness of Production and Trade Flows." *American Economic Review* 102 (3): 412–16.

Arnold, J. M., B. S. Javorcik, and A. Mattoo. 2011. "Does Services Liberalization Benefit Manufacturing Firms? Evidence from the Czech Republic." *Journal of International Economics* 85 (1): 136–46.

Arnold, J. M., B. Javorcik, M. Lipscomb, and A. Mattoo. 2016. "Services Reform and Manufacturing Performance: Evidence from India." *Economic Journal* 126 (590): 1–39.

Beverelli, C., M. Fiorini, and B. Hoekman. 2017. "Services Trade Policy and Manufacturing Productivity: The Role of Institutions." *Journal of International Economics* 104: 166–82.

Borchert, I., S. Gootiiz, and A. Mattoo. 2014. "Policy Barriers to International Trade in Services: Evidence from a New Database." *World Bank Economic Review* 28 (1): 162–88.

Broadman, H. G. 2007. "Performance and Patterns of African-Asian Trade and Investment Flows." In *Africa's Silk Road: China and*

India's New Economic Frontier, edited by H. G. Broadman, 59–128. Washington, DC: World Bank.

Burgess, R., and A. J. Venables. 2004. "Toward a Microeconomics of Growth." Policy Research Working Paper 3257, World Bank, Washington, DC.

Collier, P., and A. J. Venables. 2007. "Rethinking Trade Preferences: How Africa Can Diversify Its Exports." *World Economy* 30 (8): 1326–45.

Constantinescu, C., A. Mattoo, and M. Ruta. 2017. "Does Vertical Specialization Increase Productivity?" Policy Research Working Paper 7978, World Bank, Washington, DC.

Coulibaly, S. 2017. "Differentiated Impact of AGOA and EBA on West African Countries." Working paper, Office of the Chief Economist of the Africa Region, World Bank, Washington, DC.

De Melo, J., and A. Portugal-Perez. 2014. "Preferential Market Access Design: Evidence and Lessons from African Apparel Exports to the United States and the European Union." *World Bank Economic Review* 28 (1): 74–98.

Duggan, V., S. Rahardja, and G. Varela. 2013. "Service Sector Reform and Manufacturing Productivity: Evidence from Indonesia." Policy Research Working Paper 6349, World Bank, Washington, DC.

ECDPM (European Centre for Development Policy Management). 2010. "African Regional and SubRegional Economic Integration Groupings and the Regional Economic Partnerships Agreement (EPA) Negotiations Configurations." Online infographic, ECDPM, Maastricht, the Netherlands. https://ecdpm.org/publications/regional -groupings-epa-negotiation-configurations/.

Ehrich, M., B. Brümmer, and I. Martínez-Zarzoso. 2015. "Do Food Standards Enhance the Concentration of Food Export Markets? A Quantile Regression Approach." Paper presented at the European Trade Study Group 17th Annual Conference, Paris, September 10–12.

Fernandes, A., H. Maemir, A. Mattoo, and A. Forero. 2019. "Are Trade Preferences a Panacea? The African Growth and Opportunity Act and African Exports." Policy Research Working Paper 8753, World Bank, Washington, DC.

Formai, S., and F. Vergara Caffarelli. 2016. "Quantifying the Productivity Effects of Global Sourcing." Economic Working Paper No. 1075, Economic Research and International Relations Area, Bank of Italy, Rome.

Francois, J. F. 1990. "Producer Services, Scale, and the Division of Labor." *Oxford Economic Papers* 42 (4): 715–29.

Francois, J. and B. Hoekman. 2010. "Services Trade and Policy." *Journal of Economic Literature* 48 (3): 642– 92.

Frazer, G., and J. Van Biesebroeck. 2010. "Trade Growth under the African Growth and Opportunity Act." *Review of Economics and Statistics* 92 (1): 128–44.

Freund, C., A. Mulabdic, and M. Ruta. 2019. "Is 3D Printing a Threat to Global Trade? The Trade Effects You Didn't Hear About." Policy Research Working Paper 9024, World Bank, Washington, DC.

Hoekman, B., and B. Shepherd. 2015. "Services Productivity, Trade Policy and Manufacturing Exports." *World Economy* 40 (3): 499–516.

Humphrey, J., and H. Schmitz. 2002. "How Does Insertion in Global Value Chains Affect Upgrading in Industrial Clusters?" *Regional Studies* 36 (9): 1017–27.

Kassa, W., and S. Coulibaly. 2019. "Revisiting the Trade Impact of the African Growth and Opportunity Act: A Synthetic Control Approach." Policy Research Working Paper 8993, World Bank, Washington, DC.

Kassa, W., and W. Owusu. 2019. "Rules of Origin as Double-Edged Sword: Evidence from Textile GVC under AGOA." Paper presented at the Centre for the Study of African Economies (CSAE) Conference 2019, "Economic Development in Africa," St. Catherine's College, Oxford, UK, March 17–19.

Koopman, R., W. Powers, Z. Wang, and S.-J. Wei. 2010. "Give Credit Where Credit Is Due: Tracing Value Added in Global Production Chains." Working Paper 16426, National Bureau of Economic Research, Cambridge, MA.

Lenzen, M., K. Kanemoto, D. Moran, and A. Geschke. 2012. "Mapping the Structure of the World Economy." *Environmental Science & Technology* 46 (15): 8374–81.

Mattoo, A., D. Roy, and A. Subramanian. 2003. "The Africa Growth and Opportunity Act and Its Rules of Origin: Generosity Undermined?" *World Economy* 26 (6): 829–51.

Melitz, M. J. 2003. "The Impact of Trade on Intra-Industry Reallocations and Aggregate Industry Productivity." *Econometrica* 71 (6): 1695–1725.

Melitz, M. J. 2008. "International Trade and Heterogenous Firms." In *The New Palgrave Dictionary of Economics*, 2nd ed., edited by S. Durlauf and L. E. Blume, 3231–34. London: Palgrave Macmillan.

Mutambara, T. E. 2013. "Africa-Asia Trade versus Africa's Trade with the North: Trends and Trajectories." *African Review of Economics and Finance* 4 (2): 273–99.

OECD (Organisation for Economic Co-operation and Development). 2021. "OECD Services Trade Restrictiveness Index." Trade Policy Brief, OECD, Paris.

Ouattara, N., and A. Zeufack. 2019. "Africa in the New Trade Environment: Tapping into Trade Potential with Asia." Unpublished manuscript, World Bank, Washington, DC.

Robert-Nicoud, F. 2008. "Offshoring of Routine Tasks and (De) Industrialisation: Threat or Opportunity—And for Whom?" *Journal of Urban Economics* 63 (2): 517– 35.

Segerstrom, P. S. 2013. "Trade and Economic Growth." In *Palgrave Handbook of International Trade*, edited by D. Greenaway, R. Falvey, U. Kreickemeier, and D. Bernhofen, 594–621. Basingstoke, UK: Palgrave Macmillan.

Tajoli, L., and G. Felice. 2018. "Global Value Chains Participation and Knowledge Spillovers in Developed and Developing Countries: An Empirical Investigation." *European Journal of Development Research* 30 (3): 505–32.

Viner, J. 1950. *The Customs Union Issue*. London: Stevens and Sons.

World Bank. 2009. *World Development Report 2009: Reshaping Economic Geography*. Washington, DC: World Bank.

World Bank. 2020a. *Poverty and Shared Prosperity 2020: Reversals of Fortune*. Washington, DC: World Bank.

World Bank. 2020b. *World Development Report 2020: Trading for Development in the Age of Global Value Chains*. Washington, DC: World Bank.

WTO (World Trade Organization). 2018. *World Trade Statistical Review 2018*. Geneva: WTO.

PART I

Access to Traditional Markets: Taking Stock of Nonreciprocal Trade Agreements and the Way Forward

The US African Growth and Opportunity Act (AGOA) and the European Union's Everything but Arms (EBA) preference program have been operational for nearly two decades. Yet few studies have investigated the impacts of preferential market access on creating trade as well as the subsequent implications for economic transformation through exports, particularly manufacturing exports. This book attempts to fill this gap and derive policy implications for the Sub-Saharan Africa region.

The AGOA provides duty-free access to the US market for a selected group of products from eligible Sub-Saharan African countries. Most of the region's countries have registered gains in exports owing to the AGOA. However, the results have varied across countries, and most of the export gains have been unsteady. The EBA covers only least developed countries (LDCs); it excludes countries that could cross the threshold to access global markets. So far, exports of natural resources, mainly oil, account for the bulk of Africa's exports through these preferences. The next-largest boost has been for textile and apparel products, which have benefited from the largest tariff preferences.

The findings of this book suggest that preferential market access granted to Sub-Saharan African countries has the potential to foster their economic transformation through exports. Success would be conditional on changes in infrastructure, connectivity, the fundamental institutions of legal frameworks and property rights protection, and smart macroeconomic management with stable and competitive exchange rates and low inflation.

Achieving durable gains from trade would also entail reducing the uncertainties associated with preferential trade agreements (PTAs) and expanding preferential access to products in which African countries could have a comparative advantage.

The World Bank and donor countries should take the lead in reorienting the debate on Africa's development challenge—by moving from a "country-specific" to a "neighborhood-specific" approach—to maximize the gains from PTAs as well as aid-for-trade initiatives. This would have the added advantage of reducing the risk of cross-border conflicts by increasing the economic interdependence of the member countries, which would raise the costs of conflict.

The following key messages emerge from the chapters in Part I (chapters 1–3) of the book:

- PTAs must be reinforced with specific reform of how high-income countries extend the preference to select beneficiary countries. PTAs need to be integrated with other efforts to deepen trade and investment between Sub-Saharan African countries and the Organization for Economic Co-operation and Development countries, mainly the United States and the European Union. This includes integrating the AGOA and EBA with foreign aid policy instruments to address the structural challenges limiting export capacity.
- Expansion to non LDCs of quota-free, tariff-free access to the products in which most African countries may have comparative advantage, such as agriculture and nontextile manufacturing, may expand the benefits for African firms.
- The appeal of preferences should be reoriented toward building a competitive manufacturing sector. Ethiopia's recent success in attracting foreign direct investment and exploiting the AGOA is an important milestone in improving the competitiveness of the manufacturing sector, which supports the growth of manufacturing for exports.
- Sound macroeconomic policies to maintain stable, competitive exchange rates and low inflation and improvements in the quality of infrastructure (especially information and communications technology) provide the underpinnings necessary to allow economies to take advantage of the export opportunities provided by the AGOA. Reforms to improve the business environment should focus more on improving the quality of the judiciary, infrastructure, and macroeconomic stability.

CHAPTER 1

Trade Impact of the AGOA: An Aggregate Perspective

Souleymane Coulibaly and Woubet Kassa

Introduction

Since the introduction of the Generalized System of Preferences (GSP) in the 1970s,[1] there has been widespread interest in understanding the impacts of nonreciprocal trade preferences provided to Sub-Saharan African countries. This interest stems from robust evidence that expansion of trade boosts growth and development.

Recent economic growth success stories in countries including China, the Republic of Korea, Malaysia, and Singapore are often attributed to those countries' effective participation in international trade (Commission on Growth and Development 2008; Connolly and Yi 2015). Firms' participation in global trade spreads the benefits of new technology to improve overall welfare (Segerstrom 2013). The rise in exports following improved access to foreign markets may lead to the growth of more-efficient firms, further inducing increased productivity among firms and across the economy (Melitz 2003). In addition, increased access to foreign markets, because it induces entry, yields increases in the productivity of industry.

In line with this evidence, the United Nations Conference on Trade and Development (UNCTAD) has advocated for extension of the preferential trade access of least developed countries (LDCs) to high-income economies' markets (UNCTAD 2012). A few preferential trade agreements (PTAs) have emerged, aimed at providing duty-free, quota-free market access for Sub-Saharan African countries' exports. These include the GSP, the European Union's Everything but Arms (EBA) preference program, and the US African Growth and Opportunity Act (AGOA).

This chapter revisits the impact of the most important PTA in the region, the AGOA, which provides duty-free and quota-free access to the

US market for a selected group of products from eligible countries in Sub-Saharan Africa. The objectives of the chapter are twofold: First, we evaluate the total trade effect of the AGOA using the synthetic control method (SCM), a quasi-experimental approach that addresses some of the limitations in existing empirical approaches to examining the impacts of PTAs (a method further discussed in annex 1A). Second, we explore possible determinants of the variations in the estimated impact across countries and review the underlying mechanisms driving the variations. We attempt to account for the AGOA's heterogeneous impacts in the region. These findings could inform policy in the design and structure of PTAs as well as the design of domestic policy instruments to enhance the capacity of African economies to optimize their access to export markets, whether traditional or new ones.

The AGOA has been considered essential for promoting trade and hence for the transformation of economies in Sub-Saharan Africa. The underlying basis for the AGOA is that "increased trade ... [has] the greatest impact ... in which trading partners eliminate barriers to trade and capital flows and encourage the development of a vibrant private sector that offers ... the freedom to expand economic opportunities."[2] PTAs are also central in foreign policy strategy as well as the international development objectives of developed economies, including the United States and the European Union (EU).

Methodological Rationale

After close to five decades of implementation of PTAs, the findings on their impacts have largely been mixed (Klasen et al. 2015). In Sub-Saharan Africa, in particular, there has been little empirical evidence. Limitations in the empirical approaches used to analyze the impacts are also evident. The gravity model has been the workhorse framework for analyzing the impact of PTAs on trade (Aiello, Cardamone, and Agostino 2010; Anderson and Van Wincoop 2003; Brenton and Hoppe 2006; Cipollina and Salvatici 2010; Cirera, Foliano, and Gasiorek 2016; Gil-Pareja, Llorca-Vivero, and Martínez-Serrano 2014).

The predominant empirical literature on the impact of PTAs on trade or exports augments the traditional gravity model with a dummy variable representing participation in a particular PTA. The estimated coefficient of the dummy variable represents a measure of the PTA's impact. However, there is ample evidence that participation in PTAs is endogenous (Cipollina and Salvatici 2010; Egger et al. 2011; Magee 2003). Results based on the augmented versions of the gravity model suffer from the nonexperimental nature of the available data. The models fail to address underlying country differences due to observed (but not accounted for) and unobserved heterogeneity across countries. Hence, the results might have provided only an imperfect estimation of the impact.

Among recent efforts examining the impact of the AGOA, Frazer and Van Biesebroeck (2010) employ a triple difference-in-differences (DD) approach to address these issues. DD estimators provide unbiased *treatment* effect estimates when, in the absence of *treatment*, the average outcome for the *treated* and *control* groups would have followed parallel trends. However, in the absence of proper matching of the *control* and *treatment* groups, trade flows might not have followed parallel trends. In addition, DD estimates rely on the average impact, with a focus on only two points in time—before and after the AGOA—with limited consideration of the evolution of export trends or the gap in export trends between the control and treated groups over time.

Even without the AGOA, we would expect trade flows to change because of changes in observable and unobservable characteristics of the economies. We attempt to address some of these empirical challenges using SCM to supplement and inform existing work.

Summary Findings

The main finding suggests that the AGOA has contributed to increased exports in most Sub-Saharan African countries. However, the impacts have varied over time and across countries, and the gains have been unsteady. Much of the gains are accounted for by expansion of exports of fuel and other minerals, whereas, in a few successful cases, countries were able to diversify exports into manufactured goods.

Among the major factors explaining variations in the AGOA's trade impact are (a) the physical infrastructure, such as information and communication technology (ICT); (b) the rule of law and legal frameworks, such as property rights protection and contract enforcement; (c) a conducive macroeconomic environment, such as low inflation and exchange rate stability; and (d) the ease of labor market regulations.

More recent changes in high-income economies toward more-reciprocal trade agreements may deter the gains and potential gains of these nonreciprocal trade agreements between African countries and high-income economies.

The African Growth and Opportunity Act

The AGOA was enacted toward the end of 2000 as part of the US Trade and Development Act of 2000. It provides duty-free access to the US market for a selected group of products from eligible Sub-Saharan African countries. It initially provided eligibility to 34 countries on October 2, 2000, and has since been renewed and extended to 39 countries, although 3 countries are currently ineligible (table 1.1). In 2015, the AGOA was reauthorized for the fifth time, for 10 more years, to 2025.

AGOA Provisions

The AGOA has two key provisions—a broad provision and a narrower apparel- and textile-specific provision.

Broad product coverage. First, the AGOA provides eligible countries duty-free and quota-free access for selected product groups, expanding the list of products under the GSP. The GSP is a nonreciprocal trade preference

Table 1.1   AGOA-Eligible Countries, 2016

Country	AGOA eligibility start date	Apparel provision eligibility start date[a]	Special rule for apparel[b]
Angola	December 2003		
Benin	October 2000	January 2004	Yes
Botswana	October 2000	August 2001	Yes
Burkina Faso	December 2004	August 2006	Yes
Burundi	Ineligible January 2016	n.a.	n.a.
Cabo Verde	October 2000	August 2002	Yes
Cameroon	October 2000	March 2002	Yes
Chad	October 2000	April 2006	Yes
Comoros	June 2008	n.a.	n.a.
Congo, Dem. Rep.	Ineligible January 2011[c]	n.a.	n.a.
Congo, Rep.	October 2000	n.a.	n.a.
Côte d'Ivoire	Restored October 2011[d]	n.a.	n.a.
Djibouti	October 2000	n.a.	n.a.
Ethiopia	October 2000	August 2001	Yes
Gabon	October 2000	n.a.	No
Gambia, The	Ineligible January 2016	April 2008	Yes
Ghana	October 2000	March 2002	Yes
Guinea	October 2000[e]	n.a.	n.a.
Guinea-Bissau	Ineligible January 2013	n.a.	n.a.
Kenya	October 2000	January 2001	Yes
Lesotho	October 2000	April 2001	Yes
Liberia	December 2006	January 2011	n.a.
Madagascar	June 2014[f]	n.a.	n.a.
Malawi	October 2000	August 2001	Yes
Mali	Restored December 2013	n.a.	n.a.
Mauritania	October 2000[g]	n.a.	n.a.
Mauritius	October 2000	January 2001	Yes
Mozambique	October 2000	February 2002	Yes
Namibia	October 2000	December 2001	Yes
Niger	October 2000	n.a.	n.a.
Nigeria	October 2000	July 14, 2004	Yes
Rwanda	October 2000	March 2003	Yes
São Tomé and Príncipe	October 2000	n.a.	n.a.
Senegal	October 2000	April 2002	Yes
Seychelles	October 2000	n.a.	No
Sierra Leone	October 2002	April 5, 2004	Yes

(Table continues on next page)

Table 1.1   **AGOA-Eligible Countries, 2016** *(continued)*

Country	AGOA eligibility start date	Apparel provision eligibility start date[a]	Special rule for apparel[b]
South Africa	October 2000	March 2001	No
South Sudan	Ineligible 2015	n.a.	n.a.
Tanzania	October 2000	February 2002	Yes
Togo	April 2008	n.a.	n.a.
Uganda	October 2000	October 2001	Yes
Zambia	October 2000	December 2001	Yes

Source: US GAO 2015.

Note: Since 2000, 13 countries have lost eligibility, of which 7 eventually regained eligibility. Five countries—Guinea, Guinea-Bissau, Madagascar, Mali, and Mauritania—lost eligibility following coups. AGOA = African Growth and Opportunity Act; n.a. = not applicable.

a. The apparel provision provides duty-free, quota-free access to the US market for eligible apparel and textile articles made in a subset of AGOA-eligible countries, subject to a cap. This eliminates the average most-favored nation tariff of about 11.5 percent on apparel and textile imports to the United States. These include products that are not eligible under the Generalized System of Preferences or the AGOA's broader product-coverage provision.

b. The Special Rule for Apparel provides 22 lesser developed countries in Sub-Saharan Africa (those with per capita gross national product below US$1,500 in 1998) with additional duty-free preferential access for apparel made from fabric originating anywhere in the world.

c. Democratic Republic of Congo was eligible in 2000, lost eligibility in 2011 but was reinstated in 2020.

d. Côte d'Ivoire was ineligible between 2005 and 2011, owing to political unrest and armed conflict.

e. Guinea lost eligibility in 2009, regained it in 2014, and lost eligibility again in 2022.

f. Madagascar was ineligible from 2010 to 2014 because of a political coup.

g. Mauritania lost eligibility in 2006 but was reinstated in 2009.

program of the EU and the US that permits duty-free imports of a range of products (more than 4,600 products at the Harmonized System 8-digit classification) from designated low- and middle-income countries (LMICs)—currently about 130 countries, including most of those in Sub-Saharan Africa. The AGOA expanded this list to a total of more than 6,400 product groups.

In addition, AGOA countries are exempt from caps on preferential duty-free imports set by the GSP's Competitive Need Limitations program. The United States limits imports under the GSP program by placing thresholds on the quantity or value of commodities entering duty free.

Despite the AGOA's broad product coverage, there are still important exclusions from preferential access, particularly for agricultural products. Important exclusions include certain meat products, dairy products, sugar, chocolate, peanuts, prepared food products, tobacco, and other agricultural goods that could potentially be major export commodities for many Sub-Saharan African countries.

Apparel and textile coverage. Second, the AGOA provides duty-free and quota-free access for eligible apparel and textile articles made in qualifying Sub-Saharan African countries for a subset of AGOA-eligible countries, subject to a cap. This eliminates the average most-favored-nation tariff of about 11.5 percent on apparel and textile imports to the United States.

These include products that are not eligible under the GSP or the first (broader-coverage) provision of the AGOA.

These articles include apparel made of US yarns and fabrics; apparel made of Sub-Saharan African yarns and fabrics; textiles and textile articles produced entirely in Sub-Saharan Africa; certain cashmere and merino sweaters; and eligible hand-loomed, handmade, and printed fabrics. This AGOA provision represents a significant change in the inclusion of manufactured products—textiles and apparel—from that of the GSP. With a few exceptions (such as leather products, headgear, glass, and glassware), the AGOA provides access for a wide range of textiles and apparel products.

Moreover, under the Special Rule for Apparel for lesser developed beneficiary countries,[3] 22 countries in Sub-Saharan Africa enjoy additional duty-free preferential access for apparel made from fabric originating anywhere in the world. The rules of origin requirement has been relatively more liberal for this group of countries. For the remaining Sub-Saharan African countries, the rules of origin requirements are such that the yarn and fabric may be sourced only from other AGOA beneficiaries or the United States to be eligible for preferential access.

The rules of origin have unclear effects on exports and subsequent gains in trade and investment. When they are a binding constraint and more restrictive, they may restrict export opportunities. They could also benefit countries by encouraging domestic manufacturing and sourcing of apparel from domestic production and processing. The subsequent impact on the local economy of having more liberal or more restrictive rules of origin is still an open question. In addition to the rules of origin, preferential treatment for textiles and apparel requires that all beneficiary countries adopt an effective visa system and related procedures that assist in complying with the rules of origin requirements. Complying with these requirements could impose additional costs on exporting through the AGOA.

AGOA Amendment and Reviews

The most recent amendment, the AGOA Extension and Enhancement Act of 2015, calls for greater reciprocity in the elimination of barriers to trade and investment in Sub-Saharan Africa. It puts forward an out-of-cycle review mechanism, such that "at any time" the Office of the US Trade Representative (USTR) "may initiate an out-of-cycle review of whether a beneficiary country is making continual progress in meeting the requirements" for eligibility.[4] This mechanism allows entities from the private sector or "any interested person, at any time," to file a petition regarding a country's failure to comply with the "eligibility requirement."

In June 2017, the USTR initiated an out-of-cycle review of the eligibility of Rwanda, Tanzania, and Uganda after a trade group representing second-hand clothing exporters—the Secondary Materials and Recycled Textiles Association—filed a petition to challenge a proposed tariff increase and decision to phase in a ban on imports of secondhand clothing and footwear by the three East African countries. Following the risk of suspension, Tanzania and Uganda backtracked on the tariff hike and import ban, whereas Rwanda maintained its position. As a result, the United States has suspended the application of duty-free treatment for all AGOA-eligible goods in the apparel sector from Rwanda. Such developments indicate the beginning of a shift in the reciprocity of the trade agreements, although the AGOA is often considered a nonreciprocal trade agreement. These recent changes might adversely affect future export opportunities by raising uncertainty.[5]

Trade Flows from Sub-Saharan Africa to the United States

In 2017, US imports from AGOA-eligible countries totaled US$24.9 billion (equivalent to about US$20.2 billion in constant 2000 US$), compared with about US$17.9 billion in 2002 (equivalent to about US$19 billion in constant 2000 US$). Although the region made significant export gains in the first decade following the AGOA, total exports over the longer time horizon increased only marginally (figure 1.1, panel a). Petroleum products continued to account for the largest portion of US imports under the AGOA, with 86 percent of overall AGOA exports principally accounted for by only five countries, as further discussed below.

Between 2013 and 2015, there was a significant decline—more than 25 percent—in AGOA exports to the United States, mainly because of the massive decline in commodity prices. In 2017, total non-oil US imports under the AGOA were about US$4.3 billion (equivalent to about US$3.5 billion in 2000 constant US$), an increase of more than 140 percent in real terms for the period since 2001 (figure 1.1, panel b). A few non-oil sectors, including apparel, footwear, and agricultural produce, experienced increases in US imports from AGOA countries during this period. In order of importance, among non-oil exports, the biggest shares came from transportation equipment, minerals and metals, textiles and apparel, agricultural products, and chemicals and related products.

Table 1.2 presents the average annual exports to the United States (in constant 2000 US$) for the countries included in the study for four periods between 1993 and 2015. Similarly, figure 1.2 presents the average annual exports (in constant 2000 US$) of AGOA beneficiaries before and after AGOA for the entire period, 1993–2015, where the year of eligibility varies across countries. Among the major exporters, Nigeria, Angola, South Africa, the Republic of Congo, and Chad registered significant increases in exports to the United States after the AGOA (figure 1.2, panel a). Other countries that increased exports most significantly include (in order of average annual exports) Kenya, Lesotho, Ghana, Cameroon, Botswana, Namibia, Ethiopia, and Liberia (figure 1.2, panel b).

The next section discusses whether the rise in exports was associated with the AGOA, by presenting the estimated impact using SCMs.

Figure 1.1   Sub-Saharan Africa's Exports to the United States, by Type, 2000–17

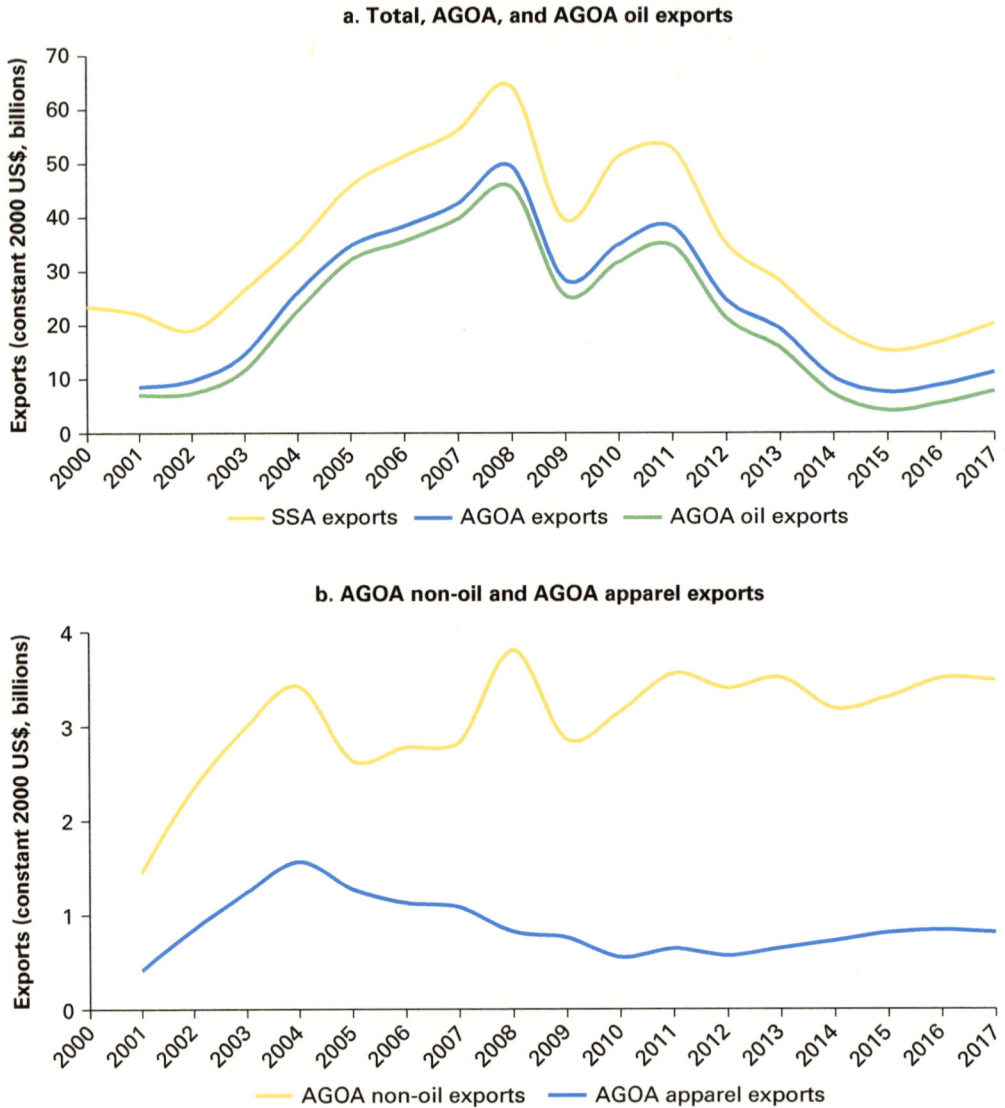

a. Total, AGOA, and AGOA oil exports

b. AGOA non-oil and AGOA apparel exports

Source: Calculations based on data from the US International Trade Commission (USITC) database.
Note: In panel a, the difference between total SSA exports and AGOA exports reflects exports that do not use AGOA preferences. In panel b, AGOA non-oil exports include AGOA apparel exports. AGOA = African Growth and Opportunity Act; SSA = Sub-Saharan Africa.

Table 1.2   Exports to the United States of AGOA-Eligible Countries, 1993–2015
Constant 2000 US$, millions

Country	1993–2000	2000–05	2006–11	2011–15
Angola	2,597	4,614	10,272	4,903
Benin	10	1	5	3
Botswana	22	60	165	189
Burkina Faso	1	2	2	3
Cameroon	80	191	270	181
Congo, Rep.	407	689	2,663	610
Côte d'Ivoire	311.4	607.8	730.2	797
Ethiopia	38	37	93	166
Ghana	192	138	230	228
Kenya	108	250	265	371
Lesotho	88	359	295	250
Madagascar	74	332	188	154
Malawi	64	80	51	49
Mozambique	22	9	23	58
Namibia	36	116	208	151
Niger	8	19	77	17
Nigeria	5,890	12,814	24,013	6,549
Rwanda	4	5	14	27
South Africa	2,745	4,964	6,607	6,018
Tanzania	25	27	38	70
Togo	5	6	8	15
Uganda	23	24	31	36
Zambia	46	20	28	37

Source: Calculations based on data from the US International Trade Commission (USITC) database.
Note: Table shows average annual export value in US$, millions (in constant 2000 US$) to the United States before and after the 2000 enactment of the African Growth and Opportunity Act (AGOA). Numbers are rounded to the nearest million. Various countries joined in different years, although most were eligible toward the end of 2000.
Note: Sixteen countries listed in table 1.1 are excluded from this table either because data are incomplete for the entire period or because the countries lost their eligibility during 2001–15, except Madagascar, which retained eligibility at least until 2010.

Impact of the AGOA: Results from the Synthetic Control Method

Would Sub-Saharan African countries have experienced similar export trends without the AGOA? If so, the trade creation or lack thereof in the post-AGOA period might not be fully attributable to the AGOA. To answer this question, we use synthetic controls—that is, estimated country experiences of trade flows had those countries not been treated preferentially under the AGOA.[6]

Figure 1.2   Average Annual Exports from AGOA-Eligible Countries to the United States, before and after the AGOA

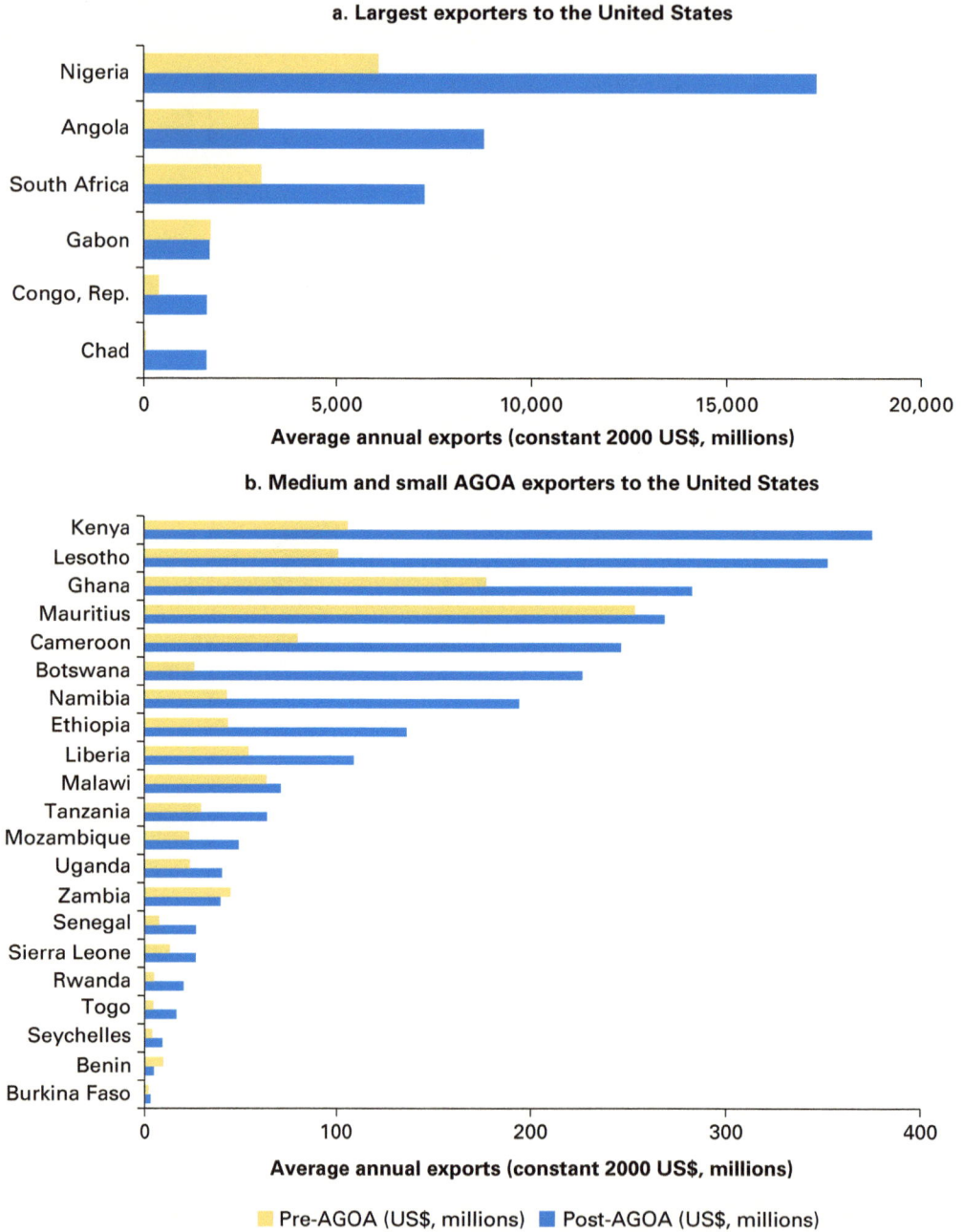

a. Largest exporters to the United States

Average annual exports (constant 2000 US$, millions)

b. Medium and small AGOA exporters to the United States

Average annual exports (constant 2000 US$, millions)

■ Pre-AGOA (US$, millions)   ■ Post-AGOA (US$, millions)

Source: Calculations based on data from the US International Trade Commission (USITC) database.
Note: Pre-AGOA refers to the period before a country became eligible (that is, 1993–2000): post-AGOA refers to the period after AGOA eligibility (that is, from 2001 up to 2015). AGOA = African Growth and Opportunity Act.

Overall Results of the SCM Estimation

To estimate the treatment effect, the SCM procedure follows table 1.1 in identifying when countries became eligible. Most of the countries in the sample were eligible toward the end of 2000 or 2001; a few others were eligible in later years. The estimation is based on specific years of entry into the AGOA framework, which may vary across countries.

Figure 1.3 presents the results of the SCM estimation for 16 AGOA-eligible countries, depicting the export trajectories of each country and its synthetic counterfactual for 1993–2015, where 1993–2001 is the pre-AGOA period.[7] The solid yellow line in the figure represents the observed trajectory of a country's exports to the United States, measured by imports to the United States (in constant 2000 US\$, millions). The broken blue line depicts the export trajectory of the synthetic country that captures the estimated aggregate value of exports a country would have attained if it had *not* been eligible for the AGOA. The vertical broken line indicates the year of AGOA eligibility.

Our estimate of the treatment effect—that is, of the AGOA's trade impact—is the difference between the country's exports and its synthetic counterpart after treatment. This gap represents how much higher or lower exports would be than what they would have been without preferential access to the US market under the AGOA. In most cases, the synthetic country closely reproduces the export trajectory of actual exports before treatment. This suggests a better fit and hence a better estimation of the impact in the posttreatment period.[8]

The results suggest that most of the countries that were eligible for AGOA expanded their exports to the United States after they gained preferential access. A few others failed to register any gains in exports due to AGOA. However, there are significant variations in the impact over time and across countries. The common trend in most countries is a rise in exports immediately after eligibility, followed by an eventual decline in exports. This pattern was largely due to the fall in US demand for exports from Africa and elsewhere in the wake of the 2008–09 Global Financial Crisis—a decline further exacerbated by the subsequent substantial collapse of commodity prices. However, a few countries registered significant gains in exports continuously, even in the midst of the financial crisis and declining commodity prices. In addition, following the expiration of the Multifiber Arrangement (MFA) in early 2005, exports of textiles and apparel have declined in some countries and stagnated in others.[9]

Angola, South Africa, Kenya, Namibia, Ethiopia, Botswana, and Tanzania (in that order) registered the biggest gains in exports as a result of the AGOA. Relative to their small size, Gabon, Togo, and Lesotho also saw large gains in exports because of the AGOA. Still, there were variations within these groups of countries across product types and by the volatility of the gains.

Figure 1.3   Export Trends and Synthetic Controls Applied to AGOA-Eligible Sub-Saharan African Countries, 1993–2015

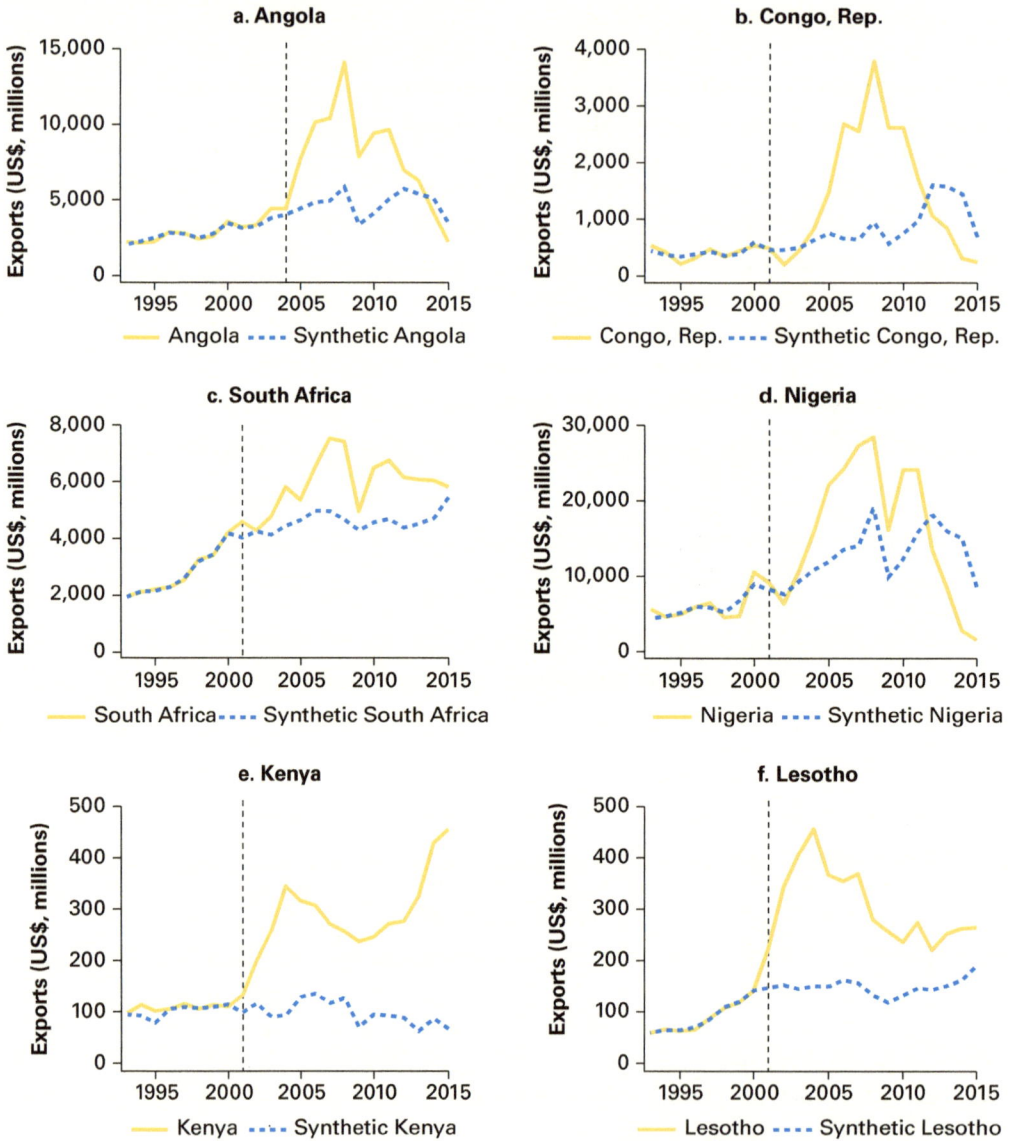

a. Angola

b. Congo, Rep.

c. South Africa

d. Nigeria

e. Kenya

f. Lesotho

(Figure continues on next page)

Figure 1.3   Export Trends and Synthetic Controls Applied to AGOA-Eligible Sub-Saharan African Countries, 1993–2015 *(continued)*

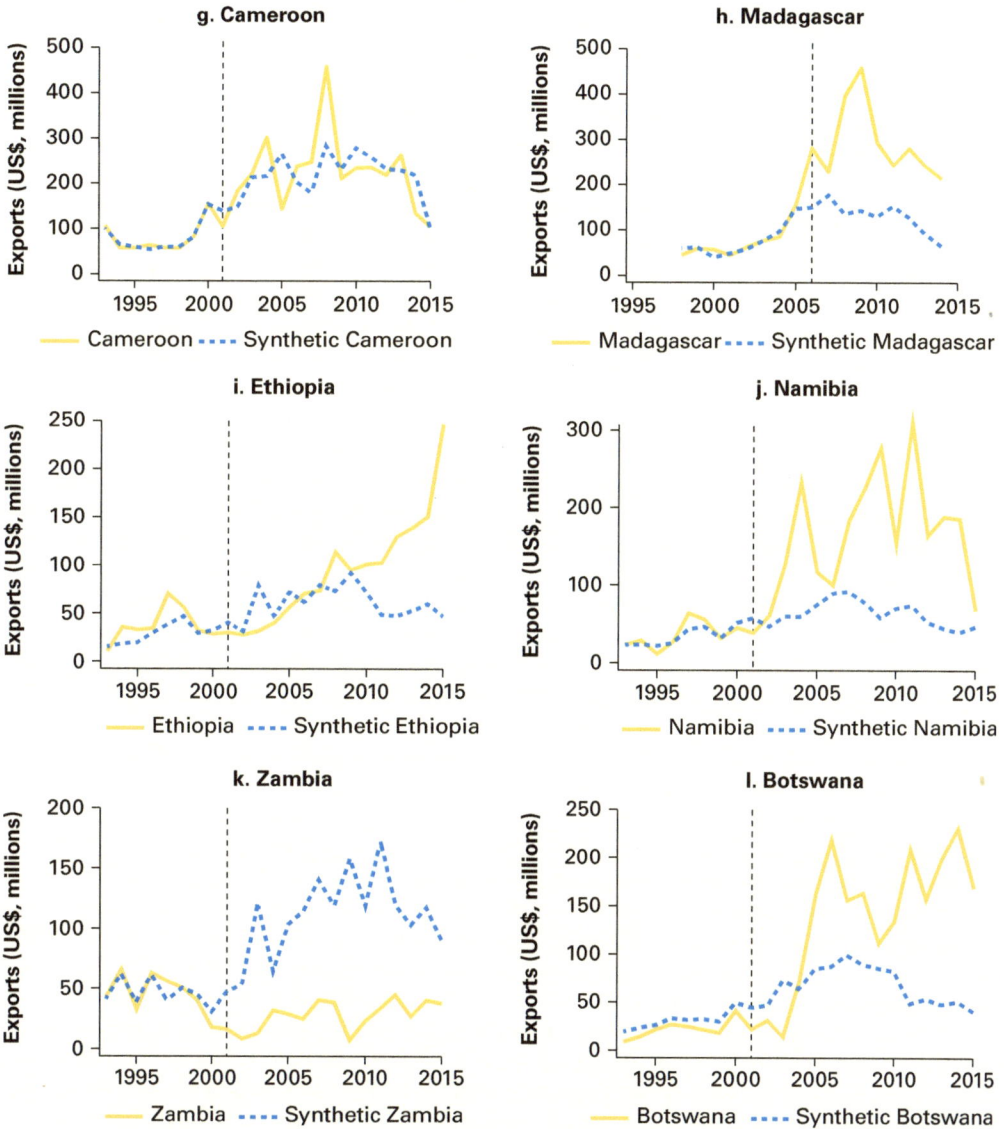

g. Cameroon

h. Madagascar

i. Ethiopia

j. Namibia

k. Zambia

l. Botswana

(Figure continues on next page)

Figure 1.3   Export Trends and Synthetic Controls Applied to AGOA-Eligible Sub-Saharan African Countries, 1993–2015 *(continued)*

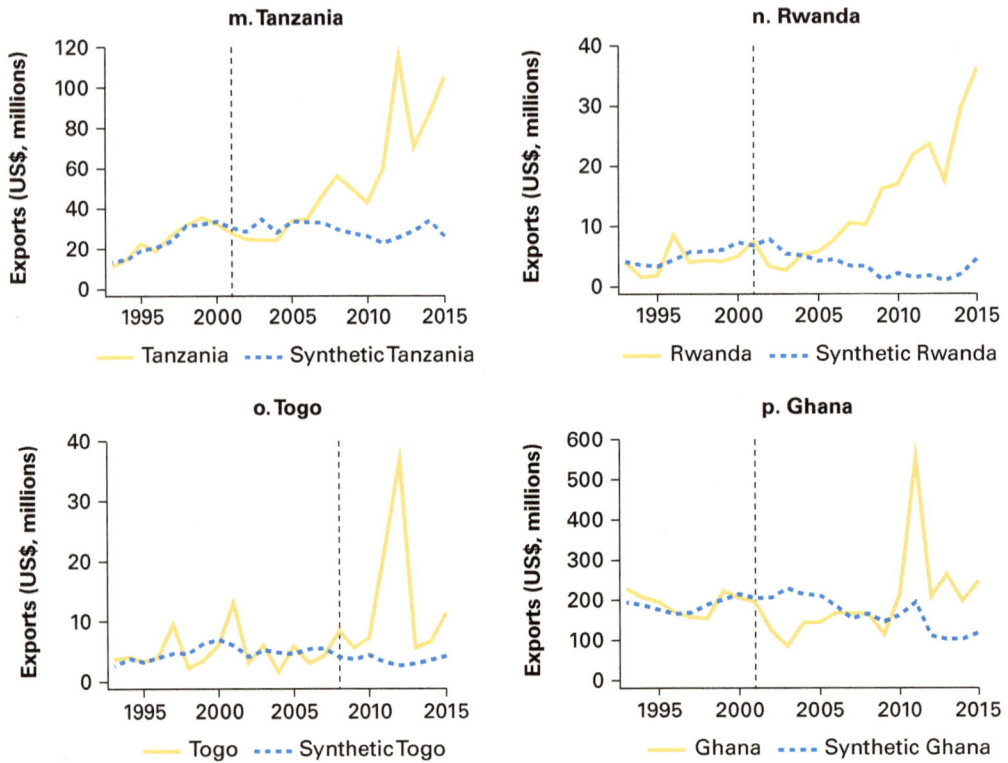

Source: World Bank calculations.
Note: The figure panels show the synthetic control method (SCM) estimation for 16 AGOA-eligible countries, depicting each country's export trajectory (solid yellow line) and its synthetic counterfactual (broken blue line) from 1993 to 2015, where 1993–2001 represents the pre-AGOA period. The counterfactual depicts the export trajectory of the synthetic country, capturing the estimated aggregate value of exports a country would have attained if it had not been eligible for preferential access to the US market under the African Growth and Opportunity Act (AGOA). The vertical dashed rule designates the country's AGOA eligibility start date. Excluded countries failed to satisfy the criteria for SCM estimation in terms of size, level of income, or other characteristics of their economies. Countries that lost their eligibility during 2001–15 are also excluded, except Madagascar, which retained eligibility at least until 2010.

Most of the gains were associated with an increase in exports of petroleum, and only a few countries registered gains in exports of manufactured goods. For countries such as Angola, the Republic of Congo, Gabon, and Nigeria, for example, all the gains resulted from a rise in exports of commodities, including petroleum and other minerals. A drastic fall in the total value of exports was evident in the immediate aftermath of the Global Financial Crisis, in the wake of which US demand fell and commodity prices declined drastically. This contributed to the biggest decline in export gains from the AGOA and reflects the risks of heavy exposure to a single export market—the United States—as well as dependence on a single commodity export. Although the AGOA has substantially raised commodity exports, it also exposed countries to the shocks of US demand as well as shocks to commodity prices—both of which are reflected in the disappointing growth performance of most of the economies.

Variations by Country and Product Category

The few success stories that registered relatively large increases in aggregate exports also registered expansions in exports of a diverse set of commodities, including manufactured goods and other consumer goods. This group comprises (in order by size of increase) South Africa, Kenya, Ethiopia, Tanzania, Botswana, Rwanda, and Lesotho. There is some variation in gains within this group as well, with South Africa benefiting the most, whereas Rwanda and Tanzania increased their exports and diversity of exports only after 2005. The rise in Ethiopia's exports is a more recent phenomenon: it has been benefiting from the expansion of its textile manufacturing as well as agricultural goods exports ever since the development of industrial parks, which serve as export processing zones.

Figure 1.4 shows the export trajectories of major product categories to the United States from countries that have expanded exports other than petroleum or natural gas. In textiles and apparel exports, Kenya registered the biggest gains (figure 1.4, panel b). Kenya also expanded its exports of agricultural produce and other manufactured non-apparel products. For Ethiopia, Rwanda, and Tanzania, the biggest share of export gains accrued from exports of agricultural commodities (figure 1.4, panels a, c, and d). Tanzania saw a sharp rise in 2012 followed by a sudden decline in 2014–15 of exports of pearls, precious stones, precious metals, and jewelry (Harmonized System [HS] Code 71). Ethiopia and Tanzania also expanded exports of textiles and apparel, whereas Rwanda's secondary export items included minerals.

East African countries registered more significant gains than other parts of the region in terms of their expansion of exports and diversification into light manufacturing, particularly textiles and apparel. In contrast, South Africa's major exports to the United States were dominated by advanced manufactured goods, such as transportation vehicles, while other minerals and textile exports accounted for smaller shares (figure 1.4, panel e).

An examination of the exports from countries registering the biggest gains from the AGOA reveals the importance of diversifying exports from commodities toward agricultural produce, apparel, and other manufactured products. In contrast, countries that depend almost exclusively on fuel or other minerals for their exports to the United States faced the worst decline in the wake of the Global Financial Crisis and subsequent commodity price shocks.

In sum, when the export gains were based on nonfuel exports, the gains were steady and increased consistently over the years of AGOA eligibility. In the long term, the AGOA could further boost exports and support the transformation of Sub-Saharan African economies if the countries diversify their exports toward nonfuel products such as manufacturing and agroprocessing.

Figure 1.4 Trajectories of Nonfuel Exports from Leading East African Countries to the United States, by Product Category, 2000–15

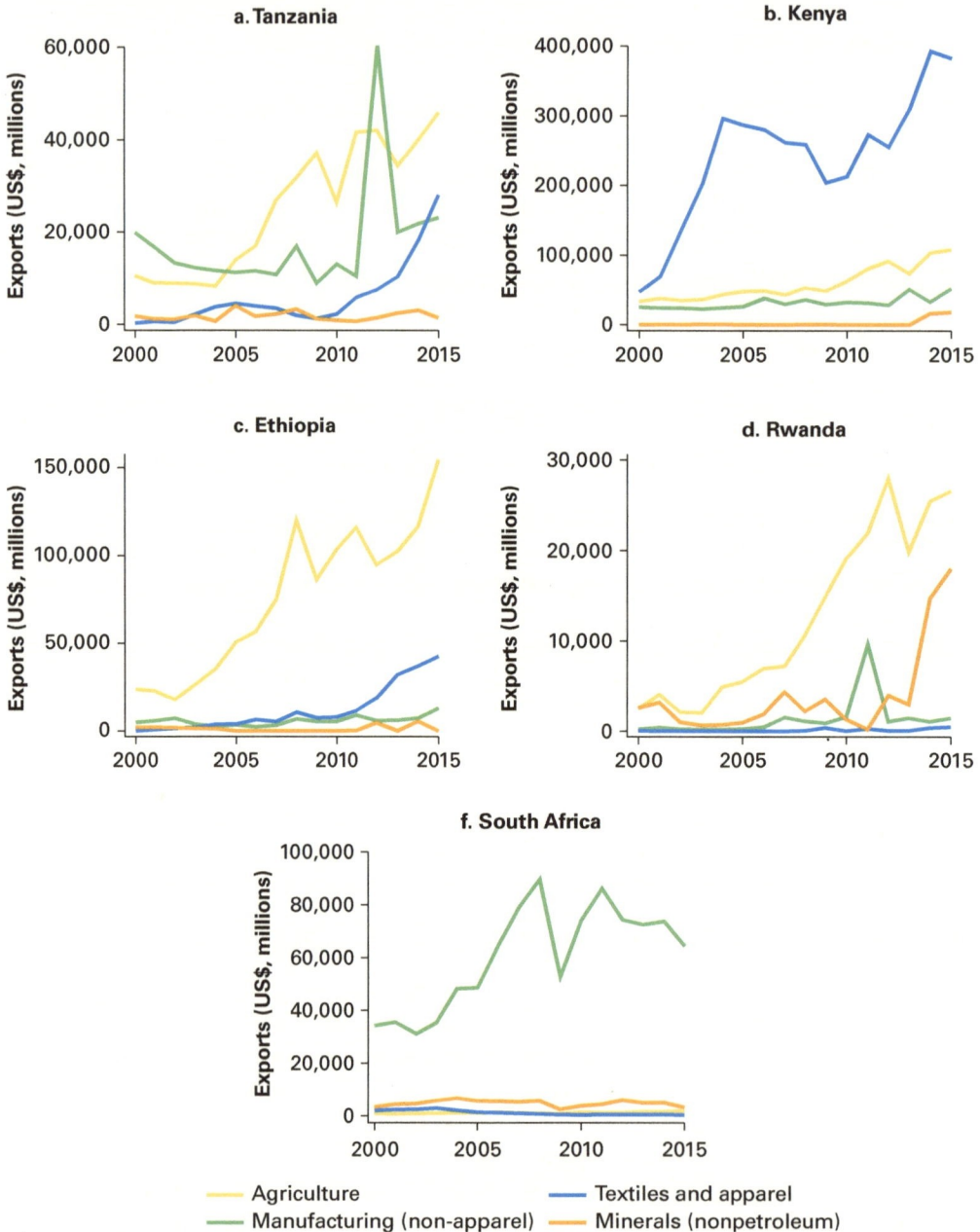

Source: Calculations based on data from the US International Trade Commission (USITC) database.

Pros and Cons of Further Relaxing the AGOA Rules of Origin

Like Lesotho, four of the successful East African economies—Ethiopia, Kenya, Rwanda, and Tanzania—have shown a rapid increase in textile exports to the United States. All these countries enjoy preferential access to the AGOA's apparel provision as well as the Special Rule for Apparel. The more liberal rules of origin requirements through the Special Rule for Apparel may have contributed to the expansion of apparel exports. This suggests that further relaxation of the AGOA's rules of origin requirements would lead to increased apparel exports by relaxing the sourcing of imported inputs.

The results from these more-liberal requirements also imply that there are prospects for expanding exports by further relaxing the rules of origin in nontextile manufacturing. In line with this, studies have shown that preferential trade regimes with strict rules of origin discourage export flows by restricting the sourcing of inputs from low-cost producers (Augier, Gasiorek, and Lai Tong 2005; Brenton and Manchin 2003; De Melo and Portugal-Perez 2008).

This reasoning may point toward a simple policy implication: that relaxing the AGOA's rules of origin is good for exports and hence for industrialization and growth prospects. However, sourcing a relatively larger share of the export components from foreign value added (FVA)—in other words, increasing the use of imported inputs to disproportionately higher levels to produce intermediate or final goods for export—under more-liberal rules of origin may create a strong disincentive for domestic industries to flourish. It could discourage local value addition and restrict the development of strong links to local industries.

Although lax rules of origin may increase exports in the short run, it is questionable whether this would lead to the expected dynamic growth benefits by enhancing backward and forward links with domestic industries. In the extreme case, lax rules of origin may encourage trade deflection and transshipment of final goods from low-cost producers to take advantage of preferential market access (Rotunno, Vézina, and Wang 2013). A recent study shows that countries that benefited from the more-liberal rules of origin under the Special Rule for Apparel have a large share of their export contents sourced from FVA (Kassa and Owusu 2019), though they also expanded textile exports.

Figure 1.5 presents the FVA share of the total textile exports of selected Sub-Saharan African countries to the United States over 1998–2015, using global value chain (GVC) trade data from the Eora multiregional input-output table. For countries such as Lesotho, Rwanda, and Tanzania, the share of FVA has more than doubled in the post-AGOA period. For South Africa, however, the FVA share in textile exports has not changed noticeably. This difference may be attributed to variations in the application of the rules of origin: although all these countries are eligible for the AGOA's broad-based and apparel provisions, only South Africa is not also a

Figure 1.5   Share of Foreign Value Added in Total Textile Exports from Selected Sub-Saharan African Countries to the United States, 1998–2015

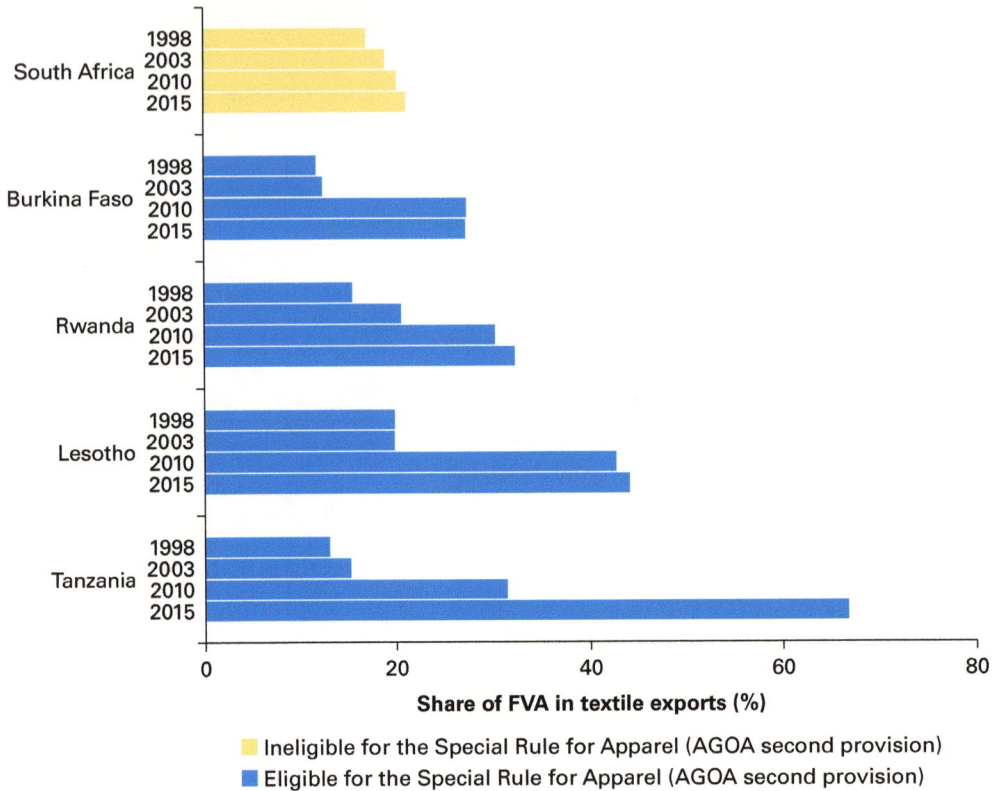

Share of FVA in textile exports (%)

■ Ineligible for the Special Rule for Apparel (AGOA second provision)
■ Eligible for the Special Rule for Apparel (AGOA second provision)

Source: Kassa and Owusu 2019, based on data from the Eora database (https://worldmrio.com/).
Note: Foreign value added (FVA) refers to the share of a country's imports that are used as inputs to produce intermediate or final goods for export. All countries except Burkina Faso were eligible starting in October 2000 for preferences under the US African Growth and Opportunity Act (AGOA). Burkina Faso's eligibility began in December 2004. All except South Africa are also covered by the AGOA's Special Rule for Apparel, which provides lesser developed countries in Sub-Saharan Africa with additional duty-free preferential access for apparel made from fabric originating anywhere in the world.

beneficiary of the Special Rule for Apparel and hence is subject to stricter rules of origin.

The impact of the flexibility of the rules of origin requires further investigation. It may be a double-edged sword in that when it is liberal it promotes exports, but it could also discourage building a strong and competitive manufacturing sector that has strong links with domestic industries.

The widely publicized upsurge in foreign direct investment (FDI) and the ensuing expansion of Lesotho's apparel industry due to the AGOA indicate the AGOA's significant potential. Following AGOA enactment, Lesotho—one of the region's smallest countries—became Sub-Saharan Africa's largest exporter of apparel to the United States. In the wake of the MFA expiration, however, textile exports declined from countries such as Lesotho, whose primary exports are textiles. This has raised concerns about the prospects of industrialization based on FDI-seeking preferential access rather than other comparative advantages. With the erosion of the preferences, as shown by the expiry of the MFA, there is a greater risk of losing a large part of the manufacturing sector because of the footloose nature of such manufacturing FDI.

Countries that have not seen gains in trade from preferential market access include Benin, Cameroon, Guinea, Mozambique, and Zambia. For example, US imports of goods from Cameroon declined by about 16 percent between 2005 and 2013. Cameroon's main exports included wood, mineral fuels, and cocoa. Zambia has a relatively bigger share of exports to the United States than many Sub-Saharan African countries. However, the estimated rise in exports that was expected over the past two decades, even without the AGOA, was much higher than the stable and constant export performance the country registered after the AGOA. This suggests that Zambia is one of the countries that would have expanded exports to the United States regardless of the AGOA. Hence, any increase in the country's exports should not be attributed to the AGOA.[10]

The AGOA's Aggregate Impact

Overall, the AGOA has had considerable trade creation impact, albeit driven largely by commodity exports. An average annual treatment (AGOA) effect in export gains for the region closely follows fluctuations in commodity prices and global demand, whereas the trade impact exhibits considerable variation across countries in the post-AGOA period. Map 1.1 shows the aggregate measure of gains in exports from 2001 to 2015, broken into three periods: 2001–05, 2006–11, and 2012–15. The map indicates the change in the trade impact over time as measured by the average annual treatment effect (in export gains) over the three periods.

AGOA impacts were largest in South Africa, Nigeria, Angola, and the Republic of Congo. A few countries that have also had resilient growth performance, particularly in East Africa, registered a continuous rise in exports, whereas a few others registered significant declines associated with the commodity price decline during the 2012–15 period. Nigeria, Angola, and the Republic of Congo registered the biggest declines after large early gains due to the AGOA. South Africa, Botswana, Kenya, Ethiopia, and Tanzania registered consistently increasing gains at various levels of trade. An often-cited AGOA success story—Lesotho—registered significant increases in exports, which lessened only slightly following the expiration of the MFA beginning in 2005 and declined further following the Global Financial Crisis.

Because this is the first attempt to use SCM to estimate the impact of a unilateral trade agreement for each country, the results from this study may not be directly comparable to those of previous studies. Previous average effects of PTAs may be hiding cross-country heterogeneity or variations across time. We calculate a comparable measure—the average treatment

Map 1.1   Average Annual Trade Impact of the AGOA in Sub-Saharan African Countries, by Period, 2001–15

a. Average annual trade impact, 2001–05

b. Average annual trade impact, 2006–11

c. Average annual trade impact, 2012–15

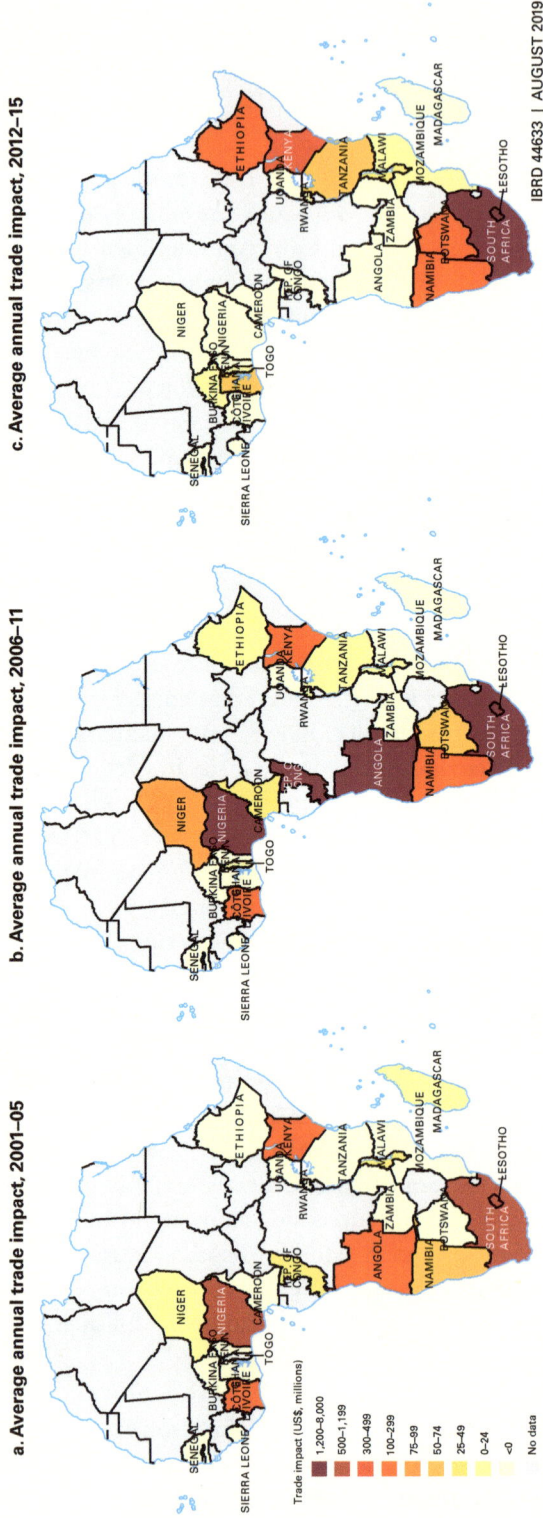

IBRD 44633 | AUGUST 2019

Source: World Bank.

Note: "Trade impact" is the annual average value of exports to the United States in US$, millions. AGOA = African Growth and Opportunity Act.

effect of the AGOA on all eligible countries included in the study. Although the measure hides extensive variations across time and countries, the significantly large trade-creation impacts suggest that the results are in line with those of previous studies (Cirera, Foliano, and Gasiorek 2016; Frazer and Van Biesebroeck 2010; Mattoo, Roy, and Subramanian 2003). The results are similar to those of earlier studies that found a significantly large, positive impact of the AGOA.

What explains the AGOA's successes and failures in Sub-Saharan African countries? The next section explains the observed variation in the impact of the AGOA in order to derive useful policy lessons for Sub-Saharan African countries seeking to expand their export capacity and take advantage of preferential access opportunities such as the AGOA.

Main Drivers of Exports under the AGOA

External trade barriers continue to be vital in understanding trade flows among countries. Despite the easing of trade barriers through preferential access such as the AGOA, fundamental supply-side factors could still limit a country's capacity to engage robustly in international trade and exports.

Using the AGOA's estimated trade effects, we provide a test to identify countries' fundamental characteristics in the effort to evaluate the heterogeneity in the effects. The goal is to understand which factors, after controlling for basic country characteristics, are more important in explaining variation in the AGOA's impact. We control for specific features of countries that could determine their participation in trade with the United States. Using country fixed effects might help account for some of these time-fixed variations across countries. It is important to exercise caution in considering the results as robust causal mechanisms because most of the determinants are correlated and endogenous. However, the similarities in the countries considered suggest that any significant difference in the determinants could be useful in understanding the heterogeneity in exploiting the AGOA and other export opportunities.

Tables 1.3 and 1.4 present the results of fixed-effect models using panel data for Sub-Saharan African countries covering the post-AGOA years, 2001–15. The data form an unbalanced panel because the years of eligibility vary across countries (as detailed earlier in table 1.1). All the coefficients in tables 1.3 and 1.4 have been standardized to allow comparisons of the relative strength of each factor. A 1-standard-deviation increase in an independent variable leads to a rise or fall in the trade impact by the value of the coefficient. Samples are included for the period after AGOA eligibility because the focus is on analyzing the correlates to the trade impact of the AGOA. We include only AGOA-eligible countries because we are interested in explaining the variations in the estimated trade gains. The dependent variable is the estimated trade impact due to the AGOA following our SCM estimations, after accounting for potential trends in trade in the AGOA's absence.

Table 1.3 Determinants of Export Gains under the AGOA

Variables	(1)	(2)	(3)	(4)	(5)	(6)	(7)	(8)
Inflation (annual %)	-0.015***	-0.067	-0.068	-0.040***	-0.033***	-0.033***	-0.035***	-0.111***
	(0.004)	(0.764)	(0.764)	(0.002)	(0.006)	(0.006)	(0.010)	(0.207)
Exchange rate stability	-0.186***	-0.118***	-0.117***	-0.230***	-0.205***	-0.205***	-0.206***	-0.219***
	0.000	0.000	0.000	0.000	0.000	0.000	0.000	0.000
External debt (% of GNI)	-0.124	0.038	0.040	-0.151	-0.159	-0.159	-0.152	-0.081
	(0.876)	(0.580)	(0.738)	(0.645)	(0.767)	(0.767)	(0.619)	(0.525)
Mobile subscription (per 100 people)	0.284***	0.205***	0.203***	0.369**				
	(0.009)	(0.001)	(0.002)	(0.032)				
Access to telecom					0.331*	0.331*	0.297*	0.198*
					-0.089	-0.089	-0.078	-0.079
Legal and property rights	-0.103**	0.036**	0.033**	-0.052*	-0.042***	-0.0421***	-0.121***	0.200***
	(0.045)	(0.047)	(0.075)	(0.002)	(0.002)	(0.002)	(0.001)	(0.001)
Transparency index	0.0134**	0.106*	0.104*	0.0140**				
	(0.022)	(0.063)	(0.095)	(0.018)				
Political corruption	0.083		0.008	0.118	0.122	0.122		
	(0.130)		(0.126)	(0.404)	(0.199)	(0.199)		

(Table continues on next page)

Table 1.3 Determinants of Export Gains under the AGOA *(continued)*

Variables	(1)	(2)	(3)	(4)	(5)	(6)	(7)	(8)
Political stability	0.035	0.103	0.105	0.045	0.049	0.049	0.069	0.117
	(0.369)	(0.332)	(0.244)	(0.541)	(0.754)	(0.754)	(0.926)	(0.810)
Quality of government (ICRG)				0.0126	−0.0168	−0.0168	−0.0221	−0.112
				−0.411	−0.793	−0.793	−0.803	−0.907
Labor regulations				−0.149***	−0.132***	−0.132***	−0.107***	−0.050***
				(0.000)	(0.000)	(0.000)	(0.000)	(0.000)
Net oil exports per capita								0.532
								−0.33
GDP		yes	yes					
Year FE	yes	yes	yes	yes	yes	yes	yes	yes
Country FE	yes	yes	yes	yes	yes	yes	yes	yes
Observations	313	292	292	298	298	298	298	298
R^2	0.448	0.260	0.261	0.486	0.470	0.470	0.469	0.484
F-stat	4.349	4.349	4.349	4.349	4.349	4.349	4.349	4.349

Source: World Bank.

Note: The dependent variable is the treatment effect (gap) in terms of export/trade due to the African Growth and Opportunity Act (AGOA) (in US$, millions); *p*-values are in parentheses. All specifications include both country and year fixed effects (FE). All coefficients have been standardized, allowing comparison as to the relative strength of each factor. A 1-standard-deviation increase in an independent variable is associated with a rise or fall of the trade impact by β standard deviation, where β is the value of the coefficient. GNI = gross national income; ICRG = International Country Risk Guide.

* $p < 0.10$; ** $p < 0.05$; *** $p < 0.01$.

Table 1.4 Sensitivity Analysis of Determinants of Export Gains under the AGOA

Variables	(1)	(2)	(3)	(4)	(5)	(6)	(7)	(8)
Inflation (annual %)	−0.061**	−0.013	−0.068					−0.111
	(−0.012)	(0.108)						.033***
Exchange rate stability	0.186		−0.182***	−0.229***	−0.192***	−0.200***	−0.192***	−0.195***
	(0.000)		(0.000)	(0.000)	(0.000)	(0.000)		(0.000)
Trade costs	0.060	0.108				0.021	0.035	0.035
	(0.713)	(0.978)				(0.973)	(0.780)	(0.651)
External debt (% of GNI)	0.070	0.086	0.083	0.066	0.086	0.067	0.100	0.099
	(0.747)	(0.661)	(0.599)	(0.305)	(0.482)	(0.348)	(0.191)	(0.196)
Labor regulation	−0.018***	0.044***		0.021***	0.021***	0.018***	0.042***	0.044***
	(0.002)	(0.004)		(0.001)	(0.006)	(0.010)	(0.004)	(0.009)
Mobile subscription (per 100 people)			0.208***	0.233*				
			(0.002)	(0.064)				
Legal and property rights		0.002	0.040**					
		(0.519)	(0.022)					(0.011)
Political stability		0.111	0.010					
		(0.951)	(0.392)					(0.455)
Access to telecom					0.226**	0.201*	0.153**	0.156**

(Table continues on next page)

Table 1.4 Sensitivity Analysis of Determinants of Export Gains under the AGOA *(continued)*

Variables	(1)	(2)	(3)	(4)	(5)	(6)	(7)	(8)
Political corruption					−0.001*			
					(0.035)	(0.062)	(0.013)	(0.010)
					(0.092)	(0.017)		
						(0.147)		
Quality of government (ICRG)				0.211				
				(0.727)				
Transparency index							0.147*	0.151*
							(0.052)	(0.086)
Net oil exports per capita						0.064	0.101	0.099
						(0.527)	(0.340)	(0.369)
Year FE	yes	yes	yes	yes	yes	yes	yes	yes
Country FE	yes	yes	yes	yes	yes	yes	yes	yes
Observations	303	303	294	266	294	290	290	290
R^2	0.241	0.288	0.296	0.295	0.297	0.297	0.293	0.296
F-stat	4.133	4.133	4.133	4.133	4.133	4.133	4.133	4.133

Source: World Bank.

Note: Dependent variable is the treatment effect (gap) in terms of export/trade due to the African Growth and Opportunity Act (AGOA) (in US$, millions), and p-values are in parentheses. All specifications include both country and year fixed effects (FE). All coefficients have been standardized, allowing comparison as to the relative strength of each factor. A 1-standard-deviation in an independent variable is associated with a rise or fall of the trade impact by β standard deviation, where β is the value of the coefficient. GNI = gross national income; ICRG = International Country Risk Guide.

* $p < 0.10$; ** $p < 0.05$; *** $p < 0.01$.

The findings suggest that various forms of infrastructure, the quality of institutions, and the macroeconomic environment explain much of the variation in export gains from the AGOA. These results are consistent in various specifications and robustness checks. (See table 1.4 for sensitivity checks.)

The Role of Infrastructure

The results show that infrastructure—in the form of access to telecommunications services and other ICTs—is critical in expanding countries' export capacity to take advantage of the preferential access created by the AGOA. Growth in digital technology reduces the costs of communications and various services, making every step of the production process more productive. Without integration into digital platforms, it would be difficult to engage actively and benefit from trade opportunities such as the AGOA.

The recent rise of GVCs, associated with falling trade and investment barriers, is also boosted by the advancement and expansion of digital technology. Digital technologies, in addition to their productivity-enhancing effects, provide the connectivity required to facilitate transactions and transfer goods and services. Hence, digital connectivity infrastructure and services are critical components in the drive toward greater engagement in trade and exports.

Similar analyses of African trade flows indicate that the region's relatively low export performance is largely due to poor infrastructure, particularly in transportation, and poor trade facilitation (Limão and Venables 2001; Wilson, Mann, and Otsuki 2005). Raising capacity in four areas of trade facilitation—port infrastructure (air and maritime), the customs environment, the regulatory environment, and communications infrastructure—would significantly improve trade performance (Wilson, Mann, and Otsuki 2005). Trade facilitation in the form of hard or soft infrastructure is found to have improved export performance for LMICS (Portugal-Perez and Wilson 2012). Hence, improving the quality and quantity of infrastructure is critical in the effort to raise the utilization rate of preferences such as the AGOA.

The Importance of Institutional Quality

Various forms of institutional quality are essential determinants of trade performance (Francois and Manchin 2013; Levchenko 2007; Nunn 2007). These include contract enforcement, property rights protection, judicial quality, ease of regulations, transparency, and anticorruption enforcement. There is strong evidence that contract enforcement explains more of the pattern of trade than physical capital and skilled labor combined (Nunn 2007), although Anderson and Marcouiller (2002) and Francois and Manchin (2013) argue that hard physical infrastructure is much more important than the rest. For Sub-Saharan Africa, issues of security and fragility are often considered significant determinants of trade performance because insecurity may act as a hidden tax on trade (Anderson and Marcouiller 2002).

We find that the quality of rule of law and other legal structures plays a significant role in enhancing export capacity. Indicators of political corruption and aggregate indicators of the quality of government are not shown to have any significant impact on trade. Neither does political stability. Yet the evidence on the role of the rule of law, legal structures, and security of property rights is robust. This can be attributed to the importance of confidence in contract enforcement and the effectiveness of judicial procedures in facilitating business-related transactions and resolving conflicts. The findings provide useful insights in determining policy priorities for improving the investment climate as well as strengthening legal institutions to enhance export capacity in the continent. Although corruption often takes center stage in discussions on improving institutions for trade, policy would have much more significant impacts if it was focused more on improving the legal institutions that are necessary to enforce contracts, maintain security, and ensure property rights protection.

In addition, we find that countries with more flexible labor market institutions—measured by the ease of regulations on minimum wages, flexibility of working hours, ease of hiring and firing, and other associated costs of managing labor transactions—tend to exhibit higher export gains. Countries with stricter labor market regulations impose costs on providing opportunities for expanding export capacity. Aidt and Tzannatos (2008) show that the package of formal and informal labor market and wage bargaining institutions matters in the effort to attract investment and expand export capacity. This suggests an essential role for the reform of labor market institutions in reducing labor costs and the associated costs of doing business.

The Robust Effect of a Sound Macroeconomic Environment

Another factor that we find to have significant impact on promoting greater investment and export capacity is the macroeconomic environment, with stable and competitive exchange rates and stable prices. Poorly managed exchange rates can have unfavorable outcomes by limiting investment and export opportunities (Rodrik 2008). Our estimations show that the role of sound macroeconomic conditions, as captured by stable and competitive exchange rate prices and lower inflation, has a strong impact on performance.

The significance of the effect is robust across various specifications. Hence, there is room for policy interventions to improve the competitiveness of the exchange rate regime and reign in domestic price fluctuations to promote exports. However, there is no significant impact of external debt accumulation on export performance related to the AGOA.

A Final Element: Policy Prioritization

Although there is some understanding that all the factors—including institutions, regulatory frameworks, and infrastructure—are critical, it is essential for policy makers to identify priorities. Reform that focuses on a few priorities would have a greater impact. We show that many countries in Sub-Saharan Africa have taken advantage of the opportunities provided by the AGOA, but the results vary across countries and over time within countries. Countries with better ICT infrastructure; a relatively better functioning and effective judiciary, and hence better contract enforcement institutions; and a better macroeconomic environment (including stable exchange rates) have registered the most significant AGOA-related export gains.

Increasing exports and improving trade—and hence promoting growth—in Sub-Saharan Africa require improvements in a set of institutions for property rights protection and legal structures. Although improvements in other institutional areas, such as reduction of corruption, are also important for trade and exports, policy priorities focused on the rule of law, the quality of the judiciary, and contract enforcement seem to generate greater returns. Sub-Saharan African countries also need to adopt a set of sound macroeconomic policies to keep inflation low and exchange rates stable and competitive. Finally, building on the quality and quantity of physical infrastructure, ICT, and other infrastructure presents opportunities for expanding exports for international trade. These represent the critical mass of reforms needed to boost the AGOA's transformation impact on beneficiary Sub-Saharan African countries.

Conclusion

This chapter has examined the AGOA's aggregate impact using SCM, a quasi-experimental approach. The novelty in the empirical approach is that it addresses the fundamental problems of estimation that are prevalent in nonexperimental methods such as the gravity model.

The main finding is that most of the eligible countries registered gains in exports due to the AGOA. However, the results were varied and the export gains largely unsteady. Much of the gains were attributable to petroleum exports, although a few countries expanded into exports of manufactured and other industrial goods. When the gains were derived from exports of fuel, they were largely unsteady. When they were based on nonfuel exports, the gains increased consistently over the years of AGOA eligibility. The erosion of preferences, particularly the expiration of the MFA, has lessened successes in the latter group.

In the long term, the AGOA's impact on exports could support the transformation of economies as long as there is diversification of exports into nonfuel sectors such as manufacturing and agroprocessing. The variation in the trade impacts is largely explained by infrastructure, institutions of legal frameworks, ease of labor market regulations, and a sound macroeconomic environment including stable exchange rates and low inflation. The results suggest that preferential market access granted to Sub-Saharan African countries has the potential to foster their economic transformation, conditional on changes in the fundamental institutions that govern legal frameworks including contract enforcement and property rights protection.

However, preferential access through PTAs such as the AGOA is not a panacea. The same underlying factors that explain the success of countries in other spheres of economic enterprise are critical. Sound macroeconomic policies to maintain a stable and competitive exchange rate, low inflation, and improvement in the quality of infrastructure (especially ICT) provide the underpinnings that are necessary to allow the economies to take advantage of the export opportunities provided by the AGOA. Reforms to improve business should focus more on improving the quality of the judiciary, infrastructure, and macroeconomic stability. In part, this approach contrasts with the widespread push on the World Bank's Doing Business indicators, which are focused on more-general business climate interventions. The study suggests the need for further disaggregated analysis of changes in exports, by product category, under similar PTAs.

As for either redesigning the next generation of the AGOA and other PTAs or reshaping existing ones, the United States and other Organisation for Economic Co-operation and Development countries could consider incorporating policy commitments along with preferential access. Commitments to reforms across a range of areas to create an enabling environment for private investment and trade could enhance export capacity. To that end, we suggest that PTAs be reinforced with specific reform-based eligibility criteria. PTAs should be integrated with other efforts to deepen trade and investment between Sub-Saharan African countries and the United States. For example, integrating the AGOA with foreign aid policy instruments would help to address the structural challenges limiting export capacity.

Efforts to ease supply constraints and support the integration of African economies into global trade require the augmentation of quota-free, tariff-free *preferential* agreements with additional instruments to strengthen the capacity and competitiveness of the region's firms. Recent initiatives such as the Compact with Africa—an effort of the Group of Twenty (G-20) to promote private investment in the region by focusing on improving the business environment, building infrastructure, and promoting effective regulations and institutions—seem to be in line with this comprehensive approach. Furthermore, expansion of quota-free, tariff-free access to the products in which most African countries have comparative advantage, such as agriculture and relevant manufacturing, may expand the benefits for African firms. There is also an urgent need to combine aid with trade to maximize the gains from preferential access.

In addition, in line with the World Trade Organization's goal of providing support to LMICs, high-income economies need to maintain the unilateral concessions provided under the special and differential treatment. This requires reversing the recent trends toward greater reciprocity in traditionally nonreciprocal trade agreements including the AGOA.

Annex 1A The Synthetic Control Method

Following Abadie, Diamond, and Hainmueller (2010, 2015), the rationale underlying the SCM is described here.

Let Y_{it}^N be the outcome in terms of exports that would be observed in the absence of the intervention or participation in the AGOA for country $i = 1, 2,\ldots, J + 1$ and time periods $t = 1,2,\ldots,T$. Let T_0 be the number of preintervention periods, where $1 \leq T_0 < T$. Let Y_{it}^I be the outcome observed for country i at time t if country i is exposed to the intervention in periods T_{0+1} to T. Participation in the AGOA is assumed to have no effect on the outcome of trade before the implementation period. Then, we can define the difference between Y_{it}^I and Y_{it}^N as the effect of participation in the PTA for country i at time t, if country i is participating in the PTA in periods $T_{o+1},T_{o+2},\ldots,T$, as follows:

$$\alpha_{it} = Y_{it}^I - Y_{it}^N. \tag{1A.1}$$

Because only Y_{it}^I is observed in periods T_{0+1} to T, we use SCM to estimate the counterfactual Y_{it}^N, which is the level of trade of a country that has participated in the PTA had the country not participated in the PTA. Assuming only country $i = 1$ is eligible for the AGOA after period T_0, we are interested in estimating $[\alpha_{1T_{0+1}},\alpha_{1T_{0+2}},\ldots\alpha_{1T}]$, the impact of the AGOA for each period following the country's AGOA eligibility.

Because no single country is like the treated unit (country) before treatment, Abadie, Diamond, and Hainmueller (2010, 2015) propose estimating optimal weights $W^*=(w^*,\ldots,w^*_{J+1})$, which can be used to obtain a suitable control from a weighted average of similar countries that did not participate in the PTA. The optimal weights vector W^* for each country can be obtained following a synthetic control algorithm[11] that minimizes the objective function, that is, a measure of the distance between the predictors of the treated unit X_1 and those of the synthetic control, X_0:

$$\underset{x}{Minimize} \sum_{m=1}^{k} v_m \left(X1_m - X_{0m}W\right)^2 subject\ to \geq 0,\ldots,w_{J+1} \geq 0;\ w_2 +\ldots+w_{j+1} = 1,$$

$$\underset{x}{Minimize} \sum_{m=1}^{k} v_m \left(X1_m - X_{0m}W\right)^2 subject\ to \geq 0,\ldots,w_{J+1} \geq 0;\ w_2 +\ldots+w_{j+1} = 1,$$

$$\tag{1A.2}$$

where v_m is a weight that reflects the relative importance that we assign to the mth variable when we measure the discrepancy between X_1 and X_0W. X_1 is a $(k \times 1)$ vector of pretreatment variables that we use to match as nearly as possible to the treated country, and X_0 is a $(k \times j)$ matrix of the values of the same variables for the countries in the donor or control pool.

To provide a theoretical foundation for the choice of these variables, we follow a well-established literature in gravity models that explains trade flows (Anderson 1979; Bergstrand 1985; Head and Mayer 2014). The relevant model suggests including incomes measured by the gross domestic product (GDP) and GDP per capita of trading partners, population, weighted distance between trading partners, and a host of idiosyncratic factors, including common language and size of country, to explain trade flows.

SCM employs an iterative cross-validation method to select the optimal weights, so that the synthetic controls closely reproduce the actual outcome variable before treatment. If the synthetic country and the counterfactual have similar behavior over extended periods of time before the treatment, the gap in the outcome variable after the treatment is interpreted as the impact of participation in a PTA or treatment.

Conditional on a good match in the periods before treatment, Abadie, Diamond, and Hainmueller (2010) show that the bias in SCM is bounded by an expression that converges to zero with the number of pretreatment periods, even when treatment or eligibility is correlated with unobserved heterogeneity. That is, $\hat{\alpha}_{it} = Y_{it}^I - \sum_{j=2}^{J+1} w_j^* Y_{jt}$ is an unbiased estimator of α_{it} in equation (1A.1). Hence, $\hat{\alpha}_{it}$ represents the estimated trade impact of the AGOA.

Notes

1. See "Generalized System of Preferences" on the Trade Agreements website of the United Nations Conference on Trade and Development: https://unctad.org/topic/trade-agreements/generalized-system-of-preferences.
2. Trade and Development Act of 2000, title I, 19 U.S.C. § 3701 (2000).
3. "Lesser developed countries" are those whose per capita gross national product was less than US$1,500 per year in 1998, as measured by the World Bank.
4. AGOA Extension and Enhancement Act of 2005, Pub. L. 114–27, title I, § 101, 129 Stat. 363 (2015).
5. In a 2019 US–Africa Trade and Investment Forum in Addis Ababa, Ethiopia, many African governments and businesses expressed discontent over the increasing uncertainty associated with the AGOA. A few textile manufacturers indicated the importance of the AGOA in their choice of location for investment and the challenges of the unpredictable continuity of the AGOA from then until its expiration in 2025.
6. Annex 1A presents a brief introduction to SCM and its application for evaluating the AGOA's impact on exports to the United States.
7. A few countries are excluded because they fail to satisfy the criteria for basic fit in terms of their size, level of income, or other characteristics of their economies. Countries that lost their eligibility during 2001–15 are also excluded, except Madagascar, which retained eligibility at least until 2010.

8. In addition to simple observation and because traditional inference is not feasible, we undertake placebo tests to check the fitness of our model. We also estimate the root mean square error before treatment to evaluate the fit of the estimated synthetic control to the observed data. As a result, we dropped countries when there was a poor fit.

9. The MFA was an international trade agreement regarding textiles and clothing that was in place from 1974 to 2004. It imposed quotas on the amount of clothing and textile exports from LMICs to high-income countries.

10. This is the type of impact that would have otherwise been associated with the AGOA in traditional empirical frameworks.

11. The synthetic control $W^* = (w_2,...,w_{j+1})$ is selected to minimize $\| X_1 - X_0 \|$ subject to $w_2 \geq 0$, ..., $w_{j+1} \geq 0$ and $w_2 + ... + w_{j+1} = 1$, where for any $(k \times 1)$ vector u, $\| u \| = \sqrt{u'Vu}$.

References

Abadie, A., A. Diamond, and J. Hainmueller. 2010. "Synthetic Control Methods for Comparative Case Studies: Estimating the Effect of California's Tobacco Control Program." *Journal of the American Statistical Association* 105 (490): 493–505.

Abadie, A., A. Diamond, and J. Hainmueller. 2015. "Comparative Politics and the Synthetic Control Method." *American Journal of Political Science* 59 (2): 495–510.

Aidt, T. S., and Z. Tzannatos. 2008. "Trade Unions, Collective Bargaining and Macroeconomic Performance: A Review." *Industrial Relations Journal* 39 (4): 258–95.

Aiello, F., P. Cardamone, and M. R. Agostino. 2010. "Evaluating the Impact of Nonreciprocal Trade Preferences Using Gravity Models." *Applied Economics* 42 (29): 3745–60.

Anderson, J. E. 1979. "A Theoretical Foundation for the Gravity Equation." *American Economic Review* 69 (1): 106–16.

Anderson, J. E., and D. Marcouiller. 2002. "Insecurity and the Pattern of Trade: An Empirical Investigation." *Review of Economics and Statistics* 84 (2): 342–52.

Anderson, J. E., and E. van Wincoop. 2003. "Gravity with Gravitas: A Solution to the Border Puzzle." *American Economic Review* 93 (1): 170–92.

Augier, P., M. Gasiorek, and C. Lai Tong. 2005. "The Impact of Rules of Origin on Trade Flows." *Economic Policy* 20 (43): 568–624.

Bergstrand, J. H. 1985. "The Gravity Equation in International Trade: Some Microeconomic Foundations and Empirical Evidence." *Review of Economics and Statistics* 67 (3): 474–81.

Brenton, P., and M. Hoppe. 2006. "The African Growth and Opportunity Act, Exports, and Development in Sub-Saharan Africa." Policy Research Working Paper 3996, World Bank, Washington, DC.

Brenton, P., and M. Manchin. 2003. "Making EU Trade Agreements Work: The Role of Rules of Origin." *World Economy* 26 (5): 755–69.

Cipollina, M., and L. Salvatici. 2010. "Reciprocal Trade Agreements in Gravity Models: A Meta-Analysis." *Review of International Economics* 18 (1): 63–80.

Cirera, X., F. Foliano, and M. Gasiorek. 2016. "The Impact of Preferences on Developing Countries' Exports to the European Union: Bilateral Gravity Modelling at the Product Level." *Empirical Economics* 50 (1): 59–102.

Commission on Growth and Development. 2008. *The Growth Report: Strategies for Sustained Growth and Inclusive Development.* Washington, DC: World Bank on behalf of the Commission on Growth and Development.

Connolly, M., and K-M. Yi. 2015. "How Much of South Korea's Growth Miracle Can Be Explained by Trade Policy?" *American Economic Journal: Macroeconomics* 7 (4): 188–221.

De Melo, J., and A. Portugal-Perez. 2008. "Rules of Origin, Preferences and Diversification in Apparel: African Exports to the US and to the EU." Discussion Paper No. 7072, Centre for Economic and Policy Research, Washington, DC.

Egger, P., M. Larch, K. E. Staub, and R. Winkelmann. 2011. "The Trade Effects of Endogenous Preferential Trade Agreements." *American Economic Journal: Economic Policy* 3 (3): 113–43.

Francois, J., and M. Manchin. 2013. "Institutions, Infrastructure, and Trade." *World Development* 46: 165–75.

Frazer, G., and J. Van Biesebroeck. 2010. "Trade Growth under the African Growth and Opportunity Act." *Review of Economics and Statistics* 92 (1): 128–44.

Gil-Pareja, S., R. Llorca-Vivero, and J. A. Martínez-Serrano. 2014. "Do Nonreciprocal Preferential Trade Agreements Increase Beneficiaries' Exports?" *Journal of Development Economics* 107: 291–304.

Head, K., and T. Mayer. 2014. "Gravity Equations: Workhorse, Toolkit, and Cookbook." In *Handbook of International Economics, Vol. 4*, edited by G. Gopinath, E. Helpman, and K. Rogoff, 131–95. Amsterdam: North-Holland.

Kassa, Woubet, and Solomon Owusu. 2019. "Rules of Origin as Double-Edged Sword: Evidence from Textile GVC under AGOA." Paper presented at the Centre for the Study of African Economies (CSAE) Conference 2019: "Economic Development in Africa," St. Catherine's College, University of Oxford, March 17–19.

Klasen, S., I. Martínez-Sarzoso, F. Nowak-Lehmann, and M. Bruckner. 2015. "Trade Preferences for Least Developed Countries: Are They Effective? Preliminary Econometric Evidence." Policy Review No. 4, Committee for Development Policy, Department of Economic and Social Affairs, United Nations, New York.

Levchenko, A. A. 2007. "Institutional Quality and International Trade." *Review of Economic Studies* 74 (3): 791–819.

Limão, N., and A. J. Venables. 2001. "Infrastructure, Geographical Disadvantage, Transport Costs, and Trade." *World Bank Economic Review* 15 (3): 451–79.

Magee, C. S. 2003. "Endogenous Preferential Trade Agreements: An Empirical Analysis." *B.E. Journal of Economic Analysis & Policy* 2 (1): 1–19.

Mattoo, A., D. Roy, and A. Subramanian. 2003. "The Africa Growth and Opportunity Act and Its Rules of Origin: Generosity Undermined?" *World Economy* 26 (6): 829–51.

Melitz, M. J. 2003. "The Impact of Trade on Intra-Industry Reallocations and Aggregate Industry Productivity." *Econometrica* 71 (6): 1695–1725.

Nunn, N. 2007. "Relationship-Specificity, Incomplete Contracts, and the Pattern of Trade." *Quarterly Journal of Economics* 122 (2): 569–600.

Portugal-Perez, A., and J. S. Wilson. 2012. "Export Performance and Trade Facilitation Reform: Hard and Soft Infrastructure." *World Development* 40 (7): 1295–1307.

Rotunno, L., P-L. Vézina, and Z. Wang. 2013. "The Rise and Fall of (Chinese) African Apparel Exports." *Journal of Development Economics* 105: 152–63.

Rodrik, D. 2008. "The Real Exchange Rate and Economic Growth." *Brookings Papers on Economic Activity* 2008 (2): 365–412.

Segerstrom, P. S. 2013. "Trade and Economic Growth." In *Palgrave Handbook of International Trade*, edited by D. Greenaway, R. Falvey, U. Kreickemeier, and D. Bernhofen, 594–621. Basingstoke, UK: Palgrave Macmillan.

UNCTAD (United Nations Conference on Trade and Development). 2012. *Handbook on Duty-Free Quota-Free (DFQF) and Rules of Origin. Part II: Other Developed Countries' and Developing Countries' Implementation of DFQF.* Geneva: UNCTAD.

US GAO (US Government Accountability Office). 2015. "African Growth and Opportunity Act: Eligibility Process and Economic Development in Sub-Saharan Africa." Report to Congressional Requesters No. GAO-15-300, US GAO, Washington, DC.

Wilson, J. S., C. L. Mann, and T. Otsuki. 2005. "Assessing the Benefits of Trade Facilitation: A Global Perspective." *World Economy* 28 (6): 841–71.

CHAPTER 2

Preferential Access to the United States and Manufacturing Export Performance: A Product-Level Analysis

Ana M. Fernandes, Hibret Maemir, Aaditya Mattoo, and
Alejandro Forero Rojas

Introduction

Did preferential access to the US market durably boost African manufacturing export performance? To address this question, this chapter uses product-level data that take advantage of two trade policy changes in the United States at the turn of the twenty-first century:

- The expansion of Generalized System of Preferences (GSP) products for least developed countries (LDCs) in 1997 and the implementation of the US African Growth and Opportunity Act (AGOA) in 2001—which together allow us to assess whether preferential access boosts the exports of all eligible products in general and of apparel specifically
- The 2005 phaseout of the Multifiber Arrangement (MFA), which allows us to assess whether any expansion in apparel exports persisted beyond the erosion of trade preferences.

The analysis relies on a highly detailed trade and tariff database that we constructed by combining US Census Bureau data on imports with US tariff data published by the US International Trade Commission (USITC), which jointly result in 26 years of data (1992–2017) on exports to the United States at the country Harmonized System (HS) 6-digit- level.

Analytical Context and Emerging Patterns

To place the US trade policy changes in context, well before the entry into force of the AGOA in 2001, nearly 30 percent of the HS 8-digit tariff lines in the United States had zero most-favored-nation (MFN) tariffs, and another 35 percent were duty-free for LDCs under the 1970s GSP regime. The expansion of GSP products for LDCs in 1997 freed another 16 percent of US tariff lines from duties.

The AGOA (a more favorable GSP arrangement) was unprecedented, allowing duty-free US entry of apparel products for the first time, as part of a further 6 percent of tariff lines being made duty-free. Under the AGOA, eligible African apparel exporters received privileged access to the US market not only because other countries continued paying tariffs but also because the main non-African exporters remained subject to quotas under the MFA.[1] These quotas were entirely phased out by 2005, unleashing competition from China and other Asian countries and eroding the preferences that African countries enjoyed in the US market.

The raw data reveal that oil accounted for the bulk of African exports to the United States under the AGOA, but we focus on manufacturing exports because boosting manufacturing was the main purpose of the AGOA. African manufacturing exports to the United States grew steadily in the first post-AGOA years and then flattened at about the time of the 2008–09 Global Financial Crisis. A more interesting pattern is seen in African apparel exports to the United States, which first boomed then declined after the end of the MFA quotas and have stagnated in recent years.

Delving deeper into apparel, we find that the aggregate picture for African exports is based on four country-level stories:

- *Missed opportunities:* Countries mostly in Central and West Africa never took meaningful advantage of the AGOA.
- *Boom-bust patterns:* Countries mostly in Southern Africa experienced a boom right after the AGOA took effect, followed by a bust.
- *Growth and stagnation:* Countries like Lesotho and Mauritius experienced a period of growth, followed by stagnation.
- *Late and sustained growth:* Countries in East Africa saw sustained success, albeit starting late in some cases.

How far are the patterns in the raw data attributable to (a) the GSP LDC and AGOA trade preferences and, (b) for apparel, the erosion of preferences when the MFA quotas were phased out? To identify a causal impact of the US trade policy changes on African countries' exports over a 26-year period (1992–2017), we take a treatment-and-control group approach. This approach relies on estimating a regression—designated as a triple-differences specification—following that proposed by Frazer and Van Biesebroeck (2010). The specification identifies the impact of GSP LDC or AGOA preferences by comparing (a) exports to the United States for eligible countries of eligible products with (b) exports to the United States for the control group (including noneligible products in eligible countries, noneligible products in control countries, and eligible products in control countries) before and after the US trade policy changes.

The specification identifies the causal impact of the AGOA and GSP LDC policy changes, because it accounts for unobserved differences and dynamics at the country-product, country-year, and product-year levels by including the corresponding large set of fixed effects.

Summary Findings

Our main findings are as follows:

- *Regarding the average impacts across all beneficiary countries* over the entire period following the US trade policy changes, the biggest boost from the AGOA to African countries' exports was for apparel products, which benefited from the largest tariff preferences. But the GSP LDC also had a positive and significant impact on exports of other African products.
- *Estimating separate impacts of the AGOA, by year,* we find that marginal impacts on African apparel exports grew sharply in the first years after AGOA but then leveled off after the end of the MFA quotas on apparel in 2005. This flattening could be a consequence of the erosion of preferences for African countries facing fiercer competition from the Asian giants in the US market.
- *The AGOA's impact on apparel exports varied* across the subregions of Sub-Saharan Africa. Countries in Central and West Africa saw little growth in exports. Countries in Southern Africa displayed a boom-bust pattern, with a stronger marginal benefit to exports in the first years followed by a decline after MFA was phased out. Countries in East Africa differed in terms of when growth took off, but some eventually saw sustained success, with large marginal impacts on exports starting in 2005.

Overall, these findings suggest that the AGOA helped to increase African exports, but the poor performance of Central and West Africa and the delayed spurt in most East African countries demonstrate that preferential access was not sufficient for export growth. Other factors—namely, favorable domestic conditions—were necessary to benefit fully from preferential access.

A preliminary exploration of the causes of the AGOA's differential impacts across African countries hints at several reasons: First, low tariffs on own imports may help explain the initial success of Southern African countries because such regimes allowed easier access to imported inputs than did other countries, where duty-drawback and other schemes involved higher transaction costs. Second, the establishment of effective special economic zones may explain not only the success of Mauritius but also the recent success of Ethiopia. Third, exchange rate regimes, and overvalued exchange rates in particular, may explain the lost opportunities in West and Central Africa.

A Product-Level Perspective from Disaggregated Export Data

The analysis in this chapter is based on a new, highly detailed database that we constructed by combining US trade data from the US Census Bureau with tariff data published by the USITC. This database—the US Trade and Market Access Database—is described briefly in the following paragraphs.[2]

The database provides detailed information on tariffs and product eligibility for trade preferences in the United States, including the applied MFN tariff the country-product faces in the United States in a particular year; the unilateral preferences the country-product can benefit from in the United States in that year (for example, the GSP and AGOA); and the best preferential tariffs that the country-product can benefit from in the United States in that year. Our tariff measures are all expressed as ad valorem because we compute ad valorem equivalents for duty variables expressed in the USITC tariff database as specific tariffs or combined tariffs (with an ad valorem component and a specific component).[3] The database also includes the value and quantity of US imports from any country of any HS 8-digit product each year from 1997 through 2017.

The new US Trade and Market Access Database offers important advantages relative to the widely used trade and tariff data sets from the World Bank's World Integrated Trade Solution (WITS):

- It provides information at a more disaggregated 8-digit level.
- It provides much better coverage of years for all types of tariffs, be they the MFN or preferential tariffs (under a large number of programs and regimes), whereas the WITS data on tariffs have many MFN and preferential tariffs missing. The imputation techniques used in the literature to correct those missing tariff data may yield inaccurate tariff rates.
- Preferential tariff rates are constructed on the basis of updated preferential trade agreements (PTAs), whereas in the WITS data they are often not updated when the preferential rates are phased in or phased out.
- It includes information on the actual imports that have entered under different trade regimes (for example, the GSP and AGOA), such that preference utilization rates can be computed. We also describe some broad patterns in Africa's export performance to the world (not just the United States) using WITS data.

For the econometric analysis, we make the following adjustments to the database: First, to capture trade flows before the GSP product coverage was expanded for LDCs in 1997, we augment the data on imports to include years from 1992 onward. Second, for computational feasibility, trade, preference eligibility, and tariff data are aggregated from the 8-digit level to the 6-digit level for most of the estimations. Third, to account for zero trade flows in our estimation, we expand the database such that it is a balanced panel in which all countries exporting to the United States have observations for all products in all years, with many recording zero trade flows. Fourth, we exclude oil products (HS chapter 27) from the estimating sample in all the regressions, although they account for a large share of AGOA-eligible exports from African countries to the United States, because the chapter focuses on the impact of US trade preferences on African manufactured products.

In addition, our long sample period presents a challenge for product classification, because HS product codes underwent several revisions between

1992 and 2017. To harmonize the product codes across years, we convert all HS 6-digit-level codes into HS 1996 revision 6-digit codes using the concordance tables provided by WITS.

The detailed tariff information allows us to examine how the trade effects of preferences under the AGOA or the GSP LDC vary with the magnitude of the preference margin offered to the beneficiary countries and how this effect changes over time. The database also provides detailed tariff information to examine how these trade effects change in response to the reciprocal and nonreciprocal preferential tariff rates granted to other countries.

A limitation of the tariff information is that it does not capture the ad valorem equivalents of quotas, such as those on apparel exports implemented under the MFA. To account for the effects of the MFA phaseout in our analysis, we complement the tariff data using quota information for 1992–2004 from Brambilla, Khandelwal, and Schott (2010). They construct quota fill rates in the United States, by exporting country and year, for 3-digit MFA categories defined by the Office of Textiles and Apparel that are mapped to 10-digit US HS codes using a concordance table.[4]

US Trade Preferences: The GSP and AGOA

GSP Programs

Over the past half century, high-income countries have aimed to support the integration of low- and middle-income countries (LMICs) into the world economy by providing them with "special and differential treatment," including nonreciprocal preferential access to their markets. The GSP has become a key instrument for such trade preferences.[5] The GSP programs were established in 1971, led by the United Nations Conference on Trade and Development (UNCTAD), under the assumption that preferential market access to high-income country markets—in the form of duty-free status or lower tariff rates for a wide range of products—could spur export-driven growth in LMICs. The argument was that the markets of high-income countries were sufficiently large to provide economic motivation and space for LMICs to achieve those goals.

The European Union (EU) was the first to establish a GSP program for LMICs in the early 1970s, and other high-income countries followed, with the United States beginning its GSP program for beneficiary LMICs in 1975.[6] In 1997, the scope of the US GSP benefits was expanded for LDC beneficiaries ("GSP LDC") by allowing duty-free entry into the United States for a larger number of products.

To be eligible for the GSP, countries must not be classified as "high income" by the World Bank.[7] As for the GSP LDC, the United Nations determines eligibility on the basis of three criteria: per capita gross national income, human assets, and economic vulnerability to external shocks.[8] In addition to the GSP programs, the EU and the United States signed other nonreciprocal PTAs with LMICs, such as, respectively, Everything but Arms (EBA) and the AGOA.

AGOA Eligibility and Benefits

General textile and apparel preferences. AGOA and country eligibility are discussed at length in chapter 1, but it is worth describing product eligibility in detail because it is crucial for the analysis conducted here. To begin with, Sub-Saharan African countries that are eligible for AGOA preferences do not automatically qualify for preferences under the general textile and apparel provisions. To be eligible for preferences under the AGOA's general textile and apparel provisions (section 112), AGOA beneficiary countries must be certified to confirm that they have in place an effective visa system and enforcement and verification procedures (USITC 2014).

These conditions ensure that the goods on which AGOA benefits are claimed are in fact produced in an eligible Sub-Saharan African country, meeting the rules of origin required to claim those benefits. As of 2017, 26 AGOA beneficiary countries also qualify for the general AGOA textile and apparel provisions. Burundi, South Sudan, and Togo, among others, do not qualify.

The Special Rule for Apparel. AGOA-eligible countries that are designated as "lesser developed beneficiary countries" (LDBCs)—those with a per capita gross national product (GNP) of less than US$1,500 in 1998—qualify for additional preferential treatment under the AGOA Special Rule. Under this rule, yarn, thread, or fabric used in manufacturing of textile and apparel articles can be sourced in any country in the world, and those articles can be eligible for duty-free access in the United States, subject to certain quantitative restrictions.[9] Although Botswana, Mauritius, and Namibia are not LDBCs under the per capita GNP definition, amendments to the AGOA designated them as LDBCs from 2004 onward.[10] As of 2017, 24 AGOA beneficiary countries also qualify for the AGOA Special Rule.

South Africa is the only Sub-Saharan African country that is eligible for preferences under the AGOA's general textile and apparel provisions but not eligible for the Special Rule, because it is not designated as an LDBC. For South Africa, the rules of origin for apparel and textile articles require (a) the use of US yarn, thread, or fabric (bilateral cumulation) for duty-free, quota-free access, or (b) the use of AGOA-originated yarn, thread, or fabric for duty-free access but with quantitative restrictions.[11]

Non-apparel products. The rules of origin for non-apparel products differ from those applied to textile and apparel articles and are similar for all AGOA-eligible countries, resembling those of the GSP program. Duty-free treatment of exports to the United States is allowed if (a) the product is the "growth, product, or manufacturing" of an AGOA beneficiary country, *and* (b) the percentage of local content in the appraised import value of the good when it enters the United States exceeds 35 percent. (This percentage can include the cost of materials and parts sourced from other AGOA-eligible countries, as well as the cost of materials and parts sourced from the United States, which can account for up to 15 percentage points of that 35 percent.)

Changes and amendments. Between 1997 and 2017, there was some degree of uncertainty about the continuity of the US GSP and AGOA, because of periodic expirations, and the AGOA also underwent amendments and changes. One such change, as noted earlier, was the addition of three countries to the list of LDBCs benefiting from the Special Rule that had not fit the LDBC per capita GNP definition in 2006 and 2008. In 2004, AGOA benefits were extended until 2015, but the Special Rule was extended only until 2007. Then the Special Rule was renewed under a series of waivers in 2006 and extended until 2012, and in 2012 it was extended until 2015. In 2015, the AGOA (including the Special Rule) was reauthorized to be in place until 2025.[12]

Tariff Structures and Changes under the GSP and AGOA

Next, we discuss product eligibility under the GSP and the changes brought by the AGOA, drawing on the US Trade and Market Access Database. Table 2.1 presents the numbers separately for Sub-Saharan African LDCs and non-LDCs in 2001. For LDCs and non-LDCs before AGOA enactment, from the universe of 10,184 tariff rate lines (HS 8-digit) on US imports, 3,131 faced a nonpreferential (MFN) zero rate of duty in the United States, and 3,507 faced a zero rate of duty in the United States for GSP-eligible countries.[13]

For LDCs, 1,670 tariff lines were added to the duty-free group under the expansion of the GSP LDC program in 1997, and from 2001 onward 780 new product lines became eligible for duty-free entry under the AGOA—divided into 555 apparel tariff lines (which had never been duty-free under any other nonreciprocal trade preference regime before the AGOA) and 225 non-apparel tariff lines (which faced positive MFN tariffs before the AGOA).

For non-LDCs, from 2001 onward, 1,610 tariff lines (which were already duty-free under the GSP LDC program since 1997) became duty-free under the AGOA. And (similarly to the LDCs) 780 new product lines—555 apparel and 225 non-apparel—became eligible for duty-free entry under the AGOA.

The AGOA's significance seems larger when accounting for the value of Sub-Saharan African exports in eligible tariff lines. For Sub-Saharan African LDCs, the AGOA covered 11 percent of exports in 2001, mostly from apparel products (table 2.1). For Sub-Saharan African non-LDCs, the AGOA covered 67 percent of exports, of which 3 percent were of AGOA-exclusive products (mostly apparel) and 64 percent were due to the extension of the GSP LDC preferences to all Sub-Saharan African countries. For LDCs, 1,096 tariff lines remain dutiable in the United States after AGOA, whereas for non-LDCs, 1,156 tariff lines remain dutiable in the United States.[14]

The tariff structure presented in table 2.1 shows that, for AGOA-eligible countries in the US market, the bulk of the tariff lines are duty-free. Focusing on LDCs, of the 1,096 tariff lines that have no preference and positive MFN tariffs, textiles (HS 50–60) account for 753 tariff lines and textile products other than apparel for 85. The other most important categories are dairy

Table 2.1   US Tariff Schedule under MFN, GSP, and AGOA Preferences for Sub-Saharan African Countries, by LDC Status, 2001

Tariff type	Number of US tariff lines (HTS 8-digit)		Share of exports to US (%)	
	LDC	Non-LDC	LDC	Non-LDC
MFN zero	3,131	3,131	9	28
GSP duty-free	3,507	3,507	1	4
GSP LDC duty-free	1,670	n.a.	79	n.a.
AGOA apparel	555	555	11	3
AGOA non-LDC	n.a.	1,610	n.a.	64
AGOA only	225	225	0	0
No preference (MFN > 0)	1,096	1,156	0	1
Total	10,184	10,184	100	100

Source: World Bank's US Trade and Market Access Database.
Note: The number of tariff rate lines and shares of total exports are for 2001, the year after enactment of the US African Growth and Opportunity Act (AGOA). Exports from least developed countries (LDCs) and non-LDCs include only those of the 46 countries that were AGOA-eligible between 2001 and 2017. (As such, the exports do not account for country-year-specific eligibility or preference utilization.) GSP = Generalized System of Preferences; HTS = Harmonized Tariff Schedule of the United States; MFN = most favored nation; n.a. = not applicable.

produce, bird eggs, and so forth (81); sugars and confectionary (24); cocoa and preparations (38); miscellaneous edible preparations (29); and travel goods (15).

Preferential Tariff Impacts on African Exports, before and after the AGOA

In addition to product *eligibility* under the AGOA, it is important to document the tariff preferences that the regime *awarded* to Sub-Saharan African exports to the United States. Before the AGOA, across all products, the average tariff had already been reduced from the average MFN tariff of 5 percent to less than 4 percent for GSP-eligible countries and to less than 3 percent for GSP LDC–eligible countries (figure 2.1, panel a). The AGOA further reduced the simple average tariff to 1–2 percent from 2001 onward for all eligible countries. This impact was particularly large for non-LDC Sub-Saharan African countries for which the AGOA non-LDC product list (almost all GSP LDC) and the AGOA-only products were liberalized simultaneously in 2001.

The trade-weighted average tariff, which accounts for the actual export capacity of African countries, was much lower than the simple average even before the AGOA but declined further with the AGOA—more sharply than as a result of the GSP and GSP LDC programs (figure 2.1, panel b). The GSP covered products making up a small share of exports, and the GSP LDC

Figure 2.1   US Average Tariffs on Products from Sub-Saharan Africa, before and after the AGOA

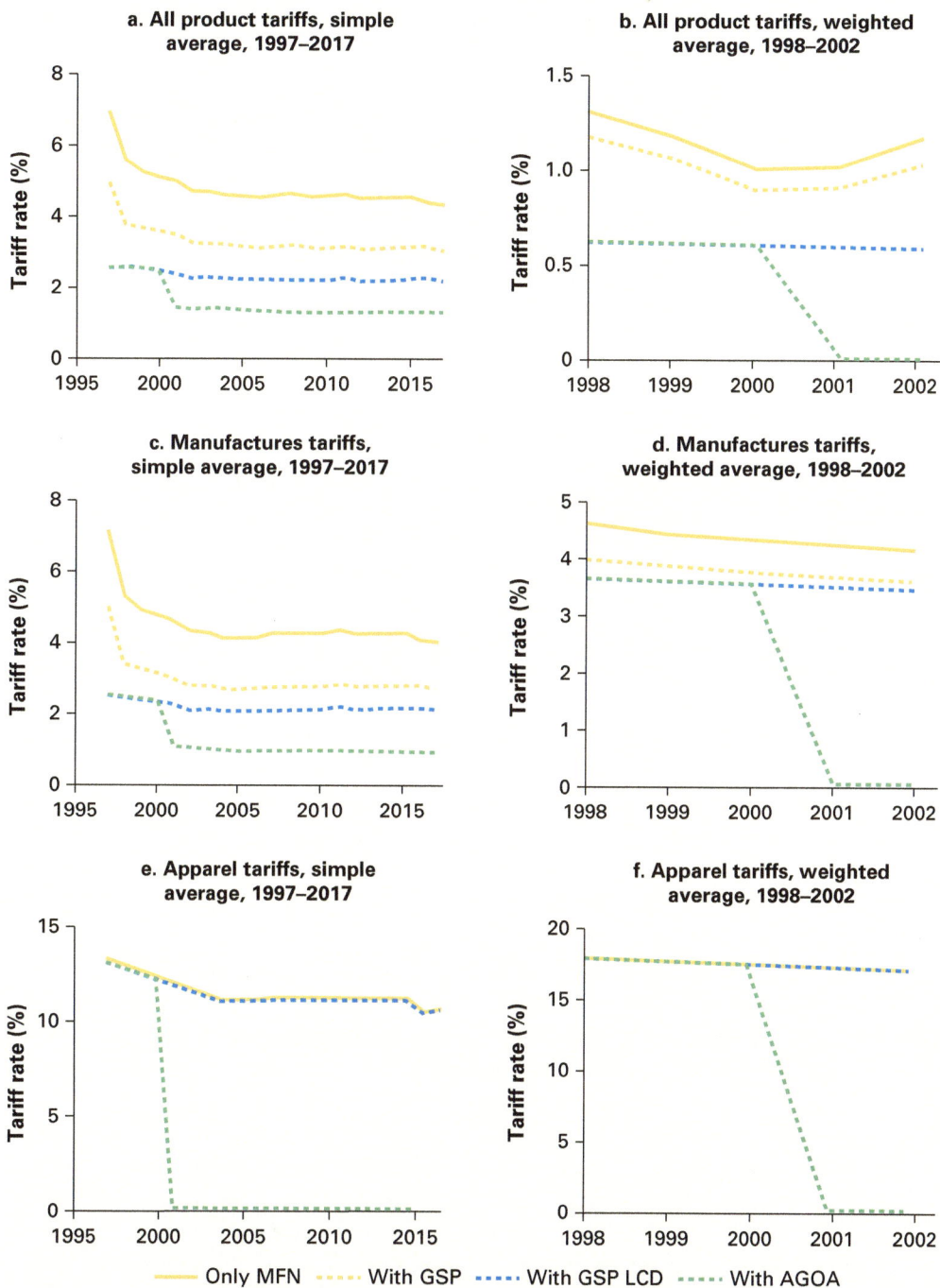

a. All product tariffs, simple average, 1997–2017

b. All product tariffs, weighted average, 1998–2002

c. Manufactures tariffs, simple average, 1997–2017

d. Manufactures tariffs, weighted average, 1998–2002

e. Apparel tariffs, simple average, 1997–2017

f. Apparel tariffs, weighted average, 1998–2002

—— Only MFN   ····· With GSP   ·-·- With GSP LCD   ·-·- With AGOA

Source: World Bank's US Trade and Market Access Database.
Note: Simple average tariffs include all 8-digit tariff lines of the Harmonized Tariff Schedule of the United States (HTS) each year. Ad valorem equivalents are calculated for tariffs with specific components (149 tariff lines with complex tariffs are not included). Trade-weighted average tariffs use Sub-Saharan Africa's total exports to the United States in 2000 as weights. The number of products per sector in 2001 HTS apparel includes Harmonized System sections 61 and 62. AGOA = US African Growth and Opportunity Act; GSP = Generalized System of Preferences; LDC = least developed country; MFN = most favored nation.

covered important products, such as oil exported by several African countries (for example, Angola). But the AGOA was the reason for the reduction of the average to zero, because of its expansion to all Sub-Saharan African countries (for example, Nigeria) and its coverage of apparel products.

The AGOA's impact on the simple average tariff on manufactured products was similar in magnitude to its impact across all products (figure 2.1, panel c), but it was much higher on the trade-weighted average tariff on manufactured products (figure 2.1, panel d). That is because (a) the corresponding trade-weighted average MFN tariff was much higher (above 4.5 percent) than across all products combined, and (b) the GSP and GSP LDC duty-free treatment covered products with seemingly little export capacity in Sub-Saharan Africa. The AGOA slashed the trade-weighted average tariff on manufactured products to almost zero, because it covered manufactured products in which African countries had the greatest export capacity.

But the most crucial tariff cuts induced by the AGOA were on apparel products (figure 2.1, panel e). These were the products most protected by US MFN tariffs (of about 12 percent), and AGOA duty-free treatment was extended to every apparel product in HS chapters 61–62. The GSP and GSP LDC had almost no effect on average tariffs because those preference programs do not cover apparel (other than a few accessories). The AGOA's impact is magnified for the trade-weighted average, which is brought to zero, relative to a trade-weighted MFN rate of 17 percent (figure 2.1, panel f).

For the AGOA's impact on the average tariffs on agricultural products and mining products, see figure 2B.1 (in annex 2B). The AGOA added a few agricultural products to those that were already duty-free under the GSP LDC program. As such, AGOA duty-free treatment was important only in reducing tariffs for non-LDC African countries that export agricultural products, like Côte d'Ivoire and Kenya. Average tariffs for mining were small because of low MFN tariffs and GSP preferences. The most important African mining exports to the United States already faced MFN tariffs that were close to zero before the AGOA. AGOA duty-free treatment became important for non-LDC, mining-intensive countries such as Botswana, Namibia, Nigeria, and South Africa.

AGOA Benefits Relative to US PTAs with Non-African Countries

Because of the proliferation of PTAs over the past two decades between the United States and non-African trading partners, the MFN tariff rates used in figure 2.1 are an imperfect benchmark against which to measure the tariff advantage that a preference program like the AGOA provided in the US market. It is therefore useful to consider a measure that captures the benefits of duty-free treatment provided by the AGOA to African countries relative to the preferential treatment provided by the United States to other exporting countries.

We construct a competition-adjusted relative preference margin (RPM), simplifying the formula used by Nicita (2011), as[15]

$$RPM_j^{US} = \frac{\sum_{hs} X_{j,hs}^{US} \left(\frac{\sum_V X_{v,hs}^{US} t_{US,hs}^v}{\sum_V X_{v,hs}^{US}} - t_{US,hs}^j \right)}{\sum_{hs} X_{j,hs}^{US}}, \tag{2.1}$$

where j is the country exporting to the United States, X is export value, v are other exporting countries competing with country j, t is the tariff paid in the United States, and hs is an HS 8-digit product. For a given country, RPM measures the difference between the trade-weighted average tariff it pays with that paid by all other competing countries, with a higher RPM indicating that the country benefits from a higher preference.

To illustrate this, we construct RPMs for apparel (HS 8-digit products within chapters 61–62) for China; Mexico (capturing the North American Free Trade Agreement, NAFTA); El Salvador (capturing the Central American Free Trade Agreement, CAFTA); and Kenya and South Africa (capturing the AGOA) and show them in figure 2.2.

Figure 2.2   Relative Preference Margins in Apparel Exports to the US from Selected Countries, 1997–2017

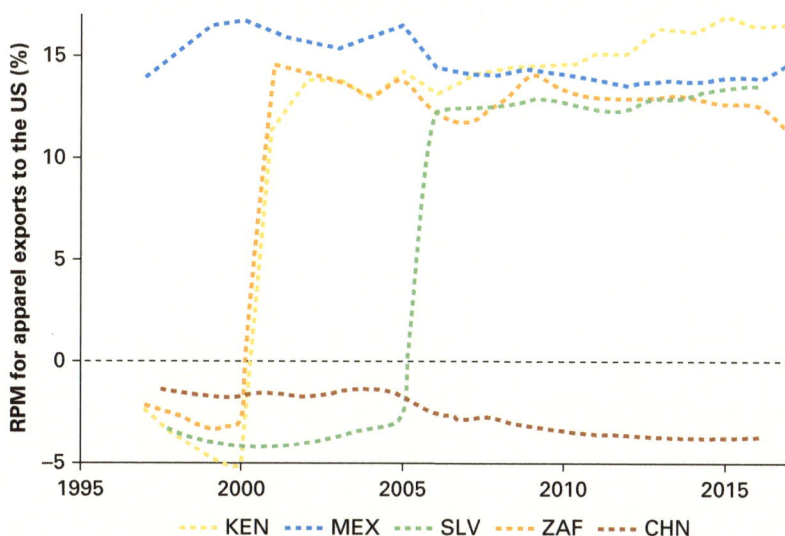

Source: World Bank's US Trade and Market Access Database.
Note: Figure shows the relative preference margin (RPM), in tariff rate differentials, for apparel exports to the United States from five countries: China (CHN), Kenya (KEN), El Salvador (SLV), Mexico (MEX), and South Africa (ZAF). The RPM measures the difference between the trade-weighted average tariff a given country pays with that paid by all other competing countries, with a higher RPM indicating that the country benefits from a higher preference. Kenya and South Africa benefited from the US Africa Growth and Opportunity Act (AGOA) of 2000, whereas El Salvador benefited from the Central America Free Trade Agreement (CAFTA) since 2005, and Mexico from the North American Free Trade Agreement since 1994.

The AGOA resulted in a large (competition-adjusted) preference margin in apparel for Sub-Saharan African countries. The AGOA gave African countries the same preference margins as NAFTA gave Mexico. The RPM received by Kenya and South Africa from the AGOA is robust to the CAFTA preferential treatment that started in 2005. Ideally, to calculate the true preference margin, we would also include the tariff equivalent of the MFA quotas and the impact of the MFA phaseout on the preference margins, but such an exercise is beyond of scope of this chapter.

African Export Performance and the Role of the AGOA

Africa's Export Performance

In describing Sub-Saharan Africa's export performance over the past two decades, we use WITS data to focus on African countries' share in world trade; the sectoral composition of their exports, emphasizing manufacturing and apparel; and the share of different destination countries.[16]

Share of world trade. Sub-Saharan Africa's low share in total world exports increased from about 0.6 percent in 1997 to almost 2.5 percent in 2011 before declining abruptly to 1 percent by 2017 (figure 2.3).

Figure 2.3   Sub-Saharan Africa's Share of World Exports, Total and Selected Sectors, 1997–2017

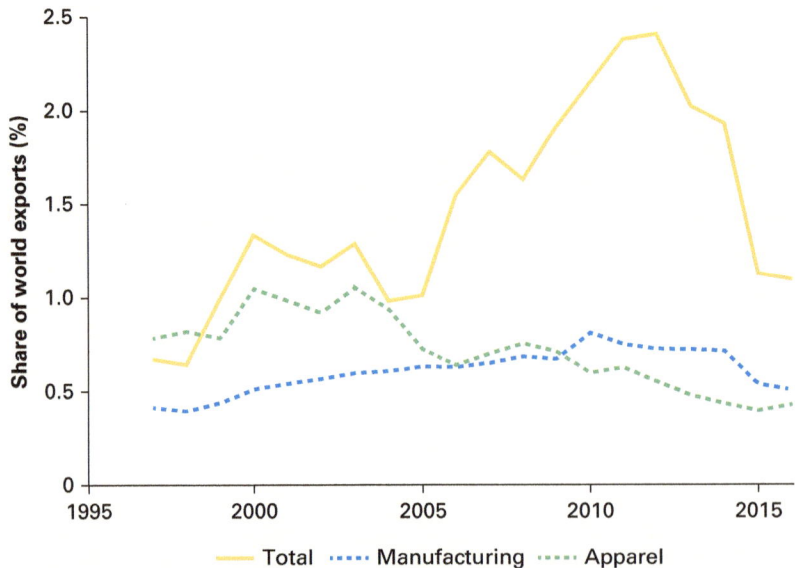

Source: World Integrated Trade Solution (WITS) data (https://wits.worldbank.org/).
Note: Graph covers 46 Sub-Saharan African countries. Data used in estimation include more countries than the number from WITS. To lessen concerns about the quality and consistency of export data from Sub-Saharan African countries, the analysis used WITS world data on imports as mirror data for the region's exports. For a list of the countries and years for which data are missing in WITS, see annex 2A, table 2A.1.

Because the region's exports are intensive in commodities, their value is sensitive to commodity prices, and the growth of African total exports follows closely the growth of commodity prices (annex 2A, figure 2A.1).

Sub-Saharan Africa's share in world manufacturing exports is much less sensitive to swings in commodity prices and has remained mostly unchanged over the past two decades, at a low 0.5 percent. However, the region's share in world apparel exports has been cut in half, from about 1 percent in 2000 to less than 0.5 percent in 2017.

Sectoral composition of exports. The share of manufacturing in Sub-Saharan Africa's total exports was close to 30 percent at the beginning of the twenty-first century, but it decreased sharply thereafter because of the boom in commodity prices. In the wake of recovery from the 2008–09 Global Financial Crisis, the share of manufacturing increased from 2012 onward, reaching 27 percent by 2016 (figure 2.4, panel a).

Individual countries exhibited diverse patterns, with manufacturing accounting for a high share of total exports for Botswana, South Africa, Madagascar, and Namibia (figure 2.4, panel b). Except for Senegal and Togo, no other African countries exhibited a meaningful increase in the share of manufacturing in their total exports between 2000 and 2016.

Share of total exports, by destination country. Africa has been shifting from its traditional trading partners, the United States and the European Union 15 (EU-15)[17] and increasing its exports to China and India (figure 2.5, panel a). For most Sub-Saharan African countries, the United States is a relatively small destination for exports, and the US share declined between 2000 and 2016 (figure 2.5, panel b).[18]

Similarly, for almost all the countries in the region, the share of total exports going to the EU-15 declined over the period: for most, it was higher than 40 percent in 2000 and less than 40 percent in 2016 (figure 2.5, panel c). The share of other Sub-Saharan African countries as a destination for Sub-Saharan African countries' exports remained relatively small and stable for most countries, but it increased substantially over 2000–16 for some countries, including Namibia and Lesotho (figure 2.5, panel d).

Share of manufacturing exports, by destination country. Sub-Saharan Africa's manufacturing exports, like its aggregate exports, have shifted away from the EU-15, whose share as a destination declined from 50 percent in 1995 to 25 percent in 2015 (figure 2.6, panel a). In contrast, the region's share of manufacturing exports to the United States remained stable, at about 10 percent. Its shares of manufacturing exports to China and India are substantially lower than those respective countries' shares of total exports, which is indicative of the recent pattern of Africa supplying raw materials to those fast-growing destinations. The share of Sub-Saharan

Figure 2.4   Share of Manufacturing in Total Exports, in Sub-Saharan Africa and by Country, circa 2000s–2010s

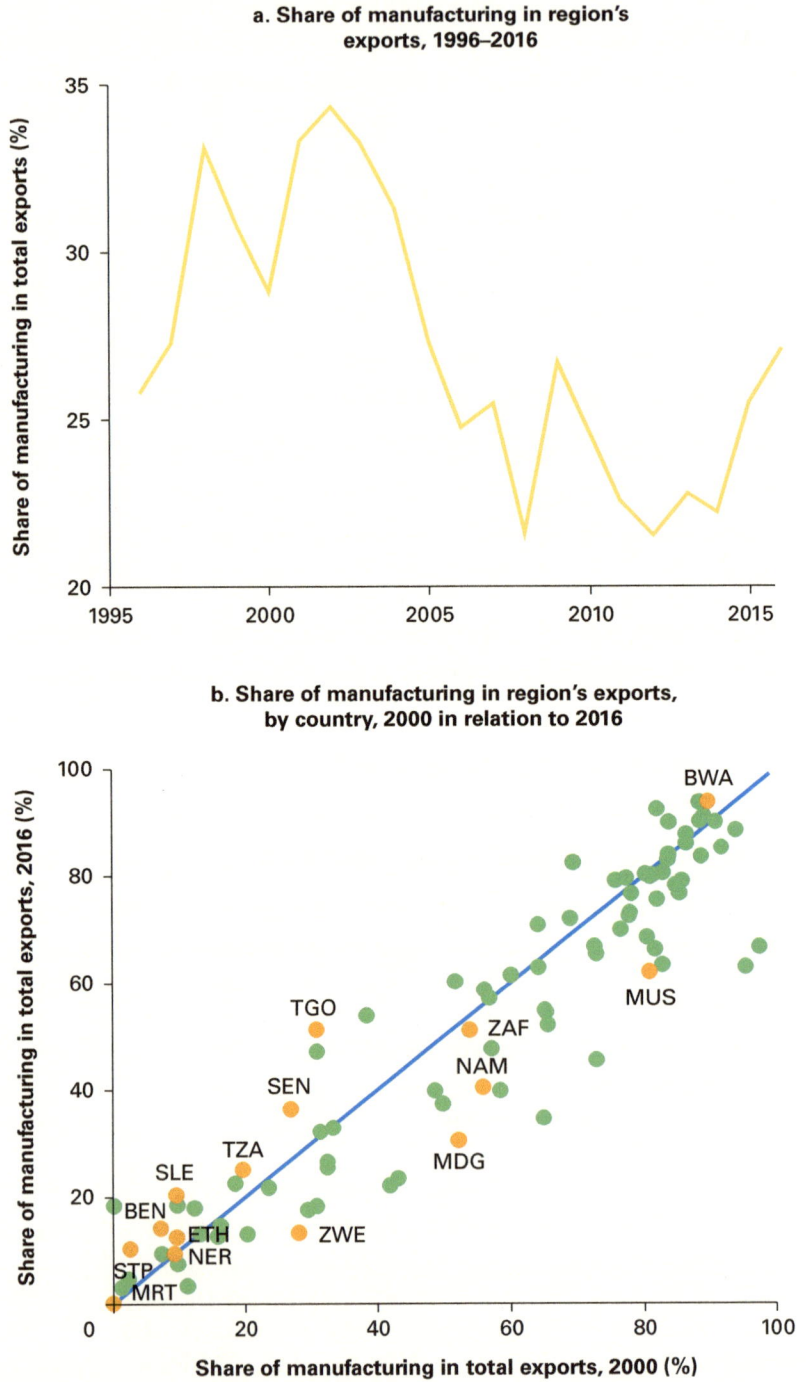

a. Share of manufacturing in region's exports, 1996–2016

b. Share of manufacturing in region's exports, by country, 2000 in relation to 2016

Source: World Integrated Trade Solution (WITS) data (https://wits.worldbank.org/); World Development Indicators database.
Note: Data for panel a cover 15 Sub-Saharan African countries. Panel b sample includes countries in all regions, but only the observations pertaining to African countries are labeled (using ISO alpha-3 codes).

Figure 2.5   Destinations of Sub-Saharan Africa's Exports

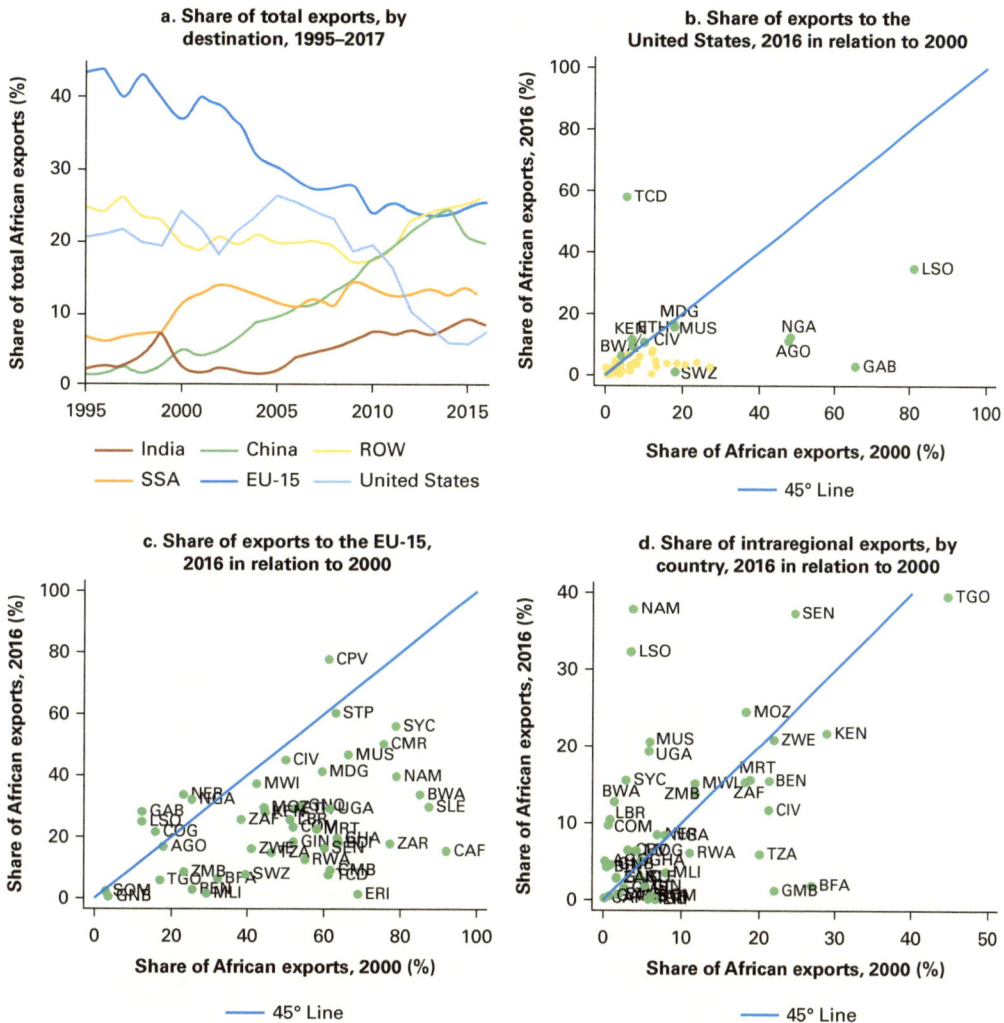

a. Share of total exports, by destination, 1995–2017

India | China | ROW
SSA | EU-15 | United States

b. Share of exports to the United States, 2016 in relation to 2000

45° Line

c. Share of exports to the EU-15, 2016 in relation to 2000

45° Line

d. Share of intraregional exports, by country, 2016 in relation to 2000

45° Line

Source: World Integrated Trade Solution (WITS) data (https://wits.worldbank.org/).
Note: Countries are labeled using ISO alpha-3 codes. Eswatini is designated by SWZ, the code for its former name of Swaziland. EU-15 = 15 member states of the European Union (EU) before 2004: Austria, Belgium, Denmark, Finland, France, Germany, Greece, Ireland, Italy, Luxembourg, the Netherlands, Portugal, Spain, Sweden, and the United Kingdom (which officially withdrew from the EU in 2020); ROW = rest of world; SSA = Sub-Saharan Africa.

Africa's manufacturing exports to other countries in the region increased substantially, from 10 percent in 1996 to 40 percent in 2010 and then declined to below 30 percent by 2016.

The share of manufacturing exports going to the United States is lower than 30 percent for most Sub-Saharan African countries. Between 2000 and 2016, the changes in the share were different for individual countries, with the United States gaining importance for Kenya, Tanzania, and Rwanda but

Figure 2.6   Destinations of Sub-Saharan Africa's Manufacturing Exports

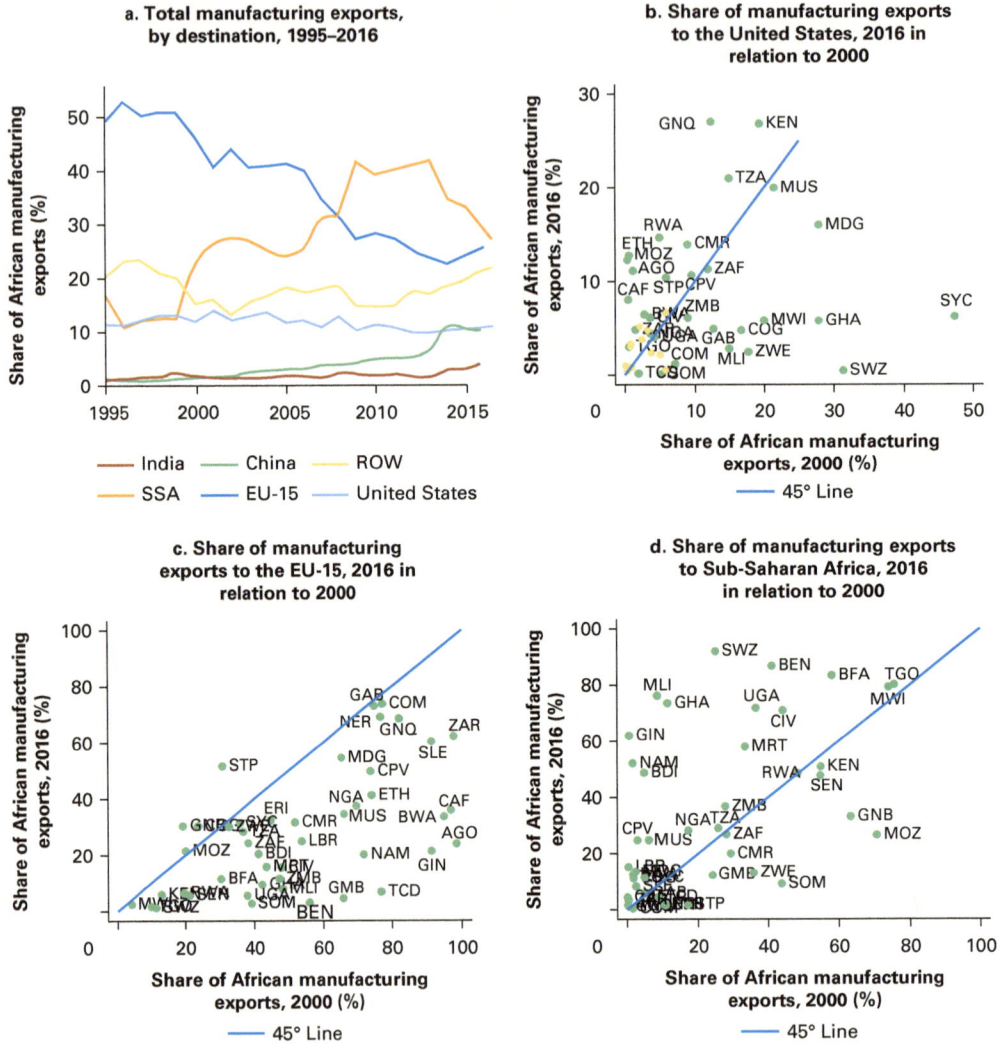

a. Total manufacturing exports, by destination, 1995–2016

b. Share of manufacturing exports to the United States, 2016 in relation to 2000

c. Share of manufacturing exports to the EU-15, 2016 in relation to 2000

d. Share of manufacturing exports to Sub-Saharan Africa, 2016 in relation to 2000

Source: World Integrated Trade Solution (WITS) data (https://wits.worldbank.org/).
Note: Countries are labeled using ISO alpha-3 codes. Eswatini is designated by SWZ, the code for its former name of Swaziland. EU-15 = 15 member states of the European Union (EU) before 2004: Austria, Belgium, Denmark, Finland, France, Germany, Greece, Ireland, Italy, Luxembourg, the Netherlands, Portugal, Spain, Sweden, and the United Kingdom (which officially withdrew from the EU in 2020); ROW = rest of world; SSA = Sub-Saharan Africa.

losing importance for the Seychelles and Eswatini (figure 2.6, panel b). The changes in shares of manufacturing exports going to the EU-15 were more uniform, decreasing for almost all countries in the region between 2000 and 2016 (figure 2.6, panel c). Increases in the share of manufacturing exports going to other Sub-Saharan African countries were observed for many countries, such as Eswatini, Mali, Uganda, and Namibia (figure 2.6, panel d).

Share of apparel exports, by destination country. The US share of Sub-Saharan Africa's apparel exports grew substantially from 1995 until 2004, especially after 2001, but it declined from 2005 onward and has hovered in the 35–40 percent range since 2010 (figure 2.7, panel a). The EU-15's share decreased throughout the period, from 60 percent to 30 percent. The share going to other Sub-Saharan African countries increased substantially and, as of 2016, it was as large as the share to the EU-15. The shares going to China and India were negligible.

For individual Sub-Saharan African countries, the shares of apparel exports to the United States changed heterogeneously between 2000 and 2016, with dramatic increases for Ethiopia, Rwanda, and Tanzania and dramatic declines for Eswatini and Namibia (figure 2.7, panel b). The share of apparel exports to the EU-15 declined for almost all countries, most notably for Rwanda and Tanzania, whose exports shifted to the United States (figure 2.7, panel c). The share going to other Sub-Saharan African countries increased substantially for Eswatini (shifting from the United States) and South Africa—the main exporter to other Sub-Saharan African countries, which shipped 90 percent of its apparel exports to those markets by 2016 (figure 2.7, panel d).

The AGOA's Impact on Export Performance

Trends in Export Value

This subsection examines in detail the exports of Sub-Saharan African countries to the United States on the basis of the US Trade and Market Access Database. We start by depicting the value of total exports and then decomposing it into three components: AGOA-eligible exports; other duty-free eligible exports (MFN zero, GSP, and GSP LDC); and dutiable exports (figure 2.8).

Total African exports to the United States increased rapidly after the start of the AGOA in 2001, reaching a peak of US$82 billion in 2008, but then declined with the Global Financial Crisis in 2009 and fell even more substantially with the decline in commodity prices from 2012 onward, reaching a nominal value in 2016 that was only slightly higher than in 1995 (figure 2.8, panel a).

Exports of AGOA-eligible products account for a high share of total exports and exhibit a similar inverted-U-shape pattern that follows the swings in commodity prices (because many AGOA-eligible products are commodities). Owing to the GSP and AGOA preferences, almost all of Sub-Saharan Africa's exports enter the United States duty-free.

African manufacturing exports, whose prices are less volatile than those of nonmanufacturing exports, grew steadily from 1997 to 2007, after which they fell because of the Global Financial Crisis and then stabilized (figure 2.8, panel c).

African apparel exports to the United States grew rapidly after 1997, accelerating in 2000 and peaking in 2004 at US$1.75 billion. From 2005 onward, apparel exports declined steadily until 2010, bottoming out at US$0.78 billion, and then picked up slightly and stabilized at about

Figure 2.7 Destinations of Sub-Saharan Africa's Apparel Exports

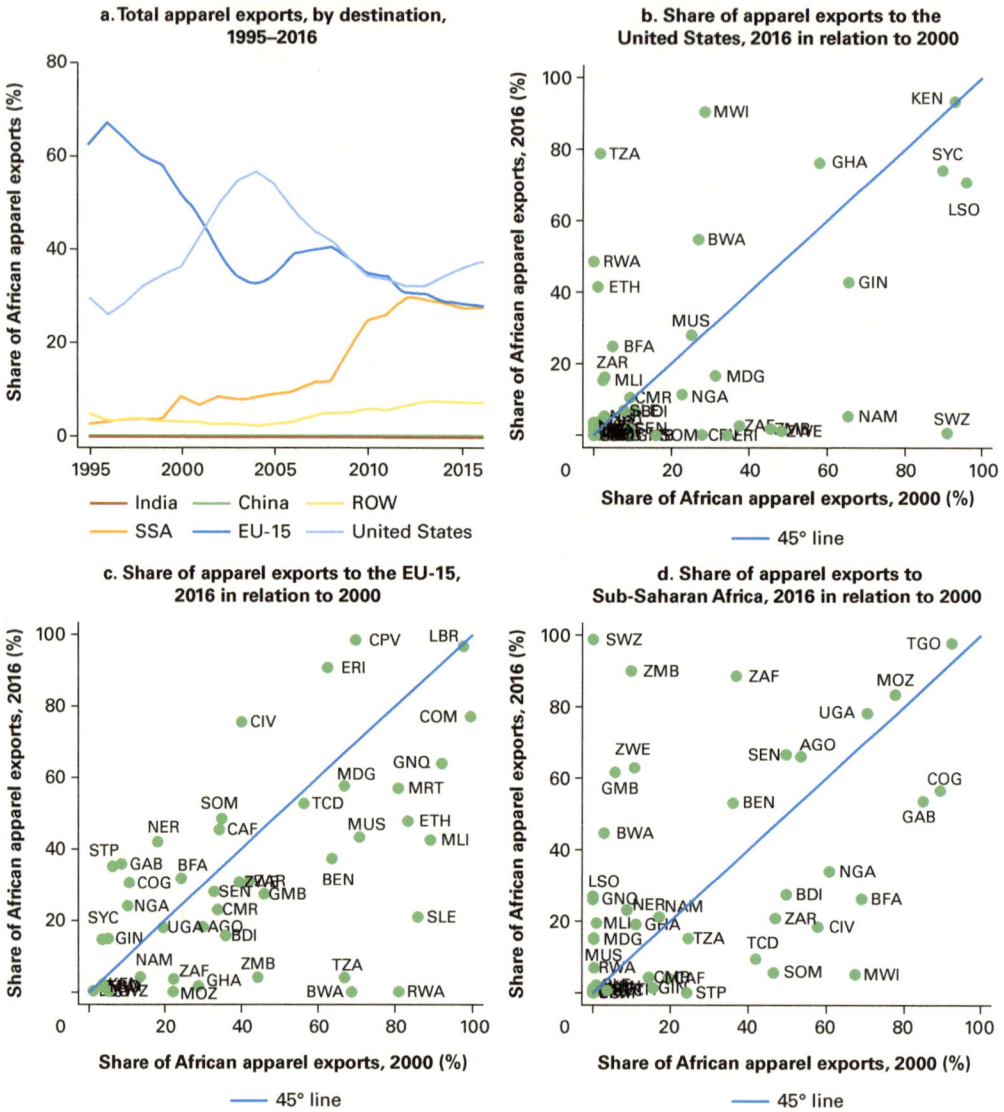

a. Total apparel exports, by destination, 1995–2016

b. Share of apparel exports to the United States, 2016 in relation to 2000

c. Share of apparel exports to the EU-15, 2016 in relation to 2000

d. Share of apparel exports to Sub-Saharan Africa, 2016 in relation to 2000

Source: World Integrated Trade Solution (WITS) data (https://wits.worldbank.org/).
Note: Countries are labeled using ISO alpha-3 codes. Eswatini is designated by SWZ, the code for its former name of Swaziland. EU-15 = 15 member states of the European Union (EU) before 2004: Austria, Belgium, Denmark, Finland, France, Germany, Greece, Ireland, Italy, Luxembourg, the Netherlands, Portugal, Spain, Sweden, and the United Kingdom (which officially withdrew from the EU in 2020); ROW = rest of world; SSA = Sub-Saharan Africa.

US$1 billion (figure 2.8, panel e). Almost all of Sub-Saharan Africa's apparel exports are eligible for duty-free treatment by the United States under the AGOA except for exports from countries that lack an approved visa system or that lost AGOA eligibility at some point between 2001 and 2017.

Figure 2.8   **Growth of Sub-Saharan Africa's Exports to the United States, circa 2000s–2010s**

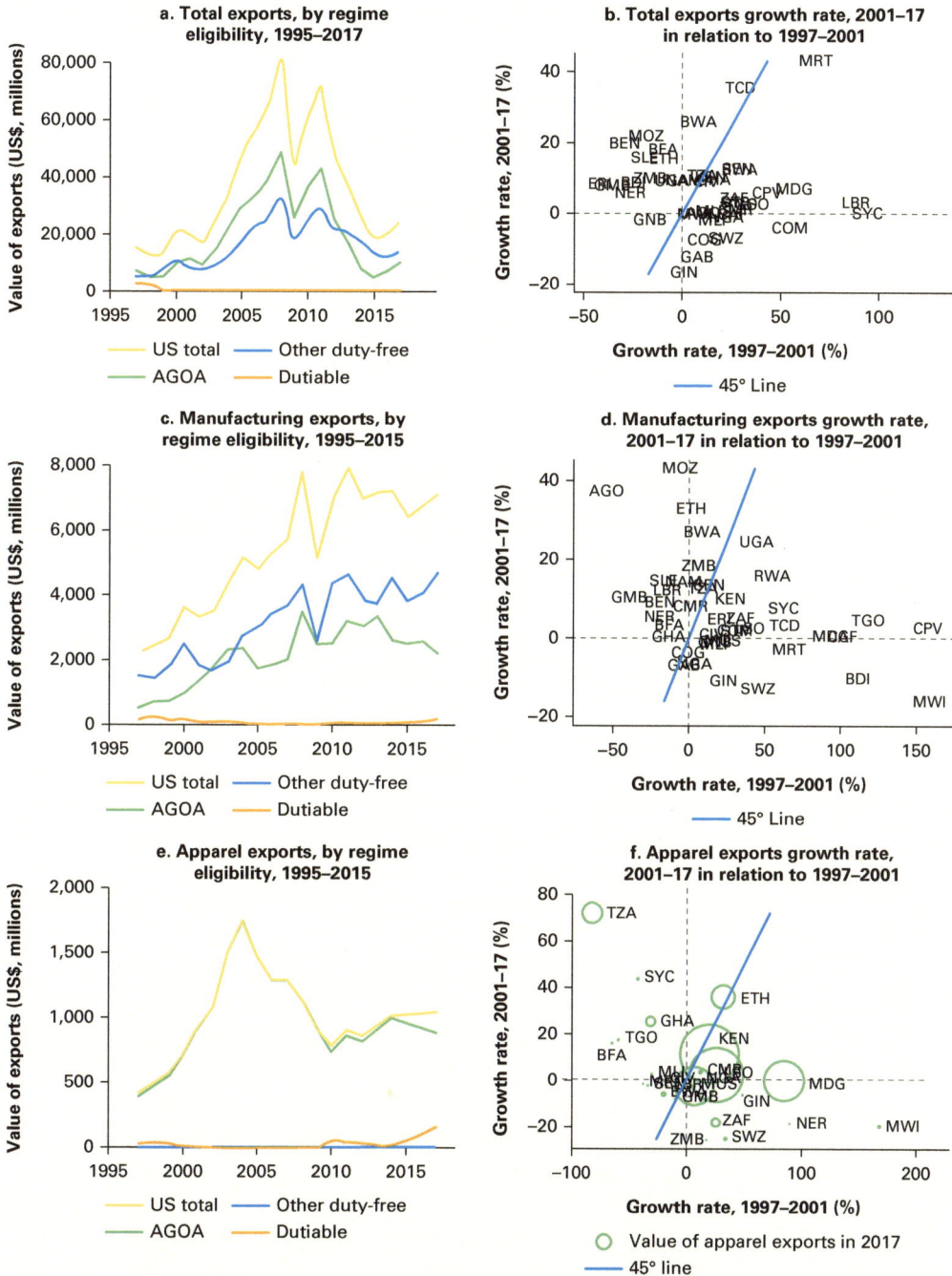

a. Total exports, by regime eligibility, 1995–2017

b. Total exports growth rate, 2001–17 in relation to 1997–2001

c. Manufacturing exports, by regime eligibility, 1995–2015

d. Manufacturing exports growth rate, 2001–17 in relation to 1997–2001

e. Apparel exports, by regime eligibility, 1995–2015

f. Apparel exports growth rate, 2001–17 in relation to 1997–2001

Source: World Bank's US Trade and Market Access Database.
Note: In panels a, c, and e, exports are classified by tariff regime eligibility by product-country-year and do not account for preference utilization. Eligibility for the US Africa Growth and Opportunity Act (AGOA) is extended to precede 2001 in the graphs for easier comparison. In panels b, d, and f, growth rates are calculated as compound growth rates between the first and last years, in nominal value of exports. Countries are labeled using ISO alpha-3 codes. Eswatini is designated by SWZ, the code for its former name of Swaziland. In panel f, circle sizes designate the value of the labeled countries' apparel exports to the US in 2017.

Rates of Export Growth

To gain greater insight into the AGOA's role, we examine the patterns of export growth for individual Sub-Saharan African countries before AGOA (1997–2001) and after AGOA (2001–17). We compute for each country, in each of these periods, average export growth as a compound growth rate (in nominal exports) for total, manufacturing, and apparel exports.[19]

For total exports to the United States, all but 3 of the 14 countries with negative average export growth before the AGOA saw positive export growth thereafter (figure 2.8, panel b).[20] But 8 countries switched from positive export growth pre-AGOA to negative export growth after AGOA. Hence, the pattern of overall export growth to the United States across periods is quite heterogeneous across Sub-Saharan African countries.

For manufacturing exports to the United States, most countries had positive growth rates before AGOA, which increased in magnitude after AGOA, with the top growers after AGOA being Ethiopia, Mauritania, and Rwanda (figure 2.8, panel d). Cameroon, Côte d'Ivoire, and Tanzania, which had close to zero growth rates before AGOA, saw rapid increases to averages of more than 10 percent per year after AGOA. In contrast, Ghana, Lesotho, and especially Madagascar saw dramatic declines—from positive pre-AGOA growth rates exceeding 20 percent per year to post-AGOA growth of less than 5 percent per year.

For apparel exports to the United States, most countries had small negative or small positive export growth rates before AGOA and maintained those rates after AGOA (figure 2.8, panel f). A few countries with negative apparel export growth switched to positive export growth after AGOA, of which Tanzania exhibited the most dramatic increase, to average growth of more than 60 percent per year. Only a couple of countries—Ethiopia and Kenya—exhibited strong positive export growth in both periods, whereas several countries (including South Africa, Eswatini, and Zambia) exhibited substantial negative export growth in both periods. The next subsection discusses in more detail the performance of Sub-Saharan African countries' apparel exports.

Finally, it is important to assess to what extent beneficiary African countries *use* the preferences granted under the AGOA and GSP LDC, because restrictive rules of origin or administrative burdens could be an obstacle for imports to qualify for duty-free treatment. The AGOA utilization rate—defined as the share of preference-eligible imports that enter using the preferential regime—was lower than 70 percent during the first years, but it increased rapidly to close to 90 percent (annex 2B, figure 2B.2).[21] Unused preferences in recent years are mostly accounted for by oil-related products—for which the US MFN duty is very low (less than 1 percent).

Apparel Exports to the United States after the AGOA: Four Stories

Four groups of countries showed different patterns of growth in apparel exports to the United States after the AGOA was introduced:

- *Missed opportunities.* Some countries were eligible for apparel preferences, engaged in some exports of apparel to the United States but with no clear pattern, and at no stage took significant advantage of the AGOA. We designate these as the "missed opportunities" group, of which Cameroon is a typical example (figure 2.9, panel a).[22]
- *Boom-bust.* Another group of countries exhibited a large boom in apparel exports to the United States immediately after the AGOA, followed by a dramatic bust soon after the end of the MFA quotas in 2005, and settled at low levels subsequently. We designate these as the "boom-bust" group, of which Eswatini is a typical example (figure 2.9, panel b).[23]
- *Growth and stagnation.* A third group of countries showed substantial post-AGOA growth in apparel exports, which was negatively

Figure 2.9 Four Stories of Apparel Exports from Selected Sub-Saharan African Countries, before and after the AGOA, 1997–2017

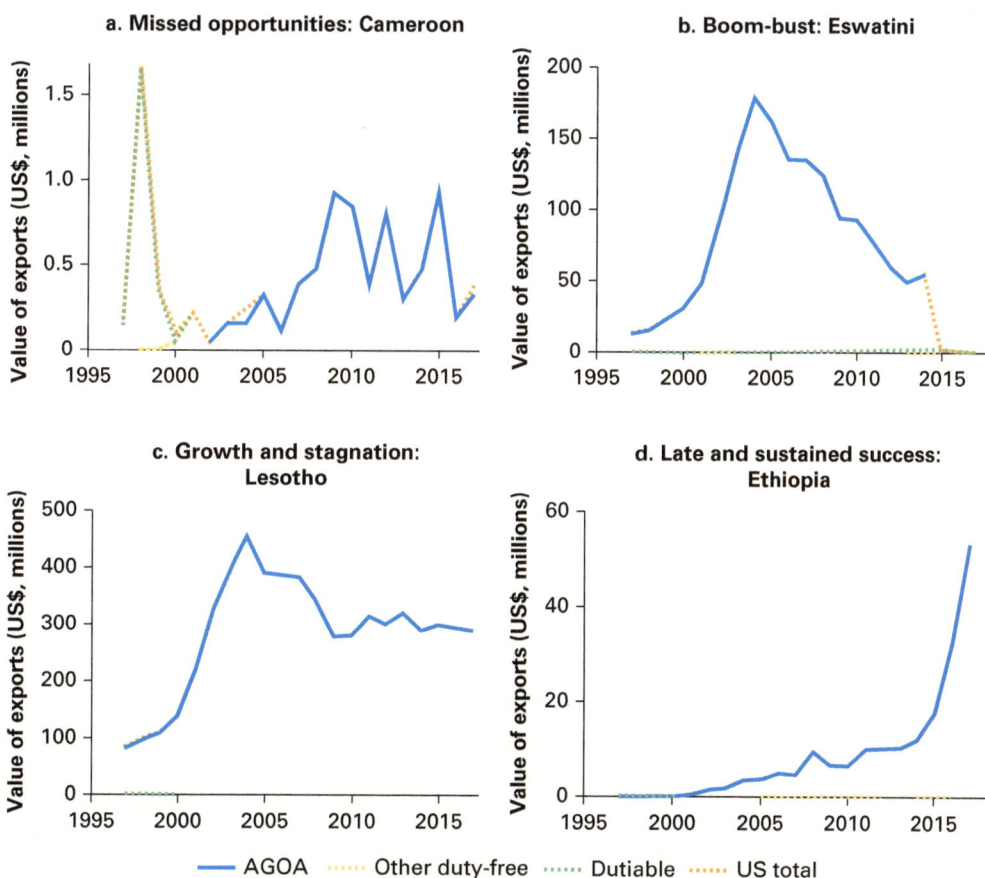

Source: World Bank's US Trade and Market Access Database.
Note: Exports are classified by tariff regime eligibility by product-country-year and do not account for preference utilization. Eligibility for the US Africa Growth and Opportunity Act (AGOA) is extended to precede 2001 in the graphs for easier comparison.

affected by the end of the MFA quotas in 2005. However, their exports did not disappear but remained stagnant. We designate these as the "growth and stagnation" group, of which Lesotho is a typical example (figure 2.9, panel c).[24]

- *Late and sustained success.* Finally, a small set of countries showed only limited growth in apparel exports to the United States immediately after the AGOA was introduced, but they have subsequently shown steady growth, which accelerated after 2010. We designate these as the "late and sustained success" group, of which Ethiopia is a typical example (figure 2.9, panel d).[25]

For the patterns in apparel exports to the United States for each Sub-Saharan African country (other than the four shown in figure 2.9) and their categorization in each of the four groups, see annex 2B, figures 2B.3–2B.6.

Estimated Impacts of the AGOA and GSP LDC

To identify a causal impact of the AGOA and the GSP LDC on African countries' exports to the United States from 1992 to 2017, we take a treatment-and-control group approach. This approach relies on estimating a regression—designated as a triple-differences specification—that compares US imports of eligible and noneligible products (first difference) before and after the AGOA and GSP LDC (second difference) and across beneficiary and nonbeneficiary countries (third difference).

The specification includes terms to capture the following: (a) the impact of the GSP policy change in 1997 that increased the number of duty-free products for GSP LDC–eligible countries and territories (designated as GSP LDC for short); (b) the impact of the AGOA policy change on non-apparel products, separately estimated for products that became eligible for duty-free treatment under the AGOA for LDC and non-LDC African countries and for products that became eligible for non-LDC African countries; and (c) the impact of the AGOA policy change on exports of apparel products.

This specification is estimated using data at the exporting country HS 6-digit product-year level, including positive as well as zero import flows to the United States. It allows us to identify the causal impact of the AGOA and GSP LDC policy changes, because it accounts for unobserved differences and dynamics at the country-product, country-year, and product-year levels, by including the corresponding large set of fixed effects:

- *Country-product fixed effects* allow us to identify the impacts relative to average pre-AGOA (or pre–GSP LDC) exports to the United States of that country-product, which implies that all coefficients are estimated on the basis of within-country-product variation over time.
- *Country-year fixed effects* account for overall demand and supply and other economywide shocks in the exporting countries, including those related to the Global Financial Crisis, which falls within our sample period.

- *Product-year fixed effects* control for differences in US demand for particular products and product-specific supply changes such as technological change. To account for the possibility of differential pretreatment time trends for the various treated groups, the specification also includes treated group-specific time trends.

The interpretation of the estimated coefficients is that they measure the increase in exports to the United States by a beneficiary African country of an eligible product after the AGOA and GSP LDC were enacted. The measure is relative to the increase in exports of all products to the United States by that country, the increase in exports of all countries to the United States of that product, and the base level of exports to the United States of that product by that country before the AGOA and GSP LDC.

We begin with baseline estimates for the impact of the AGOA. We then examine the dynamics of the impacts over time. Finally, we delve deeper into the impact of preferences on apparel and the subregional differences in the impacts.

Baseline Estimates

Before turning to the regression estimates, table 2.2 provides some statistics based on the estimating sample, focusing on characteristics before the AGOA. The estimating sample includes 27,420,560 observations, of which 87 percent have zero imports. Table 2.2 shows that, relative to control countries, AGOA-eligible countries export to the United States substantially fewer HS 6-digit products and smaller values, whether the products are AGOA-eligible or not. On average, a country that has been declared AGOA-eligible at any point has positive exports to the United States in only 97 HS 6-digit products, whereas it has 734 for the control countries. However, there is enormous variation across eligible countries.

Figure 2.10 displays the baseline regression coefficients and their 95 percent confidence intervals obtained from the triple-differences regression, which controls for country-product, country-year, and product-year fixed effects. Inference is based on standard errors that are robust to heteroscedasticity with the Huber-White approach, clustered at the product level.

The estimates show a positive and significant impact of the expansion of duty-free products for GSP LDC from 1998 onward for beneficiary countries in Africa.[26] On average, Sub-Saharan African countries increased their exports to the United States of the GSP LDC additional products eligible for duty-free treatment from 1998 onward, relative to their pre-1997 levels, by 12 percent. The AGOA's impacts are not statistically significant for non-apparel products for non-LDCs or LDCs. The important boost to exports provided by the AGOA is found for apparel products, whose exports to the United States increased by 22 percent for AGOA-eligible countries from 2001 onward, relative to their pre-AGOA levels.[27]

There are two crucial remarks about the baseline estimates in figure 2.10. First, they were obtained controlling for time-varying country and product

Table 2.2   Summary Statistics Based on the Estimating Sample

a. Number of HS 6-digit products and US imports from AGOA and control countries

	Number of HS 6-digit products and US imports			
	AGOA countries (44)		Control countries (164)	
	Mean	Standard deviation	Mean	Standard deviation
Number of HS 6-digit products per country (with imports > 0)	97	240	734	1,068
Number of AGOA-eligible HS 6-digit products per country (with imports > 0)	28	57	188	226
Log (imports) per country–HS 6-digit product	9.84	1.05	10.71	1.25
Log (imports +1) per country–HS 6-digit product	0.24	0.57	1.91	2.59

b. Share of GSP LDC–eligible or AGOA-eligible HS 6-digit products and US MFN tariff rates

		AGOA/GSP countries			
		GSP LDC (810)	AGOA non-LDC (769)	AGOA only (91)	AGOA apparel (239)
		For products with imports > 100			
Number of HS 6-digit products per country	Mean	4	26	5	23
	Max	11	195	34	120
US MFN tariff rate	Mean	5.0%	4.3%	7.3%	11.2%
	Max	21.9%	10.0%	13.3%	15.6%

Source: World Bank's US Trade and Market Access Database.
Note: The total number of products in the HS classification at 6-digits is 5,070. The numbers in parentheses in the column headings are, in panel a, the number of AGOA countries and the number of control countries, and in panel b, the number of eligible HS 6-digit products in each of the categories. AGOA = US Africa Growth and Opportunity Act; GSP = Generalized System of Preferences; HS = Harmonized System; LDC = least developed country; MFN = most favored nation.

changes in US imports. Therefore, they account for any overall surge or drop in US imports from AGOA countries for eligible and noneligible products as well any overall surge or drop in US imports of AGOA products or GSP-eligible products globally. Second, they are estimates of a response by African countries to the AGOA and GSP LDC at the intensive and extensive margins of exports to the United States, because zeros are included in the data used for the estimation.

Dynamics of the Impacts

The baseline estimates in figure 2.10 show the average impact of the GSP LDC and AGOA over the entire postimplementation period. However, one of our objectives is to understand the timing and durability of the effects of trade preferences offered by the United States. To examine how quickly and persistently African countries responded to the policy changes under the

Figure 2.10 Average Impacts of the AGOA and GSP LDC on Sub-Saharan African Exports to the United States

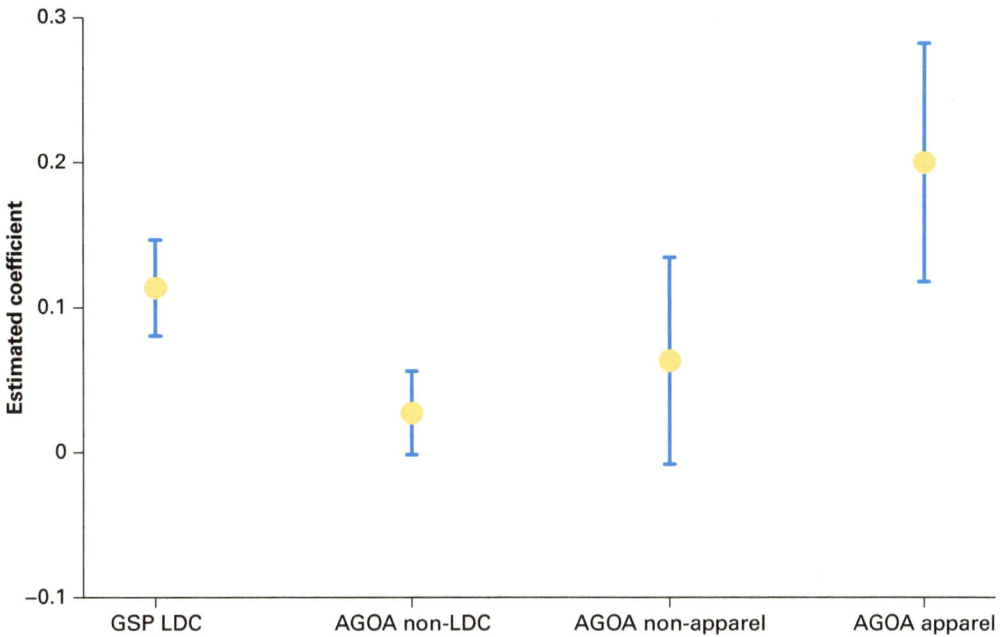

Source: Estimates based on the World Bank's US Trade and Market Access Database.
Note: The dots denote the estimated coefficients, and the bars the 95 percent confidence intervals, of impacts on exports from the Africa Growth and Opportunity Act (AGOA) and the Generalized System of Preferences (GSP), relative to pre-AGOA and pre-GSP levels. HS = Harmonized System; LDC = least developed country.

AGOA and GSP LDC, we allow the impact of the policy changes to be different each year (by allowing for a different coefficient in each year after implementation). We show the corresponding coefficients and 95 percent confidence intervals for each year in figure 2.11.

The AGOA's effect on AGOA-eligible countries' apparel exports to the United States started low but then grew rapidly over the first four years after AGOA enactment (figure 2.11, panel a). After the phasing out of the MFA quotas, the effect of the AGOA fluctuated slightly, but, in broad terms, it leveled off (and the impact decreased between 2011 and 2015). Specifically, the estimate of the AGOA's impact on apparel is zero in 2001 and increases fast thereafter, reaching 29 percent in 2004. The increase in the impact of AGOA on apparel products from 2002 to 2005 may reflect the time taken by beneficiary countries to learn about and build capacity to respond to the expanded market opportunities in the United States, or it may reflect the increase in transshipment of Chinese exports, as shown by Rotunno, Vézina, and Wang (2013). The leveling of the marginal impacts of AGOA on African apparel exports may have been a consequence of the erosion of preferences for African countries after the end of the MFA quotas, which led to fiercer competition in the US market from the Asian giants.

Figure 2.11   Impacts of the AGOA and GSP on Exports of Eligible Products from Sub-Saharan African Countries, circa 2001–17

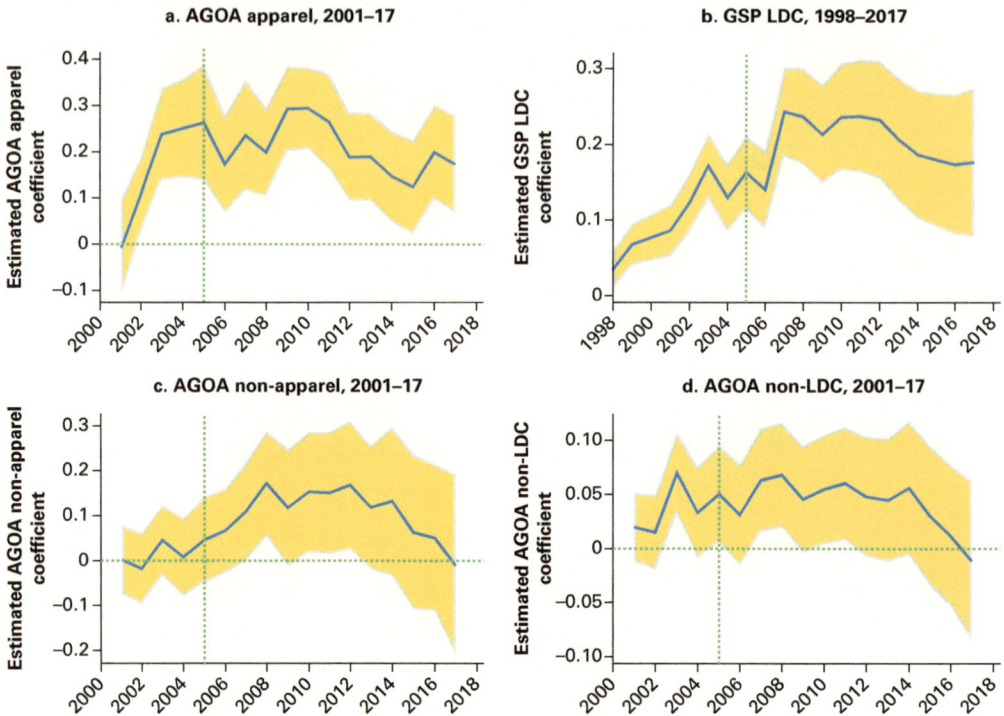

Source: Estimates based on the World Bank's US Trade and Market Access Database.
Note: The graphs show the coefficients and 95 percent confidence intervals based on robust standard errors, clustered by HS 6-digit products, obtained by estimating the triple-differences regression, which controls for country-product, country-year, and product-year fixed effects. Separate coefficients were estimated for each year after the GSP LDC (panel b) or AGOA (panels a, c, and d). The vertical dotted line marks the end of the Multifiber Arrangement (MFA) quota in 2005. AGOA = Africa Growth and Opportunity Act; GSP = Generalized System of Preferences; HS = Harmonized System; LDC = least developed country.

The impact of the GSP LDC on eligible products for African LDC countries increased over the first 10 years, starting in 1998, then leveled off and declined after 2012 (figure 2.11, panel b). Panel c shows the impact of AGOA on exports of non-apparel products that became eligible for duty-free treatment under AGOA for all African countries. Panel d shows the impact of AGOA on non-apparel products whose duty-free treatment under GSP LDC was extended to non-LDC African countries. The coefficients on these two groups are insignificant on average, and they are also insignificant in most years.

Heterogeneity in Impacts on Apparel across Subregions and Periods

The results presented so far show that the estimated impact on apparel increased over time and then became flat after 2005, which coincided with the end of the MFA quotas. We next investigate whether there was country or subregional heterogeneity in the AGOA's impact on apparel.

First, we consider country heterogeneity and return to the average impact of the AGOA from 2001 to 2017. In annex 2C, figure 2C.1 plots the coefficients on the apparel interaction term obtained by allowing the impact of each interaction term to be different for each African country. The countries exhibiting the AGOA's largest significant positive impacts on apparel exports to the United States are (in this order) Kenya, Eswatini, Madagascar, Ethiopia, and Lesotho. In contrast, South Africa, Senegal, Nigeria, and Côte d'Ivoire experience on average the most negative impacts of the AGOA on their apparel exports to the United States.

Second, we assess whether, and to what extent, the AGOA had differential impacts on exports of apparel across African subregions before versus after the liberalization of the MFA quotas. We separately estimated the AGOA's impact each year for three subregions: East Africa, Central and West Africa, and Southern Africa. We plot the corresponding coefficient estimates and 95 percent confidence intervals in figure 2.12.

The evidence shows a differential response to the AGOA and the MFA liberalization across subregions. For Central and West Africa, the AGOA's impacts on apparel exports are mostly insignificant (figure 2.12, panel b). The AGOA has a growing, positive impact on apparel exports from East Africa—although the impact is significantly lower in the early AGOA period

Figure 2.12 **Impacts of the AGOA on Apparel Exports from Sub-Saharan Africa, by Subregion, 2001–17**

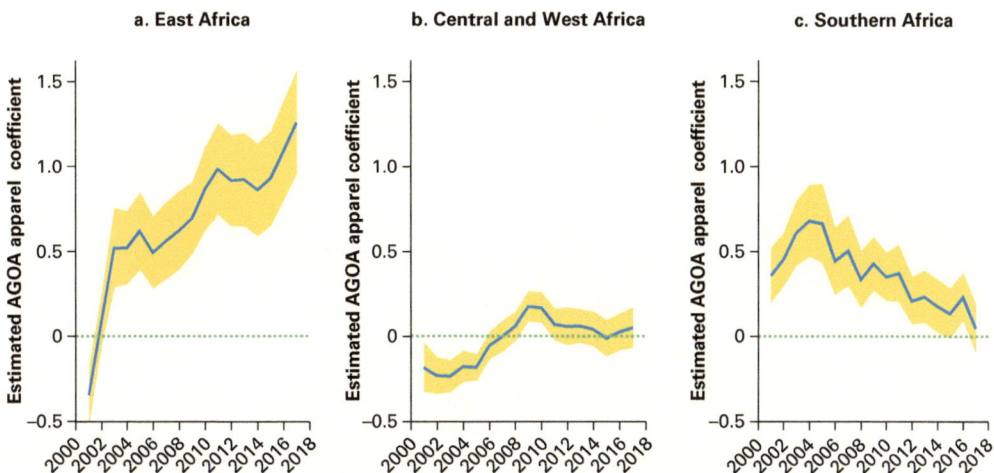

Source: Estimates based on the World Bank's US Trade and Market Access Database.
Note: The graphs show coefficients and 95 percent confidence intervals based on robust standard errors, clustered by HS 6-digit product, obtained by estimating the triple-differences regression, which controls for country-product, country-year, and product-year fixed effects allowing for separate coefficients each year after the Africa Growth and Opportunity Act (AGOA). GSP = Generalized System of Preferences; HS = Harmonized System; LDC = least developed country.

than in the years following the end of the MFA quotas (figure 2.12, panel a). In contrast, for Southern Africa, the AGOA's average impact on apparel exports is significantly higher in the early AGOA period, and it decreases after 2005—with the end of the MFA quotas—until it is not significantly different from zero (figure 2.12, panel c). Although the Southern African countries initially took advantage of the opportunities created by the AGOA, their apparel exports clearly suffered more after the end of the MFA quotas.

The decline in the AGOA's impact in the face of increased competition from previously quota-constrained countries, such as China after 2005, suggests that the US trade preferences did not help the Southern African countries to build a durable comparative advantage in apparel exports. The results show patterns that are largely consistent with the four apparel stories emerging from the raw data on exports, as described earlier.

Conclusion

This chapter analyzed the impact on African exports of preferential access to the US market by exploiting a newly developed, disaggregated product-level database. It focused mostly on apparel exports because the policy changes in that sector enable us to assess the durability of the impact of the preferences, by examining whether export gains survived the erosion of preferences. We carried out the analysis at two levels: the AGOA's average impact on beneficiary countries and the heterogeneous effects across individual countries and subregions in Sub-Saharan Africa.

Average AGOA impact. We found that the average impact of the AGOA on beneficiary countries' exports to the United States was significantly positive. Given our interest in the durability of the AGOA's impact, we considered the differences across two periods: (a) after AGOA introduction, while African countries enjoyed high preference margins over other countries, especially the quota-constrained Asian countries (2001–04); and (b) after the MFA ended, which eroded the preference margins (2005–17).

The raw data paint a picture of a rapid increase in exports over the first period and then a decline over the second. The triple-differences regression, controlling for a wide range of other factors, confirmed the increase in exports over the first period but showed a leveling off—rather than a decline—of exports over the second period.

Heterogeneity by subregion. The subregion- and country-level performances revealed considerable heterogeneity behind the "average" performance over the two periods. Central and West Africa did not take any meaningful advantage of the opportunities offered by the AGOA. Southern Africa saw rapid growth in exports during the first period and then a rapid decline or stagnation in the second period. East Africa sustained export growth over the two periods.

Heterogeneity by country. However, East Africa is made up of interestingly different country-level pictures: Kenya alone stands out as a country whose exports grew in both periods. In contrast, Ethiopia, Rwanda, and Tanzania saw hardly any growth in the first period and a growth spurt only in the second period. The finding of sustained levels of exports Africa-wide, and even for subregions, in the second period is partly because the three late bloomers in East Africa offset the decline in Southern Africa.

Understanding the precise reasons for the heterogeneous responses to trade preferences remains a challenge. Our analysis suggests that preferential access per se is not sufficient to deliver even temporary export success. The few instances of sustained export growth seem to have combined market access with domestic reforms that improved access to imported inputs through low domestic tariffs, lightened the regulatory burden, enhanced access to infrastructure through the creation of effective special economic zones, and maintained competitive exchange rates through the choice of flexible exchange rate regimes.

The next chapter focuses on West Africa to explore a comprehensive approach toward boosting exports to at least the two traditional markets: the US and the EU.

Annex 2A WITS Sectoral Definition, Sub-Saharan Africa Data, and Commodity Prices

For the descriptive and regression analyses in this chapter, we defined three sectors, following the World Trade Organization (WTO):

- *Agriculture:* Standard International Trade Classification (SITC) sections 0, 1, and 4 and divisions 22, 23, 24, 25, 26, and 27.
- *Mining:* SITC section 3 and divisions 27, 28, and 68, as defined by WTO. In addition, we include division 97 (nonmonetary gold) in mining.
- *Manufacturing:* SITC sections 5, 6, 7, and 8, minus division 68.

We drop from our data monetary gold (HS 710820) and other non-gold money and coins (HS 711810 and 711890).

In the descriptive analysis, we use WITS world data on imports as mirror data for Sub-Saharan Africa's exports, to lessen concerns about the quality and consistency of Africa's data on exports. Within Africa, the value of imports may be affected by missing data on imports in some years. Table 2A.1 shows, for each African country with missing data, the first year when the country is reported in WITS and the years for which the export data are missing. Reassuringly, for the two key years we analyze—2000 and 2016—many of the region's countries do have data in WITS, including the two largest importers, Nigeria and South Africa.

The regression analysis uses the average MFN import tariff imposed by each country under AGOA. The tariffs are taken from a newly constructed

Table 2A.1   Sub-Saharan African Countries with Missing Export Data in the World Integrated Trade Solution

Country	First year	Last year	Missing years
Angola	2007	2015	2008
Burkina Faso	1995	2016	2006
Congo, Rep.	1993	2014	1996, 1997, 1998, 1999, 2000, 2001, 2002, 2003, 2004, 2005, 2006
Ethiopia	1995	2016	1996
Gabon	1993	2009	1995
Ghana	1996	2016	2014, 2015
Guinea	1995	2015	2003, 2009, 2010, 2011, 2012
Gambia, The	1995	2016	2015
Kenya	1992	2013	1993, 1994, 1995, 1996, 2011, 2012
Lesotho	2000	2012	2005, 2006, 2007
Malawi	1990	2015	1992, 1993, 1996, 1997, 1998
Mali	1996	2016	2009, 2013, 2014, 2015
Mauritania	2000	2016	2015
Nigeria	1996	2016	2004, 2005, 2015
Rwanda	1996	2016	2000
Sierra Leone	2000	2016	2001, 2003, 2004, 2005, 2006, 2007, 2008, 2009, 2010, 2011, 2012, 2013
Seychelles	1994	2016	2009
Togo	1994	2016	2006
Zimbabwe	1995	2016	1996, 1997, 1998, 1999, 2000, 2003

Source: World Bank.

database by Felbermayr, Teti, and Yalcin (2017), which in turn is based on the UNCTAD Trade Analysis Information System (TRAINS) and Inter-American Development Bank databases. The database addresses the missing MFN tariffs by setting them equal to the nearest preceding observation or, when there is no preceding observation, to the nearest succeeding observation. However, for some countries, the MFN tariffs are still missing after these procedures. For these countries, we replace the missing MFN tariffs by linearly interpolating observations based on the World Bank's WITS database.

Figure 2A.1   Total Exports of Sub-Saharan African Countries and Commodity Price Indexes, 1996–2016

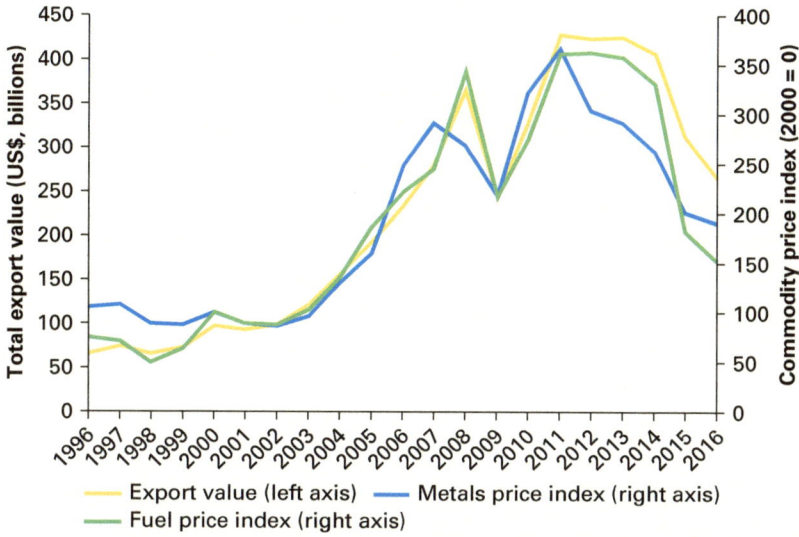

Sources: World Integrated Trade Solution (WITS) data; International Monetary Fund Primary Commodity Prices database.
Note: Sub-Saharan African exports are measured by world imports from Sub-Saharan African countries in WITS.

Annex 2B Impacts of the AGOA on Exports and Export Patterns

Figure 2B.1   US Average Agricultural and Mining Tariffs on Sub-Saharan African Exports, by Preference Type, before and after the AGOA

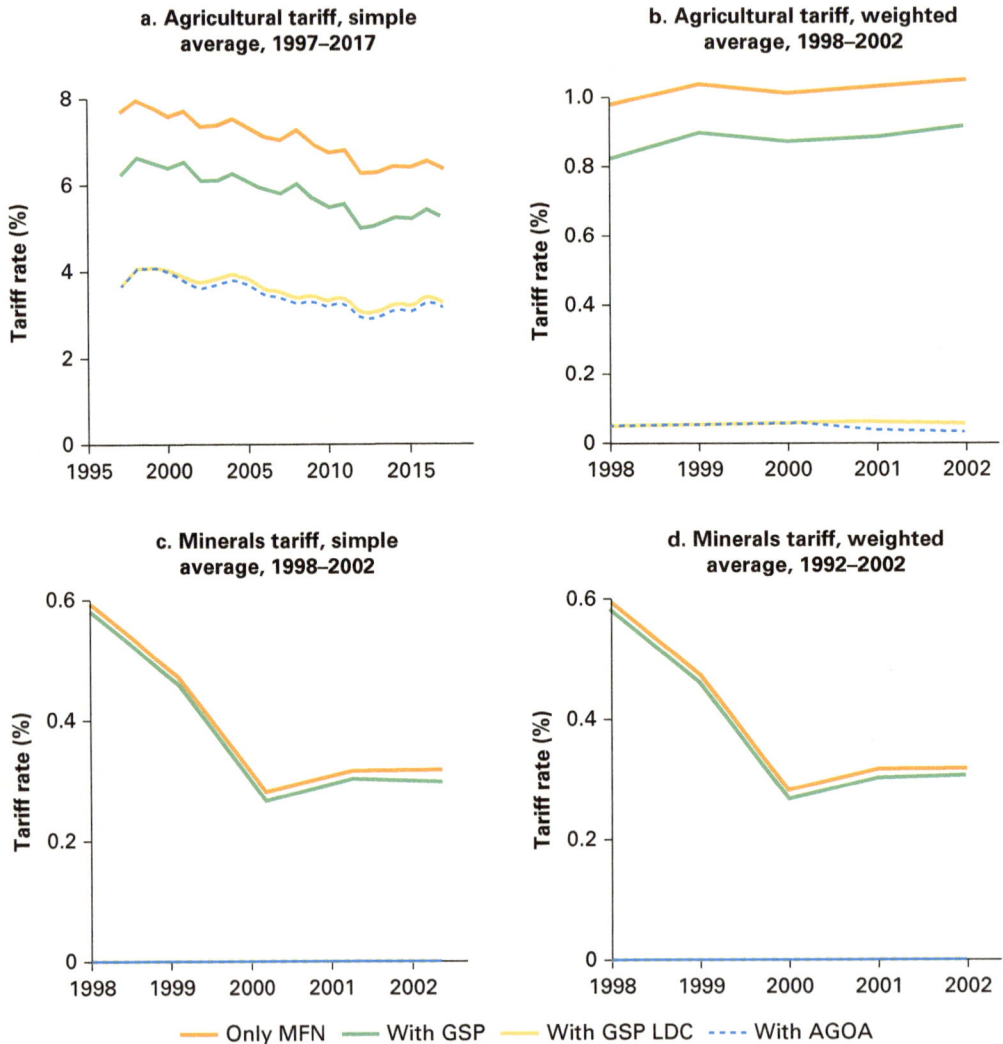

a. Agricultural tariff, simple average, 1997–2017

b. Agricultural tariff, weighted average, 1998–2002

c. Minerals tariff, simple average, 1998–2002

d. Minerals tariff, weighted average, 1992–2002

—— Only MFN   —— With GSP   —— With GSP LDC   - - - - With AGOA

Source: World Bank's US Trade and Market Access Database.
Note: The simple average tariffs include all 8-digit tariff lines of the US Trade Schedule (Harmonized Tariff Schedule, HTS) for each year. Ad valorem equivalents are calculated for tariffs with specific components (tariff lines with complex tariffs are not included). Trade-weighted average tariffs use Sub-Saharan Africa's total exports to the United States in 2000 as weights. The number of products per sector is from the 2001 HTS. AGOA = US Africa Growth and Opportunity Act; GSP = Generalized System of Preferences; LDC = least developed country; MFN = most favored nation.

Figure 2B.2   AGOA Preference Utilization by Sub-Saharan African Countries, 2001–17

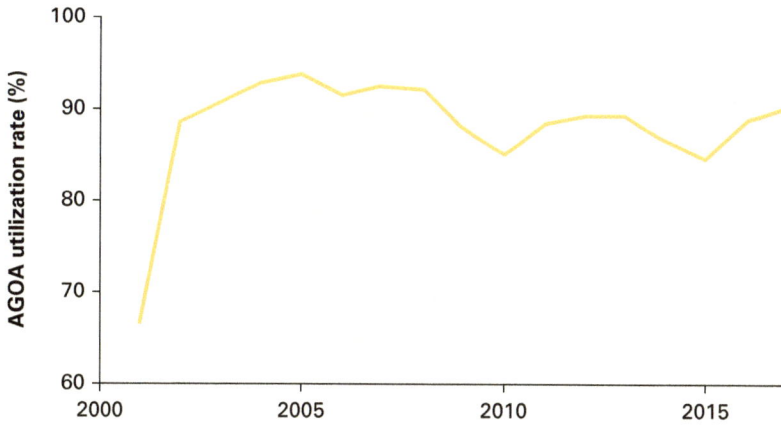

Source: World Bank's US Trade and Market Access Database.
Note: The utilization rate is defined as the share of dutiable preference-eligible imports that enter the United States (originating in Sub-Saharan African countries) using the US Africa Growth and Opportunity Act (AGOA). Imports entering under different duty-free eligible programs are excluded from the calculation.

Figure 2B.3   Sub-Saharan African Countries Exhibiting a "Missed Opportunities" Pattern, 1997–2017

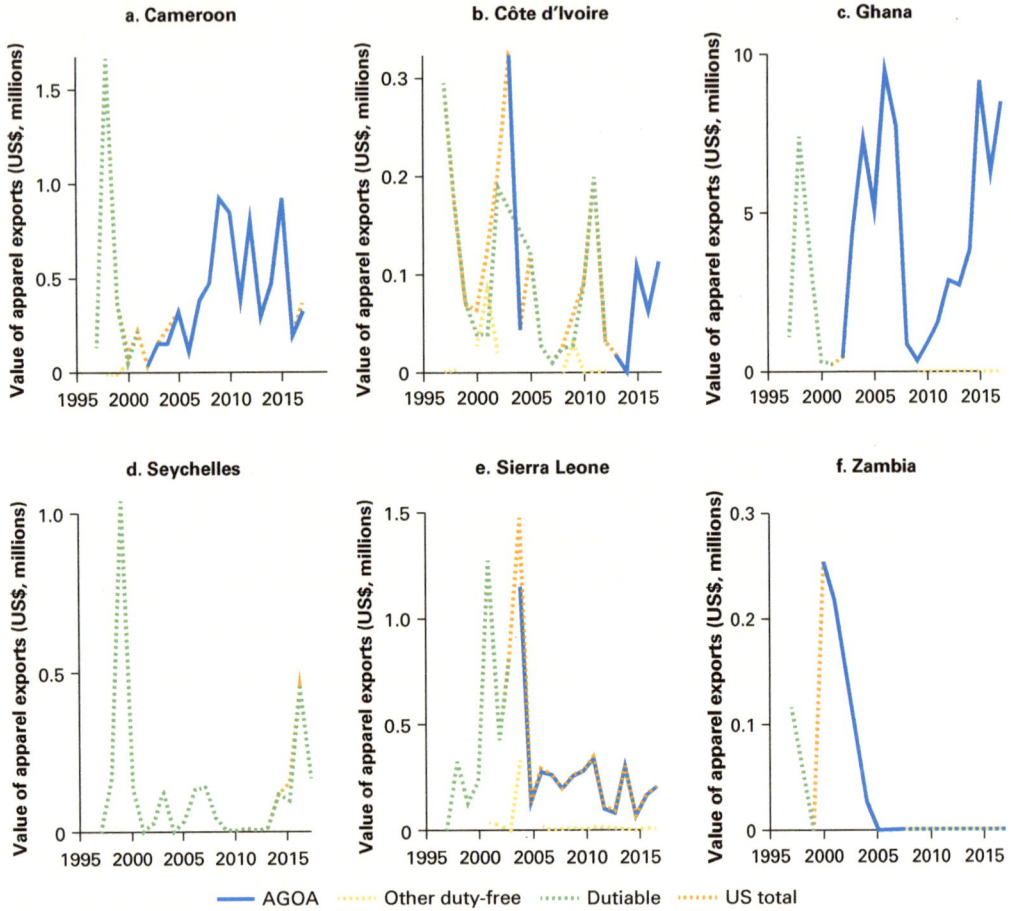

Source: US Trade and Market Access Database.
Note: In the "missed opportunities" pattern, some countries were eligible for apparel preferences, engaged in some exports of apparel to the United States but with no clear pattern, and at no stage took significant advantage of the US Africa Growth and Opportunity Act (AGOA).

Figure 2B.4   Sub-Saharan African Countries Exhibiting a "Boom-Bust" Pattern, 1997–2017

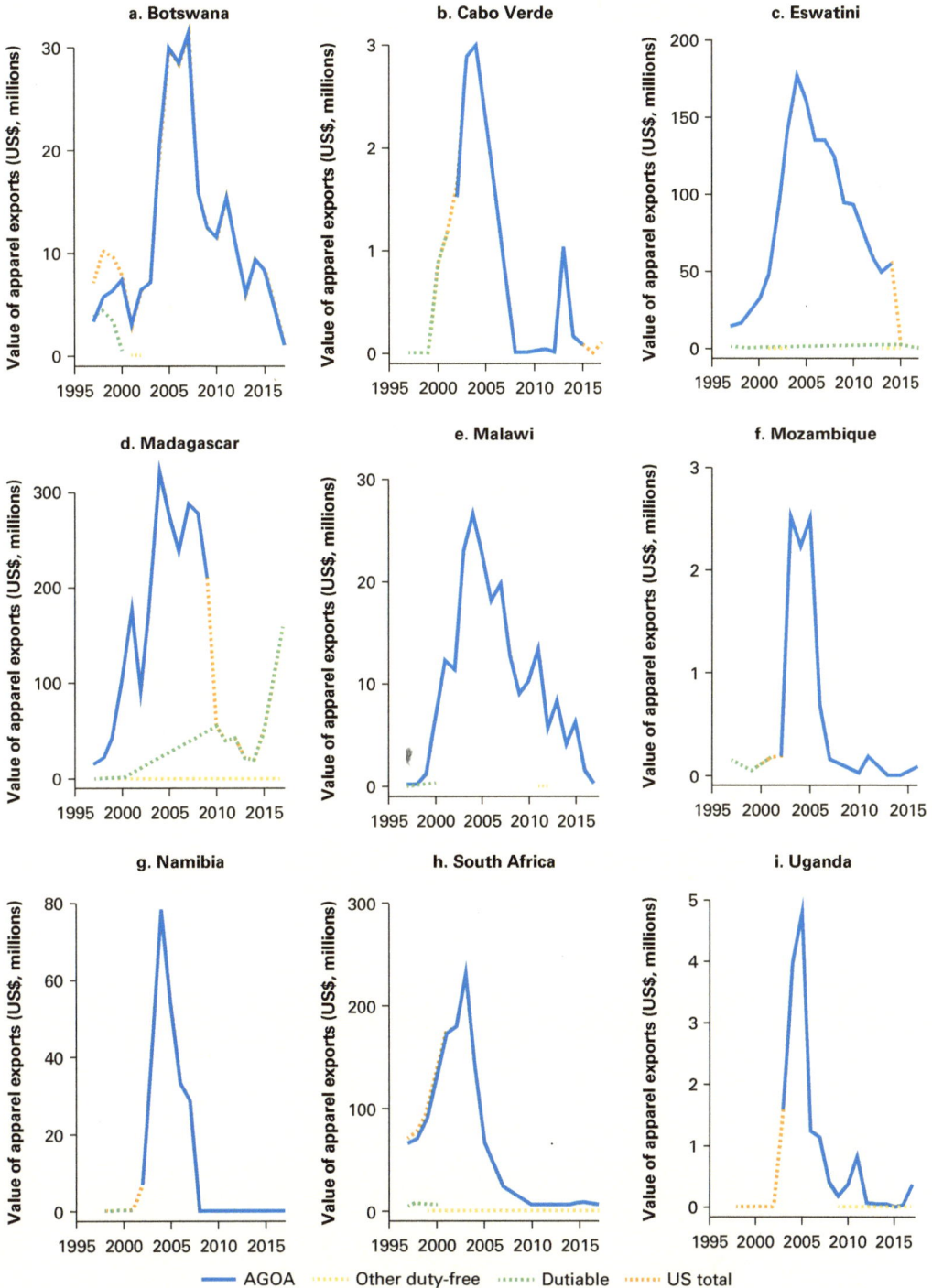

Source: World Bank's US Trade and Market Access Database.
Note: In the "boom-bust" pattern, certain countries showed a large boom in apparel exports to the United States immediately after the US Africa Growth and Opportunity Act (AGOA), followed by a dramatic bust soon after the end of the Multifiber Arrangement (MFA) quotas in 2005, and settled at low levels subsequently.

Figure 2B.5   Sub-Saharan African Countries Exhibiting a "Growth and Stagnation" Pattern, 1995–2016

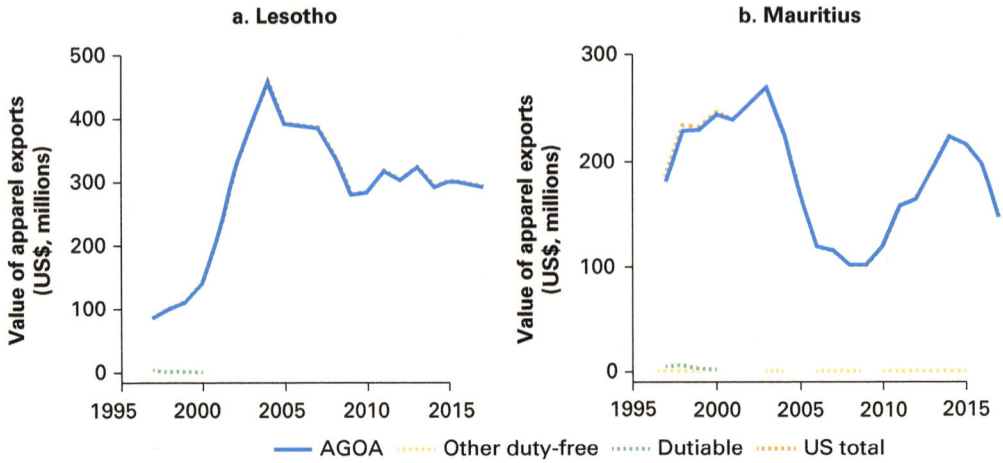

Source: World Bank's US Trade and Market Access Database.
Note: In the "growth and stagnation" pattern, some countries showed substantial growth in apparel exports after the US Africa Growth and Opportunity Act (AGOA), but this growth was negatively affected by the end of the Multifiber Arrangement (MFA) quotas in 2005. However, their exports did not disappear but remained stagnant.

Figure 2B.6 **Sub-Saharan African Countries Exhibiting a "Late and Sustained Growth" Pattern, 1995–2016**

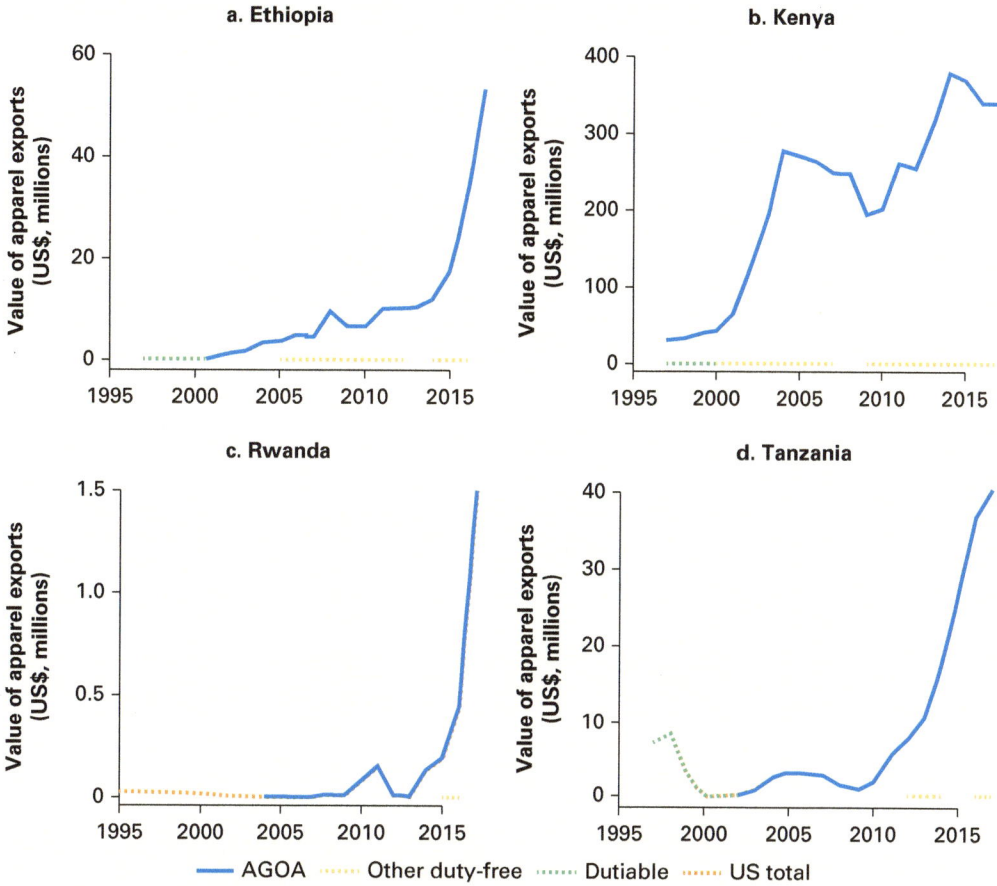

Source: World Bank's US Trade and Market Access Database.
Note: In the "late and sustained growth" pattern, a small set of countries showed only limited growth in apparel exports to the United States immediately after introduction of the US Africa Growth and Opportunity Act (AGOA), but they have subsequently shown steady growth, which accelerated after 2010.

Annex 2C AGOA Impacts, by Country

Figure 2C.1   Baseline Impacts of the AGOA on Apparel Exports from Sub-Saharan Africa, by Country

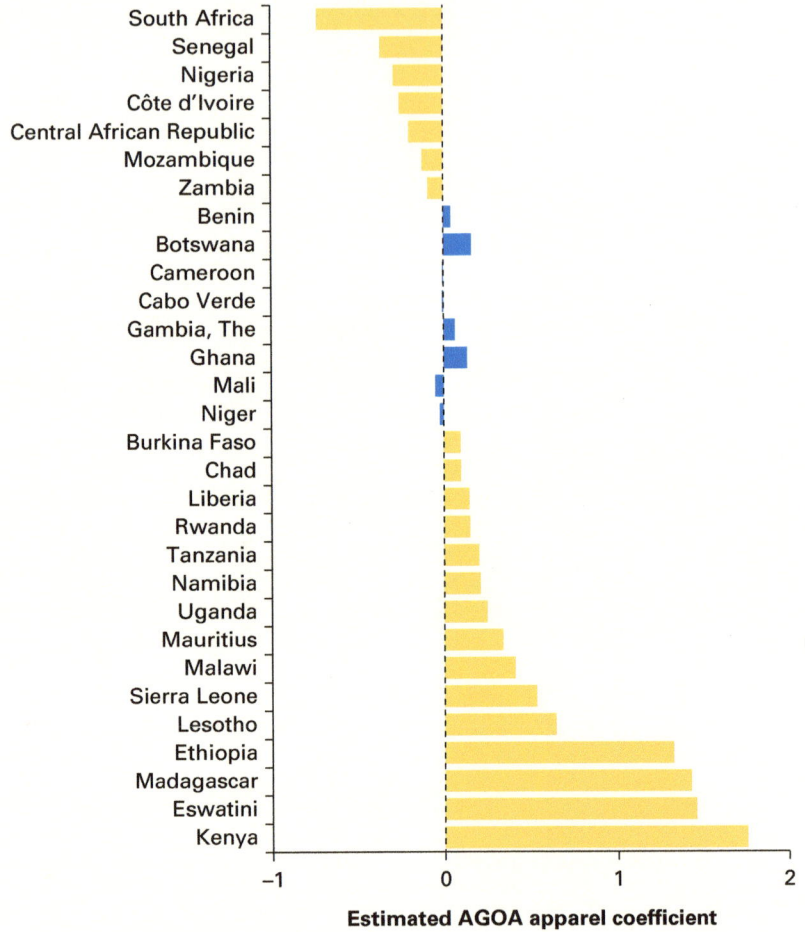

Source: Estimates based on the World Bank's US Trade and Market Access Database.
Note: The figure shows coefficients and 95 percent confidence intervals based on robust standard errors, clustered at the Harmonized System 6-digit product level. The blue bars show insignificant coefficients at the 10 percent level. AGOA = US Africa Growth and Opportunity Act.

Notes

1. The MFA governed world trade in textiles and apparel from 1974 through 2004, with quotas imposed on the totals that certain low- and middle-income countries (LMICs) could export to high-income countries.

2. A companion note provides more details (Forero-Rojas et al. 2018). The note and the database are both accessible through the World Bank's data set page, "Developing Countries' Trade and Market Access in the European Union and the United States": https:// datacatalog.worldbank.org/dataset/developing-countries%E2%80% 99-trade-and-market-access-european-union-and-united-states -introducing.

3. The ad valorem equivalents are obtained by dividing the specific tariff (or specific component) by the import unit price—itself computed as the median of the unit values of all US imports of a given HS 8-digit product in a given year across partner countries—from the US Census trade data.

4. The quota information obtained from Brambilla, Khandelwal, and Schott (2010) is available from author Peter K. Schott's website: https://sompks4.github.io/sub_data.html.

5. For an extensive discussion on "special and differential treatment" and the GSP preferences, see Ornelas (2016).

6. Under the GSP, each preference-granting country establishes specific criteria and conditions for defining and identifying the LMIC beneficiaries.

7. GSP beneficiary countries lose their beneficiary status after the US president determines they have become "high-income" countries (under World Bank income classifications).

8. For more about the GSP LDC criteria, see "Criteria for Identification and Graduation of LDCs" on the United Nations Office of the High Representative for the Least Developed Countries, Landlocked Developing Countries, and Small Island Development States (OHRLLS) website: https://www.un.org/development/desa/dpad/least -developed-country-category/ldc-criteria.html.

9. In practice, these quantitative restrictions were never binding since the onset of the AGOA (USITC 2014). The Special Rule implies that rules of origin for eligible countries are a "single transformation" requirement—that is, the only requirement is that the transformation from fabric to garment is undertaken in the eligible country.

10. The treatment of Mauritius as an LDBC was temporary between 2004 and 2005 and was not renewed in 2006, but it was granted again in 2008 without a fixed term.

11. Additional rules govern the inclusion of interlinings, findings, and trimmings of foreign origin (up to 25 percent in value is allowed) and other minimal fabrics (up to 10 percent in weight).

12. AGOA Extension and Enhancement Act of 2015, Pub. L. 114–27, title I, §101, 129 Stat. 363 (2015).
13. To be more precise, the MFN zero rate of duty was applicable to any country with normal trade relations with the United States. Exclusions to this rule included Vietnam until 2001. Currently, only Cuba and the Democratic People's Republic of Korea do not have normal trade relations with the United States.
14. The difference is explained by 60 tariff lines of the 1,670 that became duty-free under the GSP LDC program in 1997 and were not extended to non-LDC Sub-Saharan African countries after the AGOA.
15. The simplification we implement relative to Nicita (2011) is that we do not consider trade elasticities in the calculation; thus, we assume that all countries' export flows react similarly to a reduction in tariffs.
16. The definition of manufacturing used in our analysis is provided in annex 2A, which also provides some information on the availability (or lack thereof) of WITS data for Sub-Saharan African countries.
17. "EU-15" refers to the 15 European Union (EU) member states before 2004: Austria, Belgium, Denmark, Finland, France, Germany, Greece, Ireland, Italy, Luxembourg, the Netherlands, Portugal, Spain, Sweden, and the United Kingdom (which officially withdrew from the EU in January 2020).
18. As of 2000, the United States was an important destination for the exports of only a handful of countries: Lesotho, Angola, Gabon, and Nigeria.
19. For each country and subperiod, the compound growth rate r in nominal exports E between year t_0 and year T is obtained as the solution to the equation $E_T = E_{t_0} (1 + r)^{T-r_0}$.
20. The three countries with negative export growth in both periods are Gabon, Guinea, and Guinea-Bissau.
21. The low utilization rate observed in the first few years of the AGOA is likely because of an imprecision in our definition of AGOA eligibility for a given country by year, whereas the AGOA entered into force for different countries in different months of the year.
22. Other countries in this group are Côte d'Ivoire, Ghana, the Seychelles, Sierra Leone, and Zambia.
23. Other countries in this group are Botswana, Cabo Verde, Eswatini, Madagascar, Malawi, Mozambique, Namibia, South Africa, and Uganda.
24. The other country in this group is Mauritius.
25. Other countries in this group are Kenya, Rwanda, and Tanzania.
26. The specification also includes a term estimating the impact of the GSP LDC on exports of LDCs outside Africa, which is negative and significant.
27. The baseline estimates are maintained in a series of robustness checks that are presented and discussed in Fernandes et al. (2019).

References

Brambilla, I., A. K. Khandelwal, and P. K. Schott. 2010. "China's Experience under the Multi-Fiber Arrangement (MFA) and the Agreement on Textiles and Clothing (ATC)." In *China's Growing Role in World Trade*, edited by R. C. Feenstra and S-J. Wei, 345–87. Chicago: University of Chicago Press for the National Bureau of Economic Research.

Felbermayr, G., F. Teti, and E. Yalcin. 2017. "Free Trade Agreements, Customs Unions in Disguise?" Center for Economic Studies and Ifo Institute for Economic Research (CESifo) paper presented at the Midwest Economic Theory and International Trade Conference, Southern Methodist University, Dallas, November 10–12.

Fernandes, A., A. Forero, H. Maemir, and A. Mattoo. 2019. "Are Trade Preferences a Panacea? The African Growth and Opportunity Act and African Exports." Policy Research Working Paper 8753, World Bank, Washington, DC.

Forero-Rojas, A., H. Maemir, A. M. Fernandes, and A. Mattoo. 2018. "Developing Countries' Trade and Market Access in the European Union and the United States: Introducing Two New Databases." Technical note, World Bank, Washington, DC.

Frazer, G., and J. Van Biesebroeck. 2010. "Trade Growth under the African Growth and Opportunity Act." *Review of Economics and Statistics* 92 (1): 128–44.

Nicita, A. 2011. "Measuring the Relative Strength of Preferential Market Access." Policy Issues in International Trade and Commodities Study Series No. 47, United Nations Conference on Trade and Development, Geneva.

Ornelas, E. 2016. "Special and Differential Treatment for Developing Countries." In *Handbook of Commercial Policy*, Vol. 1B, edited by K. Bagwell and R. W. Staiger, 369–432. Amsterdam: North-Holland.

Rotunno, L., P-L. Vézina, and Z. Wang. 2013. "The Rise and Fall of (Chinese) African Apparel Exports." *Journal of Development Economics* 105: 152–63.

USITC (US International Trade Commission). 2014. "AGOA: Trade and Investment Performance Overview." Publication No. 4461, USITC, Washington, DC.

CHAPTER 3

Comparative Analysis of AGOA and EBA Impacts: Evidence from West Africa

Souleymane Coulibaly

Introduction

The current pace of globalization leaves small low- and middle-income countries (LMICs) with no choice: they must integrate into world markets if they wish to succeed. Sub-Saharan Africa has more than its fair share of small, poor economies because of the fragmentation it inherited from European colonizers, making Africa the continent most prone to ethnic-based conflicts (Potts, Cleaver-Bartholomew, and Hughes 2016). Yet African countries impose the heaviest artificial barriers around their borders. Except for the two dominant economies—South Africa and Nigeria—the continent is made up of countries that have small domestic markets, limited economic diversification, and generally poor connectivity with neighboring countries. These disadvantages reduce proximity between economic agents within Africa as well as between Africa and the rest of the world.

So far, the approach taken by the international community (high-income countries and international financial institutions) to helping Africa has been essentially country-specific and focused on putting out regional fires that threaten to become global: genocides, pandemics, and religious conflicts. This approach has merit, but a continent suffering permanently from the triple disadvantages of low economic density, long distance to markets, and deep divisions needs a different strategy. This chapter makes the case for a regional approach, as previously argued in the *World Development Report 2009: Reshaping Economic Geography* (World Bank 2009).

One such approach would be to grant the region preferential access to leading world markets. This is the intention of the African Growth and

Opportunity Act (AGOA) and Everything but Arms (EBA), two preferential agreements extended respectively by the United States and the European Union (EU) since 2001. But not all African countries have benefited from this access, as chapter 2 documents in the case of West African countries. Paradoxically, West Africa hosts two of the most advanced regional economic communities, demonstrating a commendable level of regional collaboration.

Regional Integration: The West African Model

Trust is indeed an important ingredient for regional integration to work, especially when some partners expect to lose out in the short run. Trust can be built on traditional ties, which are often based on a shared language or culture. West African countries share the Dioula, Peuhl, and Haoussa cultures, which, nurtured by Islam, developed an impressive regional trade network over centuries (Emmanuel and Pascal 1993). Beyond these traditional ties, the West African Economic and Monetary Union (WAEMU) and the Economic Community of West African States (ECOWAS) are two complementary regional economic communities that have built regional institutions that are working quite well. The monetary union consistently delivers a low-inflation environment in all WAEMU countries, and the regional military force (the ECOWAS Monitoring Group) and peer pressure have rooted out military coups in ECOWAS countries.

WAEMU (also known under the French acronym, *UEMOA*) comprises seven francophone countries (Benin, Burkina Faso, Côte d'Ivoire, Mali, Niger, Senegal, and Togo) and a lusophone (Portuguese-speaking) one, Guinea-Bissau. The countries share the same currency, central bank, and regional stock market; form a customs union with a compensation mechanism to uphold the common external tariff; and have a Commission that oversees macroeconomic policies and sector-specific strategies. ECOWAS comprises five English-speaking countries (The Gambia, Ghana, Liberia, Nigeria, and Sierra Leone), Cabo Verde (lusophone), and Guinea (francophone). The ECOWAS Commission is competent, and the heads of state and key ministers meet regularly to make strategic decisions and harmonize policies.

WAEMU and ECOWAS are committed to deepening regional integration. By helping West Africa to succeed in its regional integration endeavors, the international community could unleash positive spillover effects across Central Africa (starting in Cameroon, which shares a border with Nigeria) and beyond. This chapter argues that to revamp aid-for-trade initiatives—which complement preferential trade agreements, providing direct aid to address various supply-side and infrastructure constraints to LMICs' engagement in international trade—high-income countries should enact policies that offer lower trade barriers to LMICs to facilitate increased export earnings through both larger volumes of exports and more diversified exports (Persson 2015).

Changes in Exports to the European Union and the United States, by Growth Performer Group

Preferential trade with the EU and the US has helped boost Sub-Saharan Africa's exports, but not all countries have benefited equally (as discussed in chapters 1 and 2). By comparing their 1995–2008 growth performance with their 2014–16 performance, World Bank (2016) classifies Sub-Saharan African countries into five groups.[1] Focusing on four of these groups, figure 3.1 indicates the positive export response of "established" growth performers to trading with the EU and the United States. This group's exports to the EU increased by 65 percent over 2009–13, and its exports to the United States increased by 122 percent (figure 3.1, panel a). By contrast, among the "slipping" and "stuck in the middle" performers, exports to the United States decreased, and exports to the EU increased (figure 3.1, panel b). Among the "improved" performers, exports to the EU decreased, and exports to the United States increased.

This chapter examines how, or whether, the AGOA and EBA affected these export performances. It reviews the latest developments in estimation

Figure 3.1   Change in Sub-Saharan African Exports to the European Union and the United States, by "Growth Performer" Group, 2009–13

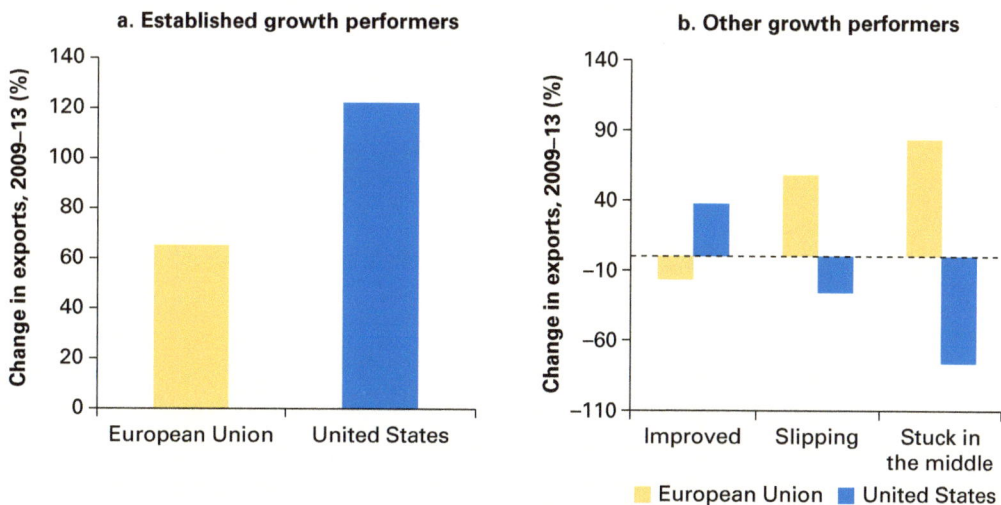

Sources: World Development Indicators database; United Nations Comtrade database; World Bank calculations.
Note: "Established," "improved," "slipping," and "stuck in the middle" are groups of Sub-Saharan African countries based on their growth performance over 1995–2008 versus 2014–16 (World Bank 2016). In panel a, "established" growth performers are countries registering annual average GDP growth exceeding the top tercile of the Sub-Saharan Africa distribution in both periods. In panel b, "other growth performers" includes (a) "improved" (with average annual GDP growth below the top tercile in 1995–2008 but greater than the top tercile in 2014–16); (b) "slipping" (countries with average annual GDP growth exceeding the bottom tercile in 1995–2008 but below the bottom tercile in 2014–16); and (c) "stuck in the middle" (countries with a growth rate in 2014–16 exceeding the bottom tercile but lower than the top tercile in both periods).

of the AGOA's and EBA's trade impacts; proposes an econometric strategy to reestimate these impacts from 2001 to 2015, covering a horizon beyond when the policies went into effect; and zooms in on West African countries to estimate their export potential and explore some policy implications for an effective regional integration process in Africa.

Estimations of the Trade Impacts of the AGOA and EBA

Several studies have analyzed the ex post trade creation impact of the AGOA and EBA. Mattoo, Roy, and Subramanian (2003) use a partial equilibrium model to estimate the AGOA's potential impact on trade. They find that the AGOA increased non-oil exports from Sub-Saharan African countries by 8–11 percent, depending on the restrictiveness of the rules of origin in the non-apparel sector. Most of this increase was accounted for by the apparel sector, whose exports increased by an estimated 8.3 percent. However, the impact varied across regions: some countries, mostly in Central and West Africa, have never taken meaningful advantage of the AGOA (Fernandes et al. 2019).

In another study, Collier and Venables (2007) focus on African countries' exports to the US relative to their exports to the EU to assess the relative trade impacts of the AGOA and EBA. They use a model expressing EU and US imports from AGOA and EBA beneficiary countries as a function of supplier countries' characteristics, importer characteristics, and some bilateral characteristics. With a triple-differences estimation approach, they show that the AGOA apparel provision had a significant and large impact on apparel exports, whereas the EBA had a significant and positive impact only when it was treated as an innovation within the Cotonou Agreement signed between the EU and all African, Caribbean, and Pacific countries for 2000–20.[2]

In addition, De Melo and Portugal-Perez (2014) delve into the specificity of the rules of origin of the AGOA and EBA to assess their impacts on African apparel trade. To benefit from these preferences, proof of sufficient transformation must be provided to the customs agencies in importing countries, by meeting the rules of origin requirements. The rules of origin are complicated and burdensome for exporters in least developed countries (LDCs). Since 2001, under the US AGOA initiative, 22 Sub-Saharan African countries that export apparel to the United States have been allowed to use fabric of any origin (single transformation) and still meet the criterion for preferential access (the so-called Special Rule on Apparel). In contrast, the EU has continued to require yarn to be woven into fabric and then made into apparel in the same country (double transformation).

De Melo and Portugal-Perez (2014) exploit this quasi-experimental change in the design of preferences to estimate the trade impacts of the AGOA and EBA from 1996 through 2004. Their estimates show that the AGOA simplification contributed to an increase in export volume of approximately 168 percent for the top seven beneficiaries, nearly quadrupling the

44 percent growth effect from the AGOA's initial preferential access (without the allowance for single transformation). This change in design was also important for diversity in apparel exports, because the number of export varieties grew more rapidly under the AGOA Special Rule.

The AGOA and EBA have been in effect for more than 15 years. They are expected to boost the exports of eligible products from eligible countries. However, the bulk of the empirical assessments of their impacts on trade have so far narrowly focused on apparel, and there has been no counterfactual assessment to estimate the boost to exports from LMICs if product and country eligibility were broadened to increase support of economic communities committed to regional and global integration. Indeed, given the "spaghetti bowl effect" of many overlapping regional integration initiatives in Africa (as depicted in the Overview, figure O.4), the EU grouped the continent's countries into five regional entities to streamline the EU's Economic Partnership Agreement negotiations with them while at the same time fostering a more effective regional integration process: ECOWAS and WAEMU in West Africa, the Central African Economic and Monetary Community (CEMAC), the East African Community (EAC), and the Southern African Development Community (SADC).

One way to expand the literature on the trade impacts of the AGOA and EBA is to assess carefully, for each of these groupings, what the trade creation impact would have been if all the members were eligible and all the products for which they have comparative advantage were covered by these two preferential agreements. Such a counterfactual analysis would highlight the potential development impact of these trade policies, particularly for regional economic communities demonstrating a strong commitment to deepening regional integration to scale up their supply capacity while pursuing global integration to scale up demand. This chapter focuses on West African countries as an initial step.

ECOWAS Exports to the European Union and the United States since 2000

ECOWAS total exports to the EU and the US increased severalfold between 2000 and 2008—from US$11 billion to US$40 billion for the US and from US$10 billion to US$30 billion for the EU—before collapsing in both cases to around US$20 billion in 2009 during the Global Financial Crisis (figure 3.2, panel a). After 2009, ECOWAS exports to the EU surged to exceed US$50 billion by 2013, whereas exports to the US plunged after reaching US$37 billion in 2011. The widening gap between exports to the EU and those to the US appears to be a systematic trend since 2010. The gap sharply increased, from US$6 billion in favor of the US in 2010, to US$40 billion in favor of the EU in 2014.

Shifts in mineral exports underlying the EU–US gap. A closer look at the composition of ECOWAS exports to the EU and the US indicates that the shift in favor of the EU resulted from the sharp decline of ECOWAS mineral

Figure 3.2   ECOWAS Exports to the European Union and the United States, 2000–15

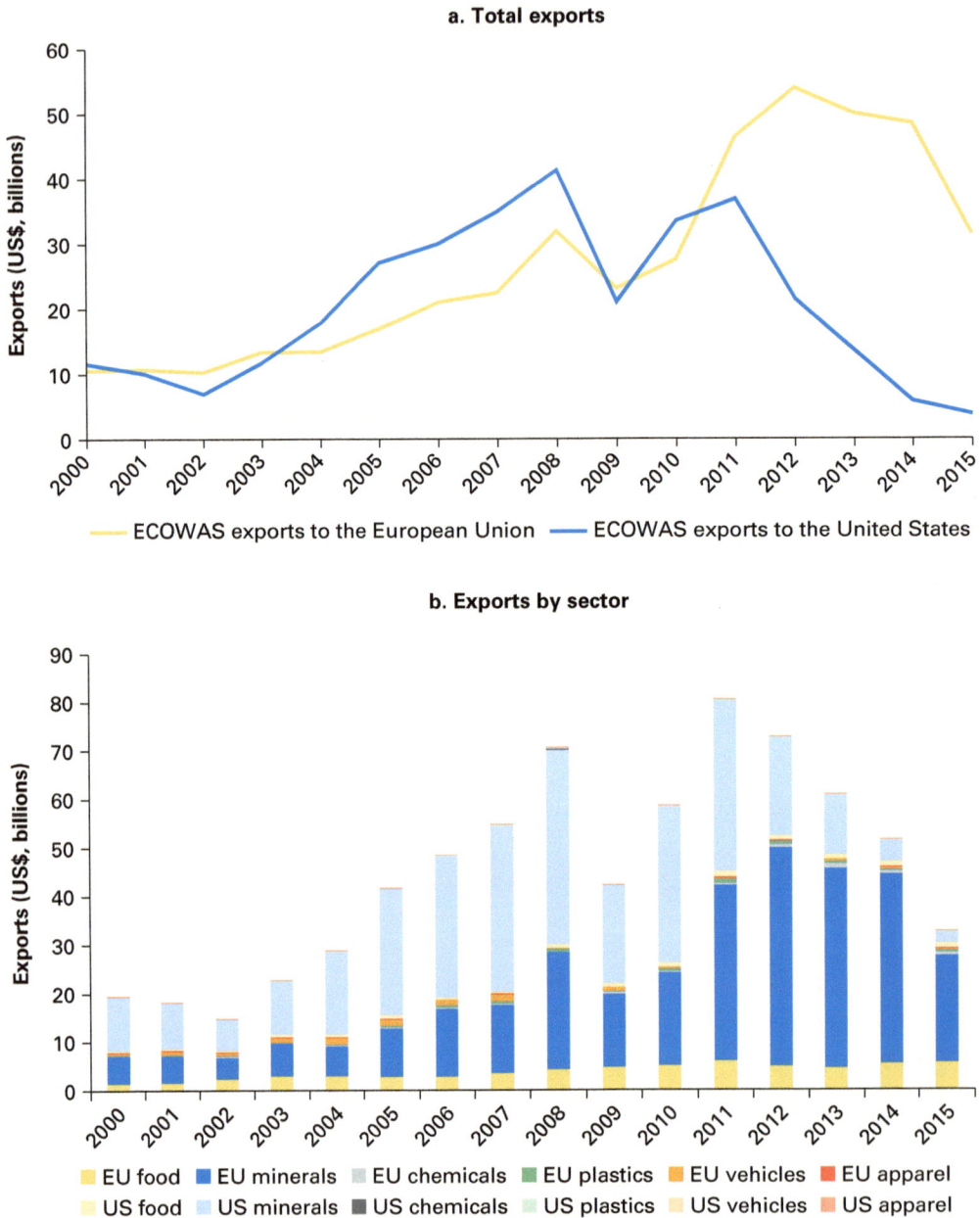

a. Total exports

— ECOWAS exports to the European Union   — ECOWAS exports to the United States

b. Exports by sector

■ EU food   ■ EU minerals   ■ EU chemicals   ■ EU plastics   ■ EU vehicles   ■ EU apparel
■ US food   ■ US minerals   ■ US chemicals   ■ US plastics   ■ US vehicles   ■ US apparel

Source: United Nations Comtrade database.
Note: ECOWAS = Economic Community of West African States; EU = European Union.

exports to the United States after 2011 (figure 3.2, panel b). This reflects the negative shock to the price and production of oil in Nigeria, the main US trading partner in ECOWAS. By contrast, ECOWAS countries' minerals exports to the EU quickly rebounded after the 2008–09 Global Financial Crisis, and they remained high.

ECOWAS exports to both the EU and the US appear to be dominated by minerals, with only exports of food products to the EU also reaching appreciable levels. In relative terms, except for minerals (figure 3.3, panel a), ECOWAS exports to the EU dominate their US-bound equivalents.

Nonmineral exports to the EU, by sector. ECOWAS food exports to the EU increased from US$1.5 billion in 2000 to US$5.7 billion in 2015, an average annual growth rate of 9 percent (figure 3.3, panel b). ECOWAS

Figure 3.3   EU and US Imports from ECOWAS Countries, by Sector, 2000–15

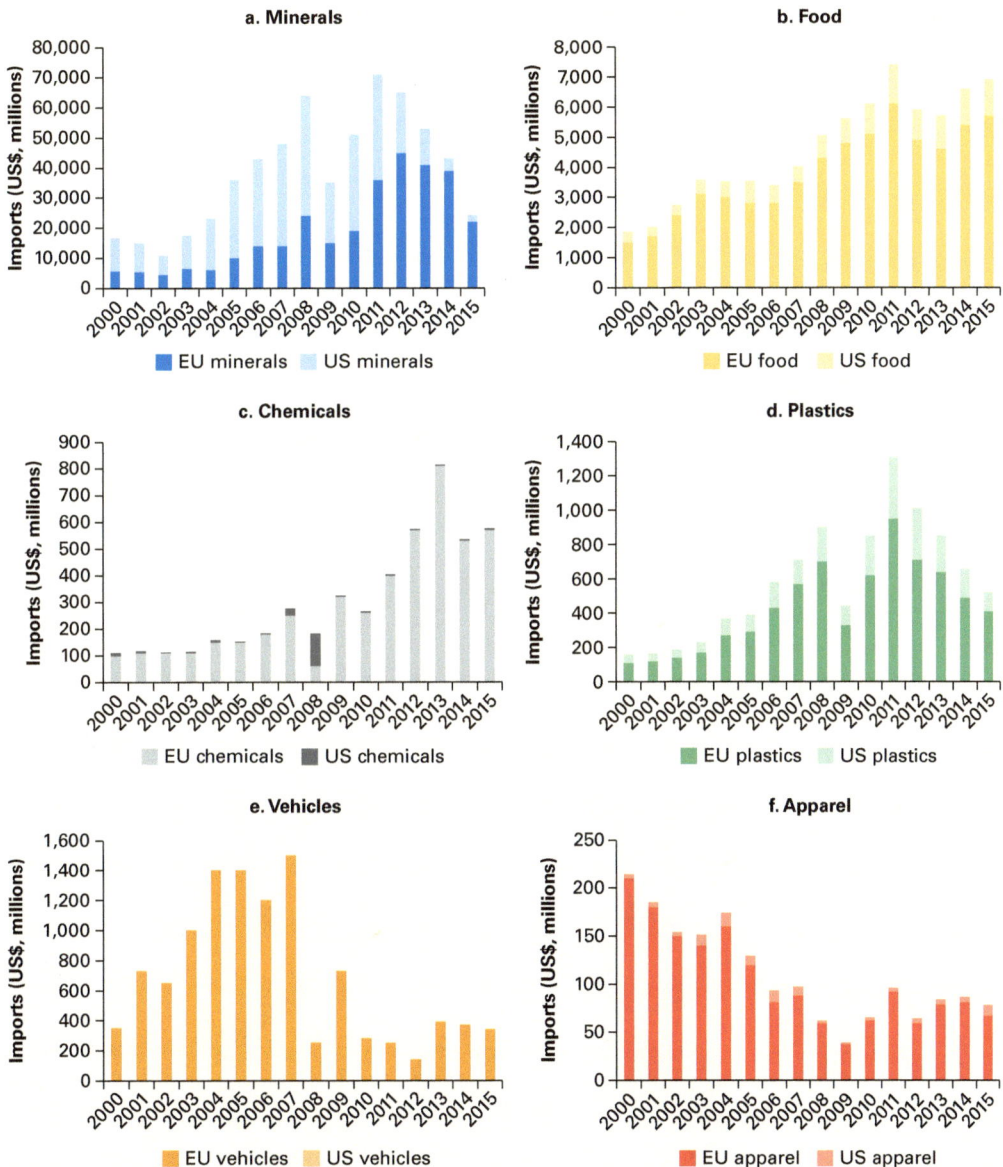

Source: United Nations Comtrade database.
Note: ECOWAS = Economic Community of West African States; EU = European Union.

food exports to the United States increased at the same pace, but from a much lower base (US$350 million in 2000, less than a quarter of the value of exports to the EU).

Similarly, ECOWAS countries' exports of chemicals to the EU increased from US$100 million in 2000 to US$810 million in 2013 (figure 3.3, panel c), and their exports of plastics to the EU increased from US$110 million in 2000 to US$910 million in 2011 (figure 3.3, panel d), posting average annual growth rates of 17 percent and 22 percent, respectively.

ECOWAS exports of vehicles and automobile parts to the EU increased from US$350 million in 2000 to US$1.5 billion in 2007, before plunging to less than US$150 million by 2012 (figure 3.3, panel d). However, ECOWAS exports of apparel to the EU consistently decreased, from US$210 million in 2000 to US$67 million in 2015 (an average annual negative growth rate of 6 percent) (figure 3.3, panel f).

Nonmineral exports to the US, by sector. By contrast, ECOWAS exports of these categories of goods to the United States have been very low, with less-marked trends except for food and plastic products (figure 3.3, panels b and d). ECOWAS exports of food to the United States increased from US$350 million in 2000 (less than one-fourth the exports to the EU) to US$1.2 billion in 2015 (one-fifth the exports to the EU), posting an average annual growth rate of 9 percent. ECOWAS exports of plastics to the United States increased from US$50 million in 2000 to a maximum of US$360 million in 2011, before declining and stabilizing at around US$100 million in 2015.

The rest of this chapter assesses whether these differences (in volume and composition) in ECOWAS exports to the EU and the US result from differences in the design and implementation of the AGOA and EBA. The chapter also makes inferences about the potential impacts on ECOWAS countries of redesigning these two preferential trade agreements.

Empirical Specifications and Data

Following Santos Silva and Tenreyro (2006), we use the Poisson pseudo-maximum likelihood estimation approach to account for the heteroscedasticity of bilateral trade flows as well as zero trade flows. The basic equation to be estimated for each year t is

$$Export_{ijpt} = \alpha_{ijt} ln\left(X_{ijpt}\right) + \sum_{k \in \{nT,T\}} \beta_{k,t} AGOA_{k,ijpt} +$$
$$\gamma_t EBA_{ijpt} + FE_i + FE_j + \varepsilon_{ijpt}, \tag{3.1}$$

where X_{ijt} is a vector of gravity variables; nT and T are nontextile and textile products, respectively; $AGOA_{nT,ijpt}$ takes the value 1 only for year t when the AGOA is in effect in country i and covers nontextile product p exported to the United States; $AGOA_{T,ijpt}$ takes the value 1 only for year t when the AGOA is in effect in country i and covers textile product

p exported to the United States; EBA_{ijpt} takes the value 1 only for year t when the EBA is in effect in country i and covers product p exported to any of the 28 EU member countries; FE_i is the full set of reporter fixed effects; and FE_j is the full set of partner fixed effects. In the empirical assessment, we also interact the AGOA and EBA variables with a dummy variable specifying West African countries, to single out the impact of the two preferential agreements on this subregion.

Given the difference in country eligibility between the AGOA and EBA— with the EBA covering only LDCs and the AGOA covering any country that is approved by the United States—it is important to be able to assess any differential treatment of countries by both preferential agreements. We focus on West African countries and compare the trade impact estimated for all the AGOA and EBA beneficiaries with that estimated only for West African countries. The final equation used for the empirical assessment of the trade impacts of the AGOA and EBA is the following:

$$Export_{ijpt} = \alpha_{ijt} ln\left(X_{ijpt}\right) + \sum_{k \in \{nT, T\}} \beta_{k,t} \times West\_Africa \times AGOA_{k,ijpt}$$
$$+ \gamma_t \times West\_Africa \times EBA_{ijpt} + FE_i + FE_j + \varepsilon_{ijpt}, \tag{3.2}$$

where $West\_Africa$ is a dummy variable taking the value 1 only if country i is a West African country. This formulation allows us to focus on ECOWAS countries and assess the differentiated trade impacts of the AGOA and EBA on them.

We use the approach suggested by Anderson and van Wincoop (2003) to account for multilateral trade resistance, focusing on all the bilateral flows between Sub-Saharan African countries, non-African LDCs, and the EU and the US to estimate the model.[3] We therefore have 91 partner countries for each of the 92 reporter countries.

Because AGOA product eligibility is granted at a fairly disaggregated (Harmonized System [HS] 6-digit) level, we use disaggregated export flows to assess the trade impacts of the AGOA and the EBA. To reduce the size of the data set, we use the 4-digit (1,241 products) instead of the 6-digit (more than 5,000 products) disaggregation level. To ensure the "square-ness" of the data set for product coverage, we complete it as needed with zero trade flows for any 4-digit product exported at least once by any of the reporter countries to any of the partner countries during 2001–15.

Finally, to deal with missing trade flows, we use the Database for International Trade Analysis (BACI), a unique data set of harmonized trade flows.[4] The data set was initially constructed by Gaulier and Zignago (2010), using United Nations Comtrade data, and is regularly updated by the Centre for Prospective Studies and International Information (CEPII). CEPII also provides a full set of traditional gravity variables (such as bilateral distance, contiguity, common language, and common colonizer), which was first used in Head, Mayer, and Ries (2010).

Estimation Results

Table 3.1 presents the results of estimating equation (3.1) for each year. Tables 3.2 and 3.3 present the estimation results for equations (3.1) and (3.2), respectively, using panel data.[5] For the panel Poisson pseudo-maximum likelihood estimation, we interpret the estimated coefficients as elasticities, in the spirit of Santos Silva and Tenreyro (2006). Table 3.4 presents the marginal effects of AGOA and EBA eligibility.

Table 3.1 **Poisson Pseudo-Maximum Likelihood Estimations of AGOA and EBA Impact on Exports in Sub-Saharan Africa, 2001–15**

Dependent variable: X_{ijpt}	(1) 2001	(2) 2002	(3) 2003[a]	(4) 2004	(5) 2005	(6) 2007[a,b]	(7) 2008
lnGdpi	−0.024	−0.363	0.422	−0.538	−0.406	1.178	1.803
	(0.02)	(0.29)		(0.90)	(0.48)		(1.15)
lnGdpj	0.471	0.794	0.119	1.024	0.662	0.893	0.704
	(1.76)	(2.42)*		(3.55)**	(2.32)*		(1.76)
lnGdppci	0.099	0.395	−0.144	0.628	0.194	−0.714	−0.951
	(0.12)	(0.42)		(1.44)	(0.33)		(0.91)
lnGdppcj	0.091	−0.191	0.293	−0.369	−0.056	−0.240	−0.074
	(0.46)	(0.74)		(1.71)	(0.30)		(0.35)
lnDistij	−0.799	−0.818	−0.849	−0.875	−0.895	−0.922	−0.927
	(14.68)**	(13.90)**		(18.14)**	(17.89)**		(20.65)**
1=Contiguity	0.126	0.138	0.119	0.113	0.129	0.117	0.150
	(1.96)	(2.14)*		(1.87)	(2.15)*		(2.77)**
1=Common official or primary language	0.573	0.593	0.606	0.595	0.556	0.582	0.539
	(5.55)**	(5.73)**		(6.03)**	(5.51)**		(5.49)**
1=Common colonizer post-1945	1.183	1.151	0.983	0.984	0.962	0.821	0.870
	(6.91)**	(6.77)**		(7.89)**	(6.86)**		(5.75)**
AGOA nontextile impact	0.613	0.403	0.114	0.286	0.410	0.461	0.504
	(1.36)	(0.94)		(0.60)	(0.80)		(0.94)
AGOA textile impact	0.593	−0.293	−0.043	−0.481	−0.842	−1.523	−1.823
	(1.44)	(0.91)		(1.55)	(2.61)**		(3.84)**
EBA impact	0.351	0.365	0.079	0.222	−0.067	−0.123	−0.150
	(1.45)	(1.58)		(0.77)	(0.25)		(0.43)
Constant	−5.235	−5.186	−5.222	−4.971	−3.880	−8.503	−10.000
	(1.94)	(1.79)		(3.06)**	(1.75)		(2.30)*
Reporter fixed effects	Yes	Yes	Yes	Yes	Yes	Yes	Yes
Partner fixed effects	Yes	Yes	Yes	Yes	Yes	Yes	Yes
R^2	0.02	0.02	0.02	0.02	0.02	0.02	0.02
N	1,361,247	1,361,247	1,361,247	1,361,247	1,361,247	1,361,247	1,361,247

(Table continues on next page)

Table 3.1   Poisson Pseudo-Maximum Likelihood Estimations of AGOA and EBA Impact on Exports in Sub-Saharan Africa, 2001–15 *(continued)*

Dependent variable: X_{ijpt}	(8) 2009	(9) 2010	(10) 2011	(11) 2012[b]	(12) 2014	(13) 2015
lnGdpi	0.647	0.749	0.466	−2.521	−2.867	−3.645
	(0.67)	(0.94)	(0.40)		(5.18)**	(5.78)**
lnGdpj	0.952	0.388	−0.148	−0.802	−0.628	−1.445
	(2.55)*	(0.71)	(0.19)		(1.12)	(2.84)**
lnGdppci	−0.161	−0.111	−0.128	1.487	1.597	2.159
	(0.25)	(0.25)	(0.22)		(7.04)**	(7.30)**
lnGdppcj	−0.350	−0.040	0.286	0.515	0.301	0.821
	(1.60)	(0.17)	(0.77)		(1.63)	(3.54)**
lnDistij	−0.912	−0.918	−0.875	−0.877	−0.898	−0.887
	(18.69)**	(19.66)**	(18.79)**		(20.60)**	(20.60)**
1=Contiguity	0.148	0.169	0.219	0.226	0.220	0.173
	(2.64)**	(3.01)**	(3.84)**		(4.06)**	(3.13)**
1=Common official or primary language	0.575	0.549	0.517	0.455	0.376	0.477
	(5.46)**	(5.47)**	(4.95)**		(4.17)**	(4.86)**
1=Common colonizer post-1945	0.712	0.631	0.704	0.757	0.813	0.947
	(4.96)**	(4.94)**	(4.74)**		(7.26)**	(8.19)**
AGOA nontextile impact	0.257	0.372	0.606	−0.008	−0.665	−0.836
	(0.50)	(0.67)	(1.09)		(2.31)*	(3.75)**
AGOA textile impact	−1.724	−1.641	−1.835	−1.988	−1.566	−1.453
	(4.27)**	(5.89)**	(4.78)**		(5.80)**	(5.47)**
EBA impact	−0.228	−0.171	−0.045	0.029	0.123	0.187
	(0.80)	(0.65)	(0.16)		(0.59)	(1.07)
Constant	−7.672	−6.292	−3.396	7.439	8.586	12.394
	(2.73)**	(2.19)*	(0.78)		(3.16)**	(4.89)**
Reporter fixed effects	Yes	Yes	Yes	Yes	Yes	Yes
Partner fixed effects	Yes	Yes	Yes	Yes	Yes	Yes
R^2	0.02	0.02	0.02	0.02	0.02	0.02
N	1,361,247	1,361,247	1,361,247	1,353,749	1,351,927	1,339,153

Source: World Bank.
Note: t-statistics are in parentheses. AGOA = African Growth and Opportunity Act; EBA = Everything but Arms.
a. t-statistics were not estimated because the variance matrix is highly singular.
b. Estimations for 2006 and 2013 are not reported because the computation could not be completed owing to name conflict (STATA error code 507).
* $p < 0.05$; ** $p < 0.01$.

Table 3.2   Poisson Pseudo-Maximum Likelihood Panel Estimations of AGOA Trade Impacts on Sub-Saharan African Countries, 2001–15, and by Three-Year Period

Dependent variable: X_{ijpt}	(1) 2001–15	(2) 2001–03	(3) 2004–06	(4) 2007–09	(5) 2010–12	(6) 2013–15
lnGdpi	−1.089	−1.558	−1.240	1.161	−0.394	−3.460
	(182.74)**	(17.84)**	(19.72)**	(18.74)**	(8.14)**	(75.17)**
lnGdpj	−0.534	0.283	−1.188	−0.092	−0.860	−0.839
	(87.68)**	(3.34)**	(18.12)**	(1.43)	(16.65)**	(24.08)**
lnGdppci	1.691	2.149	1.981	−0.781	0.847	3.957
	(267.33)**	(24.60)**	(30.18)**	(12.79)**	(16.17)**	(84.50)**
lnGdppcj	1.260	0.186	1.751	0.522	1.644	1.484
	(200.84)**	(2.23)*	(26.24)**	(8.22)**	(29.93)**	(41.77)**
AGOA nontextile impact	−0.069	0.010	−0.417	−1.134	−0.035	−0.065
	(7.93)**	(0.37)	(5.92)**	(7.60)**	(2.01)*	(3.52)**
AGOA textile impact	0.135	0.559	0.414	−0.569	0.079	0.629
	(6.88)**	(11.03)**	(9.62)**	(0.03)	(1.36)	(2.70)**
N	20,526,037	2,311,185	2,463,144	2,591,877	2,639,577	2,720,351

Source: World Bank.

Note: Reporter-partner-product and time fixed effects panel estimations. The European Union's Everything but Arms (EBA) trade preference was dropped from the estimations because of multicollinearity. Bilateral traditional gravity variables such as distance, contiguity, and common language were also dropped because of constant values in groups. *t*-statistics are in parentheses. AGOA = African Growth and Opportunity Act.
* $p < 0.05$; ** $p < 0.01$.

For the panel specifications, we estimate equations (3.1) and (3.2) for the entire period, 2001–15, and on three-year intervals. The gravity variables are dropped from the panel specifications because of constant values in the clusters. The year-by-year specifications are generally statistically significant, with the expected sign except for the gross domestic product of the reporter country, which has a negative coefficient in a few instances. The panel estimations appear to be statistically more robust than the year-by-year estimations. Therefore, the following discussion focuses on the panel specifications. The next section uses year-by-year estimated coefficients for simulation.

Over 2001–15, the estimated coefficient for AGOA[6] nontextiles is −0.069, compared with 0.135 for AGOA textiles (table 3.2, column [1]), which confirms previous results that the AGOA's textile provision has had a stronger positive impact on Sub-Saharan Africa's exports to the United States than the general AGOA provision. Looking at shorter time spans, the estimated effect of the AGOA's textile provision is even stronger: 75 percent more exports over 2001–03, 51 percent more exports over 2004–06, and 88 percent more exports over 2013–15, compared with 14 percent more exports over 2001–15 (table 3.4). In contrast, the general AGOA provision appears to have induced export diversion away from the United States.

Focusing on countries in West Africa (table 3.3), we find that the AGOA's textile provision did not induce more exports of apparel to the United States. All the estimated coefficients are not statistically significant (AGOA textile) or are statistically significant but negative (AGOA general provision). By contrast, the estimated EBA coefficients are large and positive, although not statistically significant. These findings seem to corroborate that ECOWAS countries trade more with the EU and on a more diversified basis (figure 3.3). Despite their deeper regional integration as well as fairly diversified trade with the EU, the ECOWAS countries appear to benefit less than all Sub-Saharan African countries collectively from the two major preferential trade agreements providing access to the EU and US markets.

This poor performance could have multiple explanations. Regarding the EBA, which covers only LDCs, ECOWAS's most dynamic countries (Côte d'Ivoire, Ghana, and Nigeria) are not beneficiaries. As for the AGOA, the restrictiveness of the nontextile provision seems to preclude ECOWAS AGOA beneficiaries from leveraging their potential for diversified trade.

Table 3.3 **Poisson Pseudo-Maximum Likelihood Panel Estimations of AGOA and EBA Trade Impacts on West African Countries, 2001–15, and by Three-Year Period**

Dependent variable: Xijpt	(1) 2001–15	(2) 2001–03	(3) 2004–06	(4) 2007–09	(5) 2010–12	(6) 2013–15
lnGdpi	−1.088	−1.525	−1.248	1.160	−0.391	−3.458
	(182.52)**	(17.50)**	(19.85)**	(18.73)**	(8.10)**	(75.14)**
lnGdpj	−0.534	0.283	−1.192	−0.092	−0.859	−0.839
	(87.66)**	(3.35)**	(18.18)**	(1.43)	(16.63)**	(24.08)**
lnGdppci	1.690	2.115	1.990	−0.781	0.845	3.956
	(267.12)**	(24.25)**	(30.32)**	(12.78)**	(16.13)**	(84.47)**
lnGdppcj	1.260	0.182	1.755	0.522	1.642	1.483
	(200.85)**	(2.18)*	(26.30)**	(8.22)**	(29.91)**	(41.76)**
AGOA nontextile - West Africa	−0.307	−0.000	−0.300	−1.386	−0.005	0.717
	(10.29)**	(0.00)	(4.25)**	(8.14)**	(0.09)	(0.70)
AGOA textile - West Africa	0.560	1.045	−1.182	−0.569	−1.533	
	(1.83)	(1.54)	(0.12)	(0.03)	(0.86)	
EBA - West Africa	3.918	3.064				
	(0.45)	(0.16)				
N	20,526,037	2,311,185	2,463,144	2,591,877	2,639,577	2,720,351

Source: World Bank.
Note: "West African countries" refers to members of the Economic Community of West African States (ECOWAS). Reporter-partner-product and time fixed effects panel estimations. Bilateral traditional gravity variables such as distance, contiguity, and common language were dropped because of multicollinearity. The European Union's Everything but Arms (EBA) preference is not included in specifications (3) to (6), and the US African Growth and Opportunity Act (AGOA) textiles in specification (6) because of multicollinearity. *t*-statistics are in parentheses.
* $p < 0.05$; ** $p < 0.01$.

Table 3.4 Estimated Marginal Effects of AGOA and EBA on Exports in Sub-Saharan Africa, 2001–15, by Period and by Year

Percentage change in exports

Period or year	AGOA nontextile overall	AGOA textile overall	EBA overall	AGOA nontextile West Africa	AGOA textile West Africa	EBA West Africa
2001–15	−7	14	n.a.	−26	75	4,930
2001–03	1	75	n.a.	0	184	2,041
2004–06	−34	51	n.a.	−26	−69	n.a.
2007–09	−68	−43	n.a.	−75	−43	n.a.
2010–12	−3	8	n.a.	0	−78	n.a.
2013–15	−6	88	n.a.	105	n.a.	n.a.
2001	85	81	42	184	−100	130
2002	50	−25	44	94	−94	137
2003	12	−4	8	n.a.	n.a.	n.a.
2004	33	−38	25	220	−98	49
2005	51	−57	−6	302	−99	67
2006	n.a.	n.a.	n.a.	221	−99	32
2007	59	−78	−12	314	−99	8
2008	66	−84	−14	234	−100	−30
2009	29	−82	−20	127	−100	29
2010	45	−81	−16	164	−99	−35
2011	83	−84	−4	n.a.	n.a.	n.a.
2012	−1	−86	3	−10	−98	−49
2013	n.a.	n.a.	n.a.	−36	−100	−49
2014	−49	−79	13	−78	−99	−49
2015	−57	−77	21	−83	−99	−38

Source: World Bank.

Note: The marginal effects are calculated as (e^estimated coefficient − 1). Gray highlights indicate that the marginal effect is calculated with a coefficient that is not statistically significant. AGOA = African Growth and Opportunity Act; EBA = Everything but Arms; n.a. = not applicable.

This situation suggests that the EBA could boost export growth and diversification if the rules of origin allowed countries with more diversified export portfolios to the EU to scale up their exports to this major market. It also suggests that an extension of the AGOA's provisions to cover more countries and products, coupled with a better understanding among beneficiary countries about how to use the preferential scheme, could have a major impact on ECOWAS countries.

The next section quantifies the West Africa subregion's potential exports to the EU and the US. That is, it estimates what ECOWAS countries could have expected if the best features of these two preferential agreements had not differentiated between countries and types of products.

Differentiated Impacts of the AGOA and EBA on ECOWAS Countries

We use the estimated coefficients on the AGOA and EBA variables for each year to simulate the export potential of ECOWAS countries, assuming that the AGOA and EBA had been formulated to allow full benefits for all the ECOWAS countries. For this, we first separate disaggregated bilateral exports into textiles and nontextiles, so that the EBA's impact can be estimated for textile and nontextile products. We then assume that the AGOA's full potential is estimated by the panel specifications of equation (3.1) (table 3.4). Because the largest positive and statistically significant marginal effect is obtained for 2013–15, we use the estimated 88 percent increase in exports as the full potential of the AGOA textile provision. Then, for each year, we use the difference between this marginal effect and the estimated marginal effect on ECOWAS countries of AGOA nontextile provision, AGOA textile provision, and the EBA. (For nonstatistically significant coefficients, we assume the marginal effect to be zero.) We finally aggregate each of these ECOWAS individual export flows, distinguishing between textile and nontextile products, for 2001–15 (table 3.5). Figure 3.4 plots the simulated values of exports.

Nontextile products seem to have greater potential for ECOWAS countries than textile products, and the EU seems to be the market with more potential for ECOWAS countries than the United States. Actual ECOWAS exports of nontextile products to the EU varied from less than US$10 billion in 2001 to about US$50 billion in 2014. They would have reached US$110 billion by 2014 if EBA had the same impact on ECOWAS countries as the AGOA's textile provision had on Sub-Saharan Africa as a whole from 2013 through 2015. And they would have reached US$190 billion if, in addition, this potential EBA impact had been extended to ECOWAS countries that are not currently EBA beneficiaries (table 3.5 and figure 3.4).

These findings mean that ECOWAS nontextile exports to the EU in 2014 could have been nearly four times the level registered. Similarly, ECOWAS textile exports could have reached nearly US$4 billion by 2014 instead of the registered amount of less than US$1 billion. ECOWAS exports of nontextile products to the United States in 2014 could have been about US$20 billion, more than triple the US$6 billion registered. Similarly, ECOWAS exports of textile products to the United States in 2014 could have been nearly US$100 million, about 2.5 times the registered US$40 million.

The full set of simulations indicates that ECOWAS exports of nontextile products to either the EU or the US could have averaged 2.5 times the levels registered. The subregion's exports of textile products could have quadrupled the actual levels. This potential for trade creation in a region that has demonstrated commitment to deeper regional integration calls for revisiting the AGOA and EBA provisions.

Table 3.5 Potential Impacts of AGOA and EBA on Exports from ECOWAS Countries to the European Union and the United States, by Export Type, 2001–15

Export destination	Year	Nontextile exports (US$, billions)			Textile exports (US$, billions)			Nontextiles (ratio of potential to actual)	Textiles (ratio of potential to actual)
		Actual	AGOA potential	EBA potential	Actual	AGOA potential	EBA potential		
European Union	2001	9.64	5.30	5.30	0.18	0.34	0.16	2.10	3.76
European Union	2002	9.19	4.63	4.63	0.16	0.30	0.14	2.01	3.70
European Union	2003	12.79	6.31	6.31	0.19	0.34	0.16	1.99	3.72
European Union	2004	12.19	5.47	5.47	0.20	0.37	0.17	1.90	3.74
European Union	2005	15.35	7.93	7.93	0.13	0.24	0.11	2.03	3.75
European Union	2006	21.90	12.37	12.37	0.09	0.16	0.08	2.13	3.75
European Union	2007	20.22	10.08	10.08	0.13	0.24	0.11	2.00	3.75
European Union	2008	28.83	15.51	15.51	0.10	0.19	0.09	2.08	3.76
European Union	2009	22.78	11.56	11.56	0.08	0.15	0.07	2.02	3.76
European Union	2010	27.59	14.75	14.75	0.13	0.24	0.11	2.07	3.75
European Union	2011	45.80	27.36	27.36	0.17	0.33	0.15	2.19	3.75
European Union	2012	50.66	33.28	33.28	0.11	0.21	0.10	2.31	3.74
European Union	2013	45.72	32.25	32.25	0.14	0.26	0.12	2.41	3.76
European Union	2014	48.10	62.89	81.46	0.80	1.49	1.71	4.00	5.02
European Union	2015	26.98	32.99	32.99	0.13	0.23	0.21	3.45	4.58
United States	2001	8.88	7.16	7.16	0.01	0.01	0.01	2.61	3.76
United States	2002	6.87	5.57	5.57	0.00	0.01	0.00	2.62	3.70
United States	2003	10.84	8.56	8.56	0.02	0.03	0.01	2.58	3.72
United States	2004	16.51	13.63	13.63	0.02	0.03	0.01	2.65	3.74
United States	2005	24.26	20.09	20.09	0.01	0.02	0.01	2.66	3.75

(Table continues on next page)

Table 3.5   Potential Impacts of AGOA and EBA on Exports from ECOWAS Countries to the European Union and the United States, by Export Type, 2001–15 *(continued)*

Export destination	Year	Nontextile exports (US$, billions)			Textile exports (US$, billions)			Nontextiles (ratio of potential to actual)	Textiles (ratio of potential to actual)
		Actual	AGOA potential	EBA potential	Actual	AGOA potential	EBA potential		
United States	2006	27.67	22.70	22.70	0.02	0.03	0.01	2.64	3.75
United States	2007	31.87	26.43	26.43	0.01	0.02	0.01	2.66	3.75
United States	2008	37.81	31.45	31.45	0.00	0.01	0.00	2.66	3.76
United States	2009	19.17	15.78	15.78	0.00	0.01	0.00	2.65	3.76
United States	2010	31.29	25.67	25.67	0.01	0.02	0.01	2.64	3.75
United States	2011	34.29	28.36	28.36	0.01	0.02	0.01	2.65	3.74
United States	2012	22.90	15.84	15.84	0.05	0.09	0.04	2.38	3.74
United States	2013	12.68	9.72	9.72	0.01	0.02	0.01	2.53	3.76
United States	2014	6.15	6.50	8.42	0.02	0.03	0.04	3.43	5.02
United States	2015	3.57	3.26	3.26	0.02	0.05	0.04	2.83	4.58

Source: World Bank.

Note: AGOA = African Growth and Opportunity Act; EBA = Everything but Arms; ECOWAS = Economic Community of West African States.

Figure 3.4   Differentiated Impacts of the AGOA and EBA on ECOWAS Countries, 2001–15

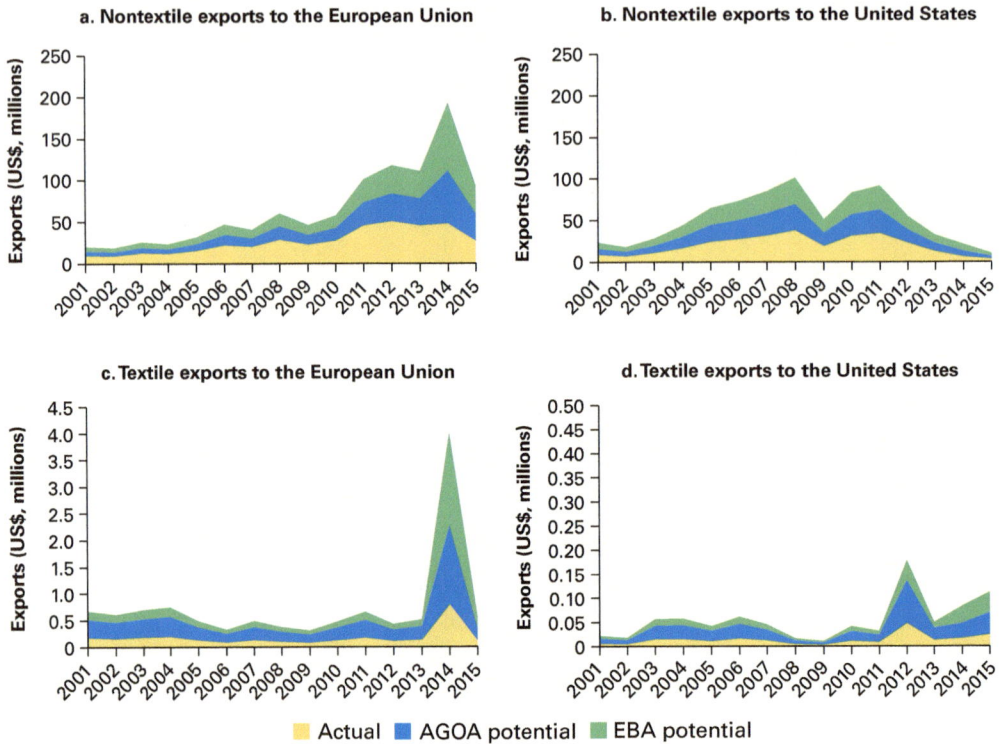

a. Nontextile exports to the European Union

b. Nontextile exports to the United States

c. Textile exports to the European Union

d. Textile exports to the United States

■ Actual   ■ AGOA potential   ■ EBA potential

Sources: United Nations Comtrade database; World Bank calculations.
Note: AGOA = African Growth and Opportunity Act (US); EBA = Everything but Arms (EU); ECOWAS = Economic Community of West African States.

Policy Implications

The EBA provides the widest product coverage ("everything but arms") but only for LDCs and with rules of origin that are more restrictive than the AGOA's (De Melo and Portugal-Perez 2014). However, given the initial cost of getting familiar with the requirements to benefit from the AGOA's general and textile provisions—because of the language barrier (most of the ECOWAS countries are former French colonies)—ECOWAS has tended to trade more with the EU. This has led to a fairly diversified export basket to that destination (as depicted earlier in figure 3.3). At the same time, however, the EBA's restrictiveness in terms of the beneficiary countries has precluded ECOWAS's most dynamic economies (namely Côte d'Ivoire, Ghana, and Nigeria) from taking advantage of this diversified export base.

Given the quite advanced regional integration processes of ECOWAS and WAEMU, and the potential to trigger 2.5 to 4 times more exports to the EU and the United States, a revision of the AGOA and EBA, or a special ECOWAS/WAEMU provision intended to tap this potential, should be considered. This section provides the rationale for such recommendation.

Unleashing the Channels of Regional Spillovers

In the spirit of the Group of Twenty (G-20) "Africa Compact" spearheaded by Germany,[7] an aid-for-trade initiative focusing on ECOWAS/WAEMU countries could accelerate exports from West African countries. It would also trigger three chain reactions that could be considered channels of regional spillovers:

1. A *distribution effect* from countries directly benefiting from the targeted aid-for-trade initiative to their regional economic partners within and outside West Africa, through trade in goods and services and cross-border labor and capital movement searching for better opportunities. For instance, this effect could boost the attractiveness of Côte d'Ivoire, Ghana, and Nigeria to major foreign investors looking for hub locations in Africa.

2. A *domino effect* that would induce countries close to ECOWAS/WAEMU to join the integration process, to take advantage of the new economic opportunities generated by the coordination of foreign aid. (Morocco's recent application for ECOWAS membership confirms the relevance of such a domino effect.) Other neighboring countries, such as Cameroon and Mauritania, might benefit from such a move too.

3. A *demonstration effect*, encouraging other subgroups of countries to deepen their regional integration processes to take advantage of the coordinated aid-for-trade initiative. For instance, countries like Cameroon and Gabon could be induced to overcome their longtime rivalries and lead the integration effort in the Central Africa neighborhood, including the Central African Republic, Chad, the Democratic Republic of Congo, and the Republic of Congo.

International financial institutions (including the World Bank) could take the lead in reorienting the debate on Sub-Saharan Africa's development challenge by moving from a country-specific to a neighborhood-specific approach for the efficient use of foreign aid. By the same token, this reorientation would help to reduce the risk of cross-border conflicts by increasing the economic interdependence of the member countries.[8]

Promoting a "Contract with African Neighborhoods"

Once these initial moves have helped to form African regional economic communities that are ready to deepen their economic cooperation, the international community could shift from the current tangle of crisscrossing trade alliances and agreements to a more streamlined "contract with African neighborhoods." This approach would encompass both leading and lagging countries of the neighborhoods as well as the donor community's provision of the right incentives to ensure developmental regional cooperation initiatives.

Under this model, in each of the African neighborhoods, governments of leading and lagging countries and the international community would participate in the contract. The governments of countries in East, Central, Southern, and West Africa would commit to the following:

- *Establishing "African Economic Areas"*—neighborhood-like blocs of countries with higher potential for integration—that would tie the economic interests of leading and lagging countries in Africa's regional neighborhoods tightly together.
- *Allowing and maintaining the free movement* of labor, capital, goods, and services within these areas.
- *Maintaining and protecting access routes* between landlocked countries and outlets for trade, as well as providing the political space to support investment in regional infrastructures that are essential for the neighborhoods.

In exchange for these cross-regional actions, bilateral and multilateral development partners would commit to the following:

- *Significantly increasing international financial assistance for improved social services* and other life-sustaining infrastructure—such as world-class secondary education—aimed at raising living standards and creating portable human capital in lagging countries.
- *Increasing financial support for growth-sustaining infrastructure*—including ports, transportation links, and information and communications technology—in the leading countries where economic takeoff is most likely, as well as infrastructure to link the markets of leading countries with labor, capital, goods, and ideas from their lagging neighbors.
- *Providing preferential access to the markets of high-income countries* for Sub-Saharan Africa's exports, without strict rules of origin or eligibility criteria that impede rapid growth of trade in intermediate inputs with other LMICs.

The large export potential estimated in this chapter for ECOWAS—if the AGOA and EBA were revised to eliminate the differentiated eligibility criteria and rules of origin—provides a rationale to jump-start the implementation of such a contract with the West Africa neighborhood.

Notes

1. *Africa's Pulse* Vol. 14 (World Bank 2016) defines several groups of growth performers: (a) "established" (countries registering an annual average gross domestic product [GDP] growth rate that exceeds the top tercile of the Sub-Saharan Africa distribution in both 1995–2008

and 2014–16); (b) "improved" (countries with average annual 1995–2008 GDP growth below the top tercile but 2014–16 growth greater than the top tercile); (c) "slipping" (countries with average annual 1995–2008 GDP growth exceeding the bottom tercile but 2014–16 growth below the bottom tercile); and (d) "stuck in the middle" (countries with 2014–16 average annual GDP growth exceeding the bottom tercile but lower than the top tercile in both periods).

2. The Cotonou Agreement is a treaty between the EU and the African, Caribbean and Pacific Group of States (ACP), under which a new scheme called the Economic Partnership Agreements (EPAs) took effect in 2008. This EPA provides reciprocal trade agreements whereby the EU provides duty-free access to its markets for ACP exports, and the ACP countries provide duty-free access to their own markets for EU exports.

3. We did not include the entire universe of trading partners because of the computational limits given the estimation method used.

4. BACI is the French acronym of "Base pour l'Analyse du Commerce International."

5. A critical issue is endogeneity. AGOA and EBA coverage (product and country eligibility) is endogenous, given reliance on economic or governance performance that can be affected by trade. We tried instrumenting for this with the United Nations Development Programme's Human Development Index and the World Bank's Worldwide Governance Indicators on corruption, but we could not reach any conclusion because of the multicollinearity of these instruments with many of the independent variables.

6. We cannot estimate the EBA's effect in the panel specification of equation (3.1) because of multicollinearity between the EBA variable and the fixed effects included in the panel estimation.

7. The G-20 Compact with Africa was launched in 2017 to promote private investment in Africa, including in infrastructure. Its primary objective is to increase attractiveness of private investment through substantial improvements in the macro, business, and financing frameworks ("About the Compact with Africa," G-20 Compact with Africa website: https://www.compactwithafrica.org/content/compact withafrica/home.html).

8. Martin, Mayer, and Thoenig (2008) show that countries with a lot of economic interaction with their neighbors are less likely to engage in an armed conflict.

References

Anderson, J. E., and E. van Wincoop. 2003. "Gravity with Gravitas: A Solution to the Border Puzzle." *American Economic Review* 93 (1): 170–92.

Collier, P., and A. J. Venables. 2007. "Rethinking Trade Preferences: How Africa Can Diversify Its Exports." *World Economy* 30 (8): 1326–45.

De Melo, J., and A. Portugal-Perez. 2014. "Preferential Market Access Design: Evidence and Lessons from African Apparel Exports to the United States and the European Union." *World Bank Economic Review* 28 (1): 74–98.

Emmanuel, G., and L. Pascal. 1993. *Grands commerçants d'Afrique de l'Ouest: logiques et pratiques d'un groupe d'affaires contemporains [Large West African Traders: Logic and Practices of a Group of Contemporary Businessmen]*. Paris: Karthala-Orstom.

Fernandes, A., H. Maemir, A. Mattoo, and A. Forero. 2019. "Are Trade Preferences a Panacea? The African Growth and Opportunity Act and African Exports." Policy Research Working Paper 8753, World Bank, Washington, DC.

Gaulier, G., and S. Zignago. 2010. "BACI: International Trade Database at the Product-Level: The 1994–2007 Version." Working Paper Series No. 2010–23, Centre for Prospective Studies and International Information (CEPII), Paris.

Head, K., T. Mayer, and J. Ries. 2010. "The Erosion of Colonial Trade Linkages after Independence." *Journal of International Economics* 81 (1): 1–14.

Martin, P., T. Mayer, and M. Thoenig. 2008. "Civil Wars and International Trade." *Journal of the European Economic Association* 6 (2–3): 541–50.

Mattoo, A., D. Roy, and A. Subramanian. 2003. "The Africa Growth and Opportunity Act and Its Rules of Origin: Generosity Undermined?" *World Economy* 26 (6): 829–51.

Persson, M. 2015. "Trade Preferences from a Policy Perspective." In *Handbook on Trade and Development*, edited by O. Morrissey, R. A. López, and K. Sharma, 111–28. Cheltenham, UK: Edward Elgar.

Potts, J. C., A. Cleaver-Bartholomew, and I. Hughes. 2016. "Comparing the Roots of Conflict in Europe, the Middle East, and Africa." *Inquiries Journal* 8 (4): 1–2.

Santos Silva, J. M. C., and S. Tenreyro. 2006. "The Log of Gravity." *Review of Economics and Statistics* 88 (4): 641–58.

World Bank. 2009. *World Development Report 2009: Reshaping Economic Geography*. Washington, DC: World Bank.

World Bank. 2016. *Africa's Pulse*, vol. 14 (October). Washington, DC: World Bank.

New Market Frontiers: Focus on East Asia

Asia, particularly East Asia and South Asia, has been the engine of global growth in the past few decades. The growing middle class and increasing demand from East Asia, accompanied by rising relative wages along with the shifting structure of global value chains (GVCs), may offer new economic opportunities for Sub-Saharan Africa. Although the region's exports to Asia remain highly concentrated in resource-intensive products such as petroleum, minerals, metals, and other primary goods, a few African countries are diversifying their export portfolios following the export boom to Asia.

Part II (chapters 4 and 5) provides important insights about Africa–Asia trade. For example, although China is the continent's key trading partner, it is not always the dominant trading partner for individual Sub-Saharan African countries. For example, since 2005, India has become the largest export destination for Ghana, Nigeria, and Tanzania. Pakistan has been the top destination for Kenya's exports. The two chapters in this part of the book present a detailed analysis of the extent of trade between the two regions, the subsequent GVC links, and prospects for the future.

To tap this rising potential, Sub-Saharan African policy makers must further deepen their trade ties with Asia. Building on the achievements of recent periods, countries should strengthen their positions in this "hub-and-spoke" pattern of trade. A careful assessment of the changing demand patterns of Asia's growing middle class could inform export diversification options for Sub-Saharan African countries. Countries that invest in reforming their institutions—including strengthening the rule of law and contract enforcement mechanisms, reducing rent-seeking activities in specific markets, and reducing risks of political instability—would see increasing trade with Asia and the benefits from such trade.

A policy of export orientation toward Asia could support faster growth and economic transformation and poverty reduction. The prospects for gains in structural transformation will be enhanced by the ongoing restructuring of economies in East Asia, mainly China, and by committed leadership for reform and the building of firm and state capabilities in African countries. Heterogeneities in the extent of gains from these changes are evidence that improving external prospects and dormant comparative advantages alone will not guarantee gains. These efforts must be accompanied by industrial, trade, and competition policies to take advantage of the opportunities.

CHAPTER 4

Unlocking East Asian Markets to Sub-Saharan Africa

Nama Ouattara and Albert G. Zeufack

Introduction

Global competition in turbulent times has seen the gradual restructuring of international trade policy. According to the World Trade Organization trade monitoring report (WTO 2019), countries have applied 75 new trade restrictions, including tariff increases, quantitative restrictions, import taxes, and stricter customs regulations. This comes at a time of increasing trade tensions and associated rhetoric. Yet countries also continue to implement trade-facilitating measures, as witnessed by the growth of trade between 2016 and 2017. In value terms, merchandise exports rose by 10.6 percent, to $17.73 trillion, and services exports grew by 7.4 percent, to $5.25 trillion.

Asia made the largest contribution to world trade volume growth in 2017, accounting for 51 percent of the increase in merchandise exports and 60 percent of the growth in merchandise imports. Interestingly, Sub-Saharan Africa's share in Asian trade has increased rapidly, a hallmark of the recent growth of South–South trade.[1]

Over the past decade, economic relationships between Sub-Saharan Africa and Asia have expanded. Historically, these two regions have shared wide similarities. Although their historical ties since the Bandung Conference in the 1950s[2] have been marked by shared ideology and political interest, contemporary Sub-Saharan Africa–Asia relations are structured around more-economic aspects, namely trade, investment, education, and technology transfer. In light of the recent trade and policy trends, it is expected that an even closer partnership could be beneficial for Sub-Saharan African countries if strategic policies are implemented. Therefore, this chapter investigates how Sub-Saharan Africa could further benefit from its growing trade relationship with Asia.

Conceptual Motivation

At the conceptual level, the chapter is motivated by two closely related strands of the trade policy literature. The first strand concerns the role of trade agreements. Preferential trade agreements (PTAs) have been on the forefront of the trade policy agenda, including in Sub-Saharan Africa. More recently, Indonesia has started negotiating PTAs with a few African countries since it has identified opportunities for increased trade. Several empirical studies have assessed the impact of PTAs using different techniques, including general equilibrium, partial equilibrium, and gravity equation models.

The second strand of literature explores the nexus between firm productivity and export behavior, which Bernard, Jensen, and Lawrence (1995) introduced in a seminal paper. Exporting firms are generally believed to be more productive than their domestically oriented counterparts. Evidence from firm-level panel data (in Malawi, Rwanda, Senegal, and South Africa) suggests that exporters have not only higher productivity than other firms but also greater productivity *growth*. These results strengthen the narrative that trade facilitation policies have long-lasting impacts on productivity.

Contributions of This Chapter

This chapter goes beyond the narrative of export promotion as an important element of growth strategy, shedding light on how Sub-Saharan African countries can mitigate economic slowdown in turbulent times and take advantage of their relationships with various trading partners.

The chapter is organized around two key questions. The first question is whether export market destination matters, because expansion into foreign markets is a major decision for a firm and involves choices about which countries to approach and which products to export. There is an extensive literature on export orientation and firm performance, but few such studies have looked at the case of Sub-Saharan Africa. Using a new and unique firm-level survey data set collected in 2010 and covering 19 Sub-Saharan African countries, the chapter analyzes the link between export markets and geographic concentration.

Along the same line of analysis on international trade and firm heterogeneity, the second question concerns how Sub-Saharan African firms can take advantage of the available opportunities in a targeted region like Asia. To address this question, we use a specific market selection strategy, drawing on the product life-cycle theory. We look at models in which demand factors, rather than supply ones, drive a firm's sales expansion and specifically focus on innovation as a potential determinant of export behavior. Are firms that want to export compelled to innovate before doing so? Or is it only because they innovate that exporters are more productive?

According to the product life-cycle theory, we could argue that *process* innovation helps to spur exports only indirectly through the productivity channel, whereas *product* innovation directly affects the propensity to export—that is, to open new markets. The chapter sheds more light on these issues in the context of Sub-Saharan Africa by investigating the extent to which the traditional measures of export premiums are sensitive to the introduction of export market destination and innovation statistics.

The rest of the chapter is structured as follows. The next section explores the main trends in the trade relationships between Sub-Saharan African countries and their main trading partners over the past two decades from a macroeconomic standpoint. The following section develops a demand-side analysis of Asian markets, focusing on the growing middle-class consumption pattern. Then, from a microeconomic standpoint, the chapter investigates the link between export strategy and market destination, using a firm-level data set to identify the potential "niche" markets for Sub-Saharan export diversification. Finally, the chapter reports the results of the estimations, summarizes the findings, and sets forth the policy implications.

Trends in Sub-Saharan Africa's Trade Relationships since the Late 1990s

Overall Trade Performance

Sub-Saharan Africa's trade flows have increased over the past two decades, with sporadic slowdowns due to macroeconomic shocks. The region's trade with the rest of the world nearly quadrupled during this period, from $157 billion in 1997 to $621 billion in 2017.[3] Until 2009, high-income economies were the region's main trading partners, but that trend progressively changed, with Sub-Saharan African countries diversifying their trade relationships toward other low- and middle-income regions (figure 4.1).

The South–South dynamics provided opportunities for expanding trade with low- and middle-income countries (LMICs) after the 2008–09 Global Financial Crisis hit the high-income economies. Since 2013, Sub-Saharan Africa's trade with Asia's emerging and developing economies has exceeded its trade with the European Union (EU).

Top Trading Partners

Between 1997 and 2020, Sub-Saharan Africa's export destinations and import origins shifted. In 1997, the top partner countries for Sub-Saharan Africa's exports were (in this order) the United States, the United Kingdom, France, and Germany. By 2020, the top export destination countries were China, India, the United States, and the Netherlands.

Meanwhile, Europe and Central Asia's share in Sub-Saharan Africa's exports went from 35 percent in 1997 to 27 percent in 2016, whereas that of the East Asia and Pacific region went from 11 percent in 1997 to 19 percent in 2016 (figure 4.2). Nevertheless, Europe remains the main export destination, accounting for 34.4 percent of the region's exports in 2017. At the country level, France and Germany were the main European destinations for Sub-Saharan Africa's exports through 2017, but France's share declined from 6.2 percent in 2014 to 4.5 percent in 2017, and Germany's share from 5.1 percent in 2014 to 3.1 percent in 2017. The share of

Figure 4.1   Trends in Sub-Saharan Africa's Exports, by Destination, 1997–2017

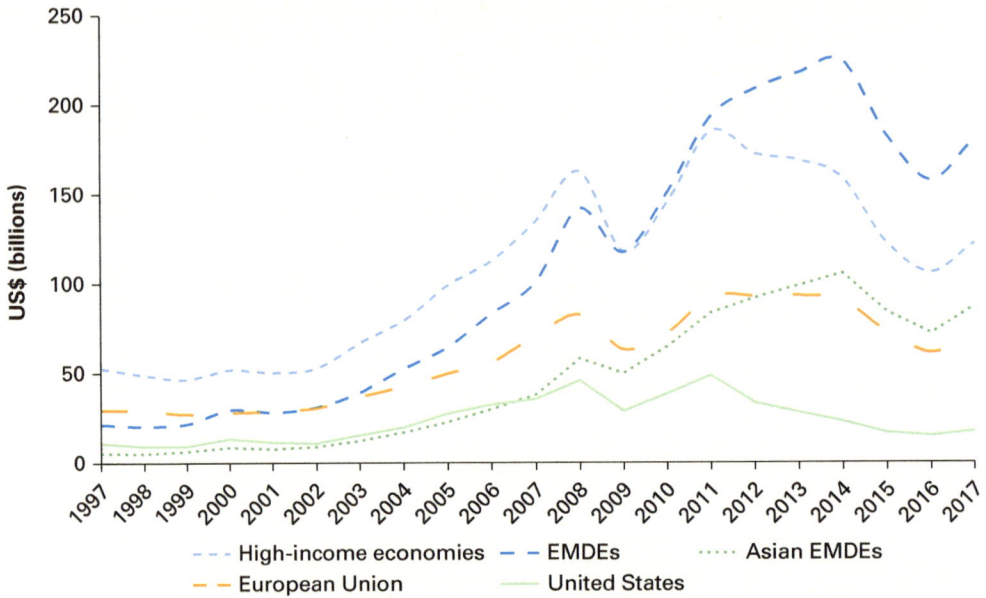

Source: Adapted from the Direction of Trade Statistics data set of the International Monetary Fund (http://data
.imf.org/).
Note: The line for all emerging market and developing economies (EMDEs) includes the Asian EMDEs.

**Figure 4.2   Decomposition of Sub-Saharan Africa's Export and Import Shares, by
Primary Partner Region, 1997–2016**

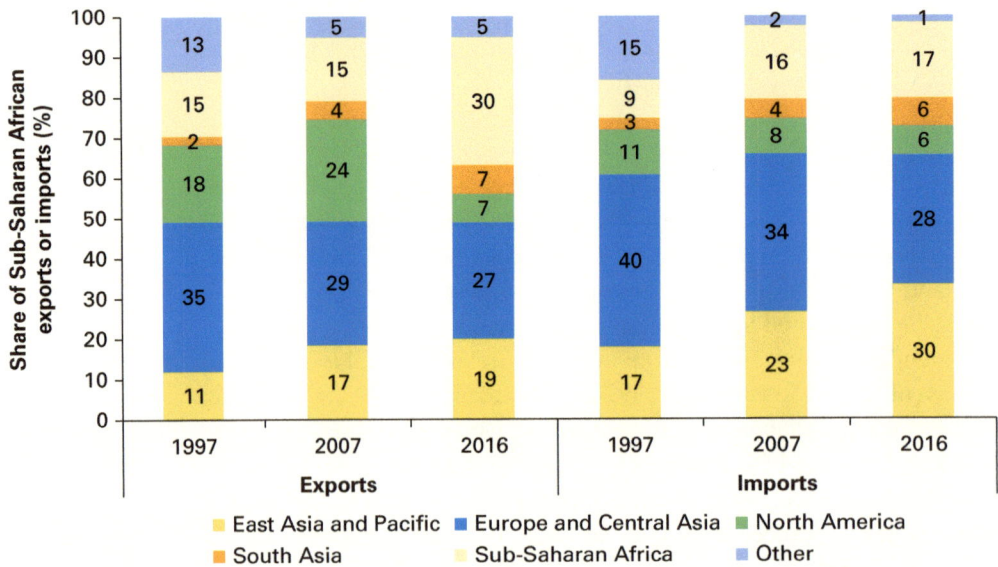

Source: Calculations based on World Integrated Trade Solution (WITS) data (https://wits.worldbank.org/).
Note: "North America" includes Bermuda, Canada, and the United States.

Sub-Saharan Africa's imports from EU countries has also declined steadily over the past three years, from 42.1 percent in 2014 to 35.6 percent in 2017. However, the EU remains an important source of imports for Sub-Saharan Africa, most of which are agricultural and mining equipment and machinery, energy-related products, vehicles, and other machinery and high-skill technology products.

North America's share of Sub-Saharan Africa's exports declined from 18 percent in 1997 to 7 percent in 2016, while its share of the region's imports fell from 11 percent to 6 percent.[4] Despite this performance, North America remained the third-largest destination for Sub-Saharan Africa's exports in 2017, behind the EU and Asia (comprising the South Asia and East Asia and Pacific regions). The overall decline was driven largely by the United States, which continued to reduce imports of commodities from the continent, especially crude oil. The US share of Sub-Saharan Africa's exports declined marginally, from 4.3 percent in 2014 to 4.1 percent in 2017. Two-way trade fell from a high of $100 billion in 2008 to $39 billion in 2017, largely owing to US energy self-sufficiency. Sub-Saharan Africa's imports from North America declined from 7 percent in 2014 to 5.3 percent in 2017. The products sourced from that region are generally machinery and transportation-related equipment.

Trade between Sub-Saharan Africa and Asia increased at a tremendous rate, from 13 percent in 1997 to 26 percent in 2016 for exports and from 20 percent to 36 percent for imports. The expansion of Asian countries in Sub-Saharan Africa's total exports is due to the intensification of trade relationships with China and India. The latter have overtaken Japan and the Republic of Korea as the most important markets for Sub-Saharan Africa's exports to Asia.

At the country level, China and India were Africa's eighth- and ninth-largest trading partners in 2000. In 2017, they were the first and second largest. China continued to dominate Sub-Saharan Africa's exports to Asia, although persistent structural challenges in the country led to a decline in its share of the continent's exports, from 12.2 percent in 2014 to 10.8 percent in 2015 and to 8.3 percent in 2016.

The composition of Africa's exports to Asia are primary commodities related to energy, metals and minerals, and agricultural raw materials. Africa has also diversified its sources of imports over the past decade. The share of imports from Asia has continued to grow, from 32.9 percent in 2014 to 34.8 percent in 2015 and to 36.0 percent in 2016. The region's imports from Asia are dominated by machinery and electrical and electronic products, which account for over 22 percent of the region's imports from Asia.

Last but not least, trade between Sub-Saharan African countries has the greatest potential for building sustainable economic development. In 2016, Sub-Saharan Africa accounted for 30 percent of the region's total exports, whereas the share was only 15 percent in 1997. The intraregional share of imports is less impressive, albeit noteworthy, with an increase from only 9 percent in 1997 to 17 percent in 2016.

Despite the substantial trade expansion, export diversification remains a challenge for Sub-Saharan Africa. The next subsection sheds light on this aspect.

Composition of Trade

Although increasing trade volume matters, the composition of exports is more important. Sub-Saharan Africa's exports are largely undiversified and heavily oriented toward raw materials. In the late 1990s, raw materials dominated the region's exports to the world, accounting for more than 50 percent of total exports. Capital goods were barely 7.0 percent, while consumer and intermediate goods represented, respectively, 12.5 percent and 20.0 percent. Almost 20 years later, the figures changed slightly, with intermediate goods taking the lead, closely followed by raw materials, consumer goods, and capital goods (figure 4.3).

Looking at disaggregated data, exports from Sub-Saharan Africa were primarily concentrated in fuels (crude oil), followed by ores and metals. It is important to underline that, for some Sub-Saharan African countries, oil and mineral exports are the dominant if not sole source of revenue for financing public expenditure. When facing commodity price shocks, these countries have limited options to fill the large finance gap created by lost oil revenues. Hence, agriculture provides jobs for more than 60 percent of the continent's workforce, yet it accounts for less than 25 percent of total exports.

As for import trends, merchandise imports are mainly consumer and capital goods. Years of reliance on the production and export of primary

Figure 4.3   Sub-Saharan Africa's Products Traded with All Countries, by Stage of Processing, 1997 and 2016

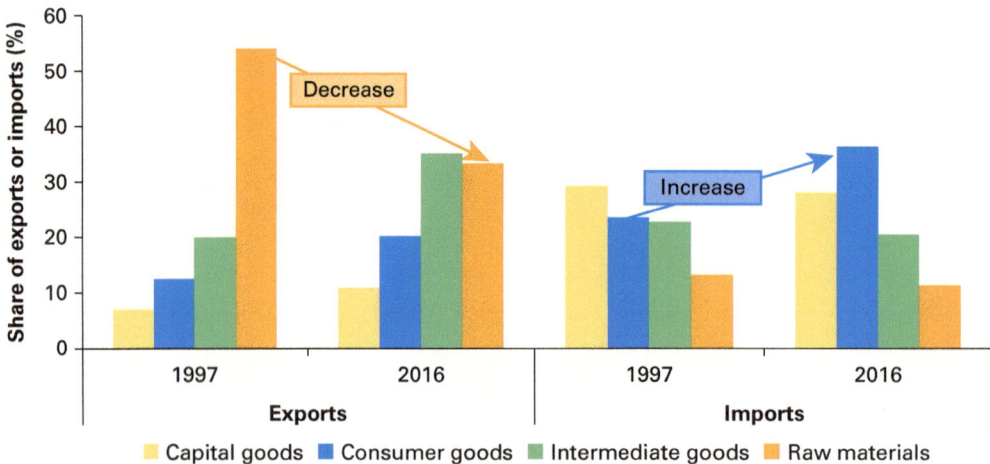

Source: World Integrated Trade Solution data (https://wits.worldbank.org/).

commodities has kept the region from exploring ways to produce the goods it currently imports. The region spent about $19 billion in 2016 on food imports alone. With the growing population in Sub-Saharan Africa, forecasts show that the annual food import bill could reach $110 billion by 2025 unless domestic production is scaled up (AfDB 2016).

Looking at bilateral flows between Sub-Saharan Africa and some of its major partners, there has been a dramatic shift in trade patterns, especially with traditional trading countries like France, the Netherlands, and the United States. In 1997, fuel accounted for 17.9 percent of Sub-Saharan Africa's total exports to France, 65.9 percent to the United States, and 33.0 percent to the Netherlands. By 2016, fuel accounted for only 5.0 percent of Sub-Saharan Africa's total exports to France, close to 1.3 percent to the United States, and 7.6 percent to the Netherlands (table 4.1). Over the years, revenues from fuel exported to these countries have decreased, whereas revenues from exports of manufactured goods, ores and metals, and machinery and transportation equipment have expanded, especially from exports to France and the United States.

For emerging partners, like China, although agricultural raw materials were Sub-Saharan Africa's most exported products in 1997, by 2016, ores and metals accounted for almost 60 percent of Sub-Saharan Africa's total exports to China. In contrast, India's demand for Sub-Saharan Africa's products changed relatively little between 1997 and 2016, as the top two products remained fuel and manufactured goods. Figure 4.4 shows data on several Asian partners' 2017 imports from Sub-Saharan Africa.

Table 4.1   Sub-Saharan Africa's Exports to Selected Partner Countries, by Product Category, 1997 and 2016
Share of total exports to a country (%)

Product category	France		United States		Netherlands		China		India	
	1997	2016	1997	2016	1997	2016	1997	2016	1997	2016
Agricultural raw materials	9.73	1.20	1.38	1.13	4.94	2.88	45.29	7.28	7.96	10.17
Chemicals	1.77	4.52	3.91	7.36	4.89	4.01	4.17	1.51	12.46	4.87
Food	34.39	30.51	6.34	12.59	33.26	49.01	5.57	5.42	13.98	14.22
Fuel	17.85	5.04	65.92	1.25	32.99	7.60	9.51	8.58	38.00	24.58
Machinery and transportation equipment	4.00	20.32	3.82	27.35	12.38	7.84	2.40	1.72	3.12	2.73
Manufactures	22.50	45.52	15.12	58.31	20.85	21.54	9.85	18.98	25.97	26.17
Ores and metals	13.54	16.71	3.43	26.36	7.64	18.90	29.38	59.22	13.96	10.43
Textiles	12.80	12.43	3.15	4.94	1.59	1.61	12.80	3.24	2.07	1.33

Source: World Integrated Trade Solution data (https://wits.worldbank.org/).

Figure 4.4   Five Asian Countries' Major Imports from Sub-Saharan Africa, 2017

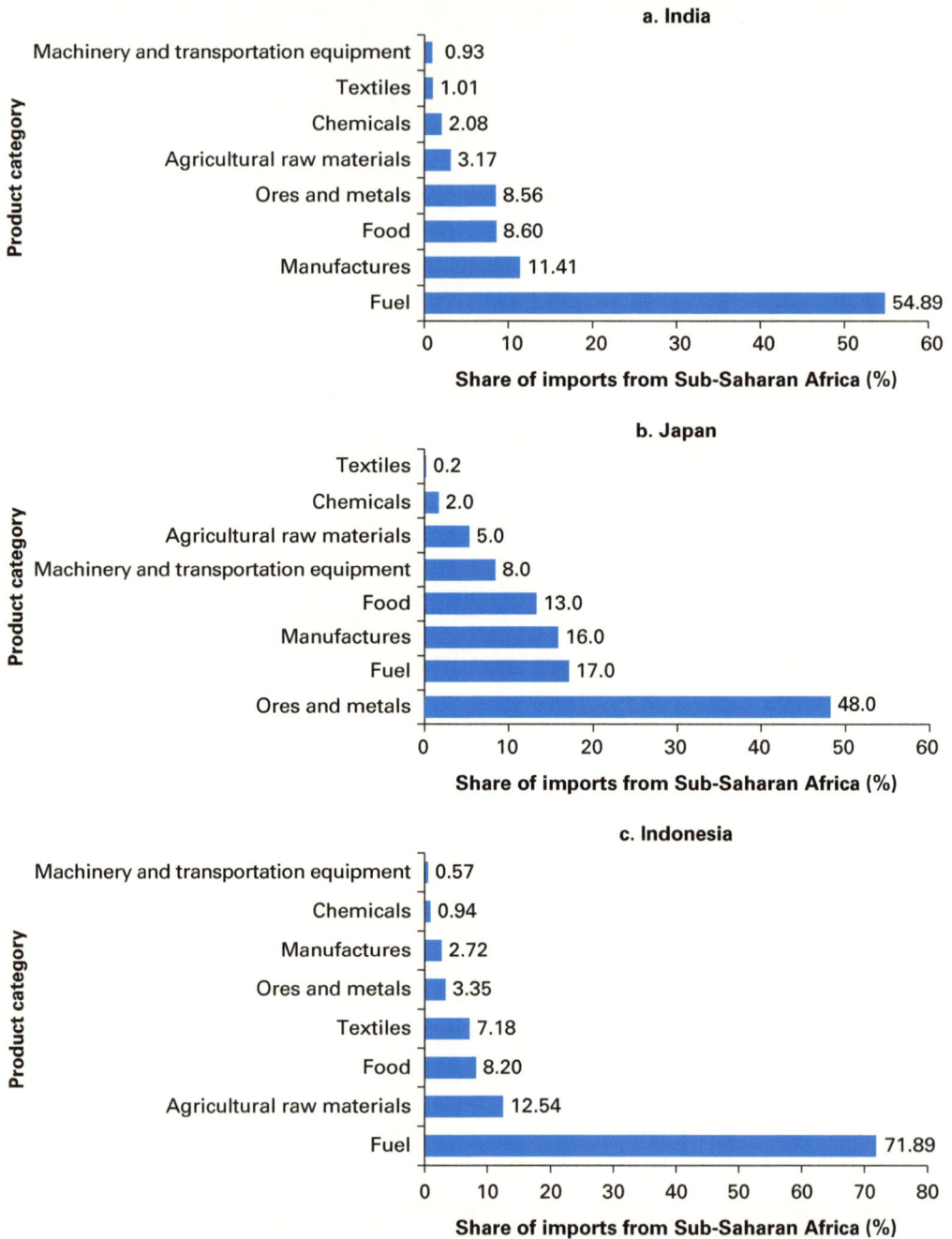

a. India

Product category	Share of imports from Sub-Saharan Africa (%)
Machinery and transportation equipment	0.93
Textiles	1.01
Chemicals	2.08
Agricultural raw materials	3.17
Ores and metals	8.56
Food	8.60
Manufactures	11.41
Fuel	54.89

b. Japan

Product category	Share of imports from Sub-Saharan Africa (%)
Textiles	0.2
Chemicals	2.0
Agricultural raw materials	5.0
Machinery and transportation equipment	8.0
Food	13.0
Manufactures	16.0
Fuel	17.0
Ores and metals	48.0

c. Indonesia

Product category	Share of imports from Sub-Saharan Africa (%)
Machinery and transportation equipment	0.57
Chemicals	0.94
Manufactures	2.72
Ores and metals	3.35
Textiles	7.18
Food	8.20
Agricultural raw materials	12.54
Fuel	71.89

(Figure continues on next page)

Figure 4.4   Five Asian Countries' Major Imports from Sub-Saharan Africa, 2017 *(continued)*

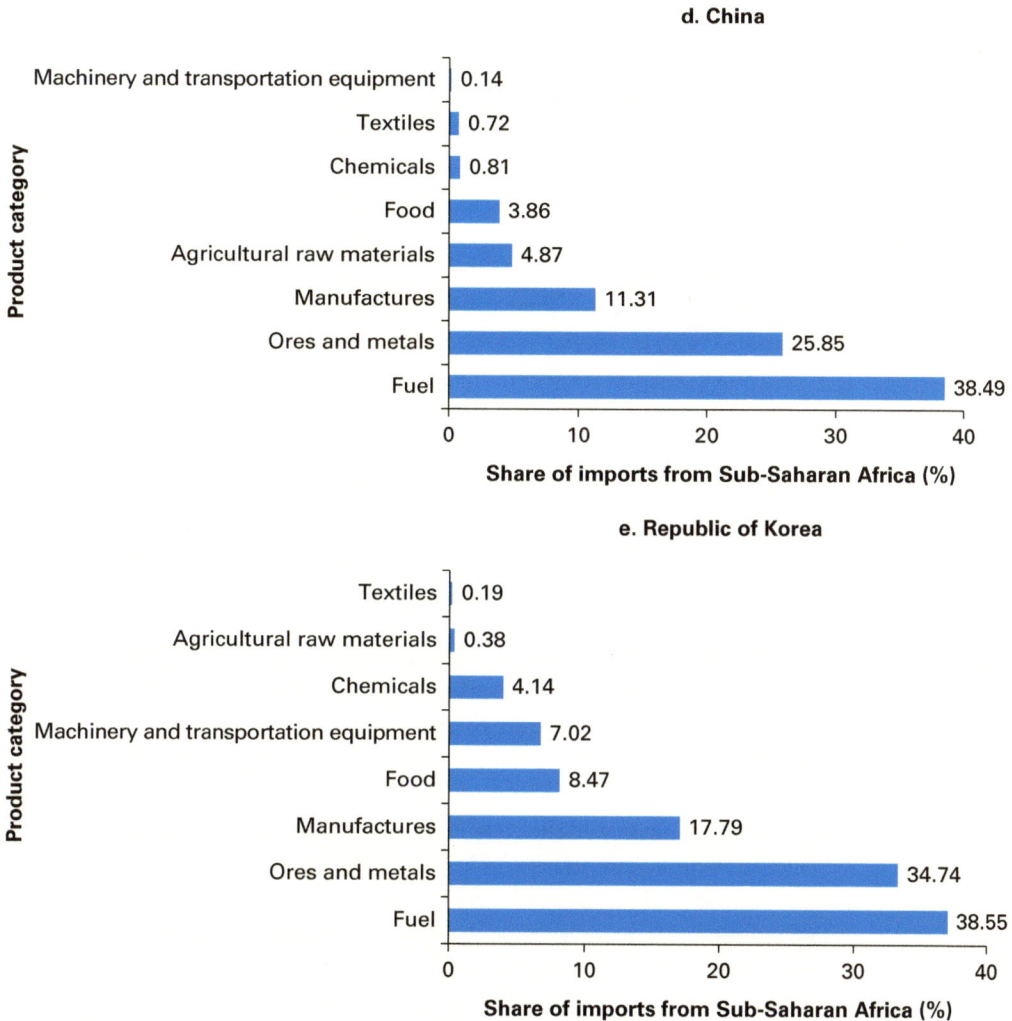

d. China

Product category	Share (%)
Machinery and transportation equipment	0.14
Textiles	0.72
Chemicals	0.81
Food	3.86
Agricultural raw materials	4.87
Manufactures	11.31
Ores and metals	25.85
Fuel	38.49

Share of imports from Sub-Saharan Africa (%)

e. Republic of Korea

Product category	Share (%)
Textiles	0.19
Agricultural raw materials	0.38
Chemicals	4.14
Machinery and transportation equipment	7.02
Food	8.47
Manufactures	17.79
Ores and metals	34.74
Fuel	38.55

Share of imports from Sub-Saharan Africa (%)

Source: World Integrated Trade Solution data (https://wits.worldbank.org/).

Overall, Sub-Saharan Africa's trade with traditional and emerging partners as a whole has not exhibited significant product diversification, because the region's rich resource endowment provides a natural comparative advantage based on raw materials and resource-based products. However, it can diversify its exports by venturing into new sectors and products or adding value to existing products. Commodity diversification and investment in goods with higher manufacturing intensity are mutually beneficial for most LMICs (Rieländer and Traoré 2015). The next section identifies potential markets for Sub-Saharan African products and comparative advantage.

Strengthening Sub-Saharan Africa's Market Position: A Demand-Side Analysis

The Expanding Middle-Class Market, Led by Asia

Although there is no commonly accepted definition of the middle class across countries, there is some agreement about a general characterization. Those in the middle class are seen as highly educated, employed, holding positions involving supervisory or managerial obligations, and, most important, as having a particular consumption level and lifestyle.[5]

From this perspective, can the growing middle class play a role in driving economic diversification and market expansion? Yes. A rising middle class brings about a rise in purchasing power and therefore a change in consumption patterns, which in turn stimulates demand for quality consumer goods (local or foreign).

Are all countries subject to the same middle-class potential? No. Although the middle class is maturing or even shrinking in high-income economies, it is the fastest-growing consumer segment in emerging markets. For example, since 2000, the Chinese middle class has expanded to twice the size of that of the United States. Kharas (2017) projects a total of about 3.7 billion middle-income consumers in the world in 2020, rising to 5.4 billion in 2030 (figure 4.5).

This expansion represents a potential mass market for Sub-Saharan African firms. In 2015, middle-class spending was about $35 trillion (in 2011 purchasing power parity terms) and approximately evenly divided between high-income countries and LMICs (Kharas 2017). By 2020, it also accounts for one-third of the global economy. By 2030, global middle-class consumption could be $29 trillion more than in 2015. Only $1 trillion of that will come from more spending in high-income economies. Lower-middle-income countries (including India, Indonesia, and Vietnam) will have middle-class markets that are $15 trillion bigger. Consumption spending by China's middle class alone is on track to pass that of the United States in 2020 and the EU in 2027, and India is on track to pass the United States in 2021 and the EU in 2026 (figure 4.6).

Trends in Middle-Class Spending

Two concepts are central when considering the purchasing power of the middle class: disposable income and discretionary consumption. Disposable income is consumers' net income after compulsory taxes and pension contributions. Thus, it captures the actual consumption capacity of the consumer. Discretionary consumption refers to expanded choices of consumer expenditures for purchases other than necessities. Typical examples of these purchases are better housing, health care, educational opportunities for children, retirement, recreation, and leisure. For instance, Chikweche and Fletcher (2014) surveyed the South African middle class and found that its prioritized discretionary spending includes housing, motor vehicles, education, luxury cars, travel, and dining out.

Figure 4.5   **Size of the Global Middle Class, by Region, 2015–30**
Millions

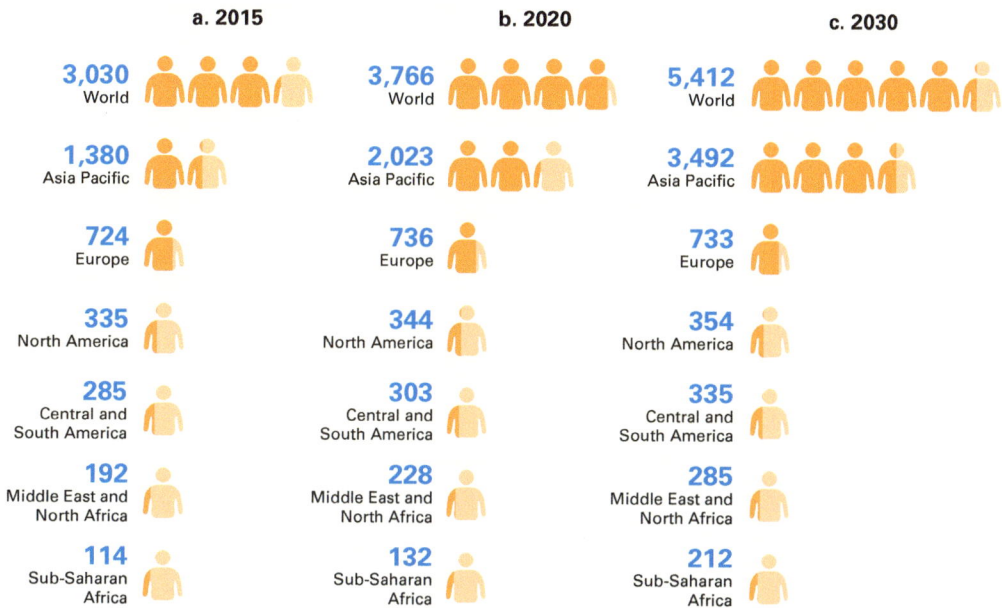

a. 2015   b. 2020   c. 2030

3,030 World
1,380 Asia Pacific
724 Europe
335 North America
285 Central and South America
192 Middle East and North Africa
114 Sub-Saharan Africa

3,766 World
2,023 Asia Pacific
736 Europe
344 North America
303 Central and South America
228 Middle East and North Africa
132 Sub-Saharan Africa

5,412 World
3,492 Asia Pacific
733 Europe
354 North America
335 Central and South America
285 Middle East and North Africa
212 Sub-Saharan Africa

Source: Adapted with permission from Kharas 2017.
Note: "Middle class" is defined as comprising those households with per capita incomes between $10 and $100 per person per day in 2005 purchasing power parity terms. "North America" includes Bermuda, Canada, and the United States. Each icon in the figure represents 1 billion people (dark orange) or a portion thereof (light orange). Panel c shows projected estimates.

The middle class not only has the resources to consume more than the poor but also is willing to pay a bit more for quality. Big changes in spending patterns occur when individuals move from very low income (annual wages of less than $1,000) to lower-middle income ($3,000–$5,000). China, India, and Indonesia are all set to cross this threshold between now and 2050 (Kharas 2017).

Moreover, economic development and rising incomes tend to coincide with increased urbanization. As people move to cities, accommodation tends to become more sophisticated and more income is spent on furnishings and powering appliances. That is followed by a large increase in spending on fuel to power the new appliances and provide heating and air conditioning (figure 4.7). In addition, rising incomes tend to accompany longer life expectancy. Therefore, as salaries rise, consumers start devoting more income to health, social protection, and insurance

Similar patterns emerge when examining food purchases at the household level: as income levels rise, consumer spending changes, shifting to foods that improve the quality of life. The amount spent on meat, fish, and dairy products increases, whereas nonprotein staples such as cereals and

Figure 4.6   Share of Global Middle-Class Consumption, by Region, 2015–30

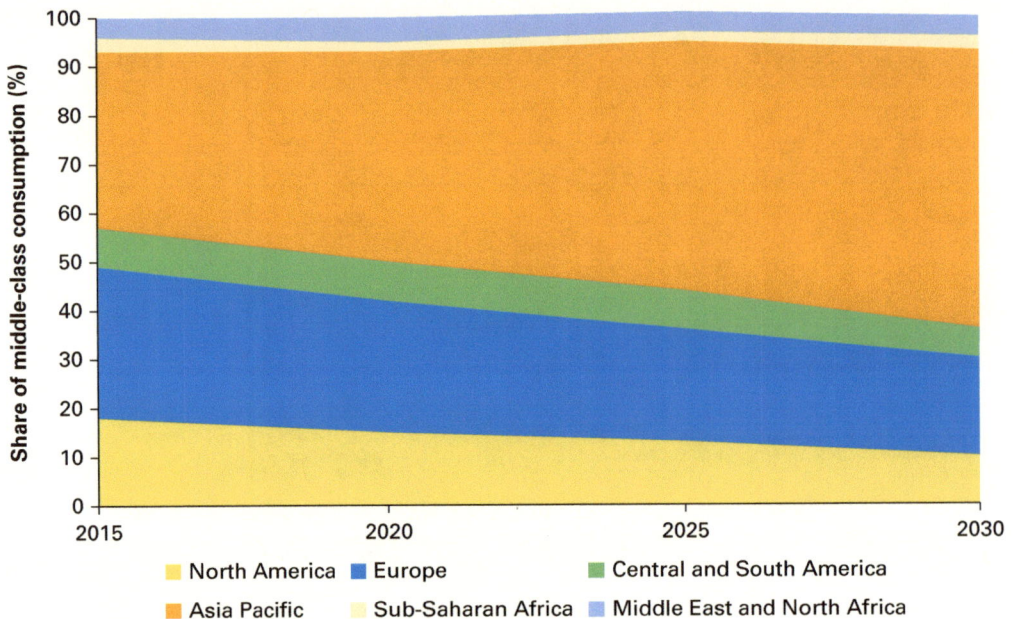

Source: Adapted from Kharas 2017.
Note: "Middle class" is defined as comprising those households with per capita incomes between $10 and $100 per person per day in 2005 purchasing power parity terms. "North America" includes Bermuda, Canada, and the United States, and "Asia Pacific" includes South Asia and East Asia and the Pacific.

vegetables play a smaller role in meeting caloric needs (figure 4.8). This transformation of consumption patterns is backed up by two well-known and related economic theories: Engel's law and Bennett's law.

Engel's law states that as income grows the share of additional income spent on food declines (as depicted in figure 4.7). Bennett's law predicts a shift in the primary source of calories from starchy staples (for example, rice, wheat, and root crops) to diverse diets that include more fat, meat, and fish as well as fruits and vegetables as the ability to afford these food groups rises. In China, the human intake of cereals and consumption of coarse grains decreased over the past two decades among the urban and rural populations, and there was a dramatic increase in the consumption of animal and fish foods (Kharas 2017). A similar but less dramatic change is occurring in India.

An important consequence of Engel's and Bennett's laws is that, as incomes increase, the demand for nonagricultural goods and services increases faster than the demand for agricultural products. This calls for a dramatic change in the structure of the domestic economy as well as in the foreign supplying economies; hence, it is a trigger for structural transformation led by the stringency of more sophisticated demand (figure 4.7).

Figure 4.7 Trends in Consumer Spending Habits, by Income Level

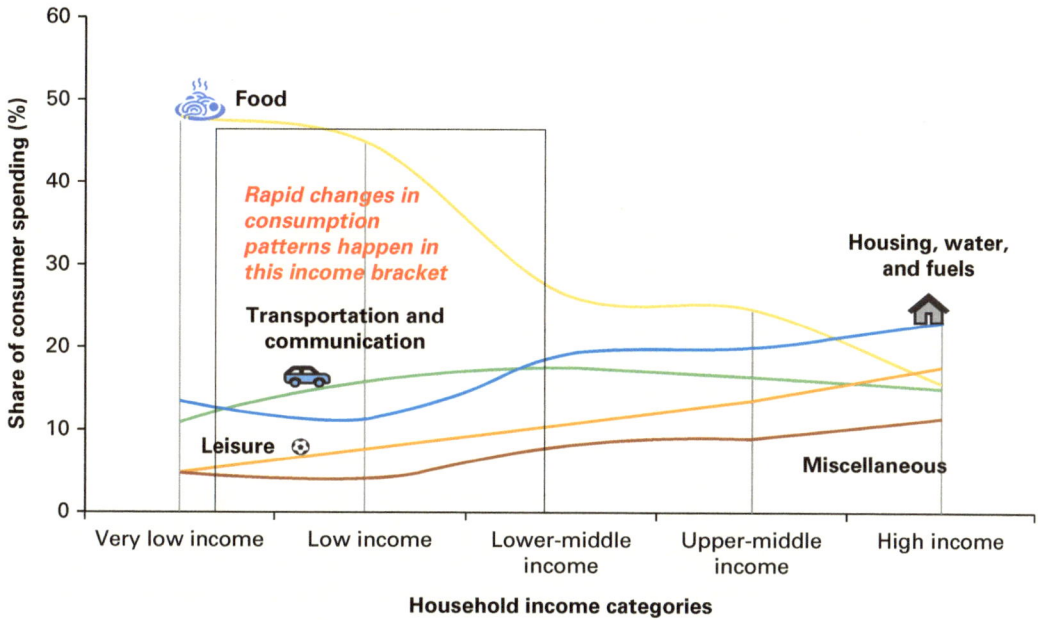

Source: Adapted from Ward and Neumann 2012.
Note: "Very low income" refers to annual household wages of less than $1,000; "low income" to $1,000–$3,000; "lower-middle income" to $3,000–$5,000; "upper-middle income" to $5,000–$15,000; and "high income" to more than $15,000. "Miscellaneous" includes expenditures such as personal care, social protection, insurance and financial services, and other services.

Figure 4.8 Share of Household Income Spent on Food, by Type and Household Income Level, 2010

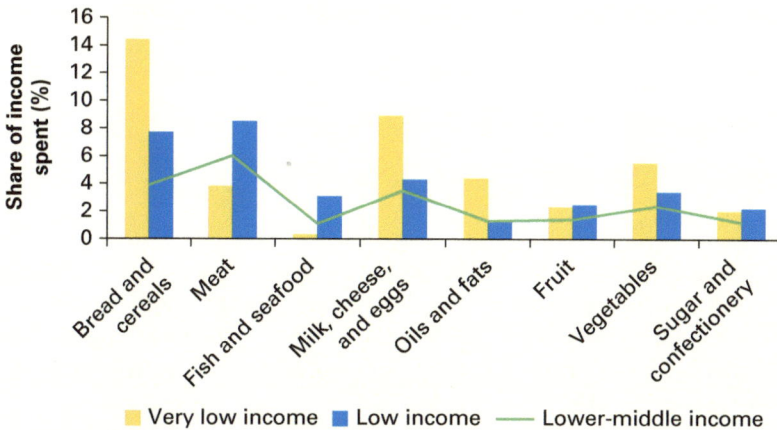

Source: Adapted from Ward and Neumann 2012.
Note: "Very low income" refers to annual household income of less than $1,000; "low income" to $1,000–$3,000; and "lower-middle income" to $3,000–$5,000.

Box 4.1   Exporting Fish to the European Union

Fishery products are among the most extensively traded food commodities in the world. For this reason, and also owing to their perishable nature, most countries have strict regulations and border inspection procedures. Freshness, hygiene, and packaging, as well as accompanying documentation, are rigorously checked. Access to markets is regulated by agreements on customs tariffs and trade, such as agreements on technical obstacles to trade, rules of origin, the application of sanitary and phytosanitary measures, and subsidies and countervailing measures.

Few countries in the Organisation of African, Caribbean, and Pacific Group of States (ACP) show recognized sanitary compliance for products intended for the markets of EU member states. Currently, 29 countries in the ACP have European approval, only 10 of which export tuna in the form of preserved tuna or tuna loin (Palin et al. 2013). Several other countries have expressed their desire to export to the EU, particularly those that have a partnership agreement in the field of fisheries (the Comoros and São Tomé and Príncipe, for example).

In addition to these sanitary and technical requirements, all marine fish products entering EU territory must be accompanied by a catch certificate attesting that the international rules concerning conservation and management of fish resources have been respected. In 2013, Ghana saw several containers returned from European ports for lack of a complying catch certificate.

Producers respond by devoting relatively more resources to industry and service activities than to agriculture. The shift to a more diverse, expensive diet—in particular to more animal- and fish-based protein intake—slows this process, but eventually the demand for more diverse diets is satisfied and further income growth is spent almost entirely on nonagricultural goods and services (box 4.1).

The next subsection looks at potential sectors that Sub-Saharan African countries could tap into based on the middle-class consumption trends.

Potential "Niche" Markets for Sub-Saharan Africa's Export Diversification

Seafood Industry

Fish is an important economic commodity in Asia. About 61 percent of the world's supply of fish comes from this region, where a large proportion of it is consumed domestically. Over the past decade, fish consumption in Asia has grown at notable rates. Much of this increase has been attributed mainly to population growth, urbanization, and expansion in per capita income.

Dey (2008) examines fish demand patterns in nine Asian countries, using a multistage budgeting framework.[6] Dey compares fish demand by income group to determine how low- and high-income households respond to price and income changes. The study finds that, as per capita income and population grow in most Asian countries, there will be tremendous increases in fish demand that are expected to come mostly from the poorer sector of the economy (tables 4.2 and 4.3). Absence of commensurate increases in the supply of fish would create pressure for fish prices to go up, which would hurt consumers. The price increases in turn would have worrisome consequences on households' protein intake, particularly among the poor. A way to circumvent this welfare loss is to expand fish production, which can be achieved through aquaculture.

The growing food market in Asia is an opportunity for Sub-Saharan African countries to seize (box 4.2). The Food and Agriculture Organization of the United Nations forecasts that world consumption of fish, which today stands at about 140 million tons, should be roughly 200 million tons on the 2030 horizon (Failler 2015). Industrialized countries whose households have high purchasing power will pull demand upward, as will the upcoming middle-class growth in emerging market countries. Full exploitation of all stocks of fish and the limited possibilities for expanding aquaculture in Europe, North America, and East Asia mean that only countries in South Asia, the Pacific, South America, and Africa will be in a position to supply the international market with additional marine products.

For some countries, fishery exports are essential to the economy. The fisheries sector operates in an increasingly globalized environment, and fish may often be produced in one country, processed in a second, and consumed in a third. Consumers typically increase their spending on animal proteins such as seafood at the expense of other food categories as their income increases. The generation of this extra demand has pushed prices upward, even as total supply continues to rise. For the average consumer, the important topics continue to be sustainability and origin certification, ease of preparation, food safety assurance, and the nutritional value of seafood.

In China, although meat products dominate as a source of animal protein intake, aquatic products occupy a relatively important share (table 4.2 and figure 4.9). From 2013 to 2017, consumption of aquatic products increased by 11.4 percent. Moreover, the proportion of the household budget spent on fish is larger for consumers in higher income groups than for those with lower incomes. Similarly, the share of expenditure on fish was found to be higher in urban areas than in rural areas.

Cotton Industry

Among the items of discretionary spending that will see a huge rise in demand are clothing and footwear (box 4.3). China, India, Malaysia, and the Philippines are all likely to see near 5 percent annual compound growth between now and 2050.

Wood Industries: Housing and Furniture

Asia's ongoing urbanization, combined with rising household incomes and an increase in the construction of new housing, continues to drive the global market for wood-based products. As a result, East Asia and Pacific is the largest and fastest-growing region in the world for sales of home improvement products. The region's home improvement market was worth

Table 4.2   Household Spending on Fish and Other Food as a Share of Budget, by Country, Income Group, and Rural or Urban Location, 2004

Share of household budget (%)

Food item	Bangladesh	China	India	Indonesia	Malaysia	Philippines	Sri Lanka	Thailand	Vietnam	Average
Food (non-fish) share										
Cereals	38	24	32	24	24	33	23	31	34	29
Meat	12	26	6	3	15	13	14	22	20	15
Fish	20	5	6	9	21	14	11	16	19	14
Others	30	45	56	64	40	40	52	31	27	43
Total share	100	100	100	100	100	100	100	100	100	100
Fish share by income group										
Lowest (first quintile)	—	—	5	—	—	16	—	15	15	13
Highest (fifth quintile)	—	—	8	—	—	12	—	18	21	15
Fish share by location										
Rural	10	3	7	—	15	—	—	—	—	9
Urban	21	7	6	—	32	—	—	—	—	16

(Table continues on next page)

Table 4.2 Household Spending on Fish and Other Food as a Share of Budget, by Country, Income Group, and Rural or Urban Location, 2004 (continued)

Share of household budget (%)

Food item	Bangladesh	China	India	Indonesia	Malaysia	Philippines	Sri Lanka	Thailand	Vietnam	Average
Fish share by species										
Freshwater fish	71	40	62	42	7	28	69	43	68	48
High-value	25	4	49	—	2	15	69	22	27	26
Low-value	46	36	13	42	5	13	—	21	41	27
Marine fish	13	35	29	30	81	41	29	16	27	33
High-value	1	17	8	13	10	23	21	8	4	12
Low-value	12	18	21	17	71	18	8	8	23	22
Non-finfish										
Shrimp	14	13	5	6	5	4	—	9	2	7
Crustaceans/mollusks	—	12	4	—	7	5	—	23	—	10
Processed fish/dried fish	2	—	—	22	—	22	2	9	3	10
Total	100	100	100	100	100	100	100	100	100	100

Source: Dey 2008.

Note: — = not available.

Table 4.3 Income Elasticities of Major Fish Groups, Selected Countries, 2004

Fish type	Bangladesh	China	India	Indonesia	Malaysia	Philippines	Sri Lanka	Thailand	Vietnam	All
Freshwater fish										
High-value	1.43	0.99	1.62	1.46	0.87	0.57	0.86	0.12	0.99	1.00
Low-value	0.91	0.99	1.62	1.46	1.94	0.56	—	0.06	0.66	1.02
Marine fish										
High-value	1.56	1.05	1.62	1.46	0.52	1.89	0.98	0.64	1.06	1.20
Low-value	1.05	0.95	1.62	1.46	1.13	0.64	1.00	0.62	—	1.06
Non-finfish										
Shrimp	0.68	1.36	1.61	—	—	1.78	—	0.66	0.94	1.17
Others[a]	—	—	1.66	1.46	0.73	1.38	—	—	—	1.31
Processed fish	1.06	—	—	1.46	—	1.01	1.01	0.62	—	1.03
Average	1.03	0.92	1.62	1.46	1.12	1.07	0.90	0.26	0.59	1.00
Lowest income group										
Freshwater fish										
High-value	2.63	0.58	1.63	3.05	1.12	0.14	0.72	0.41	0.99	1.25
Low-value	1.15	1.07	1.64	3.05	2.34	0.49	—	0.32	0.66	1.38
Marine fish										
High-value	3.07	0.90	1.14	3.05	0.69	2.14	1.19	0.91	1.14	1.58
Low-value	1.25	0.52	1.65	3.05	1.04	0.87	0.86	0.77	—	1.25
Non-finfish										
Shrimp	0.80	0.93	1.14	3.05	—	2.66	—	1.00	0.98	1.51
Others[a]	—	—	3.75	—	0.92	1.91	—	—	—	2.19
Processed fish	1.38	—	—	3.04	—	1.08	1.03	0.88	—	1.48
Average	0.70	0.66	1.35	0.53	0.68	0.73	1.04	0.13	0.73	0.73

(Table continues on next page)

Table 4.3 Income Elasticities of Major Fish Groups, Selected Countries, 2004 *(continued)*

Fish type	Bangladesh	China	India	Indonesia	Malaysia	Philippines	Sri Lanka	Thailand	Vietnam	All
Highest income group										
Freshwater fish										
High-value	0.94	0.44	1.36	0.53	0.54	0.59	1.05	0.03	0.99	0.72
Low-value	0.59	0.77	1.36	0.53	1.18	0.48	—	0.008	0.98	0.74
Marine fish										
High-value	1.00	0.87	1.37	0.53	0.40	1.54	1.00	0.37	1.04	0.90
Low-value	0.85	0.47	1.35	0.53	0.76	0.33	1.01	0.35	—	0.71
Non-finfish										
Shrimp	0.47	0.99	1.39	0.53	—	0.89	—	0.35	0.96	0.80
Others[a]	—	—	1.12	—	0.45	0.89	—	—	—	0.82
Processed fish	0.78	—	—	0.53	—	0.39	1.00	0.33	—	0.61
Average	0.70	0.66	1.35	0.53	0.68	0.73	1.04	0.13	0.73	0.73

Source: Dey 2008.
Note: The data are based on Asian Development Bank Regional Technical Assistance 5945 Country Reports. The lowest and highest income groups represent the first and fifth quintiles, respectively. — = not available.
a. The item "others" under the non-finfish category refers to crustaceans and mollusks.

Box 4.2   Growing Food Import Trends in Asia

China, India, Indonesia, and to a lesser extent the Philippines are increasingly demanding more food products. Therefore, Sub-Saharan African countries with favorable conditions for agricultural production can benefit from this excellent opportunity to market their products in Asia (table B4.2.1 and figure B4.2.1).

The surge in demand for imported food products is prompted by two main factors. First, the middle class in these countries has been growing significantly in recent decades. These consumers have high purchasing power and are increasingly exposed to international trends, resulting in a demand for imported food. Second, concerns about domestic food safety have contributed to the increase of food imports.

The products in high demand are meat, dairy products, fresh and processed fruits, oil, fish preserves, sugars, and liquors. Proper packaging is the key to success in the food sector. For instance, consumers like to see what is inside the package, which is why products such as wine and olive oil are sold in special gift boxes.

Table B4.2.1   Top Five Commodity Imports of Selected Asian Countries, 2017

Rank	India	Indonesia	Japan	China
1	Crude petroleum	Refined petroleum	Crude petroleum	Mineral fuels, including oil
2	Gold	Wheat	Copper	Iron ore
3	Diamonds	Raw sugar	Iron ore	Copper
4	Palm oil	Cotton	Corn	Oil seed
5	Copper	Soybeans	Wheat	Coal

Source: World Integrated Trade Solution (https://wits.worldbank.org/).

Figure B4.2.1   Sources of China's Fruit Imports, 2017

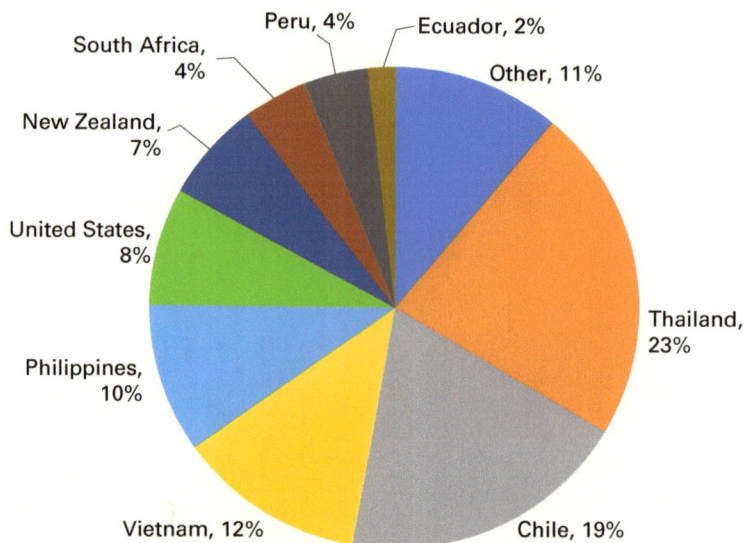

Peru, 4% — Ecuador, 2%
South Africa, 4%
Other, 11%
New Zealand, 7%
United States, 8%
Thailand, 23%
Philippines, 10%
Vietnam, 12%
Chile, 19%

Source: Produce Report data (https://www.producereport.com/region/asia/china).

Figure 4.9   Per Capita Consumption of Selected Foods in China, 2013–17

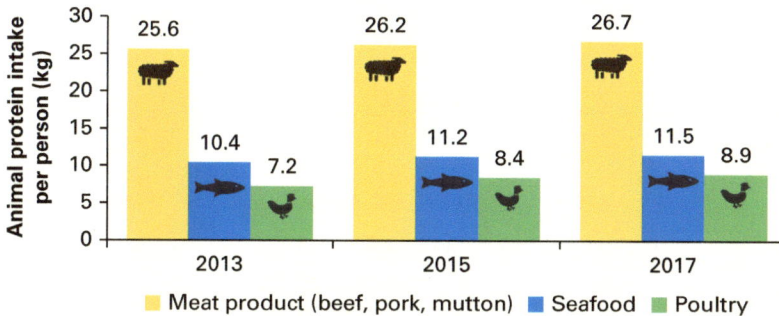

Source: National Bureau of Statistics of China data (http://www.stats.gov.cn).

$91 billion in 2016, accounting for 35 percent of global sales. The growth of the real estate industry contributes to an increase in the number of office spaces, commercial complexes, and residential buildings, leading to increased demand for wooden furniture. As such, the global wooden furniture market is expected to grow by 4.8 percent annually between 2018 and 2022 (Technavio 2018).[7]

China is the world's largest importer of logs and wood pulp, and it is the second-largest importer of lumber and wood chips. In 2016, only 7 percent of China's hardwood log imports came from Asian countries. In contrast, Africa supplies about 20 percent of China's hardwood log imports. Several countries that had been major suppliers of logs to China in the

Box 4.3   The China-Africa Cotton Industry

Established in 2009, China-Africa Cotton Development Ltd. is registered in Hong Kong SAR, China, and is a joint venture of the China-Africa Development Fund,[a] Qingdao Ruichang Cotton Industrial Co. Ltd., and Qingdao Huifu Textile Co. Ltd. The company invests in many projects in various African countries, including Chad, Malawi, Mali, Mozambique, Togo, Zambia, and Zimbabwe. It focuses on seed research, plantations, cotton purchasing and processing, cottonseed oil processing, and textile production. As the largest agricultural investment project in Africa, the company complies with the "going out to expand" trend of Chinese enterprises. It has established seven ginneries, two cottonseed oil extracting mills, and one special seed plant in Africa. With annual purchases of 100,000 metric tons of seed cotton, it uses thousands of hectares of land and benefits 200,000 local farmers, with direct hires of 1,800 local employees.

At the operational level, a small amount of the cotton is processed locally, with most of it shipped back to China as raw material for the textile industry. However, because China has import and export quotas on cotton, it cannot be traded inside the country but only internationally, facing competition from giant multinational cotton companies such as ADM, Bunge, Cargill, and Louis Dreyfus. Therefore, the company extended its operation into downstream industries, such as yarn, weaving, and clothing production. Figure B4.3.1 shows the main cotton-exporting countries in Sub-Saharan Africa.

(Box continues on next page)

Box 4.3   **The China-Africa Cotton Industry** *(continued)*

Figure B4.3.1   **Sub-Saharan African Countries' Exports of Raw Cotton, 2017**

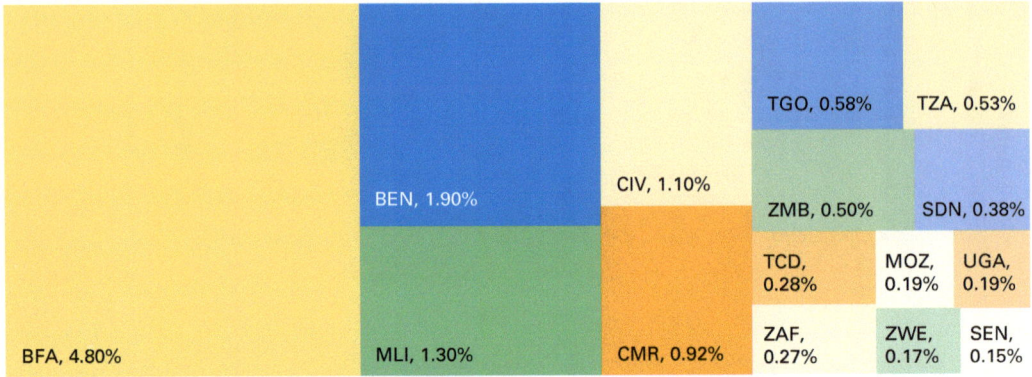

Source: Compiled from China-Africa Cotton Industry Development Co. data (http://www.ca-cotton.com).
Note: Figure shows the share of Sub-Saharan Africa's total raw cotton exports from these countries: BFA (Burkina Faso), BEN (Benin), MLI (Mali), CIV (Côte d'Ivoire), CMR (Cameron), TZA (Tanzania), ZMB (Zambia), TGO (Togo), SDN (Sudan), ZAF (South Africa), MOZ (Mozambique), UGA (Uganda), TCD (Chad), ZWE (Zimbabwe), and SEN (Senegal).

---

a.   The China-Africa Development Fund (commonly known as CAD Fund) is a Chinese private equity fund solely funded by China Development Bank, a Chinese government policy bank.

2000s declined to near zero log exports to China by 2016. These include Malaysia (during much of the 2000s), Gabon (1999 until the imposition of a log export ban in 2010), Liberia (2000–03, before UN-imposed sanctions), Myanmar (much of the two-decade period leading up to a 2014 log export ban), and others. Other countries that had few to no exports of hardwood logs to China a decade ago are now major suppliers, including Equatorial Guinea, the Lao People's Democratic Republic, Nigeria, and the Solomon Islands (Technavio 2018).

China's five largest African suppliers of hardwood logs are (in this order) Equatorial Guinea, Mozambique, Cameroon, the Republic of Congo, and Nigeria. In total, from 2006 to 2016, Gabon exported more hardwood logs to China than any other African country despite virtually ceasing all exports in 2011. During this period, Cameroon, the Republic of Congo, Equatorial Guinea, and Mozambique also each exported more than 3 million cubic meters (more than $1 billion) of hardwood logs to China. The share of China's hardwood log imports from West Africa, compared with other African subregions, was far larger by value than volume. This is because high-value species, such as *Pterocarpus erinaceus* (also known as vêne, kosso, or African rosewood, among other names), have recently been in high demand.

China's timber and forest product imports are expected to increase by 60 million cubic meters by 2025 and will eventually account for 12–13 percent of the global timber harvest. Growth in the coming decade will be more in the form of lumber rather than logs, and in wood pulp imports rather than wood chips. In total, the wood content of China's primary forest product imports will increase from an estimated 194 million cubic meters in 2015 to 254 million cubic meters by 2025 (Technavio 2018).

However, as new legislation in the global forest sector requires companies and governments to assess the risk that illegal wood will enter supply chains, Sub-Saharan African countries will have to enforce laws pertaining to timber harvesting and trade. Although more than 30 countries have enacted policies to restrict or prohibit the export of raw logs over the past several decades,[8] companies around the world (including in China) are still importing logs from these countries.

Log export bans can be difficult to enforce because of the definitional differences around what constitutes a "log" and the limitations of national control systems. As a result, a few low-risk countries (namely, the United States and EU member states) are supplying increasing volumes of hardwood species to Chinese markets (figure 4.10).

Figure 4.10   China's Hardwood Imports, by Risk Level and Source Country, 2006–16

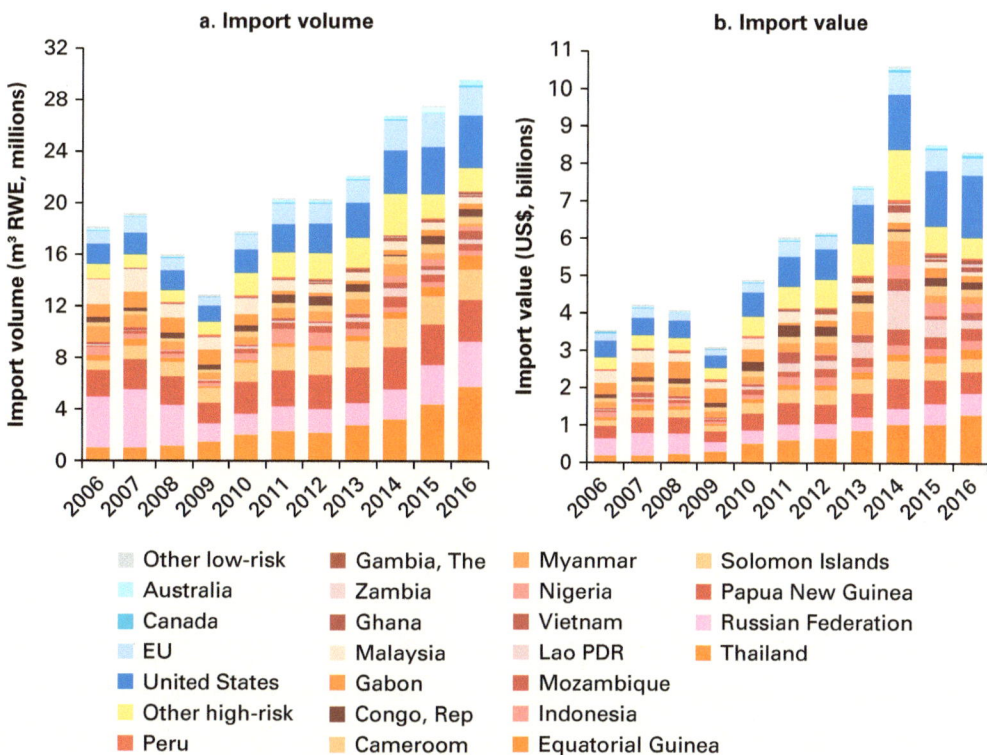

a. Import volume

b. Import value

Other low-risk	Gambia, The	Myanmar	Solomon Islands
Australia	Zambia	Nigeria	Papua New Guinea
Canada	Ghana	Vietnam	Russian Federation
EU	Malaysia	Lao PDR	Thailand
United States	Gabon	Mozambique	
Other high-risk	Congo, Rep	Indonesia	
Peru	Cameroom	Equatorial Guinea	

Source: Forest Trends (2017). Used with permission of Forest Trends; further permission required for reuse.
Note: Countries are listed in order of their relative risk level, from lowest risk (at the top) to highest risk (at the bottom). EU = European Union; m³ RWE = cubic meters of roundwood equivalent.

As the world's top importer and consumer of timber products, China is in a unique, and influential, position to take a leadership role to ensure that only legally and sustainably sourced timber—and other products sourced from forests—enters the country, thus helping to shift the global timber trade paradigm away from illegal sourcing.

Tourism and Travel

In recent years, tourism has grown faster than merchandise exports, playing a strong part in diversifying export portfolios and compensating for weaker export revenues in other sectors. As a worldwide export category, tourism ranks third after chemicals and fuels and ahead of automotive products. In many LMICs, it is the top export category. For instance, the UN Conference on Trade and Development (UNCTAD) reports that, in Africa, "The three most tourism-driven countries in terms of the sector's contribution to national GDP are Seychelles (62 percent), Cabo Verde (43 percent), and Mauritius (27 percent). These relatively small economies are also among the most dependent on the export of services" (UNCTAD 2017).

The UN World Tourism Organization (UNWTO) predicts that the number of international tourist arrivals worldwide will increase by an average of 3.3 percent per year from 2010 through 2030 (UNWTO 2017). Based on these calculations, international tourist arrivals are predicted to reach 1.8 billion by 2030 (figure 4.11).

Figure 4.11   Tourism toward 2030: Actual Trend and Forecast, 1950–2030

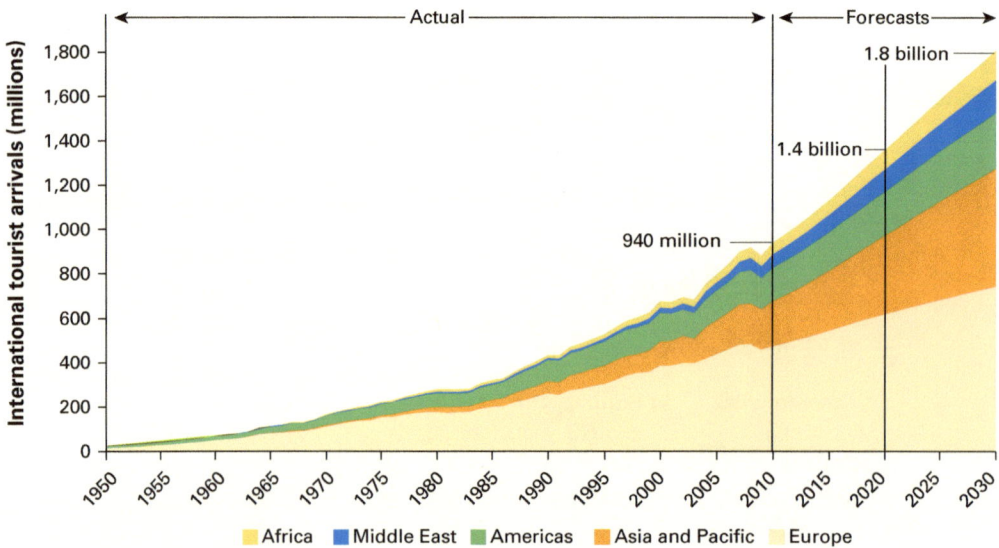

Source: UNWTO 2017.
Note: The forecasts were made before the onset of the COVID-19 (coronavirus) pandemic. International tourism has shown significant decline during the pandemic, posing a challenge to expand tourism in the Africa region.

A notable pattern in global tourism growth is the relatively faster rate of growth of arrivals in emerging economies than in high-income economies. The UNWTO predicts that international arrivals in emerging economies will grow at twice the rate (4.4 percent per year) of arrivals in high-income economies (2.2 percent per year). In absolute terms, emerging economies will add an average of 30 million arrivals per year—more than double the average of 14 million new arrivals in high-income economies. Emerging economies will surpass 1 billion arrivals by 2030, with a 57 percent share of the global tourism market (UNWTO 2017).

Sub-Saharan African countries can tap into this opportunity, because Africa is becoming an increasingly attractive destination for Asian tourists, especially Chinese tourists. A recent survey by the global travel platform Travelzoo[9] finds that the continent was the top destination of choice for Chinese tourists seeking more adventurous holidays in 2018, beating Japan and Australia. Visitors were especially drawn to (in this order) Morocco, Tunisia,[10] South Africa, Namibia, Madagascar, and Tanzania. Part of the interest in these nations came following the introduction of relaxed visa rules for Chinese citizens. And, in 2019, Kenya launched a marketing campaign to target China, hoping to boost the more than 53,000 Chinese visitors who came to the country in 2018. Chinese nationals also make up the largest group of tourists to Ethiopia, which had 45,307 Chinese visitors in 2017, a steady increase from 41,659 in 2016. The country recorded $169.6 million in revenue from Chinese tourists in 2017.

Leisure travel tends to accelerate most sharply when per capita income rises, and the Asian middle class is among the world's top tourist spenders. China consolidated its leadership as the biggest spender in travel abroad in 2017, with $258 billion in expenditure. Among the top 20 world spenders on outbound tourism (in this order), France, the United Kingdom, Australia, the Russian Federation, Spain, and India all posted double-digit growth in expenditure (UNWTO 2018). This is particularly important for Sub-Saharan African countries, because every $1 spent by visitors contributes an estimated $3.20 to the economy (Sears and Turner 2013). By tapping into this sector, Sub-Saharan African countries could expand and diversify their sources of revenues.

Fostering Trade Relations through Agreements

Interest in trading with Sub-Saharan Africa has been growing in recent years, and the region is considered a strategic trading partner for Asian countries, as numerous initiatives continue to demonstrate. Japan launched its Tokyo International Conference on African Development in 1993 to bring together African stakeholders and Japanese officials. In 2000, China renewed its engagement in Africa by establishing its Forum on China-Africa

Cooperation. Asian and African countries renewed their long-standing solidarity at the 2005 Asian-African Summit in Indonesia.

Between 2010 and 2014, 13 of the 25 fastest-growing export countries for Indonesia were in Sub-Saharan Africa: the Central African Republic,[11] Somalia, Mauritania, Djibouti, Mozambique, Kenya, Burkina Faso, Senegal, Guinea, Sierra Leone, Nigeria, the Republic of Congo, and South Africa. This has triggered meetings between Indonesian leaders and African leaders and officials to discuss opportunities to deepen their economic cooperation. Indonesia started the Indonesia-Africa Forum in 2018.

As a venture to build a bridge between Asia and Africa, the New Asian-African Strategic Partnership focuses its cooperation on the three broad pillars of partnership: political solidarity, economic cooperation, and sociocultural bonds. And, since 2008, India has been organizing the India-Africa Forum Summit, with the objective of enhancing existing partnerships between both sides.

Since 1948, the number of regional trade agreements (RTAs) in the form of free trade agreements (FTAs), PTAs, and customs unions has been increasing rapidly around the globe. As of May 2018, the WTO had been notified of 459 RTAs, of which 287 were in force. This proliferation of trade agreements has been driven partly by the desire of many countries to gain access bilaterally or multilaterally to larger markets. RTAs among non-neighborhood countries and regions go beyond goods trade and market access, by involving aspects such as investment, competition, labor standards, and the environment.

In the case of Sub-Saharan African countries, most trade agreements with non-African countries have been with high-income countries, especially the EU and the US. Some of these agreements include the EU and US Generalized System of Preferences (GSP), the EU's Everything but Arms (EBA) initiative, the EU-ACP nonreciprocal PTA under the EU's Cotonou Agreement, and the US African Growth and Opportunity Act (AGOA). Recently, efforts have been made toward establishing regional trading blocs with Asia.

Agreements with India

Under the umbrella of the most favored nation (MFN) clause, trade between the LMICs of Sub-Saharan Africa and Asia clearly grew significantly. For instance, India has bilateral trade agreements with 19 Sub-Saharan African countries (table 4.4). India introduced the Duty-Free Tariff Preference (DFTP) scheme for least developed countries (LDCs) in 2008. The DFTP scheme progressively eliminated customs duties imposed by India on its imports from LDCs on 85 percent of the country's total tariff lines (as defined at the Harmonized System 6-digit level) by 2012. An additional 9 percent of tariff lines (about 458 products) offered a margin of preference

Table 4.4   Overview of Trade Agreements between Sub-Saharan African Countries and India

Country or regional group	Agreement	Current status
Mauritius	Comprehensive Economic Cooperation and Partnership Agreement (CECPA)	The chapter on Trade in Goods (PTA) has been finalized. It includes tariffs, text of PTA with rules of origin, operational certification procedures, and a trade defense measure. Negotiations were held on Trade in Services with the view of creating a liberal, facilitative, transparent, and competitive services regime. The Trade in Investments negotiations also took place to improve the legal frameworks in both countries, including the bilateral Double Taxation Avoidance Convention (DTAC) and Bilateral Investment Promotion and Protection Agreement (BIPA). There was delay in the finalization of the chapters of "Enterprise" and treatment of "Shell Companies." This led to a standstill in the negotiations. India's proposal to modify DTAC was rejected by Mauritius, and this has put the CECPA negotiations on hold until the modifications are accepted by Mauritius.
Southern African Customs Union (SACU): Botswana, Eswatini, Lesotho, Namibia, and South Africa	Comprehensive Free Trade Agreement (CFTA)	The last round was held in October 2010, in which SACU presented a revised text of the PTA as a working document. At the round, both sides agreed on the following: the text on "Dispute Settlement Procedure"; to use the text proposed by India on "Customs Cooperation and Trade Facilitation" and "Technical Barriers to Trade (TBT)" as the working text; and to use the text "Sanitary and PhytoSanitary (SPS)" proposed by SACU as the working text. However, the fear of revenue loss from the implementation of an FTA is a sensitive issue for South Africa, which probably explains the lethargy shown by SACU authorities. This CFTA is still under consultation and study, but the hope that this PTA would concluded by the end of 2013 was dashed.
Selected Sub-Saharan African countries	Global System of Trade Preferences (GSTP)	The market access modalities adopted by the ministers are based on the principle of an across-the-board, line-by-line, linear cut of at least 20 percent on dutiable tariff lines; product coverage to be at least 70 percent of dutiable tariff lines; product coverage shall be 60 percent for participants having more than 50 percent of their national tariff lines at zero duty level; tariff cuts shall be made on the MFN tariffs applicable on the date of importation or, alternatively, participants may choose to apply the cuts on the MFN tariffs applicable on the date of conclusion of the third round; and the negotiating committee shall also consider the proposal for the revision of the GSTP rules of origin.
Common Market for Eastern and Southern Africa (COMESA)	Free trade agreement	A joint study group has been set up to look into the possibility of a free trade pact.

Source: Compiled from various sources.
Note: FTA = free trade agreement; MFN = most favored nation; PTA = preferential trade agreement.

ranging between 10 percent and 100 percent. The remaining 6 percent of tariff lines (326 products) was excluded from any tariff reduction, with LDCs enjoying MFN rates when exporting to India.

The expanded DFTP scheme offers a considerable improvement in market access for LDCs to the Asian economy. Yet, among the 97 products still on the exclusion list, some are particularly strategic for Africa, such as some fruits and vegetables, some dairy products, cashew nuts, coffee, tea, some spices, oil seeds, wheat flour, beer, wine and spirits, tobacco and cigarettes, and copper. A 100 percent DFTP would certainly provide greater opportunities to stimulate exports from Africa to India.

Only 26 of the 33 eligible African LDCs are participating in the scheme: Benin, Burkina Faso, Burundi, the Central African Republic, Chad, the Comoros, Eritrea, Ethiopia, The Gambia, Guinea, Guinea-Bissau, Lesotho, Liberia, Madagascar, Malawi, Mali, Mozambique, Niger, Rwanda, Senegal, Somalia, Sudan, Uganda, Tanzania, Togo, and Zambia. In addition, India has signed 13 bilateral investment treaties with African countries, of which, to date, 8 have come into effect.

Agreements with China

China has been promoting the reinforcement of economic partnerships with Sub-Saharan African countries since 2000. It announced the start of negotiations with the Southern African Customs Union (June 2004), but no specific negotiations have yet been held.

The China-Mauritius FTA was China's first FTA with an African country, which met comprehensive high standards and mutually beneficial objectives. The agreement covers trade in goods, trade in services, investment, and economic cooperation, among others. On trade in goods, the shares of tariff lines and trade value in duty-free trade exceed 90 percent; on trade in services, both sides have committed to open more than 100 sectors. The China-Mauritius FTA is the most liberalized FTA for Mauritius in terms of services. On the investment side, the agreement upgrades the 1996 China-Mauritius Bilateral Investment Treaty, representing the first upgrade among China's bilateral investment treaties with African countries.

Since 2005, China has provided zero import tariffs and exemptions on more than 180 product lines from 28 of the African LDCs, commodities whose average MFN tariff rate in 2004 was 9.8 percent. However, tariff escalations and peaks persist on certain African exports, such as raw cotton, which had a tariff of 27 percent in 2005 (Zafar 2007).

Agreements with Indonesia

Indonesia's promotion of bilateral trade with African countries is backed by increased official diplomatic presence on the continent. Currently, Indonesia has 11 embassies in Sub-Saharan Africa—in Ethiopia, Kenya, Madagascar, Mozambique, Namibia, Nigeria, Senegal, South Africa, Sudan, Tanzania, and Zimbabwe. It also operates a consulate-general in Cape Town, South

Africa. In addition, two Indonesian trade promotion centers—one in Lagos, Nigeria, and one in Johannesburg, South Africa—strengthen Indonesia's presence in Africa.

Although Indonesia mainly invests in bilateral agreements, it also deploys a regional approach (table 4.5). Apart from the Southern African Development Community (SADC) and the East African Community (EAC), the Economic Community of West African States (ECOWAS) offers abundant opportunities for boosting trade with Africa.

Table 4.5   Overview of Trade Agreements between Sub-Saharan African Countries and Indonesia, 1989–2019

Country or regional group	Agreement	Current status
Mozambique	Preferential trade agreement	First round discussion organized (May–June 2018).
Kenya: East African Community (EAC)	Preferential trade agreement	Upcoming negotiations (early 2019).
Nigeria: Economic Community of West African States (ECOWAS)	Preferential trade agreement	Both nations are signatories of the preferential trade agreement with the D8, which has been in effect since 2011.
Southern African Customs Union (SACU)	Preferential trade agreement with Group of Eight Developing Countries	SACU is still under negotiation since its proposal in 2017; focus on South Africa
Eight Sub-Saharan African countries	Global System of Trade Preference	In force since 1989. Countries included are Benin, Cameroon, Ghana, Guinea, Indonesia, Mozambique, Nigeria, Tanzania, and Zimbabwe. Countries applying to join the agreement are Burkina Faso, Burundi, Madagascar, Rwanda, and Uganda.
Eighteen Sub-Saharan African countries	Trade Preferential System of the Organization of the Islamic Conference (TPS-OIC)	The Committee for Economic and Commercial Cooperation is the most important multilateral economic and commercial cooperation platform of the Islamic world. Signed in 2014 but not yet in effect and not notified to the WTO. As of July 2017, Bangladesh, the Islamic Republic of Iran, Jordan, Malaysia, Pakistan, and Turkey have conveyed the updated list of concessions. The Framework Agreement, which sets out general rules and principles for negotiations on the establishment of the TPS-OIC, came into force in 2002. In February 2010, the Optional Tariff Protocol, which completed the framework agreement by determining the concrete discount rates in the tariffs for an implementation period, entered into force.

Source: Compiled from various sources.
Note: D8 = the "Group of Eight Developing Countries," which consists of eight low- and middle-income countries, namely Bangladesh, the Arab Republic of Egypt, Indonesia, the Islamic Republic of Iran, Malaysia, Nigeria, Pakistan, and Turkey; WTO = World Trade Organization.

Megaregional Agreements

Overall, the current trend for many countries is to come together into regional blocs that are significantly larger in trade and investments. These larger blocs are commonly referred to as megaregional trade agreements. Over the past few years, three major megaregional trade agreements have been under negotiation:

1. The Transatlantic Trade and Investment Partnership between the EU and the US
2. The Trans-Pacific Partnership between the United States and 11 countries in the Pacific Rim
3. The Regional Comprehensive Economic Partnership, which brings together the 10 members of the Association of Southeast Asian Nations (ASEAN) with six other countries in Asia and the Pacific, including India.

On the implications for Sub-Saharan African countries, there is a legitimate concern about market loss and trade diversion. These megaregional trade agreements could erode preferences and increase competition for African countries in Asian markets.

The next section looks empirically at how trading with different partners at different levels of development affects Sub-Saharan African manufacturing firms.

Does the Export Market Matter? A Literature Review

Aw and Hwang (1995) and Bernard, Jensen, and Lawrence (1995) pioneered the literature on firm-level characteristics and export market participation. Scholars have sought to explore whether exporting enterprises have higher performance characteristics relative to nonexporters.

Empirical studies on exporting and performance have been carried out for several high-income countries (Belgium, Denmark, France, Germany, Ireland, Italy, Portugal, Spain, Sweden, the United Kingdom, and the United States). However, there has been relatively little empirical work using firm-level data on African firms. The studies that have been done tend to concentrate on a small number of countries. Examples include Mengistae and Pattillo (2004) for Ethiopia, Ghana, and Kenya; Bigsten et al. (2004) for Cameroon, Ghana, Kenya, and Zimbabwe; Van Biesebroeck (2005) for Burundi, Cameroon, Côte d'Ivoire, Ethiopia, Ghana, Kenya, Tanzania, Zambia, and Zimbabwe; and Bigsten and Gebreeyesus (2009) for Ethiopia.

These studies find that exporters generally perform better than nonexporters. The positive productivity premium for exporters can be explained through two alternative but not mutually exclusive hypotheses: self-selection and learning by exporting.

In the self-selection hypothesis, the causality runs from productivity to exports. The most productive firms "self-select" into the export market, in the sense that they raise productivity before (not after) their entry into foreign markets. The additional costs of selling goods in foreign countries constitute an entry barrier that less successful firms cannot overcome. This self-selection hypothesis is tested empirically by looking at performance characteristics in the period before exporting. Empirical results for manufacturing exporters in Germany (Bernard and Wagner 1997), the United Kingdom (Girma, Greenaway, and Kneller 2002), and the United States (Bernard, Jensen, and Lawrence 1995) show that the exporters have significantly faster employment, shipment, and productivity growth than the nonexporters.

Learning by exporting is the alternative hypothesis to self-selection, and the causality runs now from exports to productivity. Exporters gain knowledge flows and productivity advantages through contact with international competitors and customers. Firms participating in international markets are exposed to more intense competition and must improve faster than firms that sell their products domestically only. This is tested empirically by looking at performance characteristics of exporters compared with nonexporters in the period following their entry into export markets. The empirical results vary on the impact of exporting on enterprise performance. Aw and Hwang (1995); Bernard, Jensen, and Lawrence (1995); Bernard and Wagner (1997); and Clerides, Lach, and Tybout (1998) fail to find any evidence to support the learning-by-exporting hypothesis. By contrast, studies on Canada (Baldwin and Gu 2003), Sweden (Hansson and Lundin 2004), and the United Kingdom (Girma, Greenaway, and Kneller 2002) do find evidence to support the hypothesis that exporting boosts the productivity of the exporters examined.

Lately, empirical studies have started to look at firms' exports broken down by destination regions or countries. These studies apply the standard approach used in empirical studies on the exporter productivity premium when investigating the relationship between exports and productivity by destination country or region. The productivity gains from exporting, if they exist, are likely to depend on the characteristics of the destination countries. There is a strong belief that selling in high-income country markets generates more learning opportunities, thanks to the advanced technologies used, compared with exporting to LMICs. Using a data set of Slovenian firms, De Loecker (2007) finds that new exporting companies enjoy significant productivity gains with respect to nonexporters and even greater gains for firms exporting to high-income countries. Another study, by Park et al. (2010) on Chinese firms, shows that exports increase productivity and that these gains are stronger for firms exporting to countries that are more developed.

Another strand of the literature goes deeper in this investigation, by inquiring about the sources of exporting firms' high productivity. How firms reach their ex ante productivity advantage is examined by some recent theoretical contributions in the field (Costantini and Melitz 2008).

In this chapter, technological inputs are the key variable that entails firm heterogeneity and specifically the differences in efficiency between exporters and nonexporters. From this new literature, many questions emerge about the relationship between export strategies and technological choices. Are firms that want to export compelled first to innovate? Or is it only because they innovate that exporters are more productive? From this discussion, we intend to shed more light on these issues in the context of Sub-Saharan Africa, by investigating the extent to which the traditional measures of export premiums are sensitive to the introduction of export market destination and innovation statistics.

Empirical Strategy, Data, and Preliminary Analysis

Our empirical strategy has four steps:

1. Following Bernard, Jensen, and Lawrence (1995), we first investigate whether exporters exhibit different performance characteristics than nonexporters.
2. For a more precise analysis, we follow Foster-McGregor, Isaksson, and Kaulich (2014) by estimating the productivity premium, defined as the difference in labor productivity between exporting firms and nonexporting firms.
3. We check whether the difference in the productivity of exporters and nonexporters persists when accounting for the firm-level destinations of exports. This aspect is particularly important for Sub-Saharan Africa because interaction with clients and competitors abroad allows exporting firms to absorb foreign knowledge. If most of the products shipped abroad are destined to high-income and emerging countries, the scope for improving production and quality is expected to be higher.
4. To investigate why some Sub-Saharan African firms do not export, we try to connect innovation to exporting and productivity.

The data used in this research come from the Africa Investor Survey 2010, which was carried out in 19 countries in the UN Industrial Development Organization (UNIDO) Regional Investment Program. This data set is unique in that it covers a relatively large number of African countries and a large number of firms.[12] The survey covered 6,497 agricultural, industrial, and services firms across the 19 Sub-Saharan African countries. The sample was drawn by stratifying firms by size (fewer than 50, 50–99, and 100 or more employees), ownership (domestic or foreign), and sector (2-digit level of International Standard Industrial Classification [ISIC] 7 Rev. 3.1). The questionnaire consisted of about 100 questions, which allowed the collection of more than 700 variables for each firm. Data were collected through face-to-face interviews with the top managers of the firms, and quality checks were undertaken to ensure the reliability of the data (UNIDO 2012).

Here, we consider only firms that are active in the manufacturing sector, because the propensity to export is likely to differ systematically for firms in the agriculture and services sectors, and thus they should be analyzed separately. The final, usable sample covers a maximum of 3,151 firms in ISIC sectors 15–38 that reported nonzero values for the core variables of interest. We consider the differences between domestic market–oriented firms and foreign market–oriented firms across several performance indicators identified by the literature: (a) log of labor productivity (defined as the ratio of output to employment); (b) log of total factor productivity (TFP);[13] (c) log of capital intensity (defined as the capital-to-labor ratio); (d) log of average wages; and (e) log of sales. Therefore, the basic estimating equation is of the following form:

$$\ln(X)_{ijk} = \alpha + \beta_1 \ln NEMP_{ijk} + \beta_2 \ln K/L_{ijk} + \beta_3 Exporter_{jk} + \beta_4 Foreign_{jk} + \mu_i + \delta_j = \varepsilon_{ijk}, \tag{4.1}$$

where X is our measure of firm performance (labor productivity) in firm i active in industry j from country k; $NEMP$ is the number of employees; K/L is the capital-labor ratio; $Foreign$ is a dummy taking the value 1 if the firm is foreign-owned; $Exporter$ is a dummy for exporters; and μ_i and δ_j are country- and sector-specific effects, respectively.

The regression equation is estimated using standard ordinary least squares (OLS) techniques. To control for firms' heterogeneity, as assumed by Melitz (2003), we estimate the regression model using quantile regression methods with fixed effects, which estimate the parameters of the model at different points on the (conditional) productivity distribution. We follow an approach that is similar to that suggested by Foster-McGregor, Isaksson, and Kaulich (2014) in three specific steps:

1. We center the variables by removing the country-industry-specific median from each of the variables. We then regress the centered dependent variable on the centered explanatory variables using the robust S-estimator.
2. We use the residuals from this regression and the estimated standard error of the residuals to identify outlying observations, by flagging firms that have robust standardized residuals.
3. We run a standard fixed-effects regression model, awarding a weight of zero to the outliers.

The following subsections present some descriptive characteristics of Sub-Saharan African manufacturing firms.

Ownership

Consistent with the African Investor Report (UNIDO 2012), a vast majority of investors in the manufacturing sector were foreign entrepreneurs, and only one-third of the firms were transnational corporations.[14] Nearly half of all the investors from European countries with former colonial interests began operations more than 20 years ago, confirming the persistence of long-standing economic relationships between Europe and Sub-Saharan Africa. At the other end of the spectrum, nearly 30 percent of the Chinese manufacturing firms were younger than six years. Intraregional investments from Sub-Saharan Africa and investments from India, on average, were substantially older than the Chinese investments.

At the country level, two European economies with long historical ties with Africa—France and the United Kingdom—have been displaced by India as the largest single source of foreign firms investing in manufacturing, at 17 percent of the total sample (figure 4.12). The United Kingdom and France, with 11 percent and 9 percent of foreign firms in the survey, respectively, were the second and fourth most important source countries. China was third, with 10 percent of the sample.

Eighty Chinese manufacturing firms participated in the survey. More than half of them entered the Sub-Saharan African market after 2000, through investment in new manufacturing facilities to access new markets. As with the other foreign investors, the Chinese respondents reported that they first became aware of investment opportunities mainly through existing investors.

UNIDO's Africa Investor Survey 2010 shows that Chinese investment appeared to be concentrated in East Africa (Ethiopia, Kenya, and Uganda) and in Ghana, Lesotho, and Nigeria. Three-quarters of the firms in the sample were operating in low-capital-intensive manufacturing, and half reported using low-technology production processes. The 28 exporters in the sample were concentrated in textiles and garments, wood, and paper products. The median export value was $1 million. Exports by value were divided between

Figure 4.12   Distribution of Foreign-Owned Manufacturing Firms in Sub-Saharan Africa, by Origin, 2010

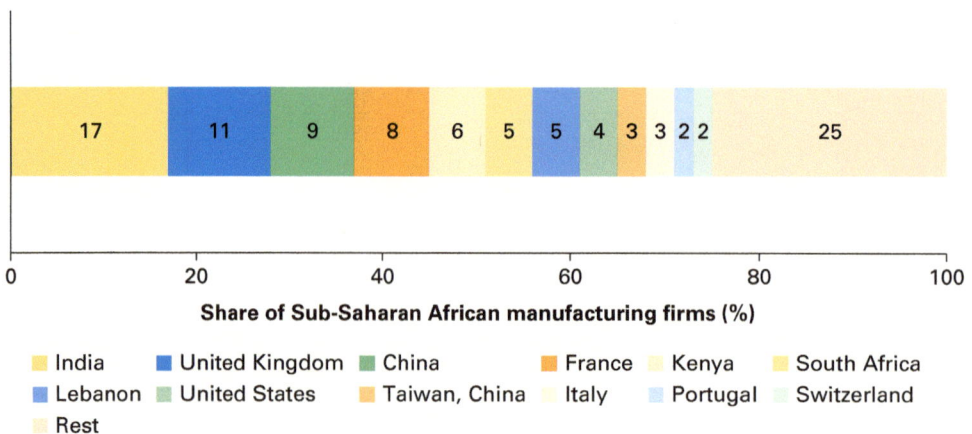

Share of Sub-Saharan African manufacturing firms (%)

India | United Kingdom | China | France | Kenya | South Africa
Lebanon | United States | Taiwan, China | Italy | Portugal | Switzerland
Rest

Source: UNIDO 2012.
Note: Data represent results from the Africa Investor Survey 2010 of the UN Industrial Development Organization (UNIDO). The survey covered 6,497 agricultural, industrial, and services firms across 19 Sub-Saharan African countries.

approximately one-third to regional markets in Sub-Saharan Africa and one-third to the United States, with the remainder divided equally among China, the EU, and South Africa. An analysis of the links of the Chinese manufacturing enterprises with their suppliers shows that more than a quarter had no domestic suppliers of raw materials or intermediate goods. By the value of their manufacturing inputs, two-thirds of all their inputs came directly from China (UNIDO 2012).

Among all of the foreign investors, half reported that they export some or all of their production, compared with less than a quarter of domestic firms. Some 270 European firms export nearly the same value of goods ($1.5 billion) as the 430 domestic Sub-Saharan African firms in the survey that export. Figure 4.13 presents the average shares of imports and exports of foreign investors according to their different countries and regions of origin—first, as the source of imported inputs used by the foreign-owned subsidiaries operating in the 19 African countries; and, second, as a destination for exports from the African host countries. Only foreign investors originating in Sub-Saharan Africa have an export surplus with their region of origin and are clearly enhancing intraregional trade.

Of the exports generated by firms owned by investors from Sub-Saharan African countries, 70 percent goes to other Sub-Saharan African countries, yet just 19 percent of inputs are imported from Sub-Saharan African countries. By contrast, Chinese firms import two-thirds of their inputs from

Figure 4.13 **Shares of Imports from and Exports to Investors' Regions or Countries of Origin, among Foreign-Owned Sub-Saharan African Firms, 2010**

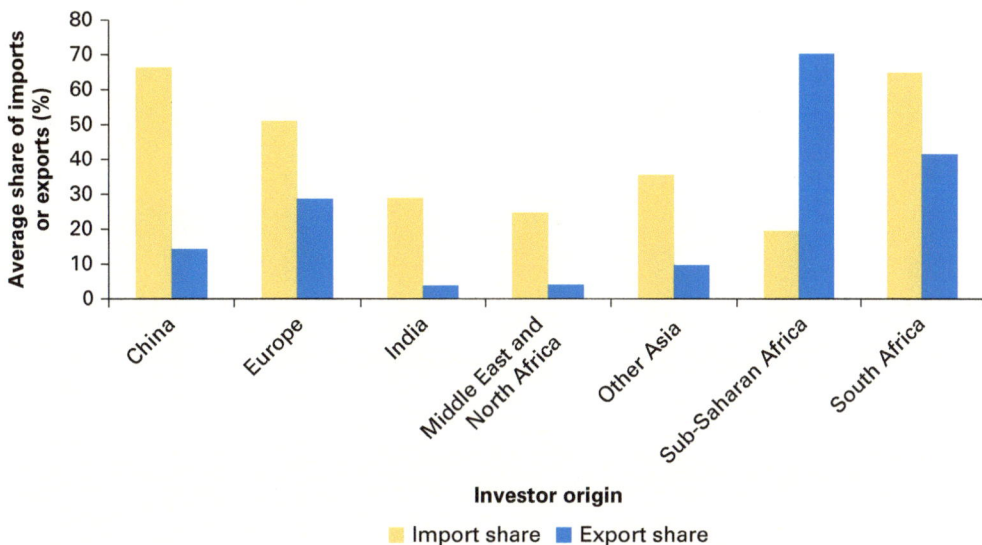

Source: UNIDO 2012.
Note: Data represent results from the Africa Investor Survey 2010 of the UN Industrial Development Organization (UNIDO). The survey covered 6,497 agricultural, industrial, and services firms across 19 Sub-Saharan African countries.

China, and just 14 percent of their exports go back to China. A modest 4 percent is imported as inputs from Sub-Saharan African countries, but 34 percent of exports go to the region. Among the European-owned firms, although about 50 percent of the imported inputs come from Europe, they source 28 percent from other Sub-Saharan African countries. Although most European firms are focused on regional markets, 30 percent of the exports still return to Europe. The firms from India and from the Middle East and North African are the most diversified in sources of imports, supplying less than 30 percent from the home country.

Overall, most of the firms reported that their largest export market is in Sub-Saharan Africa. This concentration on the Africa region suggests that there is scope for policy intervention to help regional investors diversify their exporting activity outside the region. Chinese firms and firms from elsewhere in Asia (except India) are unusual in that their exports to Sub-Saharan Africa account for only a third by value. These firms are instead major exporters to the United States, at 28 percent and 55 percent, respectively.

Exporters Are Different from Nonexporters

To identify the characteristics of exporters versus nonexporters, we follow the approach initially used by Bernard, Jensen, and Lawrence (1995) and estimate the following regression:

$$\ln(X)_{ijk} = \alpha + \beta_1 \, Exporter_{ijk} + \beta_2 Size_{ijk} \\ + \beta_3 Ind_j + \beta_4 Ctry_k + \varepsilon_i, \quad (4.2)$$

where X_{ijk} refers to the characteristics of firm i active in industry j from country k; $Exporter$ is a dummy equal to 1 when the firm is an exporter and 0 otherwise; and $Size$ is a dummy variable that takes the value 1 when the number of employees is greater than the median employment level across all firms in each industry and country and 0 otherwise.

We control for industry (Ind) and country ($Ctry$) effects, where subscripts j and k denote industry and country, respectively, and ε_i is a random error term. The interest lies in the coefficient β, which tells us whether the relevant firm characteristic is different for exporting firms relative to non-exporting ones.

The results of estimating equations (4.1) and (4.2) indicate that the export premiums are positive and significant for all the characteristics (table 4.6, panel a). Overall, exporters are more productive than nonexporters in labor productivity and TFP (39.8 percent and 17.77 percent, respectively). Foreign market–oriented firms on average pay higher wages (17.9 percent) and are more capital intensive (41 percent). These results are in line with the findings of Bernard, Jensen, and Lawrence (1995) for the United States; Bernard and Wagner (1997) for Germany; and Van Biesebroeck (2005) for Sub-Saharan Africa.

Higher Export Premiums for Multiple-Destination Exporters

In the 2010–11 UNIDO survey of investors in Sub-Saharan African firms, exporting firms were asked to specify the breakdown of their exports by destination and indicate the three Sub-Saharan African countries to which they exported the most. We draw on this information on export destination to analyze export behavior, by considering whether multiple-destination exporters differ from single-destination ones. In particular, we focus on nine export market destinations to which Sub-Saharan African manufacturing firms exported shares of their outputs: China, other Asian countries, the EU, India, the Middle East and North Africa, South Africa, Sub-Saharan Africa (excluding South Africa), the US, and other destinations.

Preliminary analysis points out that few Sub-Saharan African manufacturing firms are oriented toward one market destination. For example, 72 and 42 firms indicated that they shipped 100 percent of their exports to the EU and the US, respectively, and only 5 firms mentioned shipping 100 percent of their production to the Chinese market. For the Sub-Saharan African market as the destination, 406 manufacturing firms reported shipping 100 percent of their exports to the region. Table 4.6 (panel b) shows that multiple-destination exporters are significantly larger, have higher labor productivity, pay higher wages, and are significantly more capital intensive than single-destination exporters, as well as exhibiting superior performance characteristics relative to nonexporters even after controlling for firm size, industry, and country.

Table 4.6   Sub-Saharan African Firms' Export Market Characteristics, 2010–11

Variable	Capital intensity	Sales	Wage	Labor productivity	Total factor productivity
a. Export dummy					
Export premium	0.410*** (0.072)	0.742*** (0.095)	0.179*** (0.061)	0.398*** (0.076)	0.177*** (0.064)
Size	0.246*** (0.055)	2.560*** (0.089)	0.275*** (0.066)	0.418*** (0.056)	0.015 (0.544)
Industry dummy	Yes	Yes	Yes	Yes	Yes
Country dummy	Yes	Yes	Yes	Yes	Yes
Observations	2,941	2,989	2,812	2,463	2,440
R^2 overall	0.201	0.406	0.254	0.296	0.177
b. Multidestination dummy					
Export dummy	0.498*** (0.088)	0.812*** (0.136)	0.202** (0.087)	0.401*** (0.133)	0.245*** (0.057)

(Table continues on next page)

Table 4.6   Sub-Saharan African Firms' Export Market Characteristics, 2010/11
(continued)

Variable	Capital intensity	Sales	Wage	Labor productivity	Total factor productivity
Multidestination dummy	0.567** (0.164)	0.875 (0.151)	0.233*** (0.122)	0.489*** (0.135)	0.279* (0.107)
Intraregional dummy	0.322** (0.201)	0.678 (0.147)	0.228** (0.107)	0.454** (0.111)	0.189* (0.098)
Size	0.254*** (0.075)	2.570*** (0.090)	0.277*** (0.056)	0.432*** (0.078)	0.022 (0.055)
Industry dummy	Yes	Yes	Yes	Yes	Yes
Country dummy	Yes	Yes	Yes	Yes	Yes
Observations	2,941	2,989	2,812	2,463	2,440
R^2	0.177	0.406	0.254	0.183	0.171

Source: World Bank calculations.
* $p < 0.10$;   ** $p < 0.05$;   *** $p < 0.01$.

Higher Export Premiums for Firms Exporting to Multiple Destinations outside Sub-Saharan Africa

To test how firms' performances differ according to the type of market, we now focus on the localization of the market. We first disaggregate traders into two categories. We split the sample according to the destination market and estimate the export premium separately for firms exporting within and outside Sub-Saharan Africa. We restrict the analysis to firms serving only the regional market (South Africa included) or only outside Sub-Saharan Africa. This is important because both markets are often served by the same firms.

We then extend the analysis to other destinations. Exporters to multiple destinations outside Sub-Saharan Africa display superior characteristics relative to all other exporters. Firms that export to multiple destinations within Sub-Saharan Africa (South Africa included) are larger, more labor productive, and pay higher wages than firms that export to single destinations (inside and outside Sub-Saharan Africa). Different results are obtained and presented later, when the estimation is restricted to other market destinations, namely, China, the EU, India, the US, the Middle East and North Africa, other Asian countries, and other destinations. Interestingly, the results indicate that firms exporting to a single destination within Africa seem to perform better than firms that export to a single destination outside Africa in terms of output and labor productivity.

Export Innovations Associated with Higher Productivity

The preliminary analyses of the characteristics of exporters have clearly demonstrated the productive superiority of exporters over their nonexporting counterparts. Here, we investigate how firms make specific investments to improve their productivity and export performance.

The UNIDO data set provides information on technology transfer and innovation. The companies were asked to indicate, among other things, the average annual amount invested in process or product improvement, whether they were able to introduce on the market any newly improved product or production processes, and whether any of their products or production processes were certified by a national or international certification agency. From these data, we construct variables indicating whether the firms innovate. In particular, we use an output-based definition of innovators and noninnovators, based on the characterization of innovation as the market introduction of a new product or the implementation of a new process, as well as any investments made in acquisition of technology (patents, licenses, design, know-how, or nonpatented innovations) and research and development (R&D). In accordance with this definition, a firm is an innovator if, during 2006–10, it introduced a new or significantly improved product, introduced any new or significantly improved processes for producing or supplying products or did both.

Considering exporters and nonexporters, it appears that a large number of Sub-Saharan African firms are innovators—44 percent of the nonexporters and 27 percent of the exporters (table 4.7, panel a). As for the type of investment, acquisition of technology and adaptation of new production are the most preferred channels, followed by R&D. However, there is a clear superiority of nonexporters among firms that innovate, indicating that strategic policy targeting this subsample could be implemented to improve their export status.

To investigate the relationship between firms' export and innovation strategies (table 4.7, panel b), we discriminate among firms according to the localization of their exports, by covering the intraregional Sub-Saharan African (excluding South Africa), Asian (China and India), EU, and US markets. The data reported concern only firms that innovate.

Among firms exporting within Sub-Saharan Africa, 22 percent have acquired new technology, whereas only 10 percent have opted for R&D. Among firms that export to high-income countries, including the United States, Sub-Saharan African firms in the manufacturing sector invest more in R&D. This is consistent with high-income country market penetration usually being more challenging compared with penetration in low-income countries. In principle, high-income markets require a higher level of productivity because product differentiation and market competition are stronger and consumer requirements are more pronounced in these countries.

An interesting aspect concerns China as the destination, where 23 percent of exporters affirmed that they have acquired new technology (patents, licenses, design, and so forth), while only 18 percent have done so for more-developed destinations like the EU or the US. Why is this so? Are Asian markets easier to serve because of the comparable level of development? The next subsection presents the results of more robust analysis.

Table 4.7   Summary Statistics on Sub-Saharan African Firms: Exporters and Innovators

a. Statistics on exporters and innovators

| Variable | Export | | Do not export | | All firms |
	Innovate	Do not innovate	Innovate	Do not innovate	Total
Number of firms	767	158	1,265	657	2,847
Percent of total sample	27	6	44	23	100
Acquisition of technology	107	223	323	832	1,485
Percent of total sample	7	15	22	56	100
Adaptation of new production	110	221	319	831	1,481
Percent of total sample	7	20	22	56	100
Research and development	85	243	217	926	1,471
Percent of total sample	6	17	15	63	100

b. Export strategies conditional on innovation

| Variable | Intraregional | Farthest markets | | | | |
	Sub-Saharan Africa	China	India	European Union	United States	Total
Acquisition of technology (%)	22	23	19	18	18	100
Adaptation of new production (%)	19	13	17	27	24	100
Research and development (%)	10	17	12	35	26	100

Source: World Bank calculations.
Note: "Acquisition of technology" includes patents, licenses, design, know-how, and nonpatented innovations. "Adaptation of new production" also includes new business processes.

Productivity Gains of Sub-Saharan African Firms with a Dominant Position in the Asian Market

In the more recent literature on international trade and firm-level performance, attention has been paid to the issue of whether there are productivity differences between different types of destination markets and, in particular, between high- and low-income regions (De Loecker 2007; Serti and Tomasi 2008). To observe whether export premiums are different depending on the destination market, we split the sample into the nine locations identified. Because these markets are often served by the same firm, we consider a destination to be "dominant" if it receives the highest share of the firm's exports. Following the same approach as earlier, we estimate the productivity gains from exporting separately for the nine destination markets. Table 4.8 reports the means of kernel estimates for firms exporting to different destination markets.

Table 4.8   Sub-Saharan African Exporting Firms' Characteristics, by Dominant Destination Market

Variable	China	India	South Africa	European Union	United States	Middle East & North Africa	Sub-Saharan Africa	Other Asia	Other destinations
Labor productivity	9.28 (9.40)	8.95 (9.06)	9.01 (9.13)	9.20 (9.36)	9.03 (9.17)	8.79 (8.87)	9.50 (9.66)	9.00 (9.17)	8.61 (8.77)
Total factor productivity	5.69 (5.78)	5.66 (5.77)	5.97 (6.08)	6.01 (6.13)	6.04 (6.16)	5.70 (5.89)	5.98 (6.09)	5.70 (5.81)	5.72 (5.84)
Average wage	11.85 (11.93)	11.42 (11.44)	11.10 (11.12)	11.77 (11.78)	11.75 (11.77)	11.45 (11.45)	11.31 (11.31)	11.34 (11.36)	11.67 (11.68)
Sales	13.67 (13.78)	13.69 (13.76)	14.01 (14.13)	14.07 (14.16)	14.03 (14.17)	13.82 (13.94)	14.10 (14.22)	13.68 (13.79)	13.93 (14.07)
Capital intensity	8.74 (8.85)	8.72 (8.80)	8.75 (8.87)	9.05 (9.18)	9.01 (9.15)	8.64 (8.73)	8.76 (8.88)	8.71 (8.85)	8.84 (8.95)

Source: World Bank calculations.
Note: The table reports the mean values of the performance indicators for firms having a dominant position in one of the markets shown. The destination is considered "dominant" if it receives the highest share of the firm's exports. Median values are reported in parentheses.

The results suggest that firms selling goods to China tend to have a higher labor productivity and average wage than firms exporting to the EU or the US. However, firms with a dominant market in the EU or the US are more capital intensive and productive than the other destination subgroups.

So far, we have suggested that the country of destination matters as a source of heterogeneity among traders. To determine whether these results hold in a regression framework, where other parameters are controlled for, we estimate the following equation:

$$\ln(X)_{ijk} = \alpha + \beta_1 E_{ijk}^{China} + \beta_2 E_{ijk}^{India} + \beta_3 E_{ijk}^{SA} + \beta_4 E_{ijk}^{EU} + \beta_5 E_{ijk}^{US} + \beta_6 E_{ijk}^{MENA} + \beta_7 E_{ijk}^{SSA}$$
$$+ \beta_8 E_{ijk}^{Other\ Asia} + \beta_9 E_{ijk}^{ODest} + \beta_{10} Size_{ijk} + \beta_{11}\ Ind_j + \beta_{12} Ctry_k + \varepsilon_i, \qquad (4.3)$$

where E denotes the dummy for exporters having as their dominant market one of the nine identified destinations. The results from OLS regressions are reported in table 4.9, along with quantile and robust fixed-effects regression results. Column (1) presents the results with no specific controls, column (2) includes market destinations as well as industry fixed effects, and column (3) reports the results with innovation parameters. The results from the quantile regressions are summarized in columns (4) to (8), and the fixed-effects regression results are in column (9). The OLS results reveal positive and statistically significant effects of employment, capital intensity, and foreign ownership on firms' labor productivity, as predicted by the literature.

On the market destination parameters in table 4.9, column (2), exporters are approximatively 5 percent more productive than nonexporters. Firms that export to destinations in China, other Asian countries, and Sub-Saharan Africa as dominant markets also present a positive, large, and statistically significant effect on productivity. Firms that export mostly to the EU display additional productivity gains; however, the gains are lower than those of their counterparts exporting to the United States.

Columns (4) to (8) report the results from estimating a similar model using the fixed-effects quantile regression and the fixed-effects robust regression of Verardi and Wagner (2012). The quantile regression results are reported for the 10th, 30th, 50th (median), 70th, and 90th percentiles of the conditional productivity distribution. The results on the control variables are largely similar to those from using OLS regression in sign and significance. We also find that the size of the coefficients is generally smaller, at the median and other percentiles, when compared with the OLS results. The observations from the robust fixed-effects regression are largely similar to the OLS results for the control variables, for the size and significance of the coefficients. The coefficients on the trade dummies are positive and significant and display a similar pattern to the OLS results.

Overall, the results suggest that export market destination matters, because the productivity premiums are larger for Sub–Saharan African firms selling most of their products to less-developed regions, and this is consistent with South–South exports having increased much faster than exports from high-income countries to the South.

Productivity Gains of Innovating Sub-Saharan African Firms

To investigate the relative importance of innovation and export strategies, we next regress the dependent variable on different innovation and export variables. As expected, innovative activities are significantly correlated with firm productivity. This result is clearly in accordance with the literature on the R&D-productivity link. The quantile regression results (table 4.9) show statistically significant coefficients for the product and process innovation dummies. In addition, the results from the robust fixed-effects regression are consistent with the OLS results and indicate positive and significant coefficients for exporters and innovators.

However, the results point to the dominant importance of product innovation relative to process innovation. First, this could be explained by endogenous growth models, which endogenize the rate of innovation and predict the dynamic effects of international trade on innovative activity. The competition in international markets forces exporting firms to improve their products to remain competitive, thus increasing their probability of innovation. Second, trading with countries that have a comparable level of development smooths the diffusion of technology through imitation.

Table 4.9 Role of Innovation in Firm Productivity

| | OLS | | | Quantile regression | | | | | Fixed effects |
| | | | | 10th | 30th | 50th | 70th | 90th | |
	(1)	(2)	(3)	(4)	(5)	(6)	(7)	(8)	(9)
Log NEMP	0.425*** (0.112)	0.431*** (0.141)	0.378*** (0.121)	0.205** (0.017)	0.278*** (0.027)	0.315*** (0.036)	0.317*** (0.018)	0.399** (0.011)	0.375*** (0.21)
Log K/L	0.412*** (0.034)	0.423*** (0.0157)	0.417*** (0.0147)	0.312*** (0.035)	0.322*** (0.022)	0.335*** (0.021)	0.363*** (0.017)	0.359* (0.035)	0.377*** (0.017)
Exporter	0.048*** (0.017)	0.053*** (0.006)	0.056*** (0.012)	0.046** (0.017)	0.107 (0.028)	0.112 (0.017)	0.116 (0.010)	0.204** (0.013)	0.206*** (0.030)
Foreign	0.321*** (0.134)	0.401*** (0.135)	0.412*** (0.135)	0.339** (0.124)	0.462* (0.166)	0.398* (0.129)	0.416* (0.158)	0.411* (0.132)	0.414*** (0.176)
China		0.087*** (0.016)	0.089*** (0.0216)	0.083* (0.013)	0.081* (0.016)	0.083* (0.015)	0.087* (0.017)	0.080* (0.015)	0.098*** (0.025)
India		0.067* (0.011)	0.068** (0.021)	0.058* (0.016)	0.055* (0.009)	0.050** (0.008)	0.055** (0.010)	0.521 (0.023)	0.059*** (0.00125)
South Africa		0.068** (0.016)	0.070*** (0.012)	0.062*** (0.013)	0.063*** (0.006)	0.068*** (0.006)	0.063*** (0.007)	0.062*** (0.015)	0.049* (0.248)
European Union		0.077*** (0.078)	0.079*** (0.068)	0.061*** (0.013)	0.060*** (0.007)	0.054*** (0.006)	0.060*** (0.008)	0.063*** (0.016)	0.685*** (0.132)
United States		0.081** (0.146)	0.087*** (0.106)	0.063*** (0.013)	0.065*** (0.006)	0.062*** (0.006)	0.063*** (0.007)	0.056*** (0.014)	0.051** (0.009)
Middle East and North Africa		0.068 (0.091)	0.069* (0.061)	0.043* (0.114)	0.044* (0.136)	0.042* (0.147)	0.041* (0.207)	0.045* (0.114)	0.048*** (0.004)
Sub-Saharan Africa		0.082*** (0.003)	0.088** (0.004)	0.069** (0.015)	0.063** (0.008)	0.067** (0.008)	0.061** (0.009)	0.067* (0.018)	0.055*** (0.178)

(Table continues on next page)

Table 4.9 Role of Innovation in Firm Productivity *(continued)*

	OLS			Quantile regression					Fixed effects
	(1)	(2)	(3)	(4)	(5)	(6)	(7)	(8)	(9)
Other Asia	0.086***	0.086***	0.087***	0.049*	0.051*	0.050*	0.056**	0.069***	0.0570***
	(0.023)	(0.023)	(0.036)	(0.012)	(0.007)	(0.005)	(0.007)	(0.016)	(0.076)
Other destinations	0.068	0.068	0.069*	0.049**	0.041	0.045	0.048	0.046*	0.044*
	(0.005)	(0.005)	(0.008)	(0.030)	(0.015)	(0.113)	(0.016)	(0.038)	(0.012)
Innovation dummy			0.045***	0.033*	0.021***	0.031***	0.033**	0.030	0.338**
			(0.015)	(0.013)	(0.006)	(0.006)	(0.008)	(0.020)	(0.007)
Product innovation dummy			0.096***	0.077	0.072*	0.062**	0.068***	0.073*	0.0870**
			(0.006)	(0.014)	(0.005)	(0.006)	(0.008)	(0.017)	(0.0769)
Process innovation dummy			0.054***	0.036**	0.041**	0.043	0.049	0.043	0.041**
			(0.009)	(0.012)	(0.016)	(0.035)	(0.028)	(0.027)	(0.004)
Industry controls	No	Yes	Yes						
Observations	2,849	2,849	2,849	2,756	2,756	2,756	2,756	2,756	2,849
R^2	0.254	0.372	0.372	0.186	0.185	0.170	0.155	0.123	0.459

Source: World Bank calculations.

Note: K = capital; L = labor; NEMP = number of employees; OLS = ordinary least squares.
* $p < 0.1$; ** $p < 0.05$; *** $p < 0.01$.

Conclusion

From an empirical standpoint, this chapter looked at the growing trade relationship between Sub-Saharan Africa and its trading partners—both traditional (the EU and the US) and emerging ones (China and India, among others). This in-depth analysis of firm-level destinations of exports identified characteristics that are associated with export status, productivity, and innovation. For this exercise, we employed a rich data set of 3,151 firms in 19 countries in Sub-Saharan Africa, covering 24 manufacturing sectors.

Following the methodological approach established by Foster-McGregor, Isaksson, and Kaulich (2014), we find that exporters perform better than nonexporters. The export premium varies by the number of destinations to which countries export and the level of development of the destination market. Sub-Saharan African firms selling most of their products to China and other Asian countries (India excluded) were found to be more productive. In addition, the results point to the importance of intraregional trade between Sub-Saharan African countries because exports within the region (South Africa excluded) were associated with a strong increase in productivity. That being said, trading with the EU and the US was also found to have a positive effect on Sub-Saharan African firms' productivity, but to a lesser magnitude.

Considering these results, we investigated how Sub-Saharan African firms could tap into trade potential with Asian countries. The chapter looked at the role of innovation as a potential catalyst, given that differences in productivity are a major source of cross-country income variations and that technological change drives productivity growth. Using the same data set, our results suggest that being an exporter and an innovator is associated with productivity gains. The types of markets in which firms sell and the types of innovations the firms undertake also matter. The analysis found that product innovation has the most significant impact.

The empirical questions addressed in this chapter are important for understanding the role of trade at the enterprise level as well as for formulating policies that seek to promote growth through exporting. This analysis supports the need for enterprises to be relatively more productive and to diversify their export market destinations.

What do these results mean for Sub-Saharan Africa's trade policy? Growing exports and improving competitiveness in this turbulent time, which is characterized by increased trading blocs and trade restrictive measures, will not be an easy task; but it is surely achievable. Asia is an attractive global market, given that it is the largest exporter as well as the largest importer in South–South trade. To tap this potential, policy makers in Sub-Saharan Africa must work to deepen their trade ties with Asia. Building on the achievements of these recent years could foster the region's position in this "hub-and-spoke" pattern. Finally, at a more meso level, a careful assessment of the consumption patterns of the growing middle class in Asia is needed, to inform export diversification options for countries in Sub-Saharan Africa.

Annex 4A Sample Firms

Table 4A.1   **Number of Firms in the Data Set, by Country**

Country	Number of firms	Share in all firms (%)
Burkina Faso	49	1.56
Burundi	46	1.46
Cameroon	88	2.79
Cabo Verde	94	2.98
Ethiopia	384	12.19
Ghana	255	8.09
Kenya	350	11.11
Lesotho	87	2.76
Madagascar	104	3.30
Malawi	71	2.25
Mali	139	4.41
Mozambique	131	4.16
Niger	41	1.30
Nigeria	401	12.73
Rwanda	81	2.57
Senegal	94	2.98
Tanzania	275	8.73
Uganda	316	10.03
Zambia	145	4.60
Total	**3,151**	**100**

Source: UNIDO 2012.

Table 4A.2   **Number of Firms in the Sample, by Industry**

Sector (ISIC Rev 3.1 2-digit)	Number of firms	Share in all firms (%)
Manufacture of food products and beverages	684	21.71
Manufacture of tobacco products	20	0.63
Manufacture of textiles	118	3.74
Manufacture of wearing apparel; dressing and dyeing of fur	193	6.13
Tanning and dressing of leather; manufacture of luggage, handbags, saddles, harnesses and footwear	94	2.98
Manufacture of wood and of products of wood and cork, except furniture, manufacture of articles of straw and plaiting materials	135	4.28
Manufacture of paper and paper products	99	3.14
Publishing, printing and reproduction of recorded media	249	7.90
Manufacture of coke, refined petroleum products and nuclear fuel	12	0.38
Manufacture of chemicals and chemical products	287	9.11
Manufacture of rubber and plastics products	283	8.98
Manufacture of other non-metallic mineral products	162	5.14
Manufacture of basic metals	79	2.51
Manufacture of fabricated metal products, except machinery and equipment	320	10.16
Manufacture of machinery and equipment n.e.c.	89	2.82
Manufacture of office, accounting and computing machinery	3	0.10
Manufacture of electrical machinery and apparatus n.e.c.	48	1.52
Manufacture of radio, television and communication equipment and apparatus	9	0.29
Manufacture of medical, precision and optical instruments, watches and clocks	17	0.54
Manufacture of motor vehicles, trailers and semi-trailers	31	0.98
Manufacture of other transport equipment	14	0.44
Manufacture of furniture; manufacturing n.e.c.	178	5.65
Recycling	10	0.32
Other manufacturing	17	0.54
Total	3,151	100

Source: UNIDO 2012.
Note: ISIC = International Standard Industrial Classification; n.e.c. = not elsewhere classified

Notes

1. In this volume, "South–South trade" refers to trade among low- and middle-income economies.
2. At the 1955 Bandung Conference (also called the Asian-Africa or Afro-Asian Conference), representatives of 29 Asian, African, and Middle Eastern governments met in Bandung, West Java, Indonesia. The participants, mostly from newly independent nations, sought to promote solidarity in their economic development and decolonization and to oppose neocolonialism by any nation. The conference was a step toward formation of the Non-Aligned Movement.
3. Regional and global trade data throughout this chapter are from the Direction of Trade Statistics data set of the International Monetary Fund (http://data.imf.org/).
4. Throughout this report, "North America" follows the World Bank's regional definition, comprising Bermuda, Canada, and the United States.
5. There is no commonly accepted definition of the middle class across countries. ADB (2010) uses an absolute approach, defining the middle class as those with consumption expenditures of $2–$20 per person per day in 2005 purchasing power parity (PPP) US dollars. OECD (2010) defines middle-class households as having daily expenditure of $10–$100 per person in PPP terms.
6. In this chapter, the term "fish" refers to finfish (fresh and processed) and non-finfish—for example, shrimps, crabs, bivalves, squids, and other aquatic products.
7. The "Global Wooden Furniture Market 2018–2022" research and market study was conducted using an objective combination of primary and secondary information, including inputs from key participants in the industry (Technavio 2018). The report contains a comprehensive market and vendor landscape in addition to a Strengths, Weaknesses, Opportunities, and Threats (SWOT) analysis of the key vendors.
8. For the full set of log export bans, see the list (updated as of July 2018) on the Forest Legality Initiative's website (https://forestlegality.org/content/logging-and-export-bans).
9. The Travelzoo Travel Trends Survey was completed by 1,671 Travelzoo members in China who responded to an online questionnaire in January 2018 (Travelzoo 2018).
10. In February 2017, Tunisia decided to offer visa-free entry to Chinese tourists for stays of no more than 90 days in the country. Since then, China has become Tunisia's fastest-growing source of tourists, with arrivals rising from about 7,400 in 2016 to over 18,000 in 2017 (Xinhua 2018).
11. Based on UN Comtrade data, Indonesia's exports to the Central African Republic were valued at $2.6 million in 2010 and $2.09 million in 2014.

12. For a complete list of countries, the number of firms in each country, and the number of firms by industry, see annex 4A, tables 4A.1 and 4A.2.

13. We estimate TFP using a common definition in the literature, where TFP is defined as $TFP = VA/(Total\ employment^{2/3}\ Total\ fix\ assets^{1/3})$.

14. In this survey, a firm is considered to be part of a transnational corporation if it is the wholly owned subsidiary or joint venture of a parent firm with headquarters in another country. If the foreign investor is a foreign national or family that has invested in the firm alone or as a joint venture partner and not a subsidiary of an enterprise based in another country, it is considered to be a foreign entrepreneur firm.

References

ADB (Asian Development Bank). 2010. "The Rise of Asia's Middle Class." Special chapter of "Key Indicators for Asia and the Pacific" annual statistical report (1–57), ADB, Manila.

AfDB (African Development Bank). 2016. "Feed Africa: Strategy for Agricultural Transformation in Africa 2016–2025." Strategy document, AfDB, Abidjan, Côte d'Ivoire.

Aw, B. Y., and A. R. Hwang. 1995. "Productivity in the Export Market: A Firm Level Analysis." *Journal of Development Economics* 47: 313–32.

Baldwin, J., and W. Gu. 2003. "Export-Market Participation and Productivity Performance in Canadian Manufacturing." *Canadian Journal of Economics* 36 (3): 634–57.

Bernard, A. J., J. B. Jensen, and R. Z. Lawrence. 1995. "Exporters, Jobs, and Wages in U.S. Manufacturing: 1976–1987." *Brookings Papers on Economic Activity: Microeconomics* 1995: 67–119.

Bernard, A., and J. Wagner. 1997. "Exports and Success in German Manufacturing." *Weltwirtschaftliches Archiv* 133: 134–57.

Bigsten, A., P. Collier, S. Dercon, M. Fafchamps, R. Gauthier, J. W. Gunning, et al. 2004. "Do African Manufacturing Firms Learn from Exporting?" *Journal of Development Studies*, 40 (3): 115–41.

Bigsten, A., and M. Gebreeyesus. 2009. "Firm Productivity and Exports: Evidence from Ethiopian Manufacturing." *Journal of Development Studies* 45 (10): 1594–1614.

Chikweche, T., and R. Fletcher. 2014. "Rise of the Middle of the Pyramid in Africa: Theoretical and Practical Realities for Understanding Middle Class Consumer Purchase Decision Making." *Journal of Consumer Marketing* 31 (1): 27–38.

Clerides, S., S. Lach, and J. Tybout. 1998. "Is Learning-by-Exporting Important? Microdynamic Evidence from Colombia." *Quarterly Journal of Economics* 113 (3): 903–47.

Costantini, J., and M. J. Melitz. 2008. "The Dynamics of Firm Level Adjustment to Trade Liberalization: The Organization of Firms." In *The Organization of Firms in a Global Economy*, edited by E. Helpman, D. Marin, and T. Verdier. Boston: Harvard University Press.

De Loecker, J. 2007. "Do Exports Generate Higher Productivity? Evidence from Slovenia." *Journal of International Economics* 73: 69–98.

Dey, M. M. 2008. "Demand for Fish in Asia: A Cross-Country Analysis." *Australian Journal of Agricultural and Resource Economics* 52: 321–38.

Failler, P. 2015. "The ACP Group of States and the Challenge of Exporting Fish to the European Union." *Journal of Fisheries and Livestock Production* 3: 142.

Forest Trends. 2017. "China's Forest Product Imports and Exports 2006–2016: Trade Charts and Brief Analysis." Report, Forest Trends, Washington, DC.

Foster-McGregor, N., A. Isaksson, and F. Kaulich. 2014. "Importing, Exporting and Performance in Sub-Saharan African Manufacturing Firms." *Review of World Economics* 150 (2): 309–36.

Girma, S., D. Greenaway, and R. Kneller. 2002. "Does Exporting Lead to Better Performance? A Microeconometric Analysis of Matched Firms." GEP Research Paper vol. 02/09, University of Nottingham, UK.

Hansson, P., and N. Lundin. 2004. "Exports as an Indicator on or Promoter of Successful Swedish Manufacturing Firms in the 1990s." *Review of World Economy* 140 (3): 415–45.

Kharas, H. 2017. "The Unprecedented Expansion of the Global Middle Class, An Update." Global Economy & Development Working Paper 100, Brookings Institution, Washington, DC.

Melitz, M. J. 2003. "The Impact of Trade on Intra-Industry Reallocations and Aggregate Industry Productivity." *Econometrica* 71 (6): 1695–1725.

Mengistae, T., and C. Pattillo. 2004. "Export Orientation and Productivity in Sub-Saharan Africa." *IMF Staff Papers* 51 (2): 327–53.

OECD (Organisation for Economic Co-operation and Development). 2010. *Latin American Economic Outlook 2011: How Middle-Class Is Latin America?* Paris: OECD Publishing.

Palin, C., C. Gaudin, J. Espejo-Hermes, and L. Nicolaides. 2013. "Compliance of Imports of Fishery and Aquaculture Products with EU Legislation." Study, Directorate-General for Internal Policies, European Parliament, Brussels.

Park, A., D. Yang, X. Shi, and Y. Jiang. 2010. "Exporting and Firm Performance: Chinese Exporters and the Asian Financial Crisis." *Review of Economics and Statistics* 92 (4): 822–42.

Rieländer, J., and B. Traoré. 2015. "Explaining Diversification in Exports across Higher Manufacturing Content: What Is the Role of

Commodities?" OECD Development Centre Working Paper 327, Organisation for Economic Co-operation and Development, Paris.

Sears, Z., and R. Turner. 2013. "Travel & Tourism as a Driver of Employment Growth." In *The Travel & Tourism Competitiveness Report 2013: Reducing Barriers to Economic Growth and Job Creation*, edited by J. Blanke and T. Chiesa, 63–69. Cologny, Switzerland: World Economic Forum.

Serti, F., and C. Tomasi. 2008. "Firm Heterogeneity: Do Destinations of Exports and Origins of Imports Matter?" LEM Working Paper No. 2008/14, Scuola Superiore Sant'Anna, Laboratory of Economics and Management, Pisa, Italy.

Technavio. 2018. "Global Wooden Furniture Market 2018–2022." Market research report, Technavio, London.

Travelzoo. 2018. "Travelzoo Survey: 2018 to See Africa Boom among Avid Chinese Travelers." Press release, March 19, 2018.

UNCTAD (United Nations Conference on Trade and Development). 2017. *Economic Development in Africa Report 2017: Tourism for Transformative and Inclusive Growth*. Geneva: United Nations.

UNIDO (United Nations Industrial Development Organization). 2012. *Africa Investor Report 2011: Towards Evidence-Based Investment Promotion Strategies*. Vienna: UNIDO.

UNWTO (United Nations World Tourism Organization). 2017. *WTO Annual Report 2017*. Geneva: UNWTO.

UNWTO (United Nations World Tourism Organization). 2018. *Highlights: 2018 Edition*. Madrid: UNWTO.

Van Biesebroeck, J. 2005. "Exporting Raises Productivity in Sub-Saharan African Manufacturing Firms." *Journal of International Economics* 67 (2): 373–91.

Verardi, V., and J. Wagner. 2012. "Productivity Premia for German Manufacturing Firms Exporting to the Euro-Area and Beyond: First Evidence from Robust Fixed Effects Estimations." *World Economy* 35 (6): 694–712.

Ward, K., and F. Neumann. 2012. "Consumer in 2050: The Rise of the EM Middle Class." Report of the Global Economics unit, HSBC Global Research, London.

WTO (World Trade Organization). 2019. *WTO Trade Monitoring Report*. November 2019. Geneva: WTO.

Xinhua. 2018. "Sahara Desert in Tunisia Becomes Attractive Destination for Chinese Tourists." Xinhua New Agency, April 19, 2018. http://www.xinhuanet.com/english/2018-04/29/c_137145595.htm.

Zafar, A. 2007. "The Growing Relationship between China and Sub-Saharan Africa: Macroeconomic, Trade, Investment and Aid Links." *World Bank Research Observer* 22 (1): 103–30.

CHAPTER 5

Assessing the Global Value Chain Links between Asia and Sub-Saharan Africa

Heiwai Tang, Douglas Zhihua Zeng, and Albert G. Zeufack

Introduction

Since 2000, China and other Asian countries such as Bangladesh, Cambodia, India, and Vietnam have become important trade and investment partners with Sub-Saharan African countries. Some of these Asian trading partners have lost their own growth momentum, and there have also been concerns that their economic engagement may have reduced Sub-Saharan African countries' local industrial capability, causing them to be more dependent on Asian economies. For Sub-Saharan Africa to tap into the trade-and-growth spiral, it needs to diversify—away from some of the traditional high-income economy trading partners, whose growth is slowing, and away from commodity exports, which often exhibit high price volatility.

The growing middle class in and increasing demand from Asia, especially East Asia, along with the shifting structure of global value chains (GVCs), may offer new economic opportunities for Sub-Saharan Africa. This chapter assesses the value chain links between Sub-Saharan Africa and Asia, summarizing the current status and future potential of African products in emerging Asia. The study offers insights on how the region's economies can expand their market potential and advance their industrialization and economic diversification agendas.

Key Findings

One of the lessons from this chapter's detailed sector-level analysis of Sub-Saharan African countries' exports to Asia is that each nation in the region has its own experience of trading with Asia—in terms of structural change, diversification dynamics, and specialization patterns. Although exports from Sub-Saharan Africa to Asia remain highly concentrated in resource-intensive products such as petroleum, minerals, metals, and primary goods, there are a few exceptions. For instance, Ethiopia and Tanzania did relatively well in diversifying their export portfolios during the boom of exports to Asia. Nigeria, by contrast, has remained highly specialized in natural resources, in particular petroleum and crude oil, before and after the export boom to Asia.

We also find that each country has a distinct key trading partner in Asia. Contrary to the prevailing view, we find that China is not always the dominant trading partner for individual African nations, despite its status as the leading trading partner of the entire African continent. For instance, India is emerging as an increasingly important trading partner of Sub-Saharan Africa. Since 2005, India has become the largest export destination in Asia for Ghana, Nigeria, and Tanzania. Pakistan has been the top destination for Kenya's exports.

Structure of This Chapter

After documenting policy-relevant stylized facts, we examine the determinants of successful participation in GVCs and inclusive growth. The first part of the chapter examines how the sharply increasing engagement of Asian economies in Sub-Saharan Africa has changed the pattern of the region's exports—in the composition of destination countries (for example, between high-income countries and low- and middle-income countries); in factor intensity (for example, capital, skill, and raw material intensity); and in various value chain measures (for example, length of production, upstreamness, and domestic value added). We show that exports to Asia are positively correlated with exports to the rest of the world, using a panel data set of trade and foreign direct investment for 46 countries in Sub-Saharan Africa from 2000 to 2015.

The findings also show that increased exports from a Sub-Saharan African country to Asia, whether proportionally or in absolute value, do not appear to divert exports away from other destination countries. On the contrary, increased exports to Asia tend to raise exports to the rest of the world as well as to other African countries. We discuss the reasons why increased exports to a country (or region) would raise exports to other countries. More exports to a country usually come with more imports from the same country or other countries. The literature has shown that imports of foreign intermediate inputs can increase a firm's productivity, which in turn raises its sales and profits. So the idea of trade diversion based on a zero-sum concept is an exceptional situation. There are many reasons why a country's GVC participation with a fast-growing region can serve as an engine of growth.

The second part of the chapter assesses how Asian economic engagement changes Sub-Saharan Africa's trade patterns. First, we examine the effects of participating in Asian value chains on the factor content of exports. Using a panel data set of trade for 46 Sub-Saharan African countries over 16 years

(2000–15), we show that economic engagement with Asian GVCs raised the capital intensity of Sub-Saharan African exports but had no effect on their skill content. Such an increase in the capital content, or the so-called capital deepening, of exports was mostly driven by increased exports of capital-intensive goods to Asia rather than to the rest of the world.

By contrast, imports from Asia as a whole do not seem to have played a significant role in changing the factor intensity of African exports, although imports from Bangladesh, Cambodia, China, India, and Vietnam ("Asia-5" hereafter) have done so. Moreover, there is no evidence that increased exports to Asia led to more specialization in the resource intensity of exports, debunking the claim that Asian economic engagement in the continent is mainly resource-seeking and can potentially lead to deindustrialization.

Second, we also examine the determinants of the relative successes of some nations in Sub-Saharan Africa in terms of participation in GVCs, through Asia's economic engagement. Using panel data on trade at the country-industry level, we find that Asian economic engagement in the continent is associated with an increase in "upstreamness," a measure proposed by Antràs et al. (2012) to capture the shares of exports coming more from upstream than from downstream industries.[1] Such a process was accompanied by a reduction in the length of the production chains, implying that fewer stages and countries are now involved in the production of exported goods from Sub-Saharan Africa. However, there is no evidence that trade with Asia affects the domestic content of Sub-Saharan African nations' exports.

Third, the study also sheds some light on the policy implications for Sub-Saharan African nations to move up the value chain by participating in Asian GVCs. The results show that proportionally more *exports to* Asia, but not *imports from* Asia, can help Sub-Saharan African nations move up the value chains. The effects are particularly strong among Sub-Saharan African countries that have access to the sea but are relatively poorer than their landlocked peers in the region.

In addition, corruption appears to impede not only trade but also the benefits from GVC participation. These results suggest that export orientation toward Asia as a policy helps reduce poverty, and anticorruption policies can help enhance economic efficiency. Surprisingly, the general measure of a country's rule of law does not affect the relation between countries' trade with Asia and their GVC outcomes.

Key Trade Patterns and GVC Links between Sub-Saharan Africa and Asia

This section examines the patterns of exports from Sub-Saharan Africa as well as from five selected countries in the region (the "Africa-5": Ethiopia, Ghana, Kenya, Nigeria, and Tanzania) for which we have survey data that allow for granular GVC analyses. To this end, we aggregate the BACI trade data[2] from the Harmonized System (HS) 6-digit level to the HS 2-digit level (96 categories) in order to analyze the top sectors in Sub-Saharan Africa and the Africa-5 nations that sold to Asia in 2005 and 2015.

Top Products Exported from Sub-Saharan Africa to Asia

Focusing on the top 10 export sectors to Asia from Sub-Saharan Africa and each of the Africa-5 countries, it appears that, in both 2005 and 2015, the top sector by export value was minerals, fuels, and mining. The entire continent exported about $16.1 billion worth of goods from that sector to Asia in 2005, which increased to $54.5 billion in 2015.[3] The next sectors are natural or cultured pearls (valued at $4.1 billion and $16.3 billion in 2005 and 2015, respectively) and ores, slag, and ash (valued at $2.7 billion and $9.0 billion in 2005 and 2015, respectively). Both years exhibit a clear pattern: exports from Sub-Saharan Africa to Asia remained heavily concentrated in raw materials and primary goods, with mining and fuels always standing at the top.

Figure 5.1 shows the shares of exports from Sub-Saharan Africa to Asia by HS 2-digit sector, for 2005 and 2015. For clarity, only sectors that contributed at least 1 percent of total Sub-Saharan African exports to Asia in each respective year (or either year) are shown. Sixteen sectors (of 96) satisfied this 1 percent rule; that is, each of the 16 sectors accounted for over 1 percent of Sub-Saharan Africa's exports to Asia in *either* year.

The minerals, fuels, and mining sector (HS 27) stands out, accounting for 41 percent of Sub-Saharan Africa's total exports to Asia in 2005 and increasing to 48 percent by 2015. The second most prominent export sector in both years is natural or cultured pearls (HS 71), whose share of Sub-Saharan Africa's exports to Asia also rose, from 11 percent in 2005 to 14 percent by 2015. Among the 16 sectors shown, six increased in shares of Sub-Saharan African exports to Asia.

In addition to the top two sectors mentioned, the others include copper and copper articles (HS 74); edible fruits (HS 08); ores, slag, and ash (HS 26); and oil seeds (HS 12). The other 10 sectors declined in their shares in Sub-Saharan Africa–Asia exports. The sector that experienced the largest drop in export share between 2005 and 2015 in percentage terms is iron and steel (HS 72), which dropped from 7 percent to 2 percent. Other sectors that experienced a significant drop in export shares include aluminum and articles (HS 76), electrical machinery (HS 85), and fish and crustaceans (HS 03).

Top Exports from Africa-5 Countries to Asia

Ethiopia

Among Ethiopia's aggregate exports to Asia in 2005 and 2015, only 10 sectors (of 96 HS 2-digit sectors) made up at least 1 percent of exports in either year (figure 5.2). Two sectors stand out from the rest: coffee, tea, and maté (HS 09) and oil seeds (HS 12). The coffee sector accounted for 47 percent

Figure 5.1 Sectoral Composition of Sub-Saharan Africa's Exports to Asia, 2005 and 2015

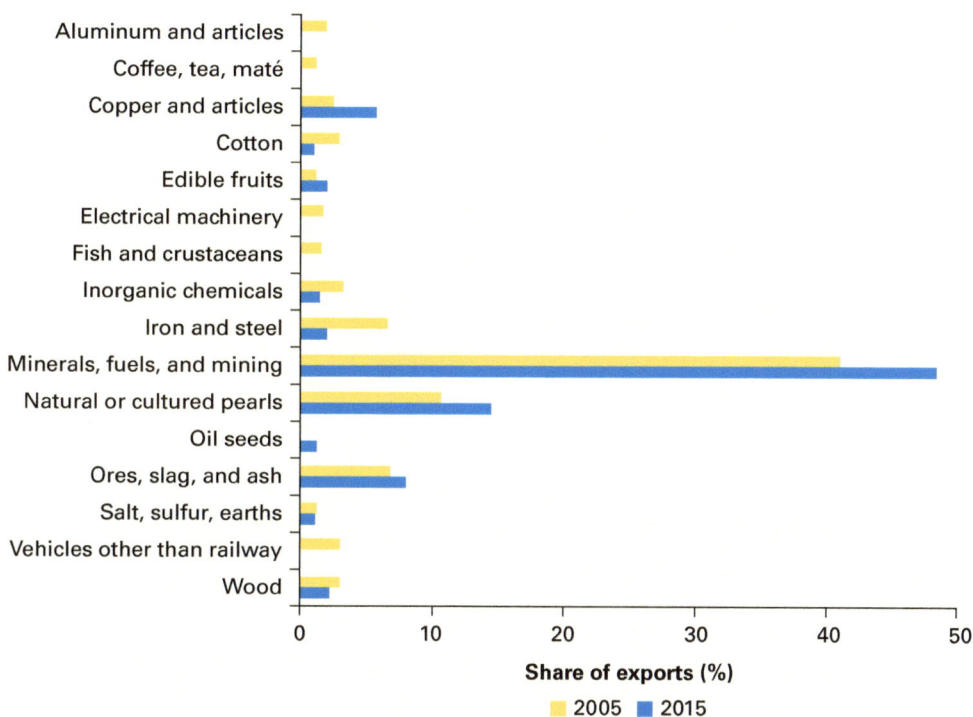

Source: Staff calculations from the Database for International Trade Analysis (BACI) of the Centre for Prospective Studies and International Information (CEPII).

Note: Shares of exports are shown by Harmonized System (HS) 2-digit sector, including only sectors that contributed at least 1 percent of total Sub-Saharan African exports to Asia in each respective year (or either year). Therefore, any sector making up less than 1 percent of exports in either year does not display a bar for that year.

of Ethiopia's total exports to Asia in 2005, but it decreased to only 18 percent in 2015. The oil seed sector instead increased its share in Ethiopia's exports to Asia, from 28 percent to 48 percent. Another notable increase was in the edible vegetables (HS 07) sector, which increased about sixfold over the 10-year period, becoming one of the top three export sectors by 2015.

Three sectors—footwear and gaiters (HS 64), natural or cultured pearls (HS 71), and railway or tramway locomotives (HS 86)—contributed less than 1 percent to Ethiopia's exports to Asia in 2005, but by 2015 they had become significant sectors in the country's exports to Asia. By contrast, another three sectors—cotton (HS 52); ores, slag, and ash (HS 26); and iron and steel (HS 72)—contributed more than 1 percent to Ethiopia's exports to Asia in 2005 but declined to less than 1 percent by 2015.

Overall, the changes in Ethiopia's export patterns are encouraging news. It is also one of the few countries in Sub-Saharan Africa that have shown

Figure 5.2   Sectoral Composition of Ethiopia's Exports to Asia, 2005 and 2015

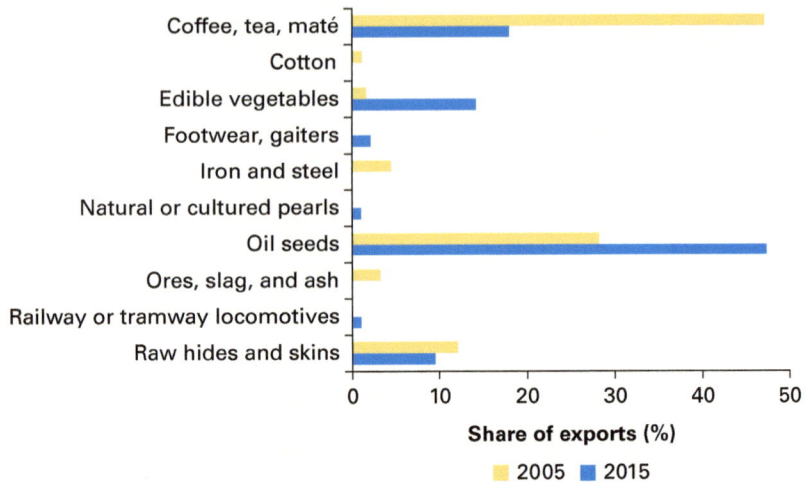

Source: Staff calculations from the Database for International Trade Analysis (BACI) of the Centre for Prospective Studies and International Information (CEPII).
Note: Shares of exports are shown by Harmonized System (HS) 2-digit sector, including only sectors that contributed at least 1 percent of total Ethiopian exports to Asia in either respective year. Therefore, any sector making up less than 1 percent of exports in either 2005 or 2015 does not display a bar for that year.

significant improvement in industrialization, at least as revealed in its movement along the GVCs with Asia.

Ghana

Only 10 of Ghana's 96 HS 2-digit sectors made up at least 1 percent of aggregate exports to Asia in either 2005 or 2015. Two sectors that clearly stand out are cocoa and cocoa prep (HS 18) in 2005, and natural or cultured pearls (HS 71) in 2015 (figure 5.3). In 2005, exports from the cocoa sector accounted for over half of Ghana's exports to Asia but declined to only 12 percent by 2015. By contrast, the natural or cultured pearls sector has emerged rapidly. In 2005, it accounted for a mere 3 percent of Ghana's exports to Asia, but it increased tremendously, to 60 percent, in 2015 because of increased demand from India in recent years.

The growth of the natural or cultured pearl sector was so substantial that it crowded out almost all other sectors, causing each of them (except for minerals, fuels, and mining) to decline in their share of Ghana's exports to Asia. Although the dominance of a single sector in a country's export basket appears to be quite common across Sub-Saharan African nations, the substantial switching of the top sector in a matter of 10 years is unique to Ghana.

Figure 5.3   Sectoral Composition of Ghana's Exports to Asia, 2005 and 2015

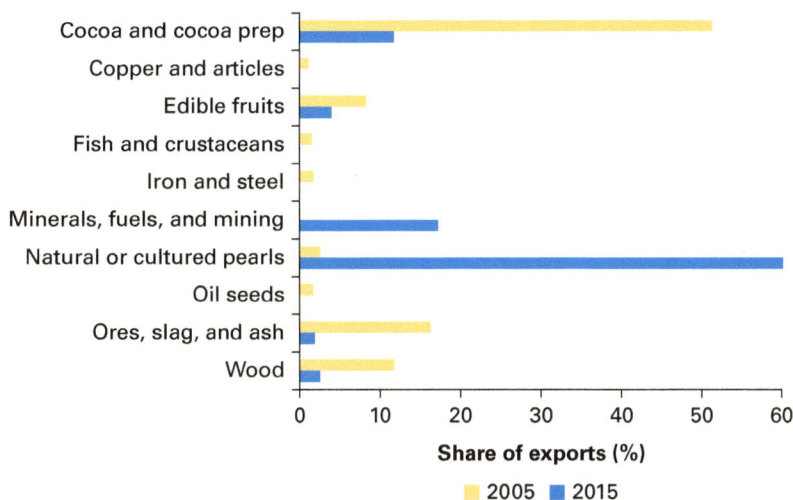

Source: Staff calculations from the Database for International Trade Analysis (BACI) of the Centre for Prospective Studies and International Information (CEPII).
Note: Shares of exports are shown by Harmonized System (HS) 2-digit sector, including only sectors that contributed at least 1 percent of total Ghanaian exports to Asia in either respective year. Therefore, any sector making up less than 1 percent of exports in either 2005 or 2015 does not display a bar for that year.

Kenya

Among Kenya's total exports to Asia in 2005 and 2015, 15 of the 96 HS 2-digit sectors made up at least 1 percent in either year, suggesting that Kenya's exports (to Asia) have been more diversified than those of Ethiopia and Ghana. Despite the country's more diversified export basket, the top sector—coffee, tea, and maté (HS09), which already accounted for over half of Kenya's exports to Asia in 2005—continued to grow in absolute value and in share, contributing about 61 percent of the country's exports by 2015 (figure 5.4).

All the other sectors appear to be much less important in Kenya's exports. Inorganic chemicals (HS 28), which was Kenya's second-largest export sector to Asia in 2005, declined from 19 percent to 5 percent of exports in 10 years. The dominance of a single sector in a country's export basket, a common feature in many Sub-Saharan African nations' exports, is particularly strong in Kenya.

Nigeria

Only 6 of Nigeria's 96 HS 2-digit sectors made up at least 1 percent of its total exports to Asia in either 2005 or 2015, suggesting that Nigeria's exports (to Asia) were much more concentrated in a few sectors than those of the four other Africa-5 countries. The top sector—minerals, fuels, and

Figure 5.4   Sectoral Composition of Kenya's Exports to Asia, 2005 and 2015

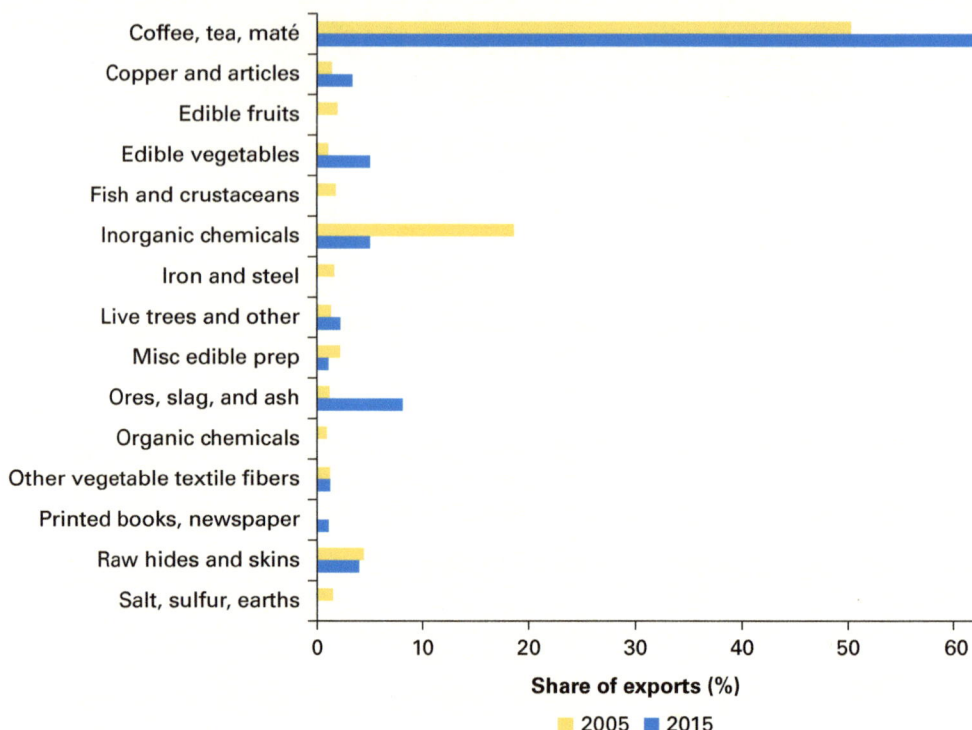

Source: Staff calculations from the Database for International Trade Analysis (BACI) of the Centre for Prospective Studies and International Information (CEPII).
Note: Shares of exports are shown by Harmonized System (HS) 2-digit sector, including only sectors that contributed at least 1 percent of total Kenyan exports to Asia in either respective year. Therefore, any sector making up less than 1 percent of exports in either 2005 or 2015 does not display a bar for that year.

mining (HS 27)—accounted for over 90 percent of Nigeria's exports to Asia in both 2005 and 2015 (figure 5.5). All the other sectors have been much less important to Nigeria's export trade, by definition.

The hyperspecialization of Nigeria's exports in petroleum and oil must be related to its rich endowment of oil. In 2015, only three sectors in Nigeria accounted for more than 1 percent of the country's exports to Asia. Aside from petroleum, they were wood (HS 44) and edible fruits (HS 08). The cotton (HS 52), oil seeds (HS 12), and ores, slag, and ash (HS 26) sectors dropped off the list because they fell below the 1 percent cutoff.

Tanzania

As for Tanzania's changing specialization pattern, 14 of the 96 HS 2-digit sectors made up at least 1 percent of the country's exports in either 2005 or 2015. This suggests that Tanzania's exports (to Asia) have been more diversified than Nigeria's and comparable to those of Ghana and Ethiopia. The more diversified export basket is illustrated not only by the number of

Figure 5.5   Sectoral Composition of Nigeria's Exports to Asia, 2005 and 2015

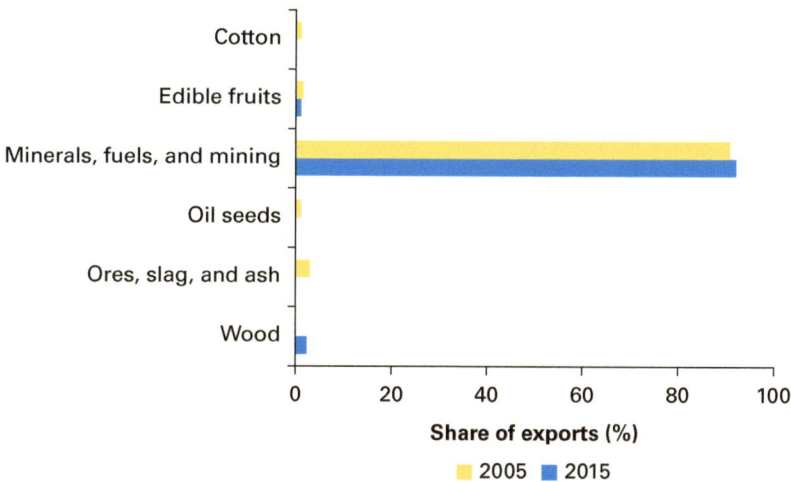

Source: Staff calculations from the Database for International Trade Analysis (BACI) of the Centre for Prospective Studies and International Information (CEPII).
Note: Shares of exports are shown by Harmonized System (HS) 2-digit sector, including only sectors that contributed at least 1 percent of total Nigerian exports to Asia in either respective year. Therefore, any sector making up less than 1 percent of exports in either 2005 or 2015 does not display a bar for that year.

"above 1 percent" sectors but also by the more even distribution of export values across sectors.

The top export sector in 2005—ores, slag, and ash (HS 26)—accounted for 35 percent of Tanzania's exports to Asia in that year (figure 5.6). But the top sector in 2015—natural or cultured pearls (HS 71)—contributed only about 22 percent to the country's exports to Asia.

An active process of dynamic reallocation of resources between sectors has contributed to the diversification of Tanzania's export portfolio between 2005 and 2015. The shares of the raw material sectors (such as ores, slag, and ash) declined substantially, whereas some light manufacturing (such as edible fruits [HS 08] and edible vegetables [HS 07]) became more prevalent sectors in Tanzania's exports to Asia.

In sum, the Africa-5 countries have been quite heterogeneous in their changing patterns of exports to Asia. Although Sub-Saharan Africa's exports to Asia, overall, have been concentrated in resource-intensive sectors, there were a few exceptions in the region. Ethiopia and Tanzania did relatively better in diversifying their export portfolios during the export boom (to Asia). Nigeria remained very specialized in natural resource exports, particularly petroleum and crude oil. The econometric assessment section later in this chapter presents regression analyses to identify the relevant policies or economic fundamentals that contributed to the positive changes.

Figure 5.6   Sectoral Composition of Tanzania's Exports to Asia, 2005 and 2015

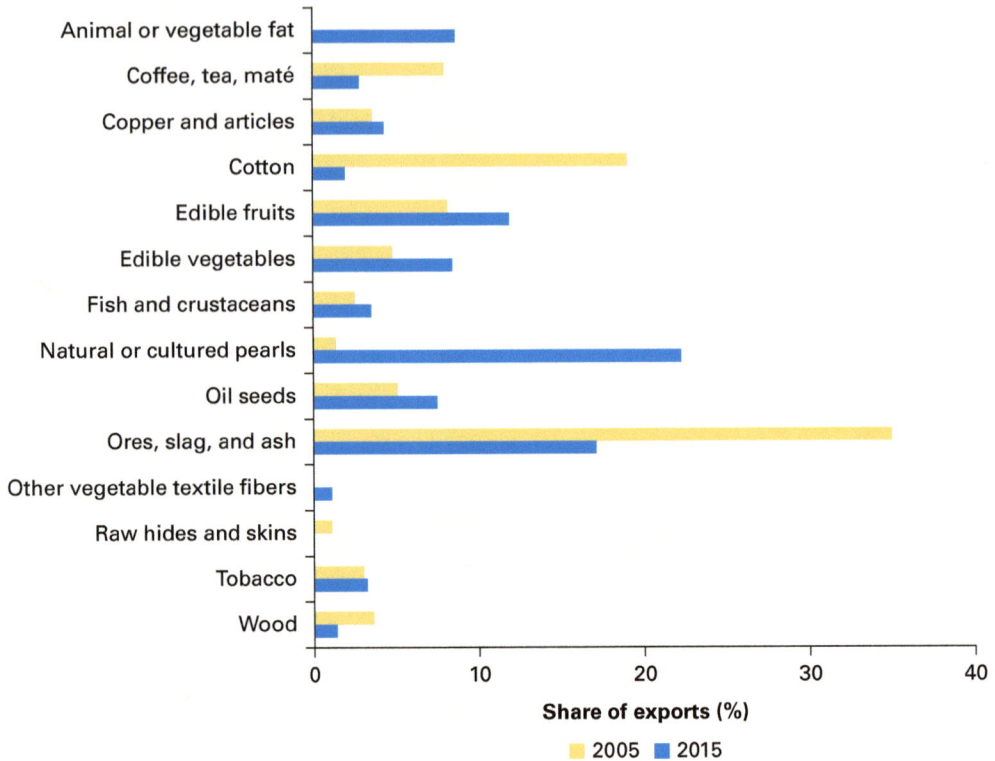

Source: Staff calculations from the Database for International Trade Analysis (BACI) of the Centre for Prospective Studies and International Information (CEPII).
Note: Shares of exports are shown by Harmonized System (HS) 2-digit sector, including only sectors that contributed at least 1 percent of total Tanzanian exports to Asia in either respective year. Therefore, any sector making up less than 1 percent of exports in either 2005 or 2015 does not display a bar for that year.

Primary versus Nonprimary Exports from the Africa-5 to Asia

This subsection summarizes the sectoral patterns in terms of the "primary" (extractive) and "nonprimary" (nonextractive) exports to Asia from the entire Sub-Saharan African continent as well as the individual Africa-5 nations. We classify sectors as primary or nonprimary on the basis of the United Nations (UN) *Classification by Broad Economic Categories Rev.5* (UN DESA 2018).

The aggregate value of the region's primary exports to Asia was $22 billion in 2005, accounting for 56 percent of Sub-Saharan African exports to Asia that year (table 5.1, panel a). The share was larger than that of primary exports from Sub-Saharan Africa to non-Asian countries, which was 52 percent. Ten years later, in 2015, the share of primary exports from

Sub-Saharan Africa to Asia remained about 55 percent, but the value tripled, to $63 billion. Among the region's exports to non-Asian countries, primary goods accounted for only 35 percent in 2015, a substantially smaller share than that to Asian destinations.

Ethiopia

The same set of statistics for Ethiopia's exports to Asian and non-Asian countries shows that the share of primary exports in the country's total exports to Asia is significantly smaller than the continent's average.

Table 5.1 Relative Importance of Primary versus Nonprimary Exports from Sub-Saharan Africa and the Africa-5 Countries to Asian and Non-Asian Destinations, 2005 and 2015

Primary or nonprimary, by origin and destination	2005		2015	
	Export value (US$, millions)	Export share, by destination (%)	Export value (US$, millions)	Export share, by destination, (%)
a. Africa				
Primary exports to Asia	22,100.00	56	62,600.00	55
Nonprimary exports to Asia	17,100.00	44	50,200.00	45
Primary exports to Non-Asia	139,000.00	52	105,000.00	35
Nonprimary exports to Non-Asia	128,000.00	48	193,000.00	65
b. Ethiopia				
Primary exports to Asia	44.87	16	36.04	5
Nonprimary exports to Asia	227.44	84	689.02	95
Primary exports to Non-Asia	155.49	15	79.89	2
Nonprimary exports to Non-Asia	866.91	85	4,643.30	98
c. Ghana				
Primary exports to Asia	112.86	32	1,133.80	23
Nonprimary exports to Asia	235.63	68	3,874.70	77
Primary exports to Non-Asia	293.15	8	1,025.84	19
Nonprimary exports to Non-Asia	3,245.80	92	4,500.94	81
d. Kenya				
Primary exports to Asia	50.72	11	127.93	16
Nonprimary exports to Asia	399.06	89	665.36	84
Primary exports to Non-Asia	157.58	5	263.98	6
Nonprimary exports to Non-Asia	3,048.19	95	4,183.62	94

(Table continues on next page)

Table 5.1   Relative Importance of Primary versus Nonprimary Exports from Sub-Saharan Africa and the Africa-5 Countries to Asian and Non-Asian Destinations, 2005 and 2015 *(continued)*

Primary or nonprimary, by origin and destination	2005		2015	
	Export value (US$, millions)	Export share, by destination (%)	Export value (US$, millions)	Export share, by destination, (%)
e. Nigeria				
Primary exports to Asia	2,682.23	95	9,357.30	66
Nonprimary exports to Asia	139.30	5	4,918.96	34
Primary exports to Non-Asia	35,200.00	89	28,700.00	85
Nonprimary exports to Non-Asia	4,271.35	11	5,128.23	15
f. Tanzania				
Primary exports to Asia	329.48	60	632.11	25
Nonprimary exports to Asia	216.07	40	1,895.78	75
Primary exports to Non-Asia	249.65	14	689.50	17
Nonprimary exports to Non-Asia	1,494.52	86	3,403.65	83

Source: Database for International Trade Analysis (BACI) and staff calculations.
Note: "Primary" products are extractive, as defined by the United Nations' Broad Economic Categories. "Nonprimary" products are nonextractive. Full Sub-Saharan Africa export values are rounded to the nearest 100 million; country export values are rounded to the nearest 10,000.

Only 16 percent of Ethiopia's exports to Asia in 2005 were primary exports, amounting to $44.9 million worth of goods (table 5.1, panel b). The share declined to 5 percent in 2015.

As for Ethiopia's exports to non-Asian countries, the share of primary goods in total exports is also much smaller than that of other Sub-Saharan African nations as a whole. The share of primary exports from Ethiopia to the rest of the world was only 15 percent in 2005, and it dropped to a mere 2 percent in 2015. In sum, Ethiopia has not been a resource-dependent exporter.

Ghana

Looking at the same set of statistics for Ghana, we see that the share of primary exports in its total exports to Asia is significantly less than the regionwide average. Primary exports made up only 32 percent of Ghana's exports to Asia in 2005, amounting to $113 million worth of goods (table 5.1, panel c). The share declined to 23 percent in 2015.

As for Ghana's exports to non-Asian countries, the share of primary goods in total exports was much smaller than that of its exports to Asia as well as the corresponding average in Sub-Saharan Africa as a whole.

The share of primary exports from Ghana to the rest of the world was only 8 percent in 2005, increasing to 19 percent by 2015.

In sum, Ghana's pattern of trade in extractive industries is very different from that of Ethiopia. Although Ghana's share of primary exports to Asian markets was larger than Ethiopia's in 2005, it has since declined. On the contrary, its share of extractive exports was small for exports to the rest of the world in 2005, but it has since increased substantially. In general, Ghana has been much more dependent than Ethiopia on primary exports.

Kenya

Kenya's share of primary exports in its total exports to Asia is significantly smaller than the region's average—only 11 percent in 2005, amounting to $51 million worth of goods (table 5.1, panel d). The share increased to only 16 percent by the end of 2015.

In Kenya's exports to non-Asian countries, the share of primary goods in total exports was also much smaller than the average share of other Sub-Saharan African nations as well as its own shares of primary exports to Asia. The share of primary exports from Kenya to the rest of the world was only 5 percent in 2005 and hovered around 6 percent in 2015. In sum, Kenya has not been dependent on resource exports, even less so than Ethiopia.

Nigeria

Looking at the same set of statistics for Nigeria's exports to Asian and non-Asian destinations, we see that the share of primary exports in Nigeria's total exports to Asia is much larger than the region's average as well as the three other countries analyzed so far. The share of primary exports in Nigeria's exports to Asia was 95 percent in 2005, amounting to $2.7 billion worth of goods (table 5.1, panel e). Nigeria has been successful in diversifying away from hyperspecialization in natural resources. As a result, in 2015, the share of primary exports declined to 66 percent.

In Nigeria's exports to non-Asian countries, the share of primary goods in total exports is still much higher than other Sub-Saharan African nations. It was 89 percent in 2005, decreasing slightly, to 85 percent, in 2015.

In sum, Nigeria's pattern of trade in extractive industries is very different from the other Africa-5 countries. Nigeria has also been more dependent on primary exports, although there are signs of diversification in its portfolio of exports to Asia.

Tanzania

Finally, we show the same set of statistics for Tanzania's exports to Asian and non-Asian destinations. The share of primary exports from Tanzania to Asia was 60 percent in 2005, which was very close to the region's average (table 5.1, panel f) and amounted to a total value of $329 million. The share declined significantly, to 25 percent in 2015, suggesting successful diversification from primary goods in its exports to Asia.

In Tanzania's exports to non-Asian countries, the share of primary goods in total exports is much smaller than that of its exports to Asia as well as the corresponding average in Sub-Saharan Africa as a whole. The share of primary exports from Tanzania to the rest of the world was only 14 percent in 2005, increasing slightly, to 17 percent, by 2015.

In sum, the Africa-5 nations represent the significant variation in the patterns of extractive exports across Sub-Saharan Africa—showing no systematic direction of the trend in concentration of natural resources in exports. Some countries, like Nigeria and Tanzania, reduced their shares of primary goods in exports to Asia, whereas other countries, like Ghana and Kenya, maintained or even increased those shares.

High-Skill- versus Low-Skill-Intensive Exports from Africa-5 to Asia

This subsection summarizes our sector-level analysis along the lines of skill intensity. We categorize sectors into high-skill and low-skill and show their shares in each Africa-5 country's total exports to Asia. We first measure a product's (HS 6-digit) skill intensity, using the share of workers with high school completion or above, in Chinese 4-digit manufacturing sectors 2002–04. The descriptions of the microdata and the concordances involved in matching the Chinese 4-digit manufacturing sectors to multiple HS 6-digit sectors are discussed in Ma, Tang, and Zhang (2014).

On the basis of this measure of product-level skill intensity, we aggregate exports from the entire Sub-Saharan African region across all HS 6-digit sectors that have a skill intensity measure above the median in the sample of more than 5,000 HS 6-digit categories. Because we have data for only manufacturing firms in China, the analysis of the skill intensity of Sub-Saharan African exports to both Asian and non-Asian countries is restricted to those from the manufacturing sector only.

By this analysis, the aggregate value of high-skill manufacturing exports to Asia was about $10.7 billion in 2005, accounting for 55 percent of Sub-Saharan Africa's exports to Asia that year (table 5.2, panel a). For the region's manufacturing exports to non-Asian destinations, the share of high-skill exports was lower (46 percent), amounting to $58.5 billion. Ten years later, in 2015, the share of high-skill exports to Asia from Sub-Saharan Africa had declined to 46 percent, although the export value more than doubled, to $24.2 billion. At the same time, the high-skill share of exports to non-Asian destinations rose, to 54 percent ($97.3 billion).

Over the same period, exports of the region's low-skill-intensive manufacturing exports to Asia increased more than threefold, from $8.7 billion in 2005 to $28.1 billion in 2015, driving the low-skill share from 45 percent to 54 percent of total manufacturing exports to Asia that year. Meanwhile, although the low-skill manufacturing exports to the non-Asian destinations increased in value, from $68.3 billion in 2005 to $83.1 billion in 2015, the low-skill share declined from 54 percent in 2005 to 46 percent in 2015.

Ethiopia

Turning to the first country in the Africa-5 group, Ethiopia's share of high-skill exports in its manufacturing exports to Asia is about the same as the Sub-Saharan African average. The share of high-skill exports from Ethiopia to Asia was 56 percent in 2005 ($150 million in goods), increasing to 59 percent by the end of 2015 and its value nearly tripling, to $424 million (figure 5.2, panel b).

Table 5.2 **High-Skill versus Low-Skill Manufacturing Exports from Sub-Saharan Africa and the Africa-5 Countries to Asian and Non-Asian Destinations, 2005 and 2015**

Skill intensity of exports, by origin and destination	2005		2015	
	Export value (US$, millions)	Export share, by destination (%)	Export value (US$, millions)	Export share, by destination (%)
a. Africa				
Skilled exports to Asia	10,700.00	55	24,200.00	46
Unskilled exports to Asia	8,690.29	45	28,100.00	54
Skilled exports to Non-Asia	58,500.00	46	97,300.00	54
Unskilled exports to Non-Asia	63,300.00	54	83,100.00	46
b. Ethiopia				
Skilled exports to Asia	150.87	56	423.92	59
Unskilled exports to Asia	118.12	44	293.48	41
Skilled exports to Non-Asia	388.01	41	1,512.57	38
Unskilled exports to Non-Asia	569.33	59	2,504.25	62
c. Ghana				
Skilled exports to Asia	78.32	65	145.23	42
Unskilled exports to Asia	41.98	35	204.57	58
Skilled exports to Non-Asia	699.60	38	1,155.22	61
Unskilled exports to Non-Asia	1,142.02	62	727.08	39
d. Kenya				
Skilled exports to Asia	147.72	34	253.16	32
Unskilled exports to Asia	285.73	66	536.85	68
Skilled exports to Non-Asia	1,176.26	38	1,449.79	33
Unskilled exports to Non-Asia	1,932.77	62	2,893.35	67

(Table continues on next page)

Table 5.2   High-Skill versus Low-Skill Manufacturing Exports from Sub-Saharan Africa and the Africa-5 Countries to Asian and Non-Asian Destinations, 2005 and 2015 *(continued)*

Skill intensity of exports, by origin and destination	2005		2015	
	Export value (US$, millions)	Export share, by destination (%)	Export value (US$, millions)	Export share, by destination (%)
e. Nigeria				
Skilled exports to Asia	58.39	40	325.40	23
Unskilled exports to Asia	89.11	60	1,064.82	77
Skilled exports to Non-Asia	1,534.22	58	1,303.40	67
Unskilled exports to Non-Asia	1,095.75	42	641. 06	33
f. Tanzania				
Skilled exports to Asia	69.37	14	620.58	37
Unskilled exports to Asia	409.67	86	1,038.86	63
Skilled exports to Non-Asia	326.51	32	1,140.51	36
Unskilled exports to Non-Asia	683.12	68	1,988.95	64

Source: Database for International Trade Analysis (BACI) and staff calculations.
Note: A product's (Harmonized System [HS] 6-digit) skill intensity is measured by using the share of "high-skilled" workers (those with high school completion or above) in that sector. The detailed methodology is discussed in Ma, Tang, and Zhang (2014). On the basis of this product-level skill intensity measure, we aggregate manufacturing exports from the entire Sub-Saharan African continent across all HS 6-digit sectors that have a skill intensity measure above the median (in the sample of more than 5,000 HS 6-digit categories) as the "skilled exports"; and the rest are referred as "unskilled exports." The data are restricted to manufacturing sectors because the Chinese data are available only for manufacturing firms. Full Sub-Saharan Africa export values are rounded to the nearest 100 million; country export values are rounded to the nearest 10,000.

In Ethiopia's exports to non-Asian countries, the share of high-skill goods in total manufacturing exports was smaller than both the Sub-Saharan African average and its own exports to Asia. The share of high-skill products in Ethiopia's exports to the rest of the world was 41 percent in 2005, declining to 38 percent in 2015.

In sum, Ethiopia's manufacturing exports to Asia have become more skill-intensive over time, whereas its manufacturing exports to non-Asian countries have become less skill-intensive. These developments were accompanied by the country's decreasing dependence on primary exports, as documented in table 5.1.

Ghana

Looking at the same set of statistics for Ghana, we see that high-skill exports made up 65 percent of its manufacturing exports to Asia in 2005, which exceeded the Sub-Saharan African average (table 5.2, panel c). Their total value amounted to $78.3 million. However, the share declined to 42 percent in 2015 (valued at $145.2 million), suggesting that exports to Asia were not related to skill upgrading in the country's manufacturing sector.

By contrast, Ghana's exports to the rest of the world started with lower skill content in 2005, because only 38 percent of its manufacturing exports were above the median level of skill intensity. But by 2015 that share reached 61 percent.

Kenya

High-skill exports made up about 34 percent of Kenya's total manufacturing exports to Asia in 2005, a significantly smaller share than the Sub-Saharan African average (table 5.2, panel d). Those exports amounted to $147.7 million in value. The share declined slightly, to 32 percent by the end of 2015 (valued at $253.2 million), consistent with the increase in the share of primary exports reported in table 5.1.

In Kenya's exports to non-Asian countries, the share of high-skill goods in total exports was also much smaller than the Sub-Saharan African average. The share of high-skill exports from Kenya to the rest of the world was only 38 percent in 2005, and it declined to 33 percent in 2015. In sum, the skill content of Kenya's exports has declined, whether going to Asian or to non-Asian destinations.

Nigeria

Nigeria's high-skill exports made up 40 percent of its total manufacturing exports to Asia in 2005, amounting to $58.4 million worth of goods (table 5.2, panel e). Despite the country's success in diversifying away from hyperspecialization in natural resources, as shown in table 5.1, the share of high-skill exports in the country's total exports to Asia declined to only 23 percent by 2015.

Nigeria's improvement in skill upgrading becomes more evident when looking at its manufacturing exports to non-Asian countries. The share of high-skill manufacturing exports from Nigeria to the rest of the world was 58 percent in 2005, increasing to 67 percent by 2015.

In sum, Nigeria's skill content in manufacturing exports to Asia declined, whereas it increased in the country's manufacturing exports to non-Asian countries—showing that growing economic engagement with Asia may not necessarily result in growth-inducing outcomes.

Tanzania

Finally, we examine the same set of statistics for Tanzania's exports to Asian and non-Asian destinations. The share of high-skill manufacturing exports from Tanzania to Asia was merely 14 percent in 2005 (valued at $69.4 million), which was much lower than the region's average (table 5.2, panel f). The share increased significantly, to 37 percent, by 2015 (valued at $620.6 million)—suggesting successful skill upgrading along with the stellar diversification from primary exports to Asia, as documented in table 5.1.

In Tanzania's exports to non-Asian countries, the share of high-skill manufactured goods in 2005, at 32 percent, was higher than its high-skill share of exports to Asia. The share to non-Asia destinations increased slightly, to 36 percent, by 2015.

In sum, similar to the pattern of extractive exports, there is significant heterogeneity in the shares of high-skill exports, and growth of the shares, across countries in Sub-Saharan Africa. There is no systematic direction of the trend in skill upgrading in exports or how it is related to economic engagement with Asia. After discussing the top Asian destinations for Sub-Saharan Africa's exports, we will turn to regression analysis to offer a more systematic investigation of the relationships.

Top Asian Destinations for the Africa-5 Nations' Exports

This subsection examines the potentially changing composition of Asian trading partners of Sub-Saharan African exporting countries. To this end, we aggregate the BACI trade data across all HS 6-digit categories to the country-pair level. For Sub-Saharan Africa as a whole and each of the Africa-5 countries, we examine the major Asian trading partners for imports and exports. Similar to our analysis of the sectoral distribution of exports from each nation, we exclude destination countries in Asia that accounted for less than 1 percent of a Sub-Saharan African nation's total exports in the respective year (2005 and 2015).

Among the Asian nations that accounted for at least 1 percent of Sub-Saharan Africa's exports in 2005 or 2015, China stands as the top destination. In 2005, China accounted for 41 percent of Sub-Saharan Africa's total exports to Asia—a share that increased modestly, to 43 percent, by 2015 (figure 5.7). Although China remains Sub-Saharan Africa's main trading partner, the small increase contrasts sharply with the media's description of China as dominating Sub-Saharan Africa's trade.

India is now the second-largest destination for the region's exports. In 2005, India ranked third in the share of exports from Sub-Saharan Africa to Asia, contributing 12 percent of Sub-Saharan Africa–Asia trade, following Japan, which accounted for 20 percent. The conventional thinking is that China has been increasing its dominance in Sub-Saharan Africa's trade. But, although China has risen rapidly as a source of investment in Sub-Saharan Africa, India is the Asian country that experienced the largest increase in export share from Sub-Saharan Africa, from 12 percent in 2005 to 29 percent in 2010.

Japan used to be a much more important trading partner for Sub-Saharan Africa, but, as China's and India's shares were growing at a much faster pace, Japan's share declined, from 20 percent to about 10 percent. Other important Asian destinations for Sub-Saharan Africa's exports in both years include the Republic of Korea, Malaysia, Singapore, and most recently Vietnam. Vietnam's share of trade with Africa was quite small (about $745 million) in 2005, but, by 2015, it had become the region's eighth-largest export destination.

Ethiopia

Similar to the region's overall pattern, China ranked as the top destination for Ethiopia's exports in 2015 (figure 5.8). However, its export pattern differed from the overall region's in 2005, when Japan rather than China was

Figure 5.7   Top Asian Destinations for Sub-Saharan Africa's Exports, 2005 and 2015

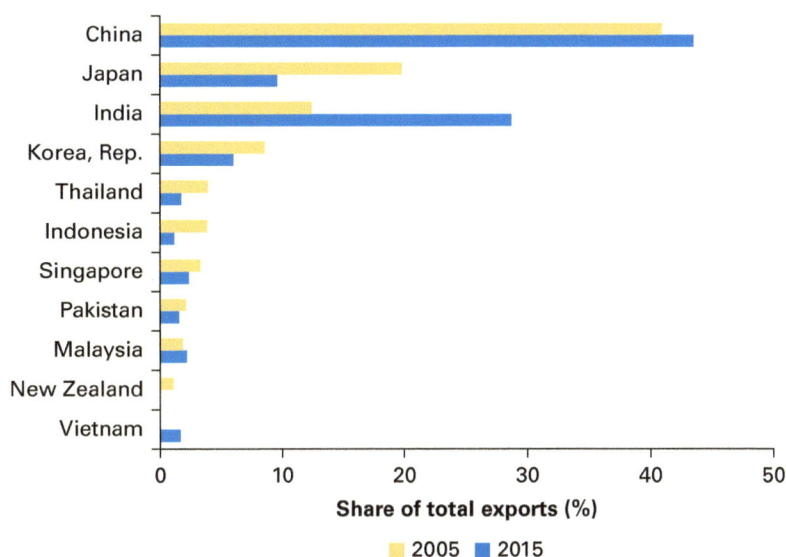

Share of total exports (%)

■ 2005   ■ 2015

Source: Staff calculations from the Database for International Trade Analysis (BACI) of the Centre for Prospective Studies and International Information (CEPII).
Note: Shares of exports are shown by Harmonized System (HS) HS 6-digit categories at the country-pair level, including only destination countries in Asia that accounted for at least 1 percent of Sub-Saharan Africa's exports in either of the respective years (2005 and 2015).

the country's top Asian destination. In 2015, Japan remained the second-largest destination for Ethiopian exports, instead of India.

Ethiopia has become increasingly dependent on China as an export market. In 2005, 36 percent of Ethiopia's total exports to Asia went to China, a share that increased to 55 percent in 2015. The share of its total exports going to India rose rapidly as well; however, because its base was much lower (only 5 percent in 2005), it accounted for only 9 percent of Ethiopia's exports to Asia in 2015. The first lesson from the comparison of Sub-Saharan Africa and Ethiopia is that what is true for the entire region may not be true for an individual country in the region.

Ghana

Among Ghana's export partners in Asia, what stands out is that India has emerged rapidly as the country's most important export destination. The country's top export destination in 2005 was China, which accounted for 26 percent of Ghana's exports to Asia. Since then, India's share has been increasing consistently, and India has become the top destination by a large margin (figure 5.9). In 2005, India was only the second-largest Asian market for Ghana's goods, accounting for 24 percent of Ghana's exports to Asia. By 2015, its share reached 64 percent, replacing China as the top destination, whose share declined to only 21 percent. The natural

Figure 5.8   Top Asian Destinations for Ethiopia's Exports, 2005 and 2015

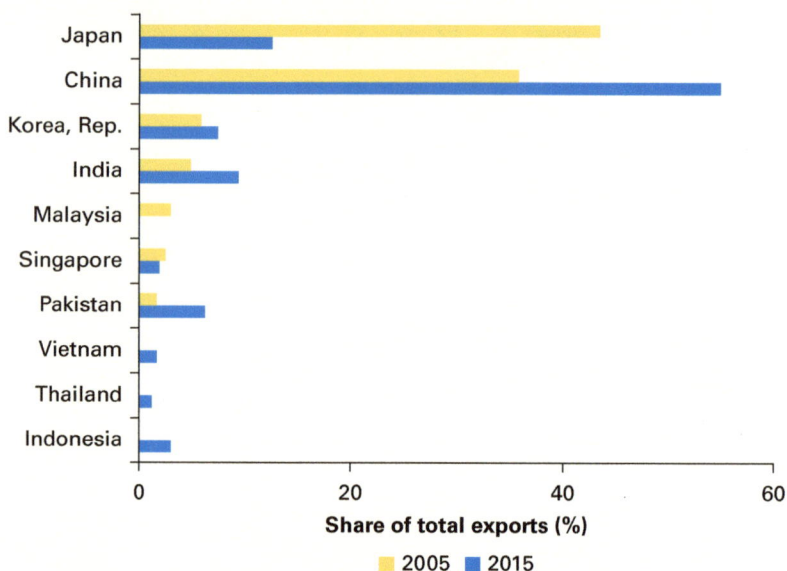

Source: Staff calculations from the Database for International Trade Analysis (BACI) of the Centre for Prospective Studies and International Information (CEPII).
Note: Shares of exports are shown by Harmonized System (HS) HS 6-digit categories at the country-pair level, including only destination countries in Asia that accounted for at least 1 percent of Ethiopia's exports in either of the respective years (2005 and 2015).

or cultured pearls sector expanded rapidly, becoming Ghana's main export sector (as shown in table 5.1). Indeed, this is a main reason why India has become Ghana's largest export destination in Asia.

Unlike Ethiopia, Ghana has not become more dependent on China but instead less dependent. This finding confirms that Asia affects the trade of each African nation in a unique way. The region's overall average trade patterns should not be relied upon to understand the experience of each individual country.

Kenya

Kenya's top Asian trading partners (for exports) are very different from those of Ethiopia and Ghana. Its top export destination in Asia is Pakistan, which in 2005 accounted for 42 percent of Kenya's exports to Asia, a share that increased to 43 percent by 2015 (figure 5.10).

Despite the significant increase in China's share of Kenya's exports, from 4.9 percent to 11.7 percent between 2005 and 2015, China remained a much less significant destination than Pakistan for Kenya's exports. India, which remains Kenya second-largest export destination, has been increasing rapidly as an export destination for other African nations.

Figure 5.9 **Top Asian Destinations for Ghana's Exports, 2005 and 2015**

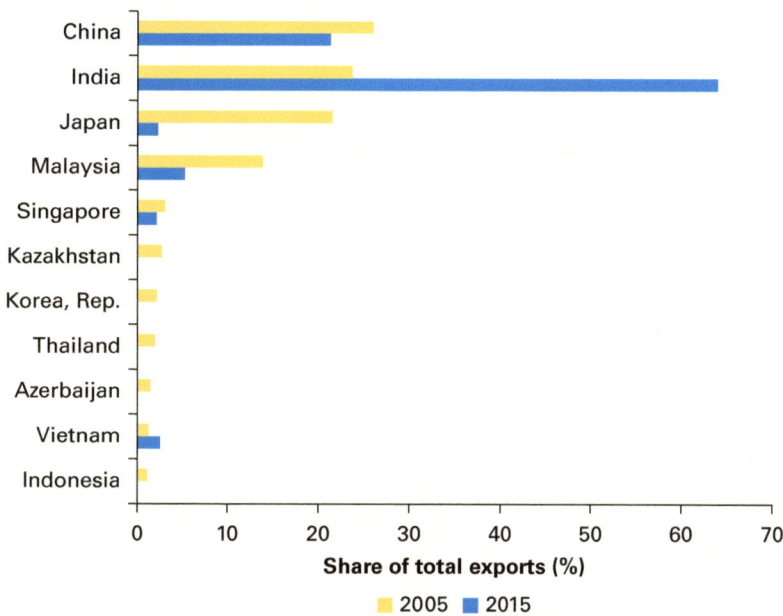

Share of total exports (%)

■ 2005 ■ 2015

Source: Staff calculations from the Database for International Trade Analysis (BACI) of the Centre for Prospective Studies and International Information (CEPII).
Note: Shares of exports are shown by Harmonized System (HS) HS 6-digit categories at the country-pair level, including only destination countries in Asia that accounted for at least 1 percent of Ghana's exports in either of the respective years (2005 and 2015).

Nigeria

For Nigeria—unlike Ethiopia, Ghana, and Kenya—China has never been a top export destination. In 2005, Nigeria's biggest Asian trading partner (in terms of exports) was Japan, accounting for 31 percent of total Nigerian exports to Asia (figure 5.11). Japan's contribution as a destination market dropped to 18 percent in 2015. India replaced Japan as the top destination in 2015. India's share of Nigerian exports to Asia was a mere 4 percent in 2005, accelerating to 64 percent in 2015.

As noted earlier (figure 5.5), the single most important sector for Nigerian exports to Asia has consistently been minerals, fuels, and mining. The sharp shift in Nigeria's main trading partners between 2005 and 2015 implies that raw materials are fairly homogeneous, making switching destination countries relatively easier for Nigeria than for other African nations that have different specialization patterns.

Tanzania

Finally, among Tanzania's Asian export destinations, China, which accounted for 42 percent of Tanzania's total exports to Asia in 2005, was replaced by India as the top destination in 2015 (figure 5.12). India

Figure 5.10   Top Asian Destinations for Kenya's Exports, 2005 and 2015

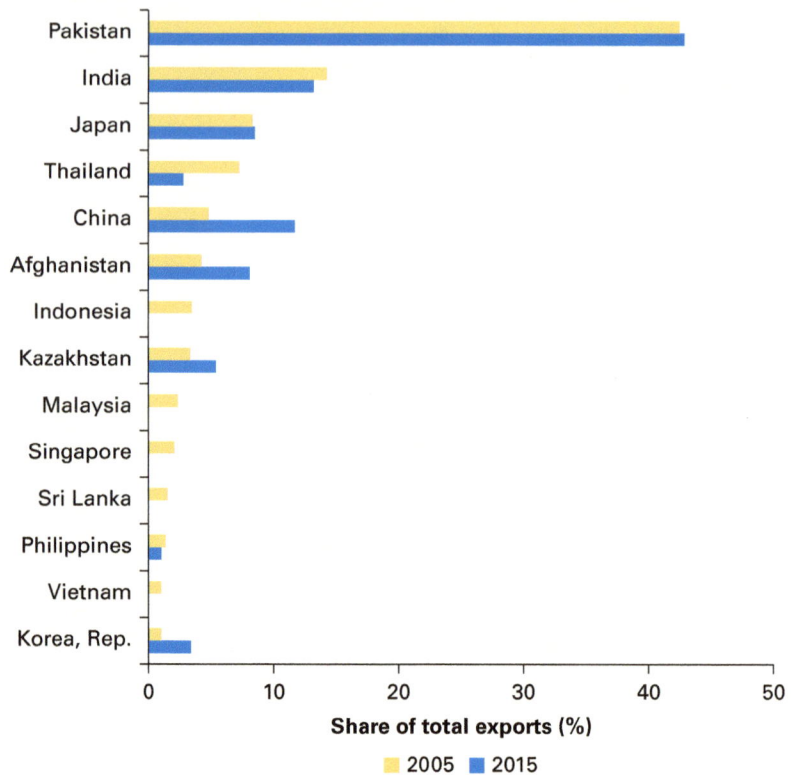

Source: Staff calculations from the Database for International Trade Analysis (BACI) of the Centre for Prospective Studies and International Information (CEPII).
Note: Shares of exports are shown by Harmonized System (HS) HS 6-digit categories at the country-pair level, including only destination countries in Asia that accounted for at least 1 percent of Kenya's exports in either of the respective years (2005 and 2015).

accounted for over 44 percent of Tanzania's exports to Asia in 2015, rising from only 20 percent in 2005.

Japan remained a stable number three market for Tanzania. Vietnam rose from an insignificant market to the fourth-largest market for Tanzania, accounting for about 5 percent of Tanzania's exports to Asia in 2015.

In sum, each of the Africa-5 countries has its own main trading partner in Asia. Contrary to the conventional wisdom, China is not always the dominant trading partner for individual African nations, although it is the case for the entire Sub-Saharan African region. India has emerged as an increasingly important trading partner of Africa. Since 2005, India has become the largest export destination in Asia for countries like Ghana, Nigeria, and Tanzania. What these three countries have in common is their high specialization in one particular raw material product—natural or cultured pearls for Ghana; minerals, fuels, and mining for Nigeria; and, to a lesser extent, ores, slag, and ash for Tanzania.

Figure 5.11 **Top Asian Destinations for Nigeria's Exports, 2005 and 2015**

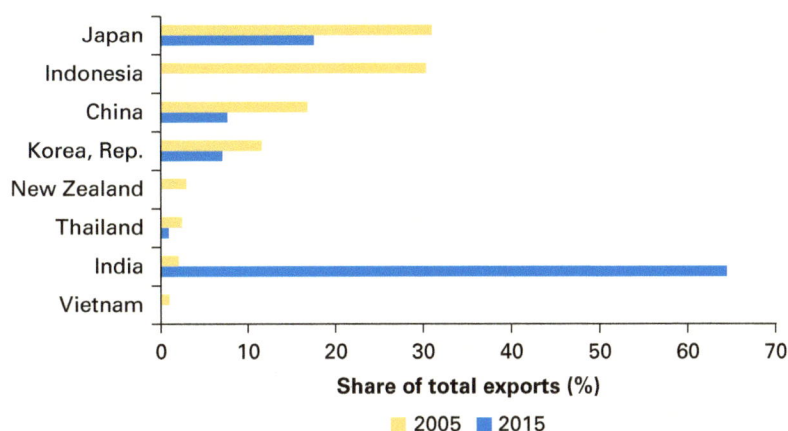

Share of total exports (%)

■ 2005 ■ 2015

Source: Staff calculations from the Database for International Trade Analysis (BACI) of the Centre for Prospective Studies and International Information (CEPII).
Note: Shares of exports are shown by Harmonized System (HS) HS 6-digit categories at the country-pair level, including only destination countries in Asia that accounted for at least 1 percent of Nigeria's exports in either of the respective years (2005 and 2015).

Figure 5.12 **Top Asian Destinations for Tanzania's Exports, 2005 and 2015**

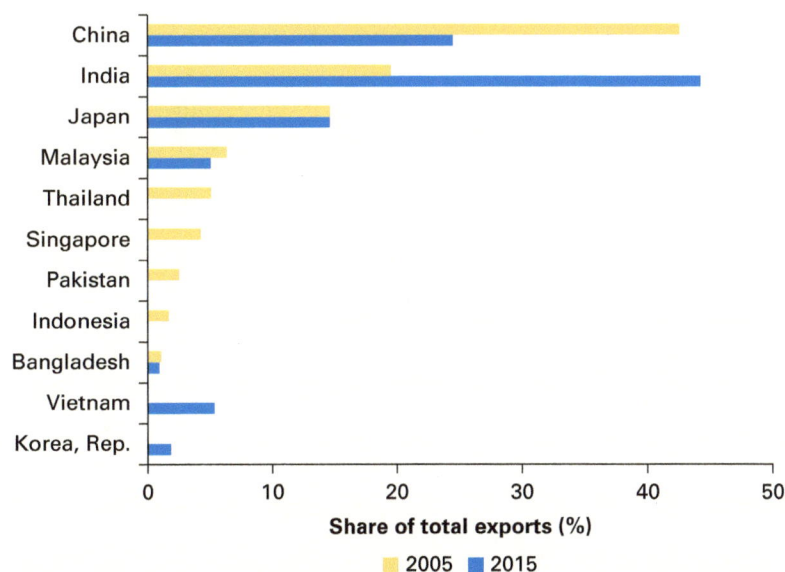

Share of total exports (%)

■ 2005 ■ 2015

Source: Staff calculations from the Database for International Trade Analysis (BACI) of the Centre for Prospective Studies and International Information (CEPII).
Note: Shares of exports are shown by Harmonized System (HS) HS 6-digit categories at the country-pair level, including only destination countries in Asia that accounted for at least 1 percent of Tanzania's exports in either of the respective years (2005 and 2015).

Econometric Assessment of Sub-Saharan African Participation in Asian GVCs

On the basis of the stylized facts described in the previous section, this section conducts an empirical analysis to understand whether economic engagement with Asia has shaped the particular trade and GVC patterns observed in individual Sub-Saharan African nations.

Our main sample covers 46 countries in Sub-Saharan Africa over a 16-year period from 2000 to 2015 (listed in annex 5A, table 5A.1). Several facts stand out from the analysis. First, Asia's economic engagement in trade with Sub-Saharan Africa increased significantly over the sample period. The share of imports from Asia in the total imports of a median Sub-Saharan African country in 2005 was 18 percent, which increased to 28 percent by 2015. The share of exports to Asia was only 12 percent in 2005, which rose to 20 percent by 2015. Of a Sub-Saharan African country's total imports, the median share *imported from* China in 2005 was 5 percent, which increased to 14 percent by 2015. The share of *exports to* China was only 2 percent in 2005, and tripled to 6 percent by 2015.

Second, we use three GVC measures as the dependent variables of interest: the ratio of domestic value added (DVA) to gross domestic product (GDP), the average length of production, and the upstreamness of exports, finding the following:

- Among the countries in our Sub-Saharan Africa sample, the median DVA declined slightly (from 0.37 to 0.35 between 2005 and 2015), consistent with the global trend of declining DVA (Johnson and Noguera 2012).
- Over the same period, the production chain of Sub-Saharan African exports became more complex, as revealed by the increasing average length of manufacturing production chains. For the median country (in terms of export volume), the export-weighted average of the number of stages (sectors) involved before final export rose from 2.31 to 2.36 between 2005 and 2015.
- Among the GVC measures, the upstreamness index—which captures the distance between the sector and final-goods consumers (at home or abroad)—increased the most. Among the countries in the sample, the median upstreamness index increased from 2.45 to 2.62.

A country's exports become "more upstream" for many reasons. One tempting explanation is that Sub-Saharan Africa's exports, partly because of China's economic engagement, have become more resource-intensive. Given that natural resource–intensive sectors tend to be more upstream, the observed increase in export upstreamness may be related to the increasing resource intensity of Sub-Saharan Africa's exports. This section empirically examines this hypothesis.

Complementarity of Exports to Asian and Non-Asian Markets

One hypothesis is that increasing demand from Asia could crowd out Sub-Saharan African countries' exports to other countries. To empirically examine this "trade diversion" hypothesis, we use as the dependent variable the log of exports from each Sub-Saharan African country to the rest of the world excluding Asia in each year (table 5.3). We subtract exports to Asia from exports to the rest of the world to remove any mechanical correlation between the dependent and independent variables of interest. Controlling for (exporting) country and year fixed effects, we find a positive and statistically significant correlation between a country's (log) exports to the rest of the world and its (lagged log) exports to Asia, as reported in column (1). This result suggests that, instead of trade diversion, exports to Asia complement exports to non-Asian countries.

In column (2), we add a country's log imports from Asia to consider the potential complementarity of imported inputs and technology from Asia on the country's exports. Controlling for country and year fixed effects, as well as (log) exports to Asia, we find that a country's imports from Asia are positively and significantly correlated with its exports to the rest of the world, suggesting that Asia may have provided intermediate inputs that facilitate individual countries' exports and participation in GVCs.

Exports to a country (or region) would complement exports to other countries for several reasons:

- In the presence of internal economies of scale, increased sales at the firm level, by tapping into more export markets, imply spreading the fixed costs of production by exporting over a larger volume of production, driving down the firm's average cost.
- In the presence of external economies of scale, increased exports may generate positive externalities between firms. Such positive externalities can take the form of labor pooling and technology spillover in exporting or special economic zones, or of information spillover between firms through learning about foreign markets.
- Participation in GVCs is a two-way game, as confirmed indirectly by the positive correlation between imports from Asia and exports to the rest of the world. More exports to a country usually come with more imports from the same country or other countries.

In general, imports of foreign intermediate inputs can increase a firm's productivity, which in turn raises its sales and profits. So the idea of trade diversion based on a zero-sum concept is a rare situation. There are many reasons why a country's GVC participation with a fast-growing region can serve as an engine of growth of the same country.

Table 5.3, columns (3) and (4), repeats the same analysis as in columns (1) and (2) but restricts it to (log) exports to and imports from, respectively, the Asia-5 countries as the regressors of interest. We adjust the dependent

Table 5.3   Correlation of Sub-Saharan Africa's Exports to Asia versus Exports to Other Countries

Dependent variable	ln(Exports to ROW except Asia)		ln(Exports to ROW except Asia-5)		ln(Exports to ROW except China)	
	(1)	(2)	(3)	(4)	(5)	(6)
ln(Exp to Asia)	0.184*** (2.749)	0.151** (2.454)				
ln(Imp from Asia)		0.204*** (4.073)				
ln(Exp to Asia-5)			0.114** (2.626)	0.106** (2.446)		
ln(Imp from Asia-5)				0.139* (1.909)		
ln(Exp to China)					0.0947*** (2.818)	0.0891*** (3.128)
ln(Imp from China)						0.185** (2.594)
Year FE	Y	Y	Y	Y	Y	Y
Country FE	Y	Y	Y	Y	Y	Y
N	710	710	698	698	681	681
R^2	0.957	0.958	0.956	0.957	0.957	0.959

Source: World Bank calculations.
Note: All independent variables are lagged one year. t-statistics, based on standard errors clustered at the country level, are in parentheses. The sample covers 46 Sub-Saharan African countries over 2000–15 (listed in annex 5A, table 5A.1). The "Asia-5" countries are Bangladesh, Cambodia, China, India, and Vietnam. FE = fixed effects; ln = natural logarithm; ROW = rest of the world.
* $p < 0.10$; ** $p < 0.05$; *** $p < 0.01$.

variable accordingly, by subtracting the exports to the Asia-5 nations from Sub-Saharan Africa's exports to the rest of the world in a year, so that the positive correlation between (log) exports to Asia and those to the rest of the world is not spurious. Within an (exporting) country and year, a country's (log) exports to the rest of the world are positively correlated with its (log) exports to and (log) imports from the Asia-5 countries, respectively.

These statistically significant results suggest that, instead of trade diversion, trade to Asia complements exports to other non-Asian countries. The elasticity of exports to the rest of the world in relation to exports to Asia-5 is smaller than that regarding exports to all of Asia. This is expected in light of the postulated spillover hypothesis. If internal and external economies of scale are the drivers, the positive effect of exporting to the entire Asian continent should be larger than exporting to only the Asia-5 countries.

Columns (5) and (6) in table 5.3 consider the potential crowding-out effect of exporting to China specifically. China has emerged as Sub-Saharan

Africa's largest trading partner. Analysts have expressed concern that Chinese economic engagement has displaced Sub-Saharan Africa's local industrial capability and made the region more dependent on economic support from China. After all, although China's increasing economic engagement in Sub-Saharan Africa has boosted the region's economic growth, it has also generated considerable controversy. We find that, contrary to the concern raised in the press and some research, more exports to and imports from China are positively related to trade with the rest of the world (with China excluded). In other words, trade with China does not divert resources away from exporting to other nations.

In table 5.4, we empirically explore the "crowding out" hypothesis, on the basis of aggregate export data from a hypothetical Sub-Saharan African country, by using the country's exports to the rest of the world at the (HS 2-digit) *sector level*. Specifically, we regress (log) Sub-Saharan African country C's exports to the rest of the world on (log) exports to Asia from the same country and sector (i). Controlling for year, country, and industry fixed effects, we find a positive and statistically significant correlation between (log) exports to Asia and (log) exports to the rest of the world in the same industry.

There may be a concern that a country's exports to Asia or any other country could be driven by a common supply shock (for example, technological shocks or government export-promotion policies). To address this concern, we control for country-year fixed effects in column (2). Or there may be a concern that a common global demand shock could lead to the observed positive correlation between a country's exports to Asia and the rest of the world. To tackle this concern, we control for industry-year fixed effects in column (3). The results reported in both columns (2) and (3) remain robust and are quantitatively similar to those reported in column (1).

In columns (4) to (6), using the same regression specifications, we find complementary effects of exports to Asia on exports to the rest of the world (excluding Asia) at the industry level. For instance, the coefficient on (log) exports to Asia in column (3) suggests that a 1 percent increase in exports to Asia is associated with a 0.413 percent increase in exports to non-Asian countries.

Following parallel specifications as in table 5.4 columns (1) to (3), we repeat the regressions with (log) exports to Asia-5 as the regressor of interest in columns (4) to (6) and (log) exports to China as the regressor of interest in columns (7) to (9), respectively. The dependent variable in each specification is adjusted accordingly by subtracting from exports to the rest of the world the exports to Asia-5 or China. Interestingly, controlling for various combinations of fixed effects, we find a negative and marginally significant correlation between exports to Asia-5 and exports to the rest of the world within the same HS 2-digit industry (columns [4] to [6]). When we restrict the analysis to exports to China only, however, we find complementarity between exports to China and exports to the rest of the world.

Table 5.4 Impact of Sub-Saharan African Countries' Exports to Asia versus Exports to Other Countries

Dependent variable	$\ln(\text{Exp}_{cit})$ to ROW			$\ln(\text{Exp}_{cit})$ to ROW except Asia-5			$\ln(\text{Exp}_{cit})$ to ROW except China		
	(1)	(2)	(3)	(4)	(5)	(6)	(7)	(8)	(9)
ln(Exp to Asia)	0.403*** (20.034)	0.406*** (19.769)	0.413*** (18.800)						
ln(Exp to Asia-5)				−0.0849** (−2.349)	−0.0733* (−1.903)	−0.0674* (−1.752)			
ln(Exp to China) (lagged)							0.327*** (17.587)	0.329*** (16.408)	0.343*** (13.870)
Year FE	Y			Y			Y		
Country FE	Y			Y			Y		
Industry (HS2) FE	Y	Y		Y	Y		Y	Y	
Country x Year FE		Y	Y		Y	Y		Y	Y
Industry x Year FE			Y			Y			Y
N	22,860	22,860	22,860	9,581	9,581	9,581	9,556	9,556	9,556
R^2	0.661	0.678	0.696	0.593	0.621	0.658	0.675	0.702	0.738

Source: World Bank data.

Note: t-statistics, based on standard errors clustered at the country level, are in parentheses. The sample covers 46 Sub-Saharan African countries over 2000–15 (listed in annex 5A, table 5A.1). The "Asia-5" countries are Bangladesh, Cambodia, China, India, and Vietnam. Exp_{cit} = exports from country c in sector i and year t; FE = fixed effects; HS2 = Harmonized System 2-digit level; ln = natural logarithm; ROW = rest of the world.

* $p < 0.10$; ** $p < 0.05$; *** $p < 0.01$.

In sum, together with the results in table 5.3, we find no empirical evidence of trade diversion due to economic exchanges with Asia as a whole or with China. However, exports to the Asia-5 countries are found to be related to trade diversion at the sector level, suggesting that exporting to one of the other four Asia-5 countries (Bangladesh, Cambodia, India, or Vietnam) could be related to trade diversion.

Factor Content in Exports

The next analysis takes a deeper look into the effects of Asian economic engagement on the pattern of Sub-Saharan Africa's exports. There have been concerns that the rapid economic growth of Asian emerging markets, by increasing the demand for natural resources, could act as a source of the "resource curse"—the paradox by which resource-rich countries fail to benefit fully from their natural resource wealth, instead facing challenges such as less economic growth and stability, poorer governance, more conflict, and worse development outcomes. If this speculation is correct, we would expect to see that more exports to Asia or selected Asian countries, such as China, are associated with deeper specialization in material-intensive exports such as ores or oils.

Material Intensity

To this end, table 5.5 regresses the weighted average of a Sub-Saharan African country's material intensity on the country's exports to Asia, Asia-5, and China (lagged by a year). We measure a sector's material intensity by the average firm's material cost per worker in the US manufacturing sector. We then compute the export-weighted average material intensity of a country in year t, using sector exports as weights. As reported in table 5.5, we find no statistically significant correlation between exports to Asia, Asia-5, or China and the weighted average material intensity of overall exports (to the rest of the world) from an individual Sub-Saharan African nation, controlling for country and year fixed effects.

Capital Intensity

Table 5.6 repeats the same set of regressions to examine whether engaging in a GVC with Asia is associated with more specialization in capital-intensive products such as ores and oils. To the extent that it is, we can argue that trade with Asia raises the demand for capital, which may lead to more investment and thus long-run growth.

As shown in columns (1) to (3), we find that proportionally more *exports to*, but not *imports from*, Asia are positively correlated with higher average capital intensity in exports to the rest of the world (including Asia), controlling for year and fixed effects. When we restrict the set of destinations to the Asia-5 countries (columns [4] to [6]) and China (columns [7] to [9]), we continue to find a positive correlation between the two variables.

In addition, we find that the shares of imports from Asia-5 and China are also positively correlated with capital deepening in countries' exports. The correlation with the share of imports from China is quantitatively larger,

Table 5.5   Correlation between Asian Economic Engagement and Material Intensity of Exports from Sub-Saharan Africa

Dependent variable	Export-weighted material intensity								
	(1)	(2)	(3)	(4)	(5)	(6)	(7)	(8)	(9)
Imp from Asia/Tot Imp	0.336 (1.070)		0.350 (1.084)						
Exp to Asia/ Tot Exp		0.239 (1.659)	0.247 (1.651)						
Imp from Asia-5/Tot Imp				0.611 (1.435)		0.680 (1.546)			
Exp to Asia-5/ Tot Exp					0.0100 (0.064)	0.0352 (0.227)			
Imp from China/Tot Imp							1.059 (1.504)		0.953 (1.434)
Exp to China/ Tot Exp								0.0965 (0.545)	0.106 (0.588)
Year FE	Y	Y	Y	V	Y	Y	Y	Y	Y
Country FE	Y	Y	Y	Y	Y	Y	Y	Y	Y
N	710	710	710	710	698	698	710	687	687
R^2	0.849	0.849	0.850	0.850	0.863	0.865	0.851	0.868	0.871

Source: World Bank data.
Note: All regressors are lagged one year. *t*-statistics, based on standard errors clustered at the country level, are in parentheses. We measure a sector's material intensity by the average firm's material cost per worker in the US manufacturing sector. We then compute the export-weighted average material intensity of a country in year *t*, using sector exports as weights. The sample covers 46 Sub-Saharan African countries over 2000–15 (listed in annex 5A, table 5A.1). The "Asia-5" countries are Bangladesh, Cambodia, China, India, and Vietnam. FE = fixed effects.

suggesting that Sub-Saharan African countries' engagement in the same value chains, with GVCs in particular, encourages investment and long-run economic growth.

Skill Intensity

Next, table 5.7 repeats the same set of regressions as in tables 5.5 and 5.6 to examine whether engaging in a GVC with Asia is positively associated with specialization in skill-intensive exports such as machinery. To the extent that it is, we can argue that trade with Asia can potentially increase the demand for skills and thus education, which may enhance a country's long-run growth.

In contrast to our encouraging findings in table 5.6, however, we find no significant correlation between (lagged) exports to Asia, Asia-5, or China and the weighted average of the skill intensity of overall exports from individual Sub-Saharan African nations.

Table 5.6 **Correlation between Asian Economic Engagement and Capital Intensity of Exports from Sub-Saharan Africa**

Dependent variable	Export-weighted capital intensity								
	(1)	(2)	(3)	(4)	(5)	(6)	(7)	(8)	(9)
Imp from Asia/ Tot Imp	0.399 (1.473)		0.422 (1.471)						
Exp to Asia/ Tot Exp		0.386** (2.640)	0.395** (2.556)						
Imp from Asia-5/Tot Imp				0.685* (1.864)		0.724* (1.889)			
Exp to Asia-5/ Tot Exp					0.317* (1.720)	0.344* (1.839)			
Imp from China/Tot Imp							1.144** (2.056)		1.051* (1.879)
Exp to China/ Tot Exp								0.506** (2.610)	0.516** (2.607)
Year FE	Y	Y	Y	Y	Y	Y	Y	Y	Y
Country FE	Y	Y	Y	Y	Y	Y	Y	Y	Y
N	710	710	710	710	698	698	710	687	687
R^2	0.855	0.857	0.858	0.856	0.866	0.869	0.858	0.873	0.878

Source: World Bank data.

Note: All regressors are lagged one year. t-statistics, based on standard errors clustered at the country level, are in parentheses. A sector's factor (capital, skilled) intensity measures are constructed on the basis of the Manufacturing Industry Database for US firms of the National Bureau of Economic Research (NBER) and US Census Bureau's Center for Economic Studies (CES). Out of 96 possible HS 2-digit sectors, 94 sectors have the sector factor intensity measures. The sample covers 46 Sub-Saharan African countries over 2000–15 (listed in annex 5A, table 5A.1). The "Asia-5" countries are Bangladesh, Cambodia, China, India, and Vietnam. FE = fixed effects.

* $p < 0.10$; ** $p < 0.05$; *** $p < 0.01$.

Patterns of GVC Participation

This subsection examines whether China's economic engagement has changed the way Sub-Saharan African nations participate in GVCs. To this end, we consider three value chain measures that are commonly used in the literature: upstreamness, the DVA ratio, and the average length of production. Although each measure captures a distinct concept of the extent of a country's GVC participation, each measure is also an indicator for whether a country has been participating in GVCs in a way to benefit the most from globalization.

As noted earlier, upstreamness captures how far a sector is from final-goods consumers. The DVA ratio captures how much of a country's GDP is generated by domestic content. The higher the DVA ratio, the more export revenue, proportionally, will be paid to domestic owners of factors or

Table 5.7 Correlation between Asian Economic Engagement and Skill Intensity of Exports from Sub-Saharan Africa

Dependent variable	Export-weighted skill intensity								
	(1)	(2)	(3)	(4)	(5)	(6)	(7)	(8)	(9)
Imp from Asia/Tot Imp	−0.00354 (−0.047)		−0.00809 (−0.106)						
Exp to Asia/Tot Exp		−0.0777 (−1.417)	−0.0779 (−1.406)						
Imp from Asia-5/Tot Imp				0.0625 (0.524)		0.0158 (0.142)			
Exp to Asia-5/Tot Exp					−0.0846 (−1.086)	−0.0840 (−1.085)			
Imp from China/Tot Imp							0.142 (0.729)		0.0809 (0.456)
Exp to China/Tot Exp								−0.0785 (−0.894)	−0.0778 (−0.879)
Year FE	Y	Y	Y	Y	Y	Y	Y	Y	Y
Country FE	Y	Y	Y	Y	Y	Y	Y	Y	Y
N	710	710	710	710	698	698	710	687	687
R^2	0.725	0.727	0.727	0.725	0.750	0.750	0.726	0.754	0.754

Source: World Bank data.

Note: All regressors are lagged one year. t-statistics, based on standard errors clustered at the country level, are in parentheses. A sector's factor (capital, skilled) intensity measures are constructed based on the Manufacturing Industry Database for US firms of the National Bureau of Economic Research (NBER) and US Census Bureau's Center for Economic Studies (CES). Out of 96 possible HS 2-digit sectors, 94 sectors have the sector factor intensity measures. The sample covers 46 Sub-Saharan African countries over 2000–15 (listed in annex 5A, table 5A.1). The "Asia-5" countries are Bangladesh, Cambodia, China, India, and Vietnam. FE = fixed effects.

suppliers of intermediates and materials. As such, any policies or shocks that enhance exports will have a larger impact on the exporting country's GDP.

The length of production of exports measures how many sector-country pairs are involved in a sector's production of exports. The longer the production process behind an exported product, the more complex it is, which implies more potential channels through which exports can benefit the rest of a country's economy.

Asian Economic Engagement and Upstreamness

We first examine whether China's economic engagement is related to the upstreamness of a country's exports. There are no direct implications about whether exports being more upstream is good for economic development, but the level of upstreamness portrays the structure of the domestic supply chain that generates the country's exports. Some of the most upstream sectors, constructed using information from the 2005 US input-output tables, include vegetable plaiting material; ores, slag, and ash; and fertilizers. These sectors have a large share of costs paid for raw materials and capital and thus have higher material and capital intensity. (For the top export sectors and trade partners of each of the Africa-5 countries—Ethiopia, Ghana, Kenya, Nigeria, and Tanzania—see annex 5A, tables 5A.2 to 5A.6.)

Using the same regression specifications and panel structure of the data as in table 5.7, table 5.8 regresses the export-weighted average of a country's upstreamness (with weights equal to the sectoral export shares in the total gross exports of a country) on a Sub-Saharan African country's (lagged) shares of imports from and exports to Asia.

In column (1), we find a positive and marginally significant (at the 10 percent level) correlation between a country's export upstreamness and the share of *imports from* Asia, after controlling for country and year fixed effects. Column (2) shows a positive and statistically more significant correlation between a country's export upstreamness and the share of *exports to* Asia. These results imply that, when a country is more engaged in GVCs with Asia, its exports on average will move upstream (away from consumers, at home and abroad). In column (3), when the shares of exports to and imports from Asia are included as regressors, in addition to the fixed effects, only the share of exports to Asia seems to matter.

In table 5.8, columns (4) to (6) repeat the same set of analyses but now consider trade with the Asia-5 countries only. Column (6) shows that imports from and exports to Asia-5 are correlated with a country's exports "moving up the value chain." According to the coefficients, the economic effects appear to be larger than those from trading with Asia only. When the share of *imports from* Asia-5 countries increases by 10 percentage points, a country's overall exports will move away from final-goods consumers by about 0.04 sector. The same magnitude increase in export share (to Asia-5 countries) implies a movement of exports toward the most upstream sector of supply chains by 0.06 sector. The effect of *exports to* Asia-5 is found to be economically significant.

The last three columns in table 5.8 consider trade shares with China. Column (9), which includes variables of imports from and exports to China, shows that the economic effects of trading with China on a country's export upstreamness seem to be even stronger. When the share of *imports from* China increases by 10 percentage points, a country's overall exports will move away from final-goods consumers by about 0.09 sector. The same magnitude increase in the share of *exports to* China implies a movement of exports toward the most upstream sector of supply chains by 0.1 sector.

Table 5.8   Correlation between Asian Economic Engagement and Upstreamness of Exports from Sub-Saharan Africa

Dependent variable	Export-weighted upstreamness								
	(1)	(2)	(3)	(4)	(5)	(6)	(7)	(8)	(9)
Imp from Asia/Tot Imp	0.333* (1.712)		0.367 (1.678)						
Exp to Asia/Tot Exp		0.584** (2.229)	0.592** (2.205)						
Imp from Asia-5/Tot Imp				0.464 (1.498)		0.586* (1.719)			
Exp to Asia-5/Tot Exp					0.631** (2.151)	0.652** (2.190)			
Imp from China/Tot Imp							0.866* (1.742)		0.895* (1.713)
Exp to China/Tot Exp								0.991*** (3.411)	0.999*** (3.418)
Year FE	Y	Y	Y	Y	Y	Y	Y	Y	Y
Country FE	Y	Y	Y	Y	Y	Y	Y	Y	Y
N	710	710	710	710	698	698	710	687	687
R^2	0.875	0.884	0.885	0.875	0.885	0.887	0.877	0.897	0.901

Source: World Bank data.

Note: All regressors are lagged one year. t-statistics, based on standard errors clustered at the country level, are in parentheses. "Upstreamness" refers to an input's average distance from final use (Antràs et al. 2012), used as a measure of a sector's distance from final-use consumers. The sample covers 46 Sub-Saharan African countries over 2000–15 (listed in annex 5A, table 5A.1). The "Asia-5" countries are Bangladesh, Cambodia, China, India, and Vietnam. FE = fixed effects.

* $p < 0.10$; ** $p < 0.05$; *** $p < 0.01$.

Asian Economic Engagement and DVA Ratio

We next examine whether trade with Asia affects Sub-Saharan African nations' movement along a GVC, as measured by the ratio of DVA to gross exports. The Global Trade Analysis Project's input-output tables are available only for 2004, 2007, and 2011. Thus, instead of using the fixed-effect models that we used to examine the other dependent variables of interest, we adopt a long-difference approach.

Table 5.9 regresses the change in the DVA ratio of a country's exports on all regressors of interest from 2004 and 2011. We find that (the change in) the share of *imports from* Asia is not related to the average DVA ratio of Sub-Saharan African countries' exports (column [1]). However, changes in the share of *exports to* Asia seem to be negatively correlated with the DVA ratio of a country's exports (column [2]). However, when we include changes in shares of imports from and exports to Asia, in column (3), the statistical significance disappears.

The rest of table 5.9 shows that there is no significant relationship between a country's DVA ratio and engagement in a GVC with Asia. A possible reason behind the lack of significant results is that the sample size covers only 23 countries, which is half the original sample of 46 Sub-Saharan African nations, because of missing data from many of the countries for the designated years.

Table 5.9 Correlation between Asian Economic Engagement and DVA Participation of Sub-Saharan Africa

Dependent variable	Weighted average ratio of DVA to gross exports								
	(1)	(2)	(3)	(4)	(5)	(6)	(7)	(8)	(9)
Change in share of imp from Asia	0.0652 (0.276)		−0.0329 (−0.129)						
Change in share of exp to Asia		−0.263* (−1.708)	−0.266 (−1.674)						
Change in share of imp from Asia-5				0.0397 (0.158)		0.0678 (0.252)			
Change in share of exp to Asia-5					0.107 (0.481)	0.111 (0.484)			
Change in share of imp from China							0.751 (1.341)		0.717 (1.246)
Change in share of exp to China								0.716 (1.192)	0.697 (1.240)
N	46	46	46	46	46	46	46	46	46
R^2	0.00098	0.0967	0.097	0.000296	0.00821	0.00906	0.0569	0.093	0.145

Source: World Bank data.
Note: t-statistics, based on standard errors clustered at the country level, are in parentheses. The sample covers the 23 Sub-Saharan African countries for which full data were available over 2000–15. The "Asia-5" countries are Bangladesh, Cambodia, China, India, and Vietnam. DVA = domestic value added.
* $p < 0.10$; ** $p < 0.05$; *** $p < 0.01$.

Asian Economic Engagement and Length of Production

In table 5.10, we use the same long-difference specification to examine the relationship between Asian economic engagement and the average length of production involved in a country's exports. An increase in the length of production implies more complex production, suggesting that there are large potential gains from trade for a country.

Similar to the findings on the relation between exports to Asia and a country's DVA ratio, we find no significant relationship between changes in the share of *imports from* Asia and the length of production for Sub-Saharan Africa's exports. However, we find a negative but marginally significant relation between the share of *exports to* Asia and the length of production. Such negative correlation is quantitatively larger when a country imports

Table 5.10 Correlation between Asian Economic Engagement and Sub-Saharan African Participation in a Complex GVC

Dependent variable	Export-weighted production length								
	(1)	(2)	(3)	(4)	(5)	(6)	(7)	(8)	(9)
Change in share of imp from Asia	−0.420 (−0.421)		−0.783 (−0.908)						
Change in share of exp to Asia		−0.933 (−1.619)	−0.981* (−1.746)						
Change in share of imp from Asia-5				−1.496** (−2.181)		−1.585* (−1.891)			
Change in share of exp to Asia-5					−0.247 (−0.229)	−0.352 (−0.321)			
Change in share of imp from China							−2.243 (−1.443)		−2.337 (−1.518)
Change in share of exp to China								1.817 (0.746)	1.881 (0.736)
N	46	46	46	46	46	46	46	46	46
R^2	0.00317	0.0944	0.105	0.0328	0.00343	0.0396	0.0395	0.0466	0.0893

Source: World Bank data.

Note: t-statistics, based on standard errors clustered at the country level, are in parentheses. The sample covers the 23 Sub-Saharan African countries for which full data were available over 2000–15. The "Asia-5" countries are Bangladesh, Cambodia, China, India, and Vietnam.

* $p < 0.10$; ** $p < 0.05$; *** $p < 0.01$.

proportionally more from the Asia-5 countries, as shown in columns (4) and (6).

These results suggest that, if anything, imports may have shortened the supply chain in Sub-Saharan Africa by replacing some of the complex intermediate inputs that used to be sourced locally. However, we find no significant correlation between trade with China and the average length of production behind Sub-Saharan Africa's exports (columns [7] and [9]).

Exports to Asia and Extent of Trade Diversion

Finally, we use export data at the country-sector level to study whether exports to Asia change the pattern of exports to other countries. In other words, we are interested in examining whether trade diversion happens in certain types of industries (or exporting countries) but not others. To this end, we regress (log) exports at the sector (HS 2-digit) level to the rest of the world or Asia (both excluding China as a destination) on (log) exports to Asia as well as their interaction with various sector factor intensities (table 5.11). Country-year fixed effects are included to capture exporting country-specific supply shocks. Industry-year fixed effects are included to control for global demand shocks for a particular product, such as a commodity.

As shown in column (1), we continue to find complementary effects of exports to Asia on exports to the rest of the world. However, we do not find stronger complementary effects in the more upstream sectors, suggesting that the increase in upstreamness of exports observed in a country's overall exports should be related to more upstream products exported to Asia rather than to the rest of the world. In column (2), we find that the complementary effects on exports to the rest of the world are weaker for skill-intensive products.

The regression results from analyzing the complementary effects of participation in Asia-5's GVCs are more intriguing. First, as reported in table 5.11, column (3), the overall complementary effects on exports are concentrated in the more-upstream sectors. Column (4) shows, in addition, that the effects are stronger in the material-intensive sectors and weaker in the skill-intensive sectors. These results appear to contrast with the findings in tables 5.6 and 5.7, which show capital deepening instead of resource intensification in overall exports in response to increased engagement in GVCs with Asia. Using the same reasoning we employed to explain the seemingly conflicting results between table 5.11 column (2) and table 5.8, we postulate the following possibility: although more exports to Asia-5 are not associated with more material-intensive exports to Asia-5, they do induce more exports of those goods to non–Asia-5 countries.

In table 5.11, the final two columns show that more exports to China are associated with more exports to the rest of the world, particularly for the more upstream sectors. However, we find no systematic change in the specialization patterns measured in terms of the three factor intensities.

Table 5.11   Effects of Increased Sub-Saharan African Exports to Asia on the Pattern of Trade to Other Countries

Dependent variable	ln(Exp$_{cit}$) to ROW except Asia		ln(Exp$_{cit}$) to ROW except Asia-5		ln(Exp$_{cit}$) to ROW except China	
	Asia		Asia-5		China	
Destination country group	(1)	(2)	(3)	(4)	(5)	(6)
ln(Exp to group) (lagged)	0.379***	0.237	−0.415***	−1.265***	0.270* **	0.170
	(8.838)	(1.595)	(−6.108)	(−6.475)	(6.845)	(1.136)
ln(Exp to group) (lagged) x w/upstreamness	0.0161		0.111***		0.0351**	
	(1.020)		(4.247)		(1.992)	
Capital intensity$_{US}$		0.0117		−0.0105		0.0160
		(0.490)		(−0.251)		(0.587)
Material intensity$_{US}$		−0.0174		0.171***		−0.00230
		(−0.635)		(3.980)		(−0.079)
Skill intensity$_{US}$		−0.157***		−0.221***		−0.0869
		(−2.770)		(−4.529)		(−1.527)
Country x Year FE	Y	Y	Y	Y	Y	Y
Industry x Year FE	Y	Y	Y	Y	Y	Y
N	30,373	29,698	13,700	13,477	13,611	13,389
R^2	0.697	0.704	0.656	0.665	0.727	0.734

Source: World Bank data.
Note: t-statistics, based on standard errors clustered at the country level, are in parentheses. The sample covers 46 Sub-Saharan African countries over 2000–15 (listed in annex 5A, table 5A.1). Asia includes all member countries of the Asian Development Bank except Australia, China, and New Zealand. The "Asia-5" countries are Bangladesh, Cambodia, China, India, and Vietnam. Exp$_{cit}$ = exports of a country c in sector i and year t; FE = fixed effects; ln = natural logarithm; ROW = rest of the world (excluding Asia, Asia-5, or China); US = the measures of intensity employ the United States' manufacturing sector as the basis.
* $p < 0.10$; ** $p < 0.05$; *** $p < 0.01$.

Country Characteristics and Policy Implications of the Trade Links between Sub-Saharan Africa and Asia

This subsection presents an empirical analysis to examine which country characteristics affect the way trade with Asia shapes Sub-Saharan African nations' participation in GVCs. We identify several key policy interventions for countries to consider for maximizing the benefits of trade with Asia. To this end, we add interaction terms between key country characteristics of economic fundamentals and institutions and the measures of trade with Asia. The country characteristics we consider include three individual country measures of institutions (rule of law, corruption, and political stability) and three measures of economic fundamentals (the natural logarithm [ln] GDP per capita, [ln] natural resources, and whether the country is landlocked).

Given that we have found that trade with Asia can increase Sub-Saharan African countries' average upstreamness and capital intensity of exports, we use these two averages as our dependent variables of interest for the policy analysis.

Implications for Upstreamness

When a country's export-weighted average of upstreamness is used as the dependent variable (table 5.12), we find that, although a larger proportion of a country's *exports to* Asia is associated with the country's overall export upstreamness, the relation is weaker for Sub-Saharan African countries that have a higher corruption index on average (column [2]). There is no significant relation between export upstreamness and individual countries' share of *imports from* Asia. However, we find that a country's measure of rule of law (column [1]) or political stability (column [3]) does not seem to be related to its export upstreamness.

As for the measures of economic fundamentals, in columns (4) through (6), we find that the positive relation between export upstreamness and the share of *exports to* Asia is weaker for countries that have a larger GDP per capita and access to the sea (that is, not landlocked), as suggested by the negative and significant coefficients on the corresponding interaction terms.

Table 5.12 Correlations between Country Institutions, Asian Economic Engagement, and Upstreamness of Sub-Saharan African Exports

Dependent variable	Export-weighted upstreamness					
	Rule of law	Corruption	Political stability	(ln) GDP per capita	(ln) Resources	Landlocked
Country characteristic	(1)	(2)	(3)	(4)	(5)	(6)
Imp from Asia/Tot Imp	0.231	0.150	0.396	1.383	0.339	0.373
	(0.622)	(0.229)	(1.588)	(1.114)	(1.205)	(1.256)
Exp to Asia/Tot Exp	0.215	2.092**	0.443	2.853**	0.440	0.815***
	(0.506)	(2.603)	(1.289)	(2.654)	(0.991)	(3.097)
Country Characteristic x Imp from Asia/Tot Imp	−0.119	0.118	0.0433	−0.145	−0.00742	0.0197
	(−0.284)	(0.378)	(0.178)	(−0.973)	(−1.006)	(0.054)
Exp to Asia/Tot Exp	−0.270	**−0.896****	−0.0269	**−0.310****	0.00465	**−0.797****
	(−0.563)	**(−2.090)**	(−0.100)	**(−2.521)**	(0.419)	**(−2.622)**
Year FE	Y	Y	Y	Y	Y	Y
Country FE	Y	Y	Y	Y	Y	Y
N	691	691	691	602	592	608
R^2	0.887	0.890	0.887	0.908	0.902	0.893

Source: World Bank data.
Note: All regressors are lagged one year. *t*-statistics, based on standard errors clustered at the country level, are in parentheses. The sample covers 46 Sub-Saharan African countries over 2000–15 (listed in annex 5A, table 5A.1). Bolded values indicate high significance. FE = fixed effects; ln = natural logarithm.
* $p < 0.10$; ** $p < 0.05$; *** $p < 0.01$.

Implications for Capital Intensity

We next consider how the same sets of countries' characteristics affect the relation between the extent of trade with Asia and the capital intensity of the countries' overall exports (to the rest of the world). As reported in table 5.13, although we find that proportionally more exports to Asia are associated with capital deepening of Sub-Saharan African countries' exports, the additional effects related to the six country characteristics are not as strong as those in table 5.12. The only country characteristic that appears to matter is GDP per capita. Sub-Saharan African countries that are relatively poorer appear to benefit more from exporting to Asia, in terms of capital deepening in their export baskets.

From the results in tables 5.12 and 5.13, we learn that countries that are relatively poorer or have access to the sea benefit more from GVC engagement with Asia. Governments of Sub-Saharan African countries, especially those along the coast of the continent, can consider policies to promote exports to Asia as a tool for poverty reduction. And policies that reduce

Table 5.13 Correlations between Country Institutions, Asian Economic Engagement, and Capital Intensity of Sub-Saharan African Exports

Dependent variable	Export-weighted capital intensity					
Country characteristic	Rule of law (1)	Corruption (2)	Political stability (3)	(ln) GDP per capita (4)	(ln) Resources (5)	Landlocked (6)
Imp from Asia/Tot Imp	−0.188	1.069	0.0194	1.843	0.236	0.255
	(−0.350)	(1.101)	(0.065)	(1.209)	(0.598)	(0.766)
Exp to Asia/Tot Exp	0.0532	1.026**	0.264	2.717***	0.220	0.489***
	(0.175)	(2.102)	(1.320)	(3.819)	(0.815)	(3.141)
Country Characteristic x Imp from Asia/Tot Imp	−0.528	−0.417	−0.391	−0.187	0.00182	0.820*
	(−0.886)	(−0.785)	(−1.172)	(−0.983)	(0.183)	(1.934)
Exp to Asia/Tot Exp	−0.317	−0.377	−0.162	−0.316***	0.00485	−0.127
	(−0.927)	(−1.285)	(−0.672)	(−3.509)	(0.646)	(−0.455)
Year FE	Y	Y	Y	Y	Y	Y
Country FE	Y	Y	Y	Y	Y	Y
N	691	691	691	602	592	608
R^2	0.862	0.856	0.861	0.870	0.863	0.863

Source: World Bank data.

Note: All regressors are lagged one year. *t*-statistics, based on standard errors clustered at the country level, are in parentheses. The sample covers 46 Sub-Saharan African countries over 2000–15 (listed in annex 5A, table 5A.1). FE = fixed effects; ln = natural logarithm.

* $p < 0.10$; ** $p < 0.05$; *** $p < 0.01$.

corruption can enhance a country's economic efficiency in general and increase the benefits of trade with Asia in particular.

Conclusion and Policy Implications

This chapter studied the effects of Asia's economic engagement on individual Sub-Saharan African nations' participation in GVCs. It first used detailed trade statistics to describe the overall GVC trends between Asia and Sub-Saharan Africa in recent years. The chapter then measured and identified the key exporting sectors driving participation in GVCs by Sub-Saharan Africa as a whole and by selected Sub-Saharan African nations (the Africa-5). The findings show that, although overall exports from Sub-Saharan Africa to Asia are still highly concentrated in resource-intensive sectors, a few countries have leveraged the export booms to Asia to diversify their export portfolios. Furthermore, each Sub-Saharan African nation has a distinct main trading partner in Asia, in contrast to the traditional thinking that China has become Sub-Saharan Africa's dominant trading partner. For example, India has emerged as a leading trading partner of many Sub-Saharan African nations.

Using a panel data set of trade for 46 Sub-Saharan African countries over 16 years (2000–15), the regression analyses show that Asian countries' economic engagement complements rather than crowds out Sub-Saharan African countries' exports to the rest of the world. In other words, the analysis does not find evidence of trade diversion due to participation in Asian GVCs.

Using panel data on trade at the country-industry level, the analysis also finds that Asian economic engagement in the continent is associated with an increase in upstreamness. In addition, proportionally more imports from Asia are associated with shortening of the production chains of a Sub-Saharan African nation's exports. However, trade with Asia has no effect on the domestic content in Sub-Saharan Africa's exports. Engagement with Asian GVCs resulted in capital deepening of Sub-Saharan African exports but not in enhancement of the exports' skill intensity. Such capital deepening of exports is mostly driven by more exports of capital-intensive goods to Asia rather than by exports of such goods to the rest of the world. The analysis also finds that the complementarity effects of trade with Asia on a country's exports to the rest of the world are concentrated in material-intensive sectors, suggesting that engagement in Asian GVCs does not necessarily enhance the economic growth of Sub-Saharan Africa.

The regression results show that proportionally more *exports to* but not *imports from* Asia can help Sub-Saharan African nations move up the value chains. The effects are particularly strong among Sub-Saharan African countries that have access to the sea but are relatively poorer than their Sub-Saharan African peers. Corruption appears to impede not only trade but also the benefits from GVC participation. This result helps explain why anticorruption policies can enhance economic efficiency. Surprisingly, the general measure of a country's rule of law does not affect the relation between countries' trade with Asia and their GVC outcomes.

As for identifying which value chains in Asia, if any, promise the largest potential for Sub-Saharan African nations to diversify their exports or move up the value chains, based on the assessment in this chapter, it is not easy to come up with a definite list of products or countries. The chapter reveals that countries that are more dependent on natural resources, like Nigeria, seem to have diversified successfully away from primary goods, thanks to trade with Asia.

The chapter also finds that the region's countries that are relatively poorer or have access to the sea benefit more from GVC engagement with Asia. Governments of Sub-Saharan African countries, especially those that are along the coast of the continent, could consider policies to promote more participation in Asian value chains as a vehicle for poverty reduction.

Annex 5A Supplementary Tables

Table 5A.1   List of Sub-Saharan African Countries in the Study Sample

ISO code	Country
DZA	Algeria
AGO	Angola
BEN	Benin
BDI	Burundi
CPV	Cabo Verde
CMR	Cameroon
CAF	Central African Rep.
TCD	Chad
COG	Congo, Rep.
CIV	Côte d'Ivoire
COD	Congo, Dem. Rep.
DJI	Djibouti
EGY	Egypt, Arab Rep.
GNQ	Equatorial Guinea
ERI	Eritrea
ETH	Ethiopia

(Table continues on next page)

Table 5A.1   List of Sub-Saharan African Countries in the Study Sample *(continued)*

ISO code	Country
GAB	Gabon
GMB	Gambia, The
GHA	Ghana
GIN	Guinea
KEN	Kenya
LBR	Liberia
LBY	Libya
MDG	Madagascar
MWI	Malawi
MLI	Mali
MRT	Mauritania
MUS	Mauritius
MAR	Morocco
MOZ	Mozambique
NER	Niger
NGA	Nigeria
RWA	Rwanda
STP	São Tomé and Príncipe
SEN	Senegal
SYC	Seychelles
SLE	Sierra Leone
ZAF	South Africa
SSD	South Sudan
SDN	Sudan
TGO	Togo
TUN	Tunisia
UGA	Uganda
TZA	Tanzania
ZMB	Zambia
ZWE	Zimbabwe

Source: International Organization for Standardization (ISO).

Table 5A.2   **Ethiopia's Top Five Sectors by Its Top Five Trade Partners, 2005 and 2015**

Top destinations	Sector rank	HS code	Sector	Exports (US$, million)
a. 2005				
Japan	1	09	Coffee, tea, maté	114.298
	2	41	Raw hides and skins	1.994
	3	12	Oil seeds	1.419
	4	15	Animal or vegetable fat	0.401
	5	05	Dairy produce	0.090
China	1	12	Oil seeds	66.360
	2	41	Raw hides and skins	14.994
	3	26	Ores, slag, and ash	8.739
	4	09	Coffee, tea, maté	5.619
	5	13	Lac, gums, resins	0.666
Korea, Rep.	1	72	Iron and steel	10.862
	2	12	Oil seeds	2.600
	3	09	Coffee, tea, maté	1.591
	4	05	Dairy produce	0.774
	5	41	Raw hides and skins	0.019
India	1	41	Raw hides and skins	4.882
	2	69	Ceramic products	1.639
	3	07	Edible vegetables	1.633
	4	12	Oil seeds	1.271
	5	09	Coffee, tea, maté	1.089
Malaysia	1	41	Raw hides and skins	6.587
	2	12	Oil seeds	1.261
	3	52	Cotton	0.252
	4	07	Edible vegetables	0.179
	5	09	Coffee, tea, maté	0.156
b. 2015				
China	1	12	Oil seeds	294.143
	2	41	Raw hides and skins	47.495
	3	64	Footwear, gaiters	15.065
	4	86	Railway/ tramway locomotives	7.555
	5	26	Ores, slag, and ash	6.911
Japan	1	09	Coffee, tea, maté	76.238
	2	12	Oil seeds	6.340
	3	06	Live trees and other	4.251

(Table continues on next page)

Table 5A.2   Ethiopia's Top Five Sectors by Its Top Five Trade Partners, 2005 and 2015 *(continued)*

Top destinations	Sector rank	HS code	Sector	Exports (US$, million)
	4	15	Animal or vegetable fat	0.932
	5	72	Iron and steel	0.792
India	1	07	Edible vegetables	39.119
	2	12	Oil seeds	8.549
	3	41	Raw hides and skins	8.243
	4	71	Natural or cultured pearls	6.422
	5	09	Coffee, tea, maté	2.869
Korea, Rep.	1	09	Coffee, tea, maté	34.924
	2	12	Oil seeds	17.733
	3	62	Apparel access, non-knitted	0.784
	4	05	Dairy produce	0.511
	5	41	Raw hides and skins	0.256
Pakistan	1	07	Edible vegetables	41.180
	2	09	Coffee, tea, maté	3.192
	3	12	Oil seeds	0.343
	4	23	Food residues and waste	0.120
	5	41	Raw hides and skins	0.030

Source: Database for International Trade Analysis (BACI) of the Centre for Prospective Studies and International Information (CEPII).
Note: HS = Harmonized System.

Table 5A.3   Ghana's Top Five Sectors by Its Top Five Trade Partners, 2005 and 2015

Top destinations	Sector rank	HS code	Sector	Exports (US$, million)
a. 2005				
China	1	26	Ores, slag, and ash	51.580
	2	18	Cocoa and cocoa prep	25.729
	3	44	Wood	3.390
	4	74	Copper and articles	2.998
	5	12	Oil seeds	1.601
India	1	44	Wood	33.820
	2	08	Edible fruits	27.367
	3	18	Cocoa and cocoa prep	8.285
	4	72	Iron and steel	5.407
	5	12	Oil seeds	4.300

(Table continues on next page)

Table 5A.3   Ghana's Top Five Sectors by Its Top Five Trade Partners, 2005 and 2015 *(continued)*

Top destinations	Sector rank	HS code	Sector	Exports (US$, million)
Japan	1	18	Cocoa and cocoa prep	65.695
	2	26	Ores, slag, and ash	4.479
	3	03	Fish and crustaceans	3.249
	4	22	Beverages, spirits, and vinegar	0.804
	5	44	Wood	0.465
Malaysia	1	18	Cocoa and cocoa prep	47.192
	2	44	Wood	0.623
	3	14	Vegetable plaiting material	0.412
	4	22	Beverages, spirits, and vinegar	0.130
	5	40	Rubber and articles	0.0474
Singapore	1	18	Cocoa and cocoa prep	8.330
	2	22	Beverages, spirits, and vinegar	1.080
	3	44	Wood	0.741
	4	14	Vegetable plaiting material	0.225
	5	82	Tools, implements, cutlery	0.199
b. 2015				
India	1	71	Natural or cultured pearls	3,010.022
	2	08	Edible fruits	86.391
	3	44	Wood	59.569
	4	76	Aluminum and articles	16.537
	5	12	Oil seeds	14.174
China	1	27	Minerals, fuels, and mining	863.683
	2	26	Ores, slag, and ash	94.994
	3	18	Cocoa and cocoa prep	50.652
	4	44	Wood	49.942
	5	12	Oil seeds	5.373
Malaysia	1	18	Cocoa and cocoa prep	244.273
	2	15	Animal or vegetable fat	14.0392
	3	40	Rubber and articles	10.391
	4	74	Copper and articles	1.086
	5	76	Aluminum and articles	0.276

(Table continues on next page)

Table 5A.3 Ghana's Top Five Sectors by Its Top Five Trade Partners, 2005 and 2015 *(continued)*

Top destinations	Sector rank	HS code	Sector	Exports (US$, million)
Vietnam	1	08	Edible fruits	112.542
	2	44	Wood	17.761
	3	12	Oil seeds	0.275
	4	03	Fish and crustaceans	0.235
	5	52	Cotton	0.185
Japan	1	18	Cocoa and cocoa prep	109.229
	2	03	Fish and crustaceans	2.854
	3	78	Lead and articles	1.612
	4	71	Natural or cultured pearls	0.934
	5	46	Straw	0.615

Source: Database for International Trade Analysis (BACI) of the Centre for Prospective Studies and International Information (CEPII).
Note: HS = Harmonized System.

Table 5A.4 Kenya's Top Five Sectors by Its Top Five Trade Partners, 2005 and 2015

Top destinations	Sector rank	HS code	Sector	Exports (US$, million)
a. 2005				
Pakistan	1	09	Coffee, tea, maté	167.767
	2	28	Inorganic chemicals	6.594
	3	41	Raw hides and skins	6.405
	4	72	Iron and steel	3.341
	5	74	Copper and articles	2.172
India	1	28	Inorganic chemicals	27.732
	2	09	Coffee, tea, maté	7.491
	3	41	Raw hides and skins	6.019
	4	25	Salt, sulfur, earths	5.593
	5	08	Edible fruits	4.979
Japan	1	21	Misc. edible prep	8.789
	2	09	Coffee, tea, maté	8.204
	3	06	Live trees and other	5.611
	4	07	Edible vegetables	3.347
	5	08	Edible fruits	2.688

(Table continues on next page)

Table 5A.4   **Kenya's Top Five Sectors by Its Top Five Trade Partners, 2005 and 2015** *(continued)*

Top destinations	Sector rank	HS code	Sector	Exports (US$, million)
Thailand	1	28	Inorganic chemicals	25.710
	2	29	Organic chemicals	4.366
	3	84	Nuclear reactors	0.834
	4	71	Natural or cultured pearls	0.647
	5	85	Electrical machinery	0.158
China	1	41	Raw hides and skins	4.515
	2	26	Ores, slag, and ash	3.828
	3	74	Copper and articles	2.995
	4	53	Other vegetable textile fibers	2.932
	5	05	Dairy produce	1.469
b.2015				
Pakistan	1	09	Coffee, tea, maté	328.432
	2	07	Edible vegetables	4.363
	3	28	Inorganic chemicals	3.732
	4	41	Raw hides and skins	1.743
	5	49	Printed books, newspapers	0.544
India	1	07	Edible vegetables	35.017
	2	28	Inorganic chemicals	18.237
	3	09	Coffee, tea, maté	16.160
	4	41	Raw hides and skins	10.494
	5	25	Salt, sulfur, earths	6.871
China	1	26	Ores, slag, and ash	52.402
	2	41	Raw hides and skins	16.785
	3	53	Other vegetable textile fibers	6.499
	4	03	Fish and crustaceans	3.947
	5	09	Coffee, tea, maté	3.622
Japan	1	09	Coffee, tea, maté	16.680
	2	06	Live trees and other	13.160
	3	26	Ores, slag, and ash	11.737
	4	74	Copper and articles	7.983

(Table continues on next page)

Table 5A.4   **Kenya's Top Five Sectors by Its Top Five Trade Partners, 2005 and 2015** *(continued)*

Top destinations	Sector rank	HS code	Sector	Exports (US$, million)
	5	21	Misc. edible prep	6.389
Afghanistan	1	09	Coffee, tea, maté	64.474
	2	48	Paper and paperboard	0.100
	3	27	Minerals, fuels, and mining	0.051
	4	62	Apparel access, non-knitted	0.003
	5	84	Nuclear reactors	0.002

Source: Database for International Trade Analysis (BACI) of the Centre for Prospective Studies and International Information (CEPII).
Note: HS = Harmonized System.

Table 5A.5   **Nigeria's Top Five Sectors by Its Top Five Trade Partners, 2005 and 2015**

Top destinations	Sector rank	HS code	Sector	Exports (US$, million)
a. 2005				
Japan	1	27	Minerals, fuels, and mining	846.493
	2	12	Oil seeds	27.650
	3	18	Cocoa and cocoa prep	0.251
	4	96	Misc manufacturing	0.162
	5	13	Lac, gums, resins	0.104
Indonesia	1	27	Minerals, fuels, and mining	849.505
	2	18	Cocoa and cocoa prep	3.396
	3	52	Cotton	2.667
	4	44	Wood	0.752
	5	78	Lead and articles	0.431
China	1	27	Minerals, fuels, and mining	452.912
	2	41	Raw hides and skins	7.634
	3	26	Ores, slag, and ash	7.120
	4	74	Copper and articles	1.821
	5	18	Cocoa and cocoa prep	1.551

(Table continues on next page)

Table 5A.5   Nigeria's Top Five Sectors by Its Top Five Trade Partners, 2005 and 2015 *(continued)*

Top destinations	Sector rank	HS code	Sector	Exports (US$, million)
Korea, Rep,	1	27	Minerals, fuels, and mining	327.906
	2	74	Copper and articles	0.123
	3	29	Organic chemicals	0.057
	4	78	Lead and articles	0.039
	5	03	Fish and crustaceans	0.030
New Zealand	1	27	Minerals, fuels, and mining	85.255
	2	84	Nuclear reactors	0.011
	3	73	Articles of iron or steel	0.008
	4	85	Electrical machinery	0.007
	5	71	Natural or cultured pearls	0.005
b. 2015				
India	1	27	Minerals, fuels, and mining	9,033.217
	2	08	Edible fruits	52.670
	3	76	Aluminum and articles	45.105
	4	41	Raw hides and skins	19.719
	5	09	Coffee, tea, maté	9.448
Japan	1	27	Minerals, fuels, and mining	2,379.100
	2	12	Oil seeds	91.010
	3	76	Aluminum and articles	60.513
	4	71	Natural or cultured pearls	0.397
	5	03	Fish and crustaceans	0.233
China	1	27	Minerals, fuels, and mining	686.931
	2	44	Wood	308.676
	3	26	Ores, slag, and ash	66.274
	4	74	Copper & articles	11.291
	5	41	Raw hides and skins	9.216
Korea, Rep.	1	27	Minerals, fuels, and mining	835.175
	2	74	Copper and articles	82.531
	3	73	Articles of iron or steel	38.676
	4	78	Lead and articles	30.073
	5	76	Aluminum and articles	19.642

(Table continues on next page)

Table 5A.5   Nigeria's Top Five Sectors by Its Top Five Trade Partners, 2005 and 2015 *(continued)*

Top destinations	Sector rank	HS code	Sector	Exports (US$, million)
Thailand	1	27	Minerals, fuels, and mining	131.715
	2	76	Aluminum and articles	3.594
	3	78	Lead and articles	2.900
	4	26	Ores, slag and ash	1.635
	5	03	Fish and crustaceans	1.087

Source: Database for International Trade Analysis (BACI) of the Centre for Prospective Studies and International Information (CEPII).
Note: HS = Harmonized System.

Table 5A.6   Tanzania's Top Five Sectors by Its Top Five Trade Partners, 2005 and 2015

Top destinations	Sector rank	HS code	Sector	Exports (US$, million)
a. 2005				
China	1	26	Ores, slag, and ash	165.113
	2	52	Cotton	36.614
	3	12	Oil seeds	11.214
	4	44	Wood	9.287
	5	05	Dairy produce	1.923
India	1	08	Edible fruits	42.952
	2	07	Edible vegetables	24.072
	3	44	Wood	8.845
	4	71	Natural or cultured pearls	6.944
	5	52	Cotton	5.331
Japan	1	09	Coffee, tea, maté	24.486
	2	26	Ores, slag, and ash	23.455
	3	12	Oil seeds	14.023
	4	03	Fish and crustaceans	11.260
	5	24	Tobacco	1.564
Malaysia	1	74	Copper and articles	16.478
	2	24	Tobacco	13.563
	3	52	Cotton	4.287
	4	51	Wool, fine or animal hair	0.110
	5	03	Fish and crustaceans	0.073

(Table continues on next page)

Table 5A.6   Tanzania's Top Five Sectors by Its Top Five Trade Partners, 2005 and 2015 *(continued)*

Top destinations	Sector rank	HS code	Sector	Exports (US$, million)
Thailand	1	52	Cotton	23.579
	2	26	Ores, slag, and ash	1.600
	3	44	Wood	1.049
	4	71	Natural or cultured pearls	0.664
	5	12	Oil seeds	0.176
b. 2015				
India	1	71	Natural or cultured pearls	550.228
	2	08	Edible fruits	198.194
	3	07	Edible vegetables	197.877
	4	03	Fish and crustaceans	65.527
	5	44	Wood	21.440
China	1	15	Animal or vegetable fat	218.457
	2	26	Ores, slag, and ash	124.055
	3	12	Oil seeds	118.440
	4	74	Copper and articles	55.195
	5	53	Other vegetable textile fibers	22.357
Japan	1	26	Ores, slag, and ash	222.449
	2	12	Oil seeds	53.242
	3	09	Coffee, tea, maté	42.038
	4	24	Tobacco	36.443
	5	03	Fish and crustaceans	10.323
Vietnam	1	08	Edible fruits	95.094
	2	52	Cotton	14.873
	3	12	Oil seeds	12.095
	4	23	Food residues and waste	10.539
	5	03	Fish and crustaceans	2.323
Malaysia	1.5	26	Ores, slag, and ash	75.137
	1.5	74	Copper and articles	31.759
	3	18	Cocoa and cocoa prep	17.543
	4	52	Cotton	1.057
	5	20	Prepared vegetables, fruits, nuts	0.599

Source: Database for International Trade Analysis (BACI) of the Centre for Prospective Studies and International Information (CEPII).
Note: HS = Harmonized System.

Notes

1. "Upstreamness" is an input's average distance from final use (Antràs et al. 2012). A relatively upstream sector is one that supplies a disproportionately large share of its output to other sectors that sell very little if any directly to final consumers.
2. BACI, the French acronym for "Base pour l'Analyse du Commerce International," is the Database for International Trade Analysis of the Centre for Prospective Studies and International Information (CEPII), available at http://www.cepii.fr/CEPII/en/bdd_modele/presentation .asp?id=37. It provides disaggregated data on bilateral trade flows for more than 5,000 products and 200 countries. The database is built from data directly reported by each country to the United Nations Statistical Division (Comtrade).
3. Data on the value of exports from Sub-Saharan Africa to Asia are from the CEPII's BACI database.

References

Antràs, P., D. Chor, T. Fally, and R. Hillberry. 2012. "Measuring the Upstreamness of Production and Trade Flows." *American Economic Review* 102 (3): 412–16.

Johnson, R., and G. Noguera. 2012. "Accounting for Intermediates: Production Sharing and Trade in Value Added." *Journal of International Economics* 86 (2): 224–36.

Ma, Y., H. Tang, and Y. Zhang. 2014. "Factor Intensity, Product Switching, and Productivity: Evidence From Chinese Exporters." *Journal of International Economics* 92 (2): 349–62.

UN DESA (United Nations Department of Economic and Social Affairs). 2018. *Classification by Broad Economic Categories Rev.5*. ST/ESA /STAT/SER.M/53/Rev.5. New York: United Nations.

PART III

Looking Inward: Deepening Regional Integration and Value Chains

Although intraregional trade still accounts for only a small share of total trade in Africa, it is becoming increasingly important. The push for regional integration is currently elevated by the potential of the African Continental Free Trade Area (AfCFTA) to significantly advance economic transformation in the region. The establishment of the AfCFTA presents major opportunities to boost intra-Africa trade, although significant challenges remain to achieve its stated goals. It is an ambitious project that requires massive investment in resources and reforms as well as increased cooperation from members and relinquishment of some control over national policies. As such, it signals the region's rising ambitions for faster growth through trade and integration.

Still, Africa suffers from challenges that most other regions do not face; hence, the region requires unprecedented levels of commitment for the AfCFTA to succeed. These challenges include the high level of geographic and political fragmentation and thick borders (a complex of both tariff and nontariff restrictions that slow down trade)—all of which increase the per unit cost of moving goods across borders.

Part III (chapters 6 and 7) shows that strengthening the integration required for a successful AfCFTA calls for a three-part approach: improving physical integration, strengthening political cooperation, and facilitating business integration. These efforts must be supplemented by the harmonization of rules and regulations through regulatory cooperation.

The post-AfCFTA gains from regional integration go beyond the traditional welfare analysis. The most important of them derive from the dynamic gains associated with benefits from increased competition, foreign direct investment inflows, economies of scale, transfer of knowledge and technology, increased productivity, and economic diversification—benefits such as the following:

- *Resilience.* Intraregional trade is expected to be more resilient to global shocks. Regional integration, particularly intra-Africa trade, has been found to strengthen the capacity of economies to absorb global shocks and build resilience to shocks emanating from high-income economies.
- *Diversification.* Regional integration promotes the exchange of a more diverse set of goods (relative to trade in more concentrated primary goods). Exports to the rest of the world are often concentrated in primary goods, but intraregional trade flows are relatively diversified, contain higher value added, and include a relatively larger share of manufactured goods.
- *Economies of scale.* Deepening intraregional trade and integration lays the groundwork to increase the region's trade and investment flows with the rest of the world by expanding economies of scale. Strengthening regional value chains through regional integration could serve as a stepping-stone to active participation in global value chains (GVCs).
- *Conflict reduction.* A high level of trade and integration may reduce the prospects of conflicts between nations by raising the opportunity cost of conflicts.

In general, low-income countries, including those in Africa, adopt traditional nontariff barriers (NTBs) less often than high-income countries. Still, numerous barriers can be categorized as NTBs that restrict trade within the region. These include inadequate infrastructure, cumbersome customs procedures, higher transportation costs, high fragmentation, thick borders, poor coordination between and within country agencies, and a multiplicity of cross-border regulations. Higher NTBs restrict the growth of intraregional trade as well as imports of essential intermediate and capital goods that are required for actively engaging in regional and global value chains.

In exporting to high-income markets, African countries also face restrictive nontariff measures (NTMs), the most predominant of which are sanitary and phytosanitary measures and other technical barriers to trade. Market access for African exports to high-income countries is restricted more by NTMs than by tariffs. Effectively, NTMs pose even higher barriers to exports because some measures, such as certification and standards requirements, are costlier to fulfill for African countries than for other, more developed partners. They have also been found to hurt low-income countries, including those in Africa, disproportionately because of their relatively higher prevalence in sectors of export interest to these economies (such as agriculture and apparel) and the lower capacity of firms in low-income countries to comply with such requirements.

Another barrier that restricts the dynamic gains from trade, particularly in the manufacturing sector, is the high level of restrictiveness in services trade. Studies show that reducing trade barriers in services has significant implications for the productivity and growth of manufacturing firms in low- and middle-income economies. In Africa, the barriers to trade in services are substantial. This poses challenges for trade and the growth of the manufacturing sector because services play a critical role in driving trade and industry.

The role of services in production and trade has gained even greater prominence with the rise of GVCs and the "servicification" of manufacturing— referring broadly to the manufacturing sector's increasing reliance on services and the associated rise in the share of services bundled in manufacturing goods. Services play a central role in the patterns of international trade and investment by enabling the creation and development of value chains, but the centrality of reform in services trade has long been ancillary in national and international policy circles. Given the role of services in enabling the creation and development of and participation in value chains, there is a need to refocus on reform strategies to ease the burden on services trade and investments in the region.

CHAPTER 6

The Promise and Challenge of the African Continental Free Trade Area

Woubet Kassa, Habtamu T. Edjigu, and Albert G. Zeufack

Introduction

In January 2012, the 18th Ordinary Session of the African Union Assembly of Heads of State and Government decided to establish the African Continental Free Trade Area (AfCFTA) by an indicative date of 2017. The summit also endorsed the Action Plan for Boosting Intra-African Trade, which identified seven program clusters: trade policy, trade facilitation, productive capacity, trade-related infrastructure, trade finance, trade information, and factor market integration. The AfCFTA aims to bring together 54 African countries with a combined population of more than 1.2 billion people and a combined gross domestic product (GDP) of more than $3 trillion. The goal is to "create a single continental market for goods and services, with free movement of business persons and investments."[1]

The draft agreement was signed in March 2018 during the 18th Extraordinary Session of the African Union Assembly of Heads of State and Government, where 44 of the 55 African countries signed the treaty. As of 2021, 54 countries had already signed the AfCFTA.[2] Twenty-two ratifications were required for the agreement to enter into force—a feat achieved as of May 2019—and 38 African Union member states have ratified it as of August 2021. Hence, Africa has put into operation the world's largest free trade area (FTA), which is expected to change the trade and investment framework of countries in the region.

The key objectives of AfCFTA include the following:[3]

- *Create a single continental market* for goods and services, with free movement of businesspersons and investments, and thus pave the way for accelerating the establishment of a Continental Customs Union.
- *Expand intra-Africa trade* through better harmonization and coordination of trade liberalization and facilitation regimes and instruments

across regional economic communities (RECs) and across Africa in general.

- *Resolve the challenges of multiple, overlapping REC memberships* and expedite regional and continental integration processes.
- *Enhance competitiveness* at the industry and enterprise levels by exploiting opportunities for scale production, continental market access, and better reallocation of resources.

Although intraregional trade still accounts for only a small share of total trade in Africa, it is becoming increasingly important. The push for regional integration is currently fostered by the AfCFTA's potential to significantly advance economic transformation in the region. The establishment of the AfCFTA presents both major opportunities from and challenges to boosting intra-Africa trade. As a part of the AfCFTA agreement, countries have committed to remove tariffs on 90 percent of goods in the first five-year phase, followed by subsequent elimination of tariffs on the remaining product groups as well as reduction of nontariff barriers (NTBs).

Following the operationalization of the AfCFTA, intra-Africa trade would increase by 52.3 percent in 2022, relative to a baseline scenario in 2022 without AfCFTA implementation, with the manufacturing sector registering the largest expansion in exports (by about 53.3 percent), higher than agriculture or services (Mevel and Karingi 2012). A more conservative estimate suggests that, in the long run, full AfCFTA implementation (without exemptions of certain sensitive products from liberalization) will likely increase intra-Africa trade by 33 percent owing to the elimination of tariffs, and cut Africa's trade deficit by 51 percent (Saygili, Peters, and Knebel 2018). By 2035, with full AfCFTA implementation, intra-Africa trade is estimated to increase by 81 percent compared with the baseline scenario without AfCFTA for the same year. Further removal of NTBs is associated with an even larger increase in intraregional trade.

The removal of tariffs will create a continental market that allows companies to benefit from economies of scale. By promoting intra-Africa trade, the AfCFTA will also foster a more competitive manufacturing sector and promote economic diversification. In turn, the region's countries will likely be able to accelerate their industrial development.

In addition, the AfCFTA could enhance economic growth and create welfare gains. Using a computable general equilibrium model (CGE) model, Saygili, Peters, and Knebel (2018) estimate that full elimination of tariffs among African countries would increase GDP by about 1 percent on average and create an overall welfare gain of about $16.1 billion in the long run.[4] These growth and welfare gains could be even larger if the scope of the agreement is extended to nontariff measures (NTMs) and trade facilitation ("the simplification, modernization, and harmonization of export and import processes," as defined in WTO [2015, 34])—the key drivers for economic growth in the region (Chauvin, Ramos, and Porto 2016). They estimate that the elimination of tariff barriers combined with reduction of

NTMs is associated with an increase in GDP of at least 5 percent on average across the region by 2027. Even with significant tariff reduction, Africa will not achieve significant gains in growth and welfare without a substantial reduction in NTMs and improved harmonization of customs procedures regionwide.

Revisiting the Theory of Regional Integration in Light of the AfCFTA

The theory of regional integration draws closely from the theories of customs unions and FTAs. There is an inherent theoretical ambiguity in the welfare impacts of regional trade agreements or FTAs (Krugman 1991). The classic theoretical framework (Viner 1950) for analyzing the impact of an FTA or customs union suggests that the welfare impact is ambiguous because of the contrasting welfare impacts of trade creation and trade diversion. Viner (1950) notes that trade creation increases welfare, and trade diversion reduces it—pointing out that an FTA could leave countries worse off as a consequence.

However, this finding has largely focused only on the static gains from trade, without due regard to the dynamic and possibly more important long-term effects (Balassa 1961; Cooper and Massell 1965). The classical analysis of welfare impact relies solely on *production* effects and ignores the *consumption* effects associated with consumer surplus resulting from price reductions (Lipsey 1960). It also considers the impact on global welfare and the efficient allocation of resources without duly considering to whom the benefits are accruing and the global distribution of income.

Overall, the modern consensus is that FTAs are considerably better in practice than in theory, particularly when viewed as alternatives to multilateral trade liberalization (Bergsten 1991; Krugman 1991). When considering the welfare impact of an FTA or regional bloc engaged in regional integration schemes, the practical evidence shows that the results are largely positive and significant for the regional blocs forming FTAs.

Trade Creation versus Trade Diversion Effects of FTAs

An FTA, by allowing competition between its members owing to reduced trade barriers, may promote a more efficient (re)allocation of resources within the FTA. This reallocation is associated with what is often referred to as *trade creation*. That is, the locus of production will shift from a high-cost producer to a low-cost, relatively more efficient producer within the FTA. And this shift brings a welfare gain associated with reduced prices, increased consumer surplus, and an overall improvement in production efficiency within the FTA.

Trade creation is hence associated with two distinct effects—the production effect and the consumption effect, both of which are expected to increase welfare. On the production side, there are greater efficiency gains, which in turn contribute to declining prices (the consumption effect) and hence to increased societal welfare.

However, another possibility is *trade diversion*—that is, a shift in the locus of production from more-efficient producers among nonmembers of the FTA to inefficient producers within the FTA, depending on the extent of the external tariffs. The impact of trade diversion could be stronger if FTA members raise external tariffs because, although high external tariffs exacerbate trade diversion, low external tariffs will reduce it (Freund and Ornelas 2010). Within the traditional theoretical framework, trade diversion is harmful because of the global efficiency losses. However, the effect within the FTA could be positive if the production gains of the new exporter outweigh the loss in consumer welfare. FTA countries that are now importing from the relatively efficient (within-FTA efficient) FTA country would have lost tariff revenue that would have been collected from the more efficient external producer, because the tariffs are very low or zero within the FTA.

The net impact of an FTA depends on the totality of trade diversion and trade creation, which is largely an empirical question. For low- to middle-income regions such as Africa, this framework alone is inadequate for understanding the impact of regional integration schemes such as the AfCFTA.

An Analytical Framework for FTAs in the African Context

In the context of African economies, the impacts of trade creation and trade diversion are expected to be minimal relative to the long-term objectives embodied in the AfCFTA. This is because, in the context of the low productivity, very high unemployment, and low investment regimes most Africans face, the previous theory is very restrictive in evaluating the impact of regional integration or FTAs.

A more suitable framework for analyzing the impacts of regional integration is to examine the welfare impacts arising from increased employment, productivity, incomes, investment, and overall structural transformation of low- and middle-income economies into, respectively, middle-income and high-income economies. The dynamic effects of an FTA such as the AfCFTA would far outweigh the static effects because it supports the growth of a strong, competitive manufacturing sector and provides economies of scale from both trade diversion and creation. In practice, it is typically countries outside the FTA that are expected to face negative trade diversion effects.

In addition, welfare impact analysis that is biased toward a globally efficient allocation of resources ignores the existing income distribution. In the wake of trade diversion, countries outside the FTA bear the brunt of the negative effects. If, through trade diversion, an FTA shifts the distribution of income or wealth in favor of the poorer economies, it would be a favorable outcome. Still, with the substantial fall in tariffs and other trade barriers globally, trade diversion may not be as predominant an outcome as expected with FTA formation. In practice, the *trade diversion* effects tend to be minimal (Clausing 2001; Freund and Ornelas 2010; Magee 2008). By contrast, the evidence for substantial *trade creation* associated with FTAs is overwhelming (Freund and Ornelas 2010). An FTA encompassing natural trading partner countries—countries with geographic proximity to each other and an already significant bilateral trade—tends to increase trade much more than otherwise (Magee 2008). This has important implications for the AfCFTA.

Arguably, the most important gains of an FTA are the dynamic gains (Baldwin 1992) associated with benefits from increased competition, foreign direct investment (FDI) inflows, economies of scale, transfer of knowledge and technology, increased productivity, and economic diversification. For FTA members in Africa and other low- and middle-income economies, the dynamic gains from trade diversion could be positive because of the production effects, leading to increased investment, job creation, and associated increases in productivity.

An important gain from regional free trade in practice arises from the increased size and hence productive efficiency and competitiveness of markets subject to economies of scale (Krugman 1991). After the European Common Market was formed in 1958, "What turned arrangement into a strong economic success was the huge intra-industry trade in manufactures, and the associated rationalization of production, that the Treaty of Rome made possible" (Krugman 1991, 9). Another benefit of an FTA, even when there is trade diversion, is that it typically enhances the region's terms of trade at the expense of the rest of the world. Given the meager size of most African economies, the regional bloc provides a much-desired improvement in their terms of trade versus the rest of the world.

Prospective Benefits from the AfCFTA

The most important motivation for the AfCFTA is the economic transformation of countries across the African continent—focused on the need to exploit economies-of-scale advantages, enlarge the size and efficiency of markets, promote industrialization, and foster transfer of production technology and knowledge. For Africa, the gains from regional integration following the AfCFTA go beyond the traditional welfare analysis. Some examples are described below.

Resilience. Intraregional trade is expected to be more resilient to global shocks. Building the resilience of national economies has become a key goal of policy makers since the 2008–09 Global Financial Crisis and emerging uncertainties in global trade. Regional integration, particularly of intra-Africa trade, has been found to strengthen the capacity of economies to absorb global shocks and build resilience to shocks emanating from high-income economies (Brixiová, Meng, and Ncube 2015).

Diversification. Regional integration promotes exchange in a more diverse set of goods (compared with trade in more concentrated primary goods). Countries in Sub-Saharan Africa, for example, that are not highly dependent on natural resources tend to be more integrated in regional trade blocs than those with greater natural resource dependence. Oil exporters are less integrated than non-oil economies with other Sub-Saharan African economies, for which intraregional exports of oil represent a mere

1.5 percent of total exports. In contrast to exports to the rest of the world, which are often concentrated in primary goods, intraregional trade flows are relatively diversified, contain higher value added, and include a relatively larger share of manufactured goods (IMF 2019).

Economies of scale. Deepening intraregional trade and integration provides the groundwork to increase the region's trade and investment flows with the rest of the world by expanding economies of scale. Economies of scale provide opportunities to attract large-scale investments, mainly FDI. Intraregional trade addresses a central challenge of many African economies, most of which are small and isolated. In half of the economies, GDP is less than $10 billion, and close to one-third of the countries are landlocked. By broadening markets and providing economies of scale, the AfCFTA boosts the region's economies by attracting large-scale FDI or reducing the costs of accessing global markets. Hence, strengthening regional value chains through regional integration serves as a stepping-stone to active participation in global value chains (GVCs).

Conflict reduction. A high level of trade and integration may reduce the prospects of conflicts between nations by raising the opportunity cost of conflicts (Martin, Mayer, and Thoenig 2008).

Key Trends in Regional Trade and Integration in Africa

Between 1995 and 2017, intra-Africa export trade increased by more than 410 percent, rising from $26.7 billion in 1995 to $137.1 billion in 2017 (figure 6.1). It registered positive growth continuously in all these years except 1998–2001, 2009, and 2015–16. The lack of growth or decline in growth in 1998–2001 and 2009 was mainly associated with global

Figure 6.1   Value of Intra-Africa Exports, 1995–2017

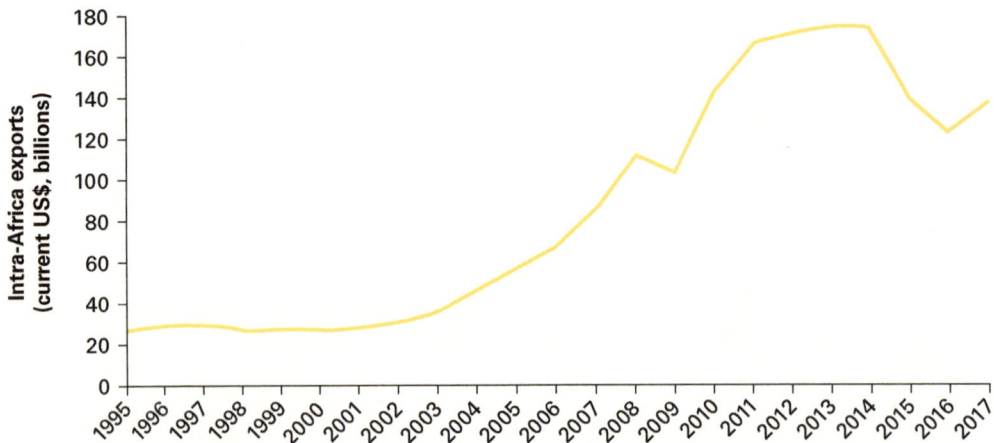

Source: Calculations from the UNCTADstat database, United Nations Conference on Trade and Development (https://unctadstat.unctad.org).

recessions, and the negative growth after 2014 resulted partly from the price shocks in global commodities, which still account for the largest share of Africa's exports. The overall trend in intra-Africa trade over the past four decades has been positive.

Still, intra-Africa trade remains a very low share of the region's total trade, most of which is with countries outside the region. Over the past two decades, the average share of intra-African in total African exports was 12 percent, compared with 56 percent of exports being intraregional in Asia, 58 percent in the Americas, and 71 percent in Europe (figure 6.2).

Moreover, Africa remains only a marginal participant in world trade. The region's share in global trade was only 2 percent over 1995–99, and it increased to 3 percent between 2011 and 2017. This is in stark contrast with Asia's share, which grew from 27 percent during 1995–99 to 37 percent between 2011 and 2017 (table 6.1).

Constraints to Intra-Africa Trade

There are several reasons for the low performance of intra-Africa trade. One is that African exporters within the region often face relatively high tariffs, with an average protection rate of 8.5 percent compared with 2.5 percent when exporting to markets outside the region (UNCTAD 2013). Moreover, African borders are relatively thick (with restrictions that slow down trade) because of NTBs in the form of excessive and unnecessary document requirements and unnecessary delays, inefficient ports, and underdeveloped infrastructure, all of which increase the cost of trading within Africa.

Figure 6.2   Intraregional Exports as a Share of Total Exports, by Region, 1995–2017

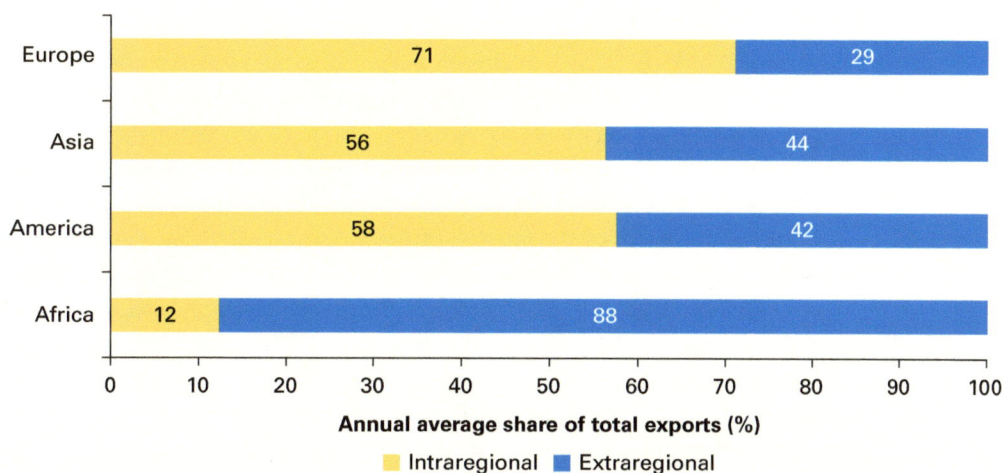

Annual average share of total exports (%)

Intraregional ■ Extraregional

Source: Calculations from the UNCTADstat database, United Nations Conference on Trade and Development (https://unctadstat.unctad.org).
Note: Regions are defined by United Nations Conference on Trade and Development classifications. "Africa" includes both Sub-Saharan and North Africa; "America" includes North, South, and Central America and the Caribbean; "Asia" includes East, Southeast, Central, and South Asia and the Middle East; and "Europe" includes Western, Eastern, Southern, and Northern Europe.

Table 6.1   Share of Global Trade, by Region, 1995–2017
Average annual share of global exports (%)

Region	1995–99	2000–04	2005–10	2011–17
Africa	2	2	3	3
America	25	26	22	21
Asia	27	28	32	37
Europe	44	43	42	36

Source: Calculations from the UNCTADstat database (https://unctadstat.unctad.org).
Note: Regions are defined by United Nations Conference on Trade and Development classifications. "Africa" includes both Sub-Saharan and North Africa; "America" includes North, South, and Central America and the Caribbean; "Asia" includes East, Southeast, Central, and South Asia as well as the Middle East; and "Europe" includes Western, Eastern, Southern, and Northern Europe.

Comparing the ease of international trade by region, Sub-Saharan Africa had the lowest score in the World Bank's *Doing Business 2018* trading across borders indicator set. Its score was 54, indicating that the region was 46 percentage points away from the best regulatory performance in the area of trading across borders (figure 6.3, panel a). This score reflects the time and cost (excluding tariffs) associated with the logistics of exporting and importing, including documentary compliance, border compliance, and domestic transportation across regions.[5] Trade among Sub-Saharan African countries costs 42 percent more than trade within the East Asia and Pacific region, 26 percent more than trade within South Asia, and 20 percent more than trade within Latin America and the Caribbean (figure 6.3, panel b). On average, exporting in Sub-Saharan Africa takes about seven days and costs $775, which is three days and $283 more than in East Asia and Pacific, five days and $519 more than in Europe and the Central Asia, and two days and $134 more than in Latin America and the Caribbean.

The relatively high cost of trading across borders in Africa is partly driven by the region's poor performance in trade logistics (figure 6.4). Sub-Saharan Africa's logistics performance index scores are, on average, 25 percent lower than those of countries in Europe and Central Asia. Looking at the six components of the World Bank's Logistics Performance Index (customs, infrastructure, international shipment, logistics quality and competence, tracking and tracing, and timeliness), Sub-Saharan Africa performs worse than all other regions in all indicators of trade logistics (as shown, by component, in annex 6A, figure 6A.1). In low- and middle-income countries, including in Africa, the trade costs associated with poor trade facilitation are equivalent to applying a 219 percent ad valorem tariff on international trade (WTO 2015).

Determinants of Intra-Africa Trade

To understand the key determinants of intra-Africa trade, we estimate a gravity model for a sample including all African countries, using the Poisson pseudo-maximum likelihood estimation.[6] Our results show that all the

Figure 6.3   Ease and Cost of Trading across Borders, Average Scores by Region, 2018

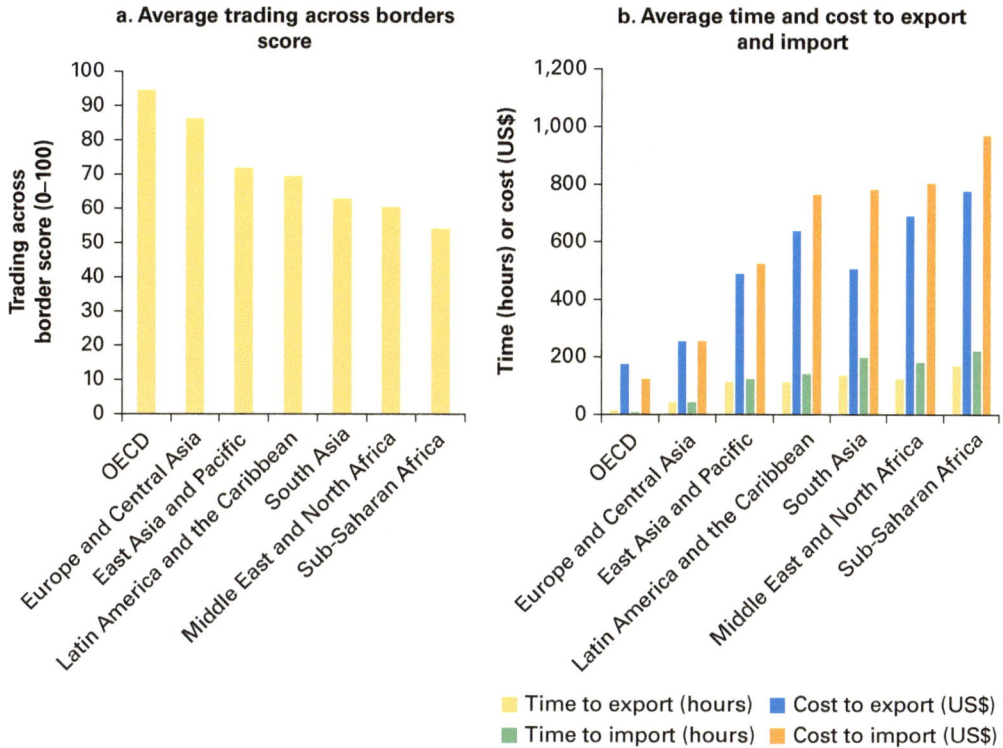

a. Average trading across borders score

b. Average time and cost to export and import

Legend:
- Time to export (hours)
- Time to import (hours)
- Cost to export (US$)
- Cost to import (US$)

Source: World Bank 2018.
Note: Among the World Bank's *Doing Business* indicator sets, the trading across borders score reflects, on a 0–100 scale, the ease of international trade logistics in day-to-day operations, where 0 represents the worst and 100 represents the best performance (panel a). In 2018, the reference measures were the time and cost to export the country's product of comparative advantage and to import auto parts (panel b). OECD = Organisation for Economic Co-operation and Development.

traditional gravity model variables are important determinants of Africa's trade (annex 6A, table 6A.1). Among these, distance and "landlockedness" (a proxy for the cost of international transportation) have the expected negative impacts on bilateral trade among African countries. In addition, the income of trading partners, sharing a border, and having a common language have positive and significant effects on intra-Africa trade.

Most important, we find that membership in a regional trade agreement or customs union tends to promote trade between countries. This explains the high cross-country trade observed *within* RECs, whereas the trade between countries *across* the various regional trading blocs is limited. This finding implies increased trade potential for members of the AfCFTA and other regional trading blocs because an FTA agreement may enhance trade between members. In addition, membership in the World Trade Organization (WTO) and its predecessor—the General Agreement on Tariffs and Trade (GATT)—has enhanced bilateral trade in Africa, indicating the potential relevance of the AfCFTA.

Figure 6.4   Performance on Trade Logistics, by Region, 2018

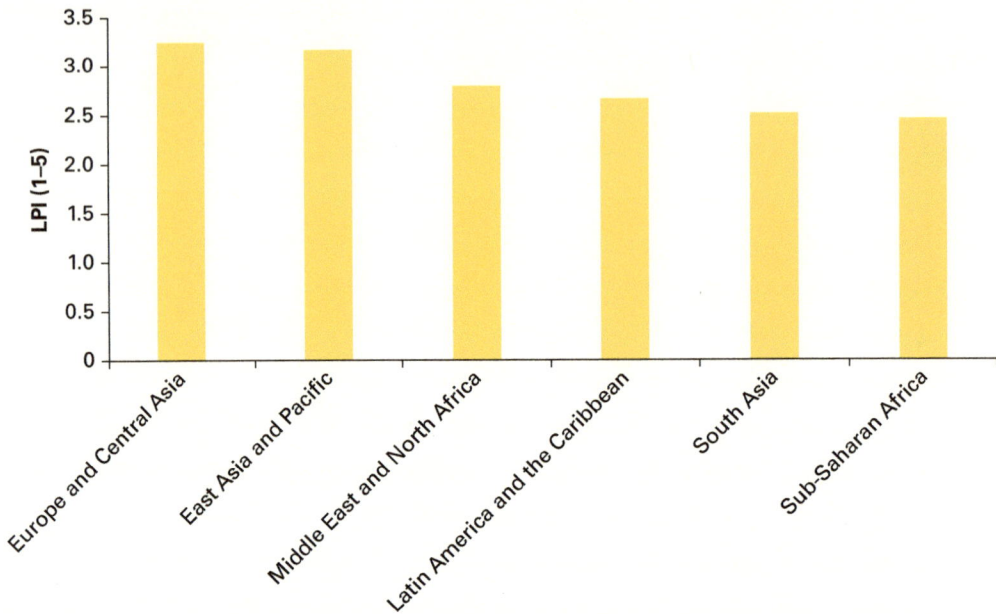

Source: Calculations using the World Bank's Logistics Performance Index (LPI) 2018 data set (https://lpi
.worldbank.org/).
Note: The aggregated 2018 LPI combines six core performance components: customs, infrastructure,
international shipment, logistics quality and competence, tracking and tracing, and timeliness. For the regional
scores on each component, see annex 6A, figure 6A.1.

The predominant finding that trade decreases with distance suggests that
policies, institutions, and infrastructure such as transportation and communications, which reduce the trade costs of distance, would ease the challenges of intraregional trade. With a few exceptions, most African countries
have low GDP. This remains one of the key challenges for expanding trade
in the region, because the countries tend to trade more with large economies. Further strengthening of regional links leading to a large-scale concentration of economic activities would eventually ease the challenge.
Expanding economies of scale through the AfCFTA could address the prob-
lem of small size that restricts trade in the region. Hence, regional integration is also the solution to the current low levels of intraregional trade.

The high level of trade within the current RECs provides an optimistic
picture for the AfCFTA's future in promoting intraregional trade. It could
also pose a challenge if the transition from RECs to the AfCFTA is sticky.

Intra-Africa Trade within Regional Economic Communities

A defining feature of intra-Africa trade is that, although it is low compared
with other regions of the world, trade within many of the RECs is high.
Between 2011 and 2017, for example, 85 percent of the trade of Southern

African Development Community (SADC) members within Africa was with other SADC member countries, and 70 percent of the trade of Economic Community of West African States (ECOWAS) countries within Africa was with other ECOWAS member countries (table 6.2). Similarly, 68 percent of the trade of the Community of Sahel-Saharan States (CEN-SAD) countries was with other CEN-SAD member countries. That RECs tend to undertake a significant portion of their trade within their own regional trading blocs demonstrates that FTAs improve trade in the region, boding well for the AfCFTA's potential to boost trade in the region.

Table 6.2 presents the share of each REC's total trade that is within Africa. The share of trade to all of Africa varies across the blocs, ranging from a high in 2011–17 of 20 percent in SADC, 10 percent in ECOWAS, 7 percent in the East African Community (EAC), 6 percent in CEN-SAD, and 6 percent in the Common Market for Eastern and Southern Africa (COMESA), to 5 percent in the Economic Community of Central African States (ECCAS), 4 percent in the Intergovernmental Authority on Development (IGAD) region,[7] and a low of 3 percent in the Arab Maghreb Union (AMU).

One of the reasons why the SADC records the highest share of Africa trade could be the subregion's relatively lower nontariff trade costs (IMF 2019). In addition, it includes such major intra-Africa traders as South Africa, Zambia, and Zimbabwe, which are also large economies, reinforcing our gravity model results (table 6.3 and, in annex 6A, table 6A.1).

Except for COMESA and ECCAS, the percentage of each REC's intra-Africa trade that happens within its own bloc decreased from 1995 to 2017

Table 6.2   Intra-Africa Trade Trends, by Regional Economic Community, 1995–2017
Percent

REC	Share of REC's exports to all African countries			Share of REC's total intra-Africa exports staying within own bloc		
	1995–2000	2001–10	2011–17	1995–2000	2001–10	2011–17
AMU	3	3	3	63	61	57
CEN-SAD	6	6	6	81	69	68
COMESA	4	6	6	31	33	42
EAC	12	10	7	84	48	49
ECCAS	3	4	5	16	16	24
ECOWAS	11	11	10	85	74	70
IGAD	8	6	4	69	45	37
SADC	17	19	20	91	88	85

Source: Calculations from the UNCTADstat database, United Nations Conference on Trade and Development (https://unctadstat.unctad.org).
Note: The first three columns show the share of total export trade by each regional economic community (REC) that stays within Africa. The last three columns show each REC's percentage of intra-Africa trade within its own bloc. AMU = Arab Maghreb Union; CEN-SAD = Community of Sahel-Saharan States; COMESA = Common Market for Eastern and Southern Africa; EAC = East African Community; ECCAS = Economic Community of Central African States; ECOWAS = Economic Community of West African States; IGAD = Intergovernmental Authority on Development (Horn of Africa, Nile Valley, and African Great Lakes regions); SADC = Southern African Development Community.

(table 6.2 and figure 6.5). However, this occurred not because their level of trade within their regional bloc was falling but simply because their level of trade with the rest of the African countries was rising faster than their trade within their bloc.

As for intra-Africa trade participation at the country level, there is significant heterogeneity. Among the top 10 intra-African exporting countries in 2017, Eswatini, Namibia, South Africa, and Zimbabwe exported at least 25 percent of their goods to other African countries—Eswatini being by far the most reliant on its intra-Africa export markets, reaching 94 percent (table 6.3, panel a). Among the top 10 intra-African importers, Botswana, Namibia, Zambia, and Zimbabwe imported at least 50 percent of their gross imports from other African countries—Botswana being the most reliant on intra-Africa imports, at 73 percent (table 6.3, panel b).

In 2017, the top 10 countries in the volume of exports to other African countries were (in this order) South Africa, Nigeria, Côte d'Ivoire, Zimbabwe, Ghana, the Arab Republic of Egypt, the Republic of Congo, Morocco, Namibia, and Eswatini. The top 10 countries in volume of imports from other African countries were South Africa, Zambia, Namibia, Botswana, Zimbabwe, Mozambique, Mali, Côte d'Ivoire, Kenya, and Cameroon.

Looking at the share of each African country in total intra-Africa trade for 2017, a few countries dominate trade in the continent (figure 6.6). The region's biggest economy, South Africa, accounts for 31 percent of the total intra-Africa trade, followed by Nigeria, Zambia, and Namibia, each of which constitute 6 percent of total intra-Africa trade. Tunisia, Algeria, The

Figure 6.5   Share of Intragroup Trade in Each REC's Total Africa Trade, 1995–2017

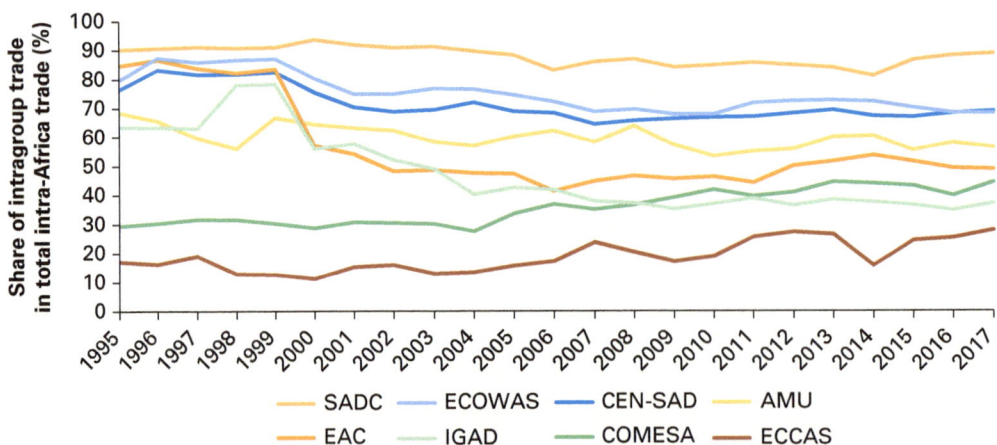

Source: Calculations from the UNCTADstat database, United Nations Conference on Trade and Development (https://unctadstat.unctad.org).
Note: Figure shows the share of intra-Africa export trade by each regional economic community (REC) that is conducted within its own REC. AMU = Arab Maghreb Union; CEN-SAD = Community of Sahel-Saharan States; COMESA = Common Market for Eastern and Southern Africa; EAC = East African Community; ECCAS = Economic Community of Central African States; ECOWAS = Economic Community of West African States; IGAD = Intergovernmental Authority on Development (Horn of Africa, Nile Valley, and African Great Lakes regions); SADC = Southern African Development Community.

Table 6.3   Exports and Imports of the Top 10 Intra-Africa Traders, 2017

	a. Top intra-Africa exporters			b. Top intra-Africa importers	
Top 10 exporting countries	Exports to rest of Africa (US$, millions)	Africa share of global exports (%)	Top 10 importing countries	Imports from rest of Africa (US$, millions)	Africa share of global imports (%)
South Africa	22,850.04	26	South Africa	7,901.03	10
Nigeria	5,048.54	11	Zambia	5,119.35	58
Côte d'Ivoire	2,781.99	22	Namibia	4,531.44	67
Zimbabwe	2,660.11	76	Botswana	3,861.92	73
Ghana	2,004.94	14	Zimbabwe	2,487.90	50
Egypt, Arab. Rep.	1,986.29	8	Mozambique	1,863.76	33
Congo, Rep.	1,893.99	23	Mali	1,749.45	40
Morocco	1,800.04	7	Côte d'Ivoire	1,661.41	17
Namibia	1,762.93	51	Kenya	1,582.98	9
Eswatini	1,696.54	94	Cameroon	1,560.92	15

Source: Calculations using data from the United Nations Comtrade database.

Figure 6.6   Shares of Total Intra-Africa Trade, by Country, 2017

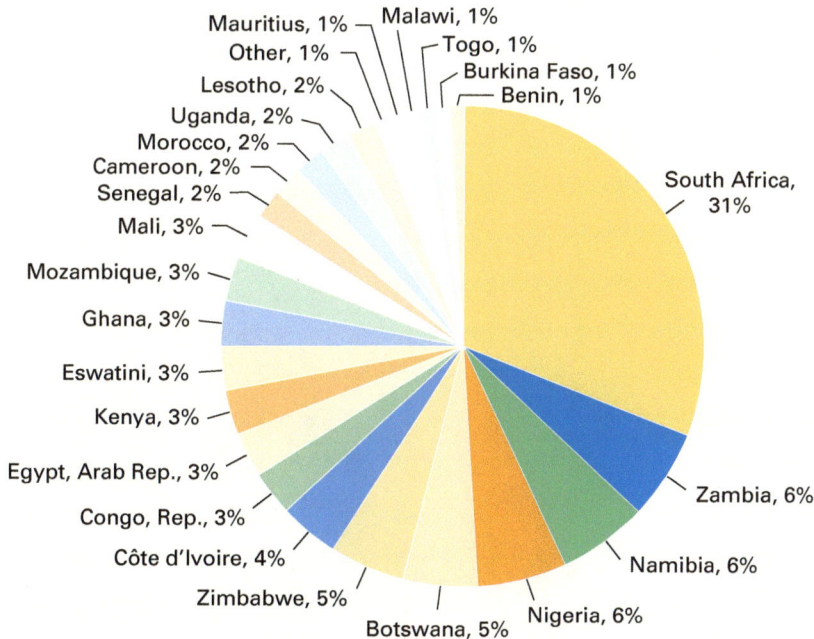

Source: Calculations using data from the United Nations Comtrade database.

Gambia, Burundi, Mauritania, the Seychelles, the Central African Republic, Sierra Leone, and Cabo Verde are among the countries with the lowest shares of intra-Africa trade.

Composition of Trade in Africa

A closer examination of the product composition of trade within Africa and the region's trade with the rest of the world provides important insights on the extent of the economic diversification of trade. Following product classification by stage of processing, raw materials are still Africa's primary export product group to the rest of the world, accounting for 45 percent of the continent's total exports (figure 6.7, panel a). In contrast, intra-Africa trade is dominated by high-value-added goods. Consumer goods and capital goods account for 32 percent and 16 percent of total intraregional exports, respectively (figure 6.7, panel b). Raw materials make up 23 percent of intra-Africa exports—about half the share of raw materials in Africa's exports to the rest of the world.

At a broader sector classification, the share of industrial (manufactured) goods in intra-Africa trade is higher than its share in Africa's exports to the rest of the world. In 2017, the share of industrial goods in total intra-Africa trade averaged 71 percent (figure 6.8, panel a), compared with a 68 percent share of Africa's exports to the rest of the world (figure 6.8, panel b). Although Africa has comparative advantage in agricultural goods exports, the composition of its exports tends to be skewed toward manufactured goods in intraregional trade. This suggests that agriculture and intra-Africa trade in agriculture are underdeveloped—signaling unexploited opportunity.

Finally, figure 6.9 explores intra-Africa trade at the Harmonized System (HS) 2-digit product level in 2017. The figure shows that fuels

Figure 6.7 **Composition of Africa's Global Exports versus Intraregional Exports, by Stage of Product Processing, 2017**

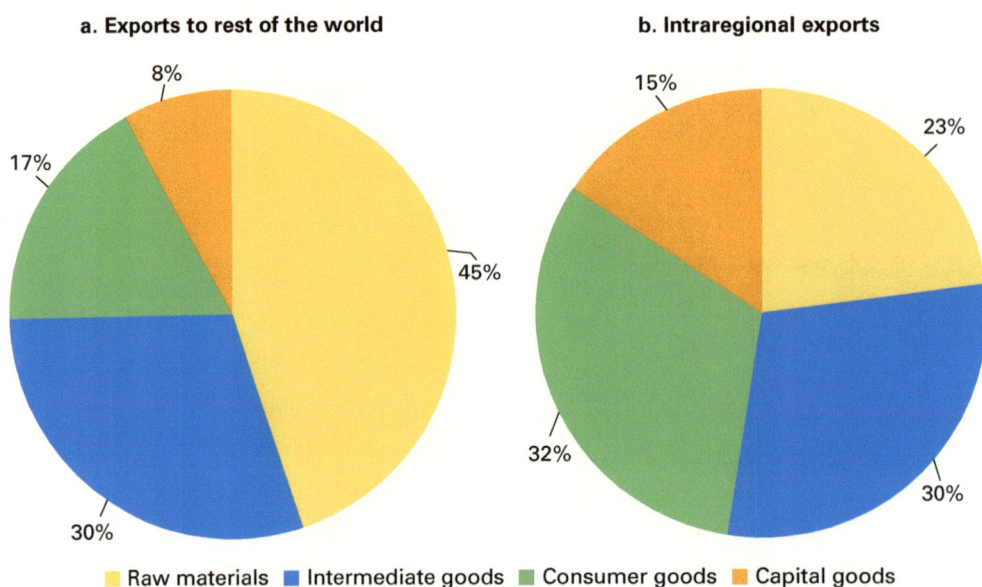

a. Exports to rest of the world

b. Intraregional exports

Raw materials   Intermediate goods   Consumer goods   Capital goods

Source: Calculations using data from the United Nations Comtrade database.

Figure 6.8   Sectoral Distribution of Goods in Africa's Global Exports versus Intraregional Exports, 2017

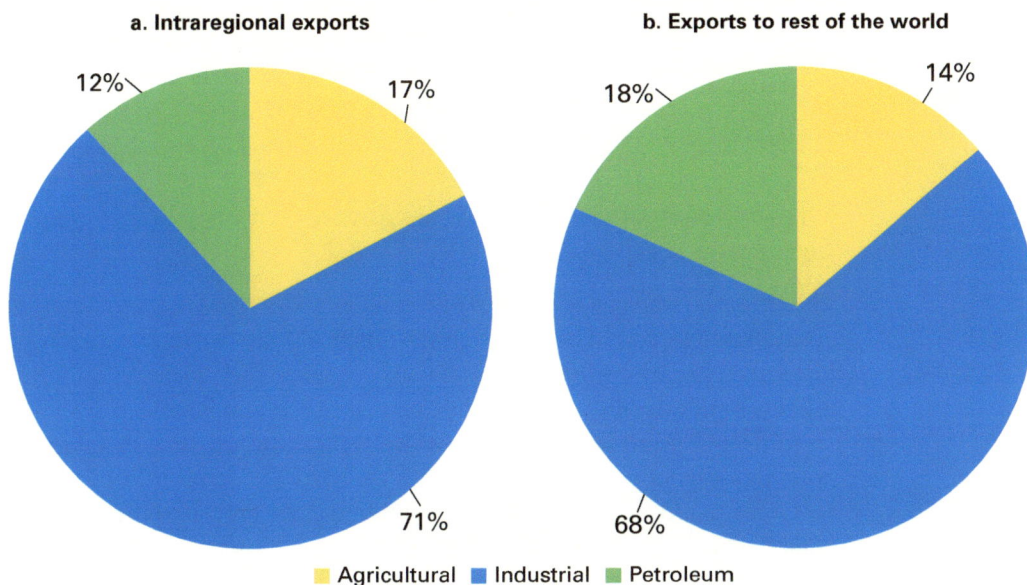

a. Intraregional exports

12%   17%
71%

b. Exports to rest of the world

18%   14%
68%

■ Agricultural   ■ Industrial   ■ Petroleum

Source: Calculations using data from the United Nations Comtrade database.

Figure 6.9   Distribution of Intra-Africa Trade, by Main Product Category, 2017

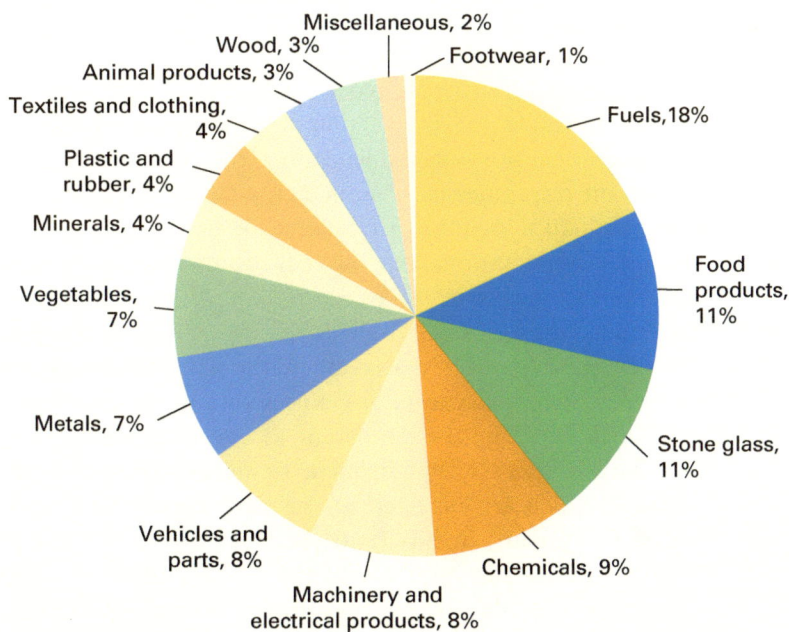

Miscellaneous, 2%
Wood, 3%
Footwear, 1%
Animal products, 3%
Textiles and clothing, 4%
Fuels, 18%
Plastic and rubber, 4%
Minerals, 4%
Vegetables, 7%
Food products, 11%
Metals, 7%
Stone glass, 11%
Vehicles and parts, 8%
Chemicals, 9%
Machinery and electrical products, 8%

Source: Calculations using data from the United Nations Comtrade database.
Note: The product groups are largely based on the World Customs Organization's sector classification for the Harmonized Sytem product nomenclature, with some minor differences.

are the top product traded within the continent, accounting for about 18 percent. Although Africa has almost half the world's uncultivated arable land and high demand for food, only 11 percent of its food products and only 7 percent of its vegetables were traded within the continent. This suggests that intraregional trade could increase the diversification of traded goods as well as production activities in the region.

The Promise of the AfCFTA: Evaluation of Its Impact on Economic Outcomes

The potential impacts of various agreements under the AfCFTA could only be estimated ex ante. Though ex ante estimations have their own limitations in terms of tracking long-term dynamic effects, they provide important insights about the directions of the potential gains and losses.

Table 6.4 summarizes a review of recent studies that estimate the potential impact of implementing the AfCFTA. The gains in total income range from a low of 0.1 percent to a high of 2.24 percent, reaching much higher when other complementary reforms such as reduction of NTMs and trade facilitation programs are included in the analysis. The studies also highlight the disparity in gains across countries, suggesting a role for the African Union to preemptively address the expected disparities in the gains and losses from such trade arrangements, both across countries and within countries.

Because the AfCFTA would boost economic growth relative to baseline GDP projections, greater openness among these countries would result in greater GDP growth in the long run. In the short run, however, there would be some economic costs, particularly in the scenario in which NTMs in goods and transaction costs are reduced intraregionally. The different scenarios for implementing the AfCFTA would also lead to important disparities in economic growth rates across African countries. The elimination of intra-Africa tariffs is not crucial to boost growth for most African countries, but the reduction in NTMs and complementary policies that facilitate trade are the key drivers for trade-led economic growth for most of them in the long run.

A review of studies that evaluate the AfCFTA's impact show that the immediate gains in income are expected to be relatively moderate, reaching a high of 4.2 percent and going as low as 0.1 percent in some studies. The largest gains accrue from a significant rise in trade, particularly exports, which are expected to rise significantly. Though estimates vary significantly, gains in exports could reach a high of 51.1 percent (AfDB 2019). And the biggest share of these trade gains is associated with the reduction of NTMs and improvements in trade facilitation rather than elimination of tariffs.

Table 6.4 Summary of Key Findings on the AfCFTA's Economic Impact

Source	Scenario for tariff and/or NTB removal	GDP gain	Intra-African trade	Total exports	Total imports
Removal of tariffs on intra-AfCFTA trade					
AfDB (2019)	Removal of all tariffs on intra-AfCFTA trade	0.10% (US$2.8b)	14.60% (US$10.1b)	1.00% (US$5.8b)	0.90% (US$5.8b)
Mevel and Karingi (2012)	Removal of all tariffs on intra-AfCFTA trade by 2017 + CET	0.20%	52.3%	4.00%	—
Jensen and Sandrey (2015)	Removal of all tariffs on intra-AfCFTA trade	0.70%	4.30%	3.11%	—
Saygili, Peters, and Knebel (2018)	Removal of all tariffs on intra-AfCFTA trade	0.97%	32.80%	2.50%	1.80%
Abrego et al. (2019)	Removal of all import tariffs	0.037%–0.053%[b]	—	—	—
World Bank (2020)	Gradual removal of 97% of tariffs on intra-AfCFTA trade	0.13% (US$12.0b)	21.76% (US$131.0b)	1.78% (US$35.0b)	2.31% (US$41.0b)
Removal of tariffs and NTBs on intra-AfCFTA trade					
AfDB (2019)	Removal of all tariffs on intra-AfCFTA trade; removal of NTBs	1.25% (US$37.0b)	107.20% (US$74.3b)	44.30% (US$107.2b)	33.80% (US$214.1b)
Jensen and Sandrey (2015)	Removal of all tariffs on intra-AfCFTA trade; 50% reduction in NTBs	1.60%	7.26%	6.28%	—
Abrego et al. (2019)	Removal of all tariffs; 35% reduction in NTBs	7.60%–1.89%–2.11%[b]	8.40%	—	—
World Bank (2020)	Gradual removal of 97% of tariffs on intra-AfCFTA trade	2.24%	51.85%	18.84%	19.58%
Removal of tariffs and NTBs on intra-AfCFTA trade and implementation of TFA					
AfDB (2019)	Removal of all tariffs on intra-AfCFTA trade; removal of NTBs; implementation of TFA	3.50% (US$100.0b)	132.70% (US$92.0b)	51.10% (US$295.6b)	46.20% (US$292.8b)
World Bank (2020)	Gradual removal of 97% of tariffs on intra-AfCFTA trade; 50% reduction in NTBs; implementation of TFA	4.20% (US$413.0b)	92.07% (US$556.0b)	28.64% (US$560.0b)	40.61% (US$714.0b)

Source: Adapted from World Bank 2020.
Note: AfCFTA = African Continental Free Trade Area; b = billions; CET = common external tariff; NTBs = nontariff barriers; TFA = trade facilitation agreement; — = not available.
a. Relative to baseline projections of GDP and trade volumes without the AfCFTA.
b. Values expressed in terms of welfare gain as equivalent variation, measured as the expenditure to attain utility in year *t* in any given simulation using base year prices.

A more recent World Bank (2020) study quantifies the short-run implications of the AfCFTA tariff reduction on trade, welfare, and tariff revenue, using a CGE model calibrated to the most recent database produced by the Global Trade Analysis Project (GTAP). The GTAP database is supplemented by additional data that quantify the impacts of NTMs that, if part of the liberalization package, would complement the elimination of tariffs, boost trade, and in most cases accelerate growth. Box 6.1 summarizes these key findings.

Box 6.1   Overview of Estimated Impacts of the AfCFTA on Welfare

The reduction of tariffs alone is expected to increase the welfare of African Continental Free Trade Area (AfCFTA) members by an average of 0.22 percent (figure B6.1.1). Further reduction of nontariff barriers (NTBs) by half would increase welfare gains to 1.4 percent. And full implementation of the World Trade Organization Trade Facilitation Agreement would bring the overall welfare gains to 4.7 percent by 2030 (relative to the baseline GDP projections without these improved conditions).

Figure B6.1.1   Estimated Welfare Gains in Africa by 2030 from Tariff Elimination, NTM Reduction, and WTO Trade Facilitation Agreement, by Country and AfCFTA Average

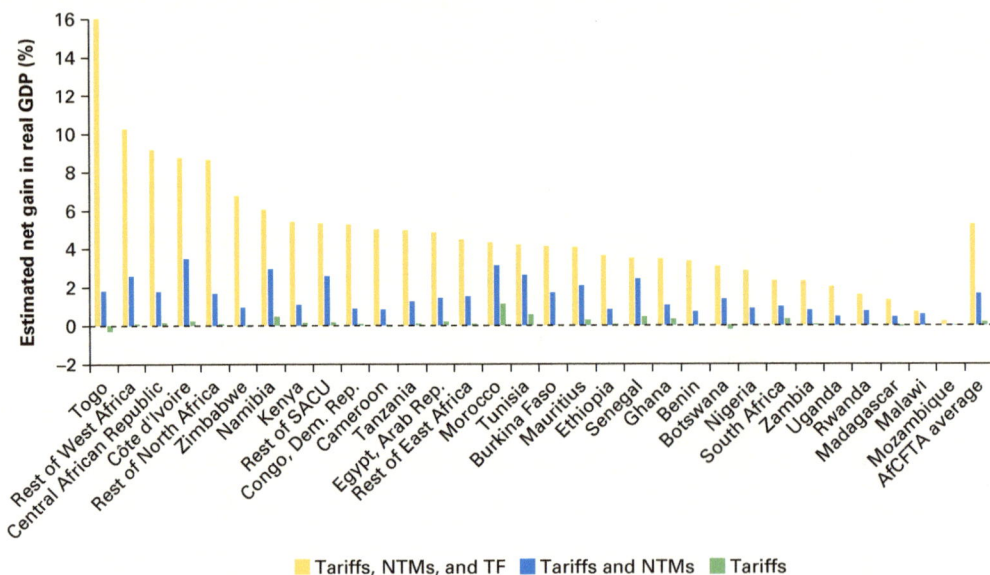

Source: World Bank 2020.
Note: "Tariffs" refers to full elimination of tariffs within the African Continental Free Trade Area (AfCFTA); "NTMs" to halving of nontariff measures in goods and services; and "TF" to full implementation of the World Trade Organization (WTO) Trade Facilitation Agreement. "Estimated welfare gains" refers to gains in real income. SACU = Southern African Customs Union. "Rest of" labels refer to the designated area's countries that are not otherwise shown in the figure.

(Box continues on next page)

Box 6.1   **Overview of Estimated Impacts of the AfCFTA on Welfare** *(continued)*

Heterogeneity of Welfare Impacts

However, the aggregate results mask the heterogeneity of impacts across countries. Although the AfCFTA is expected to benefit all members, the expected welfare gains by 2030 range from 0.2 percent to 16 percent. Thus, the impact of the agreement will depend on its depth and the extent to which it covers NTBs and services—especially in backbone sectors like transportation and logistics—and the respective export basket and economic structure of each country.

The gains are also unevenly distributed across the region. Togo is at the high end, with a gain of 16 percent, followed by the Central African Republic and Côte d'Ivoire, each gaining more than 8 percent. Several countries at the lower end are clustered around a gain of 2 percent, and Malawi and Mozambique bring up the rear with very small gains.

Impacts on Trade Volumes

The AfCFTA is also estimated to yield substantial gains in trade. Import increases are expected to remain below 0.5 percent on average. However, the volume of total exports is expected to increase by over 21 percent and intracontinental exports by over 57 percent (World Bank 2020). There is some modest trade diversion to the rest of the world, with an export decline of about 0.5 percent outside the continent. In monetary terms, intracontinental trade grows from $196 billion in 2030 in the baseline scenario to $310 billion after full implementation of the AfCFTA in 2030. Nonetheless, this raises Africa's share of intracontinental trade from only 12 percent to 16 percent of total trade. The rest of the world still remains a significant trading partner.

The AfCFTA's goal should not be to displace trade with the rest of the world. The region would benefit more from increased trade with the rest of the world, while at the same time integrating more deeply within the continent. In this respect, the finding that trade with the rest of the world remains significant is favorable for growth and welfare in the region. Long-term competitiveness of local firms will increase in response to other aspects of the AfCFTA such as nontariff measure (NTM) elimination, services liberalization, and investment provisions, among others.

Impacts of Tariff Liberalization on Tariff Revenue

For most African countries, the short-term impact of tariff liberalization on tax revenues is small. Annual tariff revenue losses will remain below 1 percent on average for roughly three-quarters of the countries (figure B6.1.2). Only three countries are expected to lose more than 2 percent: the Democratic Republic of Congo (3.4 percent), The Gambia (2.7 percent), and the Republic of Congo (2.1 percent). Even in countries experiencing the largest tariff revenue losses, the decline in total government revenues is rarely expected to rise above 0.3 percent. These results are consistent with other studies that show that, even under full liberalization, few countries will experience significant tariff revenue losses (AfDB 2019; UNECA 2017).

The small short-term revenue impact of tariff liberalization is likely to be compensated by additional long-term tax revenues from increased economic activity. The impact on fiscal revenues depends largely on the assumptions regarding NTM-related revenues. With the assumptions on the reduction in NTMs, NTM revenues would drop by 29 percent—less than the drop in the average NTM of 43 percent as import volumes rise sharply. With the default closure, the lost revenues are offset by increases in direct lump-sum taxes on households. Despite the elimination of intracontinental tariffs, import revenues would increase because trade is heavily weighted toward the rest of the world, and

(Box continues on next page)

Box 6.1   Overview of Estimated Impacts of the AfCFTA on Welfare *(continued)*

Figure B6.1.2   Estimated Average Annual Change by 2030 in Tariff Revenues under the AfCFTA, Selected African Countries

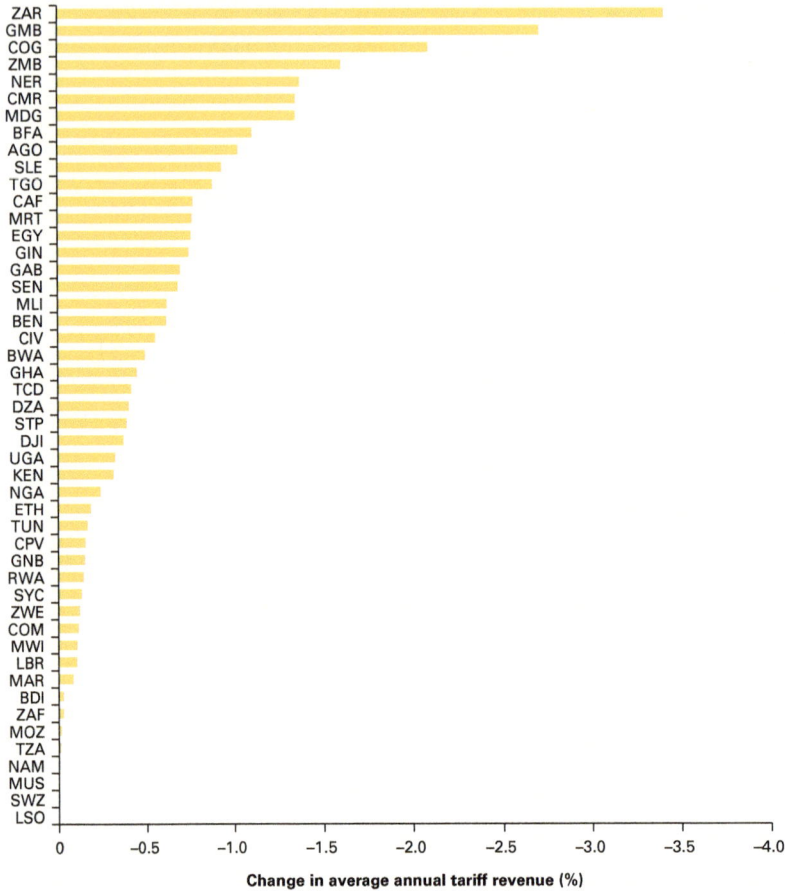

Source: World Bank 2020.
Note: Average annual changes in tariff revenues over a 10-year liberalization period are calculated using a partial equilibrium model (Tariff Reform Impact Simulation Tool [TRIST]) with statutory tariff data (Arenas and Vnukova 2019). Countries are labeled using International Organization for Standardization (ISO) alpha-3 codes. AfCFTA = African Continental Free Trade Area.

the NTM-driven rises in imports are sufficient to replace the lost tariff revenue on intracontinental trade with rising tariff revenues from trade with the rest of the world.

Source: World Bank 2020.

The Challenges Facing the AfCFTA

The AfCFTA is a bold experiment in regional integration, with ambitious goals to transform its members' economies through increased trade and increased integration in services, infrastructure, communications, and other spheres of economic activity. To achieve the AfCFTA's goals requires unprecedented commitment by national and regional institutions. Significant challenges stand in the way of achieving these goals—from building the necessary institutions and following up on the agreements to implementing national and regional strategies that require significant investment in resources and political commitment. The following subsections discuss the key challenges that African governments, international organizations, and businesses must address to realize the AfCFTA's objectives and transform the continent.

High Fragmentation and Thick Borders

As noted earlier, Africa is the most fragmented region in the world and is characterized by thick borders that pose significant challenges for regional trade and integration. With a population slightly smaller than that of China or India, Africa is home to 54 countries, more than any other continent, and the high fragmentation presents a significant geopolitical challenge for the AfCFTA. Most of the economies are small, half with GDP less than $10 billion. In addition, close to 30 percent of the countries (16 countries) are landlocked. The high cost of trading faced by landlocked countries is well documented. Trading costs for an average landlocked low- or middle-income economy are 40–50 percent higher than those for a representative coastal country (Radelet and Sachs 1998).

This severe economic and geographic fragmentation, leading to limited-scale economies, has long restricted Africa's economic expansion by restricting large-scale investment. Historical factors have also contributed to trade patterns that are currently biased toward trade outside the region.

The impact of colonization on contemporary trade patterns has been significant. Infrastructure and trade networks were designed with the goals of transferring natural resources outside the continent. As a result, the regional transportation networks are poorly developed. Most transportation networks, including rail lines (map 6.1), run from the location of a mine or agricultural production hot spot to a port, with a focus on exports to the rest of the world.

This situation still characterizes most of the region's countries and is reflected in the higher costs of trading within Africa. Transportation costs in Africa are, on average, 136 percent higher than in other low- to middle-income regions (Limão and Venables 2001).

The persistent cost of the deep fragmentation goes beyond the transportation costs. Even with increased transportation networks, the multiplicity of rules and procedures that govern trade across countries restricts trading across multiple countries and ports. The redundant procedures associated with each country's customs procedures present a significant barrier to trade. The average customs transaction involves 20–30 different parties, 40 documents, and the re-keying of 60–70 percent of all data at least once (UNECA 2010).

Map 6.1   High Fragmentation of Rail Lines in Africa, 2018

Source: Africa Infrastructure Country Diagnostic database, World Bank.

In addition, Africa's stark fragmentation—geographically and in economic size and disparity—increases the potential for conflicts of interest. In regional blocs with relatively large memberships, integration is more likely to be shallow because of disparities and the difficulty in reaching consensus (De Melo and Tsikata 2015). Another downside to the small size of African economies arises from their greater likelihood of having firms with high levels of monopoly power, given mere market size, and monopoly creates the potential for opportunistic behavior in transactions (Collier and Venables 2010). This in turn limits the birth and growth of private enterprises, a challenge that the AfCFTA intends to address by expanding markets.

Africa's large number of small countries with a multiplicity of rules and procedures, as well as the difficulties associated with crossing borders for goods, services, and people, remains one of the biggest challenges to the

AfCFTA's success. This is a continent-specific challenge that can be addressed only if the region's countries commit to minimize the costs of this high fragmentation by streamlining policies, harmonizing customs rules and procedures, and sacrificing some level of sovereignty in rule making and implementation in favor of regional frameworks.

Disparities in Potential Gains and Losses

The AfCFTA poses substantial challenges for small economies because trade liberalization may reinforce existing income disparities and create greater divergence. There are also risks that increased regional integration between low-income economies may draw manufacturing production into the relatively richer countries at the expense of the poorer members, leading to divergence of member country incomes (Venables 2003). Countries would experience uneven gains from increased liberalization, and the losses would be disproportionately allocated.

The terms of trade and income impacts would also be divergent across countries. A recent CGE simulation (Jensen and Sandrey 2015) shows that the largest AfCFTA gains would go to countries with larger manufacturing bases and developed transportation infrastructure, including South Africa ($5.7 billion), Nigeria ($2.0 billion), Kenya ($1.3 billion), Senegal ($1.2 billion), and Angola ($1.1 billion), whereas Zimbabwe and Madagascar are projected to lose about $1.5 billion and $1.0 billion, respectively. In addition, the revenue impacts of the tariff liberalization would be felt differently across countries where the revenue loss is strongest—in Angola, the Democratic Republic of Congo, Ethiopia, Ghana, Kenya, Mozambique, Nigeria, Tanzania, and Zimbabwe.

It is critical that AfCFTA countries adopt strategies so that the weaker economies are not left behind. A regional mechanism to support lagging regions may have political and social benefits. However, the long-term solution to address possible divergence in the gains is to further deepen the integration of economies within and across countries. Countries and regional entities need to implement policies that ease the constraints that inhibit the poor and poorer economies from accessing market infrastructure and facilitate better integration of leading and lagging regions and movement of people across space and skill levels. Deepening integration would better address the divergence than individually targeted compensatory mechanisms, which would help only in coping with the transitions in the short term.

Costs of Adjustment

There is now consensus that increased trade is expected to have sharp distributional implications. Job creation due to trade reform is generally accompanied by job loss because workers move from one sector to another. In a study of manufacturing jobs in 77 countries, Torres (2001) highlights that an increase in international trade is associated with increased movement of labor between industries. Relocation of workers makes finding new employment difficult and costly for displaced workers because moving into a different sector usually requires a change in skills. Economic integration enhances competition and thereby fosters structural changes. This leads to a better allocation of factors of production and productivity-enhancing innovations. Yet it could also impose certain transitional costs.

Many African countries lack the necessary financing and social protection programs to deal with the adjustment costs. Following trade, the fall in the level of output ($Y[t]$) below the initial level of output (Y_o) during the first period (t_{yo}) reflects the adjustment costs (figure 6.10). In panel a, output returns to pretrade level Y_T, where the adjustment costs are only temporary. However, the adjustment costs may persist such that output and hence employment might not return to the pretrade level. In panel b, the new long-run equilibrium would then shift from Y_T to $Y_{T,A}$, at lower levels of output and higher levels of unemployment. Increased trade may have distributive implications, with consequences for human development and welfare. This calls for national and regional active and passive labor market policies to reduce the costs of adjustment and support the transition of labor to the new, long-term equilibrium.

More recent studies have shown that, depending on labor market frictions and the mobility of capital, the duration of the transition could be longer, and the magnitude of the adjustment costs larger (Dix-Carneiro and Kovak 2017). Setting up programs in advance to address the problems arising from the adjustment costs is not only necessary to support the displaced and unemployed but also an important tool to maintain public support for the project. Recent upheavals in high-income economies, reflected in increased trade protectionism and political shifts

Figure 6.10 Adjustment Paths Following Trade Liberalization

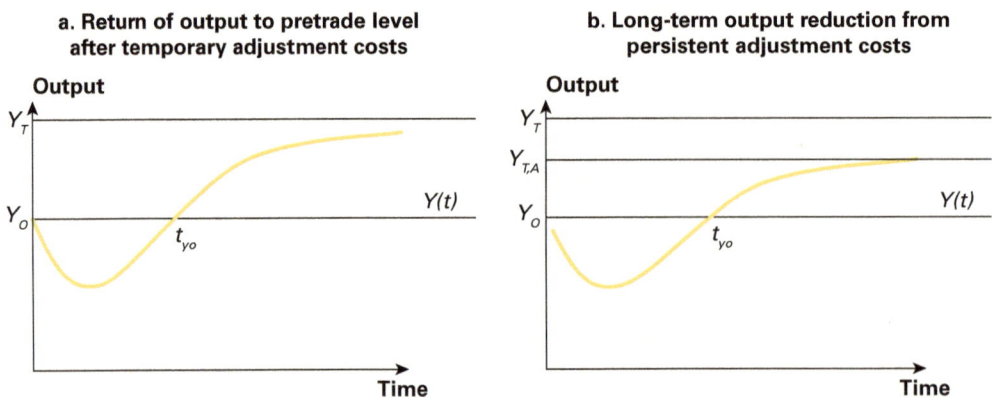

a. Return of output to pretrade level after temporary adjustment costs

b. Long-term output reduction from persistent adjustment costs

Source: Francois, Jansen, and Peters 2011.
Note: Following trade liberalization, the fall in the level of output ($Y[t]$) below the initial level of output (Y_o) during the first period (t_{yo}) reflects the adjustment costs. If the adjustment costs have a persistent negative effect in the long run, the posttrade equilibrium ($Y_{T,A}$) will be at lower levels of output.

toward the right, reflect governments' failures to address these key challenges.

Transitioning from RECs to the AfCFTA: A Sticky Process

About 80 percent of all intra-Africa trade flows through RECs and 20 percent flows outside, indicating that, although trade within the RECs is growing, intra-Africa trade across RECs has been minimal. Hence, increasing trade between the RECs remains a challenge. One of the AfCFTA's 12 core principles, stated in its founding agreement, is that the RECs serve as building blocks for the AfCFTA, and the program aims to "resolve the challenges of multiple and overlapping memberships" between the eight RECs functioning at various levels of integration.[8] The RECs may remain active during the operation of AfCFTA, although, "in the event of inconsistency, the AfCFTA agreement shall prevail."

Still, the multiplicity of rules across RECs and their distinctions from the AfCFTA rules remain a big challenge. The transition from RECs to the AfCFTA is expected to be sticky, and members must develop strategies to maximize the gains from their existing RECs while restricting the costs resulting from divergent regulations and rules governing each REC in the transition to the AfCFTA.

Tension between National Industrial Policies and AfCFTA Ambitions

The AfCFTA's success hinges on the member countries' effort to make the regional strategy part of their national policy and address the tensions that arise between the two. Short of this, the agreement remains a policy document with no meaningful national implications. Moreover, the success of other technical policy reforms such as improving regional infrastructure and easing tariff and nontariff barriers, which are critical to unleash the benefits from increased economies of scale, depends on the extent of active national AfCFTA strategies. Political tensions, both between interest groups within a country and across member countries, will always be part of the process because countries often adopt divergent economic strategies.

For example, Nigeria's early hesitation to join the AfCFTA signaled the concerns of local trade unions in manufacturing, for fear of competition from cheap imports. Nigerian President Muhammadu Buhari said in 2018 that his administration was in no hurry to enter any agreement that could make Nigeria a "dumping ground" for cheap imports from outside the FTA (Kolawole, Agbawuru, and Uzor 2018). Nigeria's concerns speak to the risks that all countries in the region face as they ease restrictions on the movement of goods, services, and people. To address these concerns, governments should find the sweet spot that reinforces national economic goals and ensures maximum gains from increased integration.

Reaching this difficult balance would require countries to look beyond a static assessment of their priorities and policies. In addition, countries need to build local consensus around the long-term benefits of integration. This is particularly important in the larger countries, which may have relatively more influence on regional decisions. National and regional initiatives to reconcile these interests would elicit a broad base of citizen support if they were preceded by an inclusive process of local consultations to evaluate the impacts of such initiatives.

(Mis)Design of Rules and Procedures

The gradual elimination of tariffs under the AfCFTA will make NTBs—including but not limited to the multiplicity of regulations across the region, such as customs clearance, standards and certification requirements, rules of origin, quotas, and export subsidies—more significant. As noted earlier, NTBs are high and prevalent in Africa and represent critical obstacles to trade in the region (Abrego et al. 2019; Mevel and Karingi 2012). These barriers generally include NTMs, infrastructure gaps, and other trade-related transaction costs. Among the NTMs, the most restrictive trade barriers in the region include sanitary and phytosanitary measures, including preshipment inspections and formalities; contingent trade-protective measures; licensing, quotas, and prohibitions; and price controls (Kee and Nicita 2016).

Underdeveloped physical infrastructure and high transaction costs due to excessive and unnecessary document requirements and unnecessary delays also remain among the main challenges of intra-Africa trade. Examining 45 AfCFTA countries, Abrego et al. (2019) find that NTB reduction has a much larger welfare effect than tariff reduction. They estimate that elimination of tariffs in Africa increases welfare by 0.05 percent, whereas an ad valorem equivalent reduction in NTBs increases welfare by 1.7 percent. A similar study by Mevel and Karingi (2012) highlights that the welfare and trade impacts of eliminating tariffs without addressing the barriers to trade would be very small and that the AfCFTA could not achieve its target of doubling the share of intra-Africa trade over the next decade without significant NTB reduction. A critical set of measures that could help in achieving the targeted outcome would be to address NTMs and improve trade facilitation.

In addition to the barriers, which are often categorized as NTMs, the AfCFTA's rules and procedures pose challenges that require clarity and close examination. Elimination of tariffs does not automatically lead to increased trade because it also depends on whether the various rules and procedures underlying trade are satisfied, including the document requirements associated with such rules and customs procedures. The AfCFTA's success depends on the ease of streamlining these rules across countries. The following discussion outlines some of the most important challenges.

Rules of Origin

The driving principle in establishing rules of origin is to ensure that firms comply with sourcing most of the intermediate and final goods from within the FTA while avoiding trade deflection or transshipment. This aims to strengthen regional value chains and support the emergence of Africa as the next factory of the world—the next frontier of global manufacturing. These rules are natural barriers to trade, although they satisfy another important goal: rules of origin, which determine the origin of products traded across borders, ensure that goods satisfy the qualification for preferential tariff treatment. The design and implementation of rules of origin are critical for the nature of trade and the emerging regional and global value chains.

Designing the rules of origin involves an important trade-off—between making them too restrictive and complex and making them too flexible and simple. Complex and stringent rules raise the costs of compliance to the extent that they may discourage the use of the FTA preferences and hence constrain the development of regional value chains. Rules with stringent requirements are even costlier in Africa because of the costs of monitoring and verification, which could be higher than in other regions. The success of stringent rules also depends on the extent to which regional production provides low-cost alternatives to the very competitive, low-cost international supply of intermediate goods for production. This is similar to using rules of origin as substitutes for industrial policies that protect domestic firms. In this case, the cost margin between local and imported content of intermediate goods would play an important role in the overall objectives of the specific rules of origin. To maximize the gains, there is a need to build the capacity of the trade administrative apparatus to enforce and verify the rules. At the same time, rules that are too flexible, particularly regarding local content requirements, may fail to deepen local production links and may limit the development of effective regional value chains with a competitive regional manufacturing sector.

Most often, there are other factors in addition to the central trade-offs that inform the current AfCFTA rules of origin negotiations. For example, high disparity in the development of the manufacturing sector across economies may have contributed to the complicated negotiations. The AfCFTA is more likely to adopt product-specific rules than ones based on broad product classifications.[9] Product-specific rules of origin are often considered more complex and require highly specified requirements for each product type, hence leading to stringent document requirements. Rules of origin that vary across products, especially at very low levels of classification, are likely to restrict the growth of regional value chains and regional industrial trade networks because production of a single item often requires multiple intermediate inputs with varying rules of origin requirements. This may impose significant costs of compliance and verification.

In addition to adopting simplified, general, and easier to administer rules, introducing an ex post verification system may help reduce the costs associated with exporting and importing. Given the multiplicity of the rules of origin across the various RECs, challenges are entailed whether in harmonizing the existing rules of origin across the RECs or in starting anew by introducing new rules of origin that govern trade within the AfCFTA.

With the newly minted AfCFTA, a more gradual approach that begins with more flexible, simpler, and easier rules of origin based on broad product classifications and then moving slowly to relatively less flexible rules seems relevant. Given the lack of a competitive manufacturing sector, stringent rules at the early stages would be too restrictive to build a vibrant regional value chain. If Africa is to become the next manufacturing frontier, very flexible rules of origin in the early phases of integration should be used to enhance production capacity and build the institutional muscle to monitor and verify the rules of origin requirements that would eventually become less flexible with increased development.

Sensitive Products and Exclusion Lists

As it stands, the AfCFTA faces uncertainties on core design issues, including the choice of the list of sensitive products (sensitive/exclusion) for tariff liberalization planned over different phases of the operation of the program. The trade-in-goods protocol has been completed. AfCFTA members have agreed to liberalize 90 percent of tariffs on goods over 10 years for least developed countries (LDCs) and over 5 years for non-LDCs. The AfCFTA is expected to have significant impacts in promoting trade and integration if tariffs are liberalized for at least 90 percent of the total value of imports corresponding to at least 90 percent of the tariff lines—that is, the double qualification approach that the AfCFTA employs.

Under the tariff line approach, the AfCFTA's success in promoting trade will be restricted, because a significant share of trade is accounted for by a very small share of the tariff lines that could be excluded from liberalization. Still, even with the double qualification, a large share of trade occurs with tariff lines that account for less than 10 percent of the tariff lines. Hence, the risk of not effectively liberalizing trade is higher depending on the choice of the exclusion and sensitive list of products. The 90 percent tariff lines may effectively represent a very small share of the total value of trade or imports in the region, or the exclusion list may account for more than half the value of imports in some countries.

Intra-Africa trade is already low; hence, the exclusion of even a small set of tariff lines could effectively exclude a significant share of imports to a country. Although the agreement toward the double qualification approach is encouraging, there is still a need for an "anticoncentration" clause to restrict the prospects that a few selected tariff lines will fall under trade regimes that are not fully liberalized.

Enforcement and Resolution of Trade Dispute Settlement Mechanisms

There is a concern among the member countries about remedial action, dispute resolution, and enforcement mechanisms within the AfCFTA. The current dispute resolution mechanism adopts a framework that is similar to the one used under the WTO. The emphasis on the WTO dispute resolution mechanisms between "state parties" limits the scope of the potential disputes that may arise beyond states, such as those between private enterprises and multinationals, for example.

In addition, the multiplicity of languages, legal institutions, and cultures poses challenges in streamlining legal systems across the region. There is a need for a continental body that addresses these challenges and has the authority to mediate and enforce decisions of arbitrations within and across countries. This body should be strongly supplemented by traditional diplomatic or political approaches to resolve disputes. In addition, there is a need for a provision in the AfCFTA agreement that allows arbitration between investors and states over claims of breaches of the trade agreement. This provision could be bolstered by a regional entity that monitors these arbitrations.

These mechanisms are essential to address not only disputes within Africa but also trade conflicts with parties outside the continent. The challenge of enforcing the rules, including border and customs rules, is reinforced by the partially arbitrary nature of the colonial borders in the region, coupled with strong ethnic connections between communities across borders. Disparities in countries' economic size also pose challenges to impartial enforcement and resolution of trade disputes—as evidenced by Nigeria's unilateral border closure in August 2019 to block the flow of goods between itself and neighboring Benin, Cameroon, Chad, and Niger. Though trade agreements are accompanied by intricate dispute resolution mechanisms, they are often underused. As the African Union works on developing the dispute settlement mechanisms for the AfCFTA, there is a need to also consider how to increase their use.

Given the ambitious industrialization agenda of the African Union and its members, disputes on rules, particularly the rules of origin, are expected to be recurrent in trading manufactured goods as the AfCFTA becomes more active. This suggests the need to address the challenges associated with origin fraud. In addition to setting the rules of regional trade, African countries need to establish national and regional institutional frameworks to monitor and ensure compliance with the rules and address illicit trade practices when they are reported. The African Union's recent online initiative to facilitate the reporting of illicit trade and trade disputes—the AfCFTA Non-Tariff Barriers Reporting, Monitoring and Eliminating Mechanism[10]—is a step in the right direction.

Policy Implications

The AfCFTA is an ambitious project that requires massive investment in resources, reforms, increased cooperation from members, and relinquishment of some control over national policies. Africa suffers from challenges that most other regions do not face; hence, the AfCFTA requires unprecedented levels of commitment to succeed. The fundamental challenges include the region's high level of fragmentation and thick borders, both of which increase the per unit cost of moving things across borders. In addition, Africa, particularly Sub-Saharan Africa, is one of the most distant regions from the large concentrations of the world economy—in North America, Europe, and East Asia—that provide much of the scale in markets and production. To overcome these challenges, the AfCFTA is the best way forward to make Africa the next regional growth frontier and provide strong grounds to engage in GVCs while also strengthening regional complementarities.

The Need for Strong Political Commitment to Regional Integration

With increasing regionalization and the rise of robust regional blocs reigning over global trade, African states operating separately would find it challenging to grow faster and reduce poverty on a large scale. Hence, the first policy implication is to understand the need for and commit to high levels of political commitment to the goals of regional integration.

The overarching policy recommendation for a successful African FTA is for member countries to make a genuine political commitment to the AfCFTA's goals. Countries should make the regional strategy part of their national policy; otherwise, the AfCFTA agreement remains a policy document with no national implications. Even with the success of all the other technical policy recommendations we often push for—improving regional infrastructure and facilitating business integration—easing NTBs on trade depends on the extent of cooperative political commitment. This often requires the pooling of national sovereignty and giving up some national policy for the larger mutual interest of the region.

Political tensions will always be part of the process. To address these, governments should engage in broad national information programs to introduce the economic benefits of regional integration. Building a strong national coalition among the elites and citizens is essential to maintain support for these goals. Regional policies may gain more traction when they align with national priorities and attract broad local support. This is particularly important in the larger countries, which may have relatively large influence on regional decisions.

The Role of Focused, Coordinated Investment in Infrastructure

The approach to strengthen the integration that is required for a successful AfCFTA should have three parts: improving physical integration, strengthening political cooperation, and facilitating business integration. Although fragmentation and political and geographic factors play key roles, growth in Africa should not be restricted by geographic determinism.

Through focused policies, the costs of distance and fragmentation can be reduced by improved regional infrastructure—roads, air travel, harbors, communication, energy, and financial services—to facilitate easy mobility of goods, services, people, and knowledge. These improvements require investments in the quality and volume of these infrastructures.

Equally important, states must ensure that national infrastructure projects are coordinated with regional frameworks, to maximize the gains and expand the economies of scale from infrastructure investments. Through collaborative frameworks, states need to reduce the administrative time and transaction costs of trading across borders by improving customs procedures, reducing customs clearance times, establishing one-stop shops, and streamlining regulations across borders.

The Importance of Simplifying the Rules

Many of the technical challenges in the AfCFTA rules and procedures are better addressed by building strong political support and commitment to the goals of regional integration. For example, given that each REC has its own distinct rules of origin, some more complex than others, there is a need to streamline and simplify the rules so that they do not restrict trade flows and investment.

Rules of origin that vary across products are likely to restrict the growth of regional value chains and regional industrial trade networks, because production of a single item often requires multiple intermediate inputs with varying rules of origin requirements. The current rules of origin under debate need to be reformed so that they are simple, are consistent across product groups, and do not impose costs on either the firms or the regional entities in administering such rules.

Similarly, given that intra-Africa trade is already low, the exclusion of even a small set of tariff lines could effectively exclude a significant share of imports to a country. Although the agreement toward implementing the double qualification approach is encouraging, there is still a need for an "anticoncentration" clause to restrict the prospects that a few select tariff lines will fall under trade regimes that are not fully liberalized.

The Use of Regional Integration to Address Disparities

It is important to picture what successful regional integration looks like in the context of Africa. This helps to monitor progress and minimizes the misperception common among economic policy circles of mistaking the goals for the end. Regional integration should be considered an instrument to achieve the goals of increasing growth and shared prosperity as well as a positive outcome by itself. A successful AfCFTA, in addition to increasing trade within the region, should not come at the cost of increased economic disparity between regions and should not restrict trade with the rest of the world.

The region's persistent high economic disparities could be further reinforced with increased trade, whereby the relatively advanced economies could dominate the production and export of goods and services. For the AfCFTA to be successful, there is a need to assess these potential impacts and signal to countries the need to build increased cooperation beyond trade.

As the policy platform shifts from national to regional or continental, it is important to institute a regional framework to address these inevitable disparities in gains and losses that would arise after integration. Regional entities need to provide a cushion for weaker economies so that they are not left behind. This will help to maintain the strength of the FTA as well as the gains from increased trade over the long term.

The emphasis on increasing trade among countries in the region should also not sway countries from further integrating into GVCs. Regional integration in Africa should not fully replace or substitute for trade with the rest of the world. Trade with countries with disparate incomes and production systems often reinforces the transfer of new knowledge and technology, compared with trade with a similar country.

Policy makers need not lose sight of the importance of trading with the rest of the world, including high-income economies as well as the newly emerging economies in Asia, mainly China and India. Integration in the region should serve as the springboard to integrate successfully with the rest of the world. Regional integration can also bring about greater peace and security as well as better bargaining power for the region, which is particularly essential with the rise of regional blocs globally.

Most of the challenges of integration before and after AfCFTA are best addressed by deeper integration within and across economies. The key instrument in deepening and broadening integration is the quality and volume of connective infrastructure and connective services across the region. This will ensure the development of strong production links and the creation and growth of regional value chains. Deeper integration is also the strategy that would ensure that most have access to market infrastructure to benefit from the potentially increasing concentration of production activities in certain places and minimize the risks of economic divergence.

The success of the AfCFTA will depend on two critical factors, one more important than the other: The fundamental challenge is the political economy of regional integration, which determines the extent of state and regional commitment by leaders, elites, and citizens. This in turn determines the second critical factor, which is the choice between more-restrictive or more-liberal rules of origin that will determine the success of AfCFTA.

Annex 6A Logistics Performance and Gravity Model Results

Figure 6A.1   Performance on Trade Logistics, by Index Component and Region, 2018

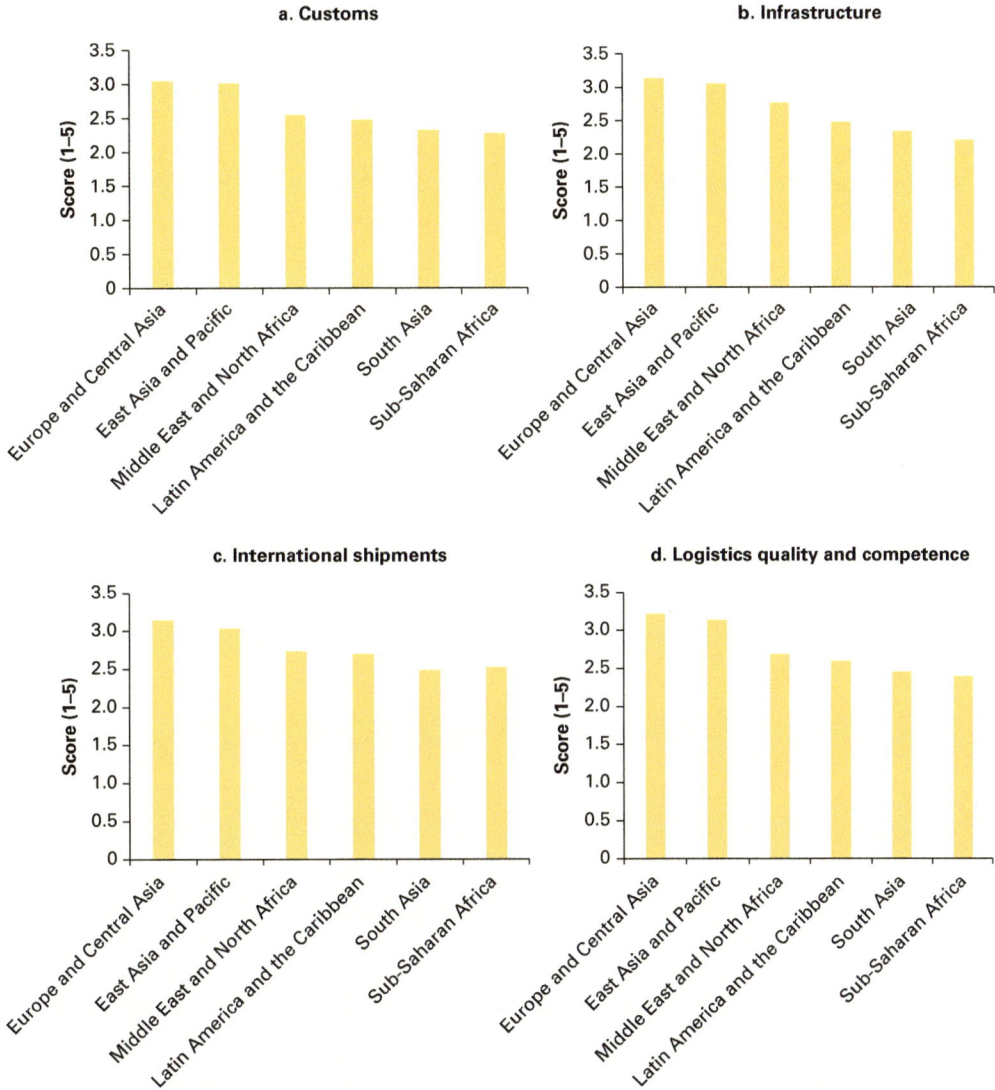

a. Customs

b. Infrastructure

c. International shipments

d. Logistics quality and competence

(Figure continues on next page)

Figure 6A.1   Performance on Trade Logistics, by Index Component and Region, 2018
(continued)

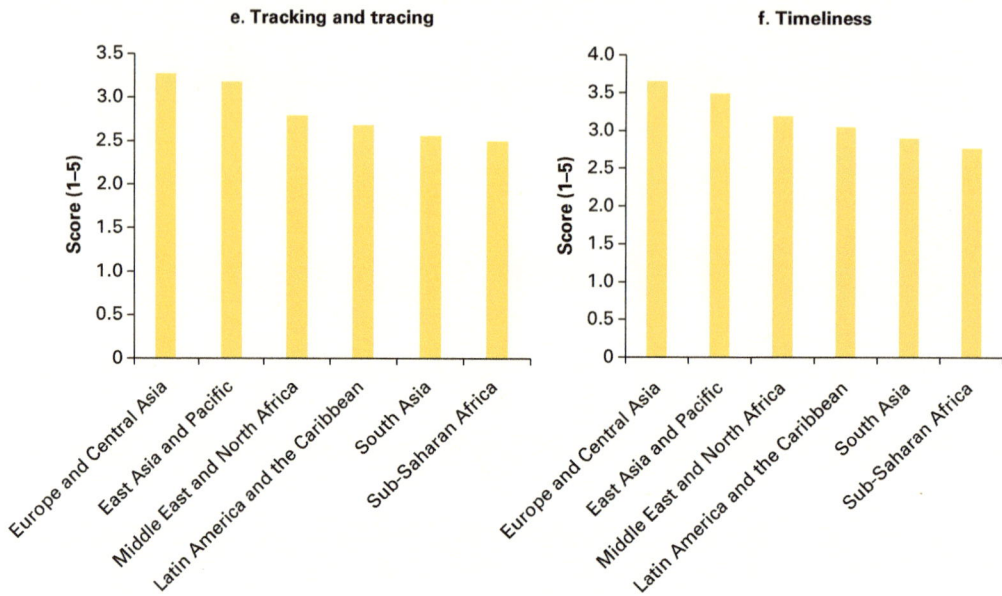

Source: Calculations using the World Bank's Logistics Performance Index (LPI) 2018 data set (https://lpi.worldbank.org/).
Note: The aggregated 2018 LPI combines six core performance components: customs, infrastructure, international shipment, logistics quality and competence, tracking and tracing, and timeliness.

Table 6A.1   Gravity Model: All African Countries, 1990–2014

	(1)	(2)	(3)	(4)
$\ln GDP_i$	0.190***	0.177***	0.173***	0.091***
	(0.002)	(0.002)	(0.002)	(0.009)
$\ln GDP_j$	0.156***	0.139***	0.137***	0.095***
	(0.002)	(0.002)	(0.002)	(0.008)
$\ln Dist_{ij}$	−0.414***	−0.362***	−0.277***	−0.399***
	(0.004)	(0.006)	(0.006)	(0.007)
1 = Common official or primary language		0.224***	0.168***	0.148***
		(0.007)	(0.006)	(0.008)
1 = Contiguity		0.106***	0.198***	0.085***
		(0.011)	(0.011)	(0.011)
1 = Landlocked$_j$		−0.192***	−0.247***	0.012
		(0.008)	(0.008)	(0.052)
1 = Landlocked$_i$		−0.135***	−0.205***	−0.202***
		(0.008)	(0.008)	(0.066)

(Table continues on next page)

Table 6A.1   Gravity Model: All African Countries, 1990–2014 *(continued)*

	(1)	(2)	(3)	(4)
1 = Both a member of at least one PTA			0.012	−0.037***
			(0.009)	(0.010)
1 = Both a member of at least one CU			0.142***	0.093***
			(0.010)	(0.012)
1 = GATT$_i$			0.389***	0.006
			(0.032)	(0.051)
1 = GATT$_j$			0.189***	0.069
			(0.033)	(0.050)
1 = Both a member of WTO			−0.049***	0.079***
			(0.011)	(0.011)
1 = Both a member of GATT			0.171***	0.123***
			(0.036)	(0.036)
Reporter fixed effects	No	No	No	Yes
Partner fixed effects	No	No	No	Yes
Constant	−2.449***	−2.201***	−3.283***	0.304**
	(0.062)	(0.066)	(0.082)	(0.155)
N	50,194	50,194	49,954	49,954
R²	0.277	0.298	0.347	0.442

Source: World Bank calculations.
Note: The subscript *i* represents the country of origin, and *j* represents the destination country. Standard errors are in parentheses. CU = customs union; GATT = General Agreement on Tariffs and Trade; PTA = preferential trade agreement; WTO = World Trade Organization.
* $p < 0.10$; ** $p < 0.05$; *** $p < 0.01$.

Notes

1. African Union, "CFTA – Continental Free Trade Area," African Union website (https://au.int/en/ti/cfta/about).
2. As of this writing, Eritrea has yet to sign the agreement establishing the AfCFTA.
3. African Union, "CFTA – Continental Free Trade Area," African Union website (https://au.int/en/ti/cfta/about).
4. The "long-run" impact accounts for the negative short-run costs of adjustment associated with short-run structural change through the relocation of labor, capital, and other factors of production. The period and the depth of the short-run costs of adjustment depend on the flexibility and structure of economies (Saygili, Peters, and Knebel 2018).
5. Document compliance captures the time and cost for obtaining, preparing, processing, presenting, and submitting documents. Border compliance records the time and cost associated with customs clearance and inspection and port or border handling.

6. The basic equation estimates $Trade\ flow_{ijt} = \alpha_{ij} + \beta_{ij}X_{ijt} + FE_i + FE_j + \varepsilon_{ijt}$, where X_{ij} represents gravity variables, including the economic size (GDP) of trading countries and the distance between trading countries and other potential determinants of trade, such as common language, contiguity, landlockedness, and membership in a preferential trade agreement, customs union, and the World Trade Organization. FE_i and FE_j represent exporting and importing country fixed effects. ε_{ijt} denotes the error term.

7. The IGAD trade bloc comprises eight countries from the Horn of Africa, Nile Valley, and African Great Lakes regions: Djibouti, Eritrea, Ethiopia, Kenya, Somalia, South Sudan, Sudan, and Uganda.

8. The eight RECs recognized by the African Union are the AMU, CEN-SAD, COMESA, EAC, ECCAS, ECOWAS, IGAD, and SADC.

9. Recent discussion (June 2019) with AfCFTA negotiators revealed that the rules of origin are likely to be product specific.

10. The AfCFTA's online Non-Tariff Barriers Reporting, Monitoring, and Eliminating Mechanism is a facility developed to enhance trade through removal of NTBs. Open to all businesses—small, medium, and large companies; informal traders; and women and youth operators—it documents reports of any impediments that businesses encounter when trading across borders, including excessive delays, ad hoc fees, cumbersome document requirements, and restrictive product standards and regulations. For more information, see the mechanism's website at https://tradebarriers.africa/.

References

Abrego, L., M. A. Amado, T. Gursoy, G. P. Nicholls, and H. Perez-Saiz. 2019. "The African Continental Free Trade Agreement: Welfare Gains Estimates from a General Equilibrium Model." Working Paper 19/124, International Monetary Fund, Washington, DC.

AfDB (African Development Bank). 2019. *African 2019 Outlook Economic*. Abidjan, Côte d'Ivoire: AfDB.

Arenas, G., and Y. Vnukova. 2019. "Short-Term Revenue Implications of Tariff Liberalization under the African Continental Free Trade Area (AfCFTA)." Unpublished manuscript, World Bank, Washington, DC.

Balassa, B. A., 1961. *The Theory of Economic Integration*. Westport, CT: Greenwood Press.

Baldwin, R. E. 1992. "Measurable Dynamic Gains from Trade." *Journal of Political Economy* 100 (1): 162–74.

Bergsten, C. F. 1991. "Commentary: The Move toward Free Trade Zones." *Economic Review* 76: 27–35.

Brixiová, Z., Q. Meng, and M. Ncube. 2015. "Can Intra-Regional Trade Act as a Global Shock Absorber in Africa?" London School of Economics (blog),

November 28, 2015. https://blogs.lse.ac.uk/africaatlse/2015/09/28/can
-intra-regional-trade-act-as-a-global-shock-absorber-in-africa/.

Chauvin, N. D., M. P. Ramos, and G. Porto. 2016. "Trade, Growth, and
Welfare Impacts of the CFTA in Africa." Proceedings of the CSAE
Conference 2016: Economic Development in Africa, St. Catherine's
College, Oxford, March 20–22.

Clausing, Kimberly A. 2001. "Trade Creation and Trade Diversion in the
Canada–United States Free Trade Agreement." *Canadian Journal of
Economics* 34 (3): 677–96.

Collier, P., and A. J. Venables. 2010. "Trade and Economic Performance: Does
Africa's Fragmentation Matter?" In *People, Politics, and Globalization:
Annual World Bank Conference on Development Economics—Global
2009*, edited by J. Y. Lin and B. Pleskovic, 51–76. Washington, DC:
World Bank.

Cooper, C. A., and B. F. Massell. 1965. "A New Look at Customs Union
Theory." *Economic Journal* 75 (300): 742–47.

De Melo, J., and Y. Tsikata. 2015. "Regional Integration in Africa:
Challenges and Prospects." In *The Oxford Handbook of Africa and
Economics: Volume 2: Policies and Practices*, edited by C. Monga and
J. Y. Lin, 222–46. Oxford: Oxford University Press.

Dix-Carneiro, R., and B. K. Kovak. 2017. "Trade Liberalization and
Regional Dynamics." *American Economic Review* 107 (10): 2908–46.

Francois, J., M. Jansen, and R. Peters. 2011. "Trade Adjustment Costs and
Assistance: The Labour Market Dynamics." In *Trade and Employment:
From Myths to Facts*, edited by M. Jansen, R. Peters, and J. M. Salazar-
Xirinachs, 213–52. Geneva: International Labour Organization.

Freund, C., and E. Ornelas. 2010. "Regional Trade Agreements." *Annual
Review of Economics* 2 (1): 139–66.

IMF (International Monetary Fund). 2019. "Is the African Continental Free
Trade Area a Game Changer for the Continent?" In *Regional Economic
Outlook, Sub-Saharan Africa: Recovery amid Elevated Uncertainty*,
39–53. Washington, DC: IMF.

Jensen, H. G., and R. Sandrey. 2015. *The Continental Free Trade Area: A
GTAP Assessment*. Stellenbosch, South Africa: tralac (Trade Law Centre).

Kee, H. L., and A. Nicita. 2016. "Trade Frauds, Trade Elasticities and Non-
Tariff Measures." Unpublished manuscript, World Bank, Washington,
DC.

Kolawole, Y., J. Agbakwuru, and N. Uzor. 2018. "CFTA: I Won't Allow
Nigeria to Be Dumping Ground—Buhari." *Vanguard*, March 22, 2018.
https://www.vanguardngr.com/2018/03/cfta-wont-allow-nigeria-dumping
-ground-buhari/.

Krugman, P. 1991. "The Move toward Free Trade Zones." *Economic
Review* 76 (6): 5–25.

Limão, N., and A. J. Venables. 2001. "Infrastructure, Geographical Disadvantage, Transport Costs, and Trade." *World Bank Economic Review* 15 (3): 451–79.

Lipsey, R. 1960. "The Theory of Customs Unions: A General Survey." *Economic Journal* 70 (279): 496–513.

Magee, C. S. P., 2008. "New Measures of Trade Creation and Trade Diversion." *Journal of International Economics* 75 (2): 34–362.

Martin, P., T. Mayer, and M. Thoenig. 2008. "Civil Wars and International Trade." *Journal of the European Economic Association* 6 (2–3): 541–50.

Mevel, S., and S. Karingi. 2012. "Deepening Regional Integration in Africa: A Computable General Equilibrium Assessment of the Establishment of a Continental Free Trade Area followed by a Continental Customs Union." Paper presented at the 7th Annual African Economic Conference, Kigali, Rwanda, October 30–November 2.

Radelet, S. C., and J. D. Sachs. 1998. "Shipping Costs, Manufactured Exports, and Economic Growth." Report No. 111639, World Bank, Washington, DC.

Saygili, M., R. Peters, and C. Knebel. 2018. "African Continental Free Trade Area: Challenges and Opportunities of Tariff Reductions." Research Paper No. 15, United Nations Conference on Trade and Development, New York.

Torres, R. 2001. *Towards a Socially Sustainable World Economy: An Analysis of the Social Pillars of Globalisation.* Geneva: International Labour Office.

UNCTAD (United Nations Conference on Trade and Development). 2013. *Economic Development in Africa Report 2013: Intra-African Trade: Unlocking Private Dynamism.* Geneva: UNCTAD.

UNECA (United Nations Economic Commission for Africa). 2010. *Assessing Regional Integration in Africa IV: Enhancing Intra-African Trade.* Addis Ababa, Ethiopia: UNECA.

UNECA (United Nations Economic Commission for Africa). 2017. *Assessing Regional Integration in Africa VIII: Bringing the Continental Free Trade Area About.* Addis Ababa, Ethiopia: UNECA.

Venables, A. J. 2003. "Winners and Losers from Regional Integration Agreements." *Economic Journal* 113 (490): 747–61.

Viner, J. 1950. *The Customs Union Issue.* London: Stevens and Sons.

World Bank. 2018. *Doing Business 2018: Reforming to Create Jobs.* Washington, DC: World Bank.

World Bank. 2020. *The African Continental Free Trade Area: Economic and Distributional Effects.* Washington, DC: World Bank.

WTO (World Trade Organization). 2015. *World Trade Report 2015: Speeding Up Trade: Benefits and Challenges of Implementing the WTO Trade Facilitation Agreement.* Geneva: WTO.

CHAPTER 7

Nontariff Measures and Services Trade Restrictions in Global Value Chains

Souleymane Coulibaly, Alejandro Forero Rojas, Hiau Looi Kee, and Daniel Mirza

Introduction

In an increasingly connected world of global value chains (GVCs), the trade policies of one country may affect the GVC participation of many countries, including itself, given that products are crossing borders multiple times. For certain products, the more relevant trade policy barriers could be tariffs, whereas for others, such as agricultural products, the more impeding trade policies could be in the form of nontariff measures (NTMs). But in the real world—as documented in *World Development Report 2020: Trading for Development in the Age of Global Value Chains* (World Bank 2020)—it is firms, not countries or industries, that participate in international trade. In line with this simple observation, economic research on international trade has transformed dramatically in the past 20 years, placing firm-level international strategies at center stage.

The expansion of GVCs entails not only a finer international division of labor but also several additional features, four of which are particularly important:

1. *Matching of buyers and sellers*. In GVCs, this is not a frictionless process. The fixed costs of importing and exporting partly reflect the costs of finding, respectively, suitable suppliers of parts and components or suitable buyers of one's products. For this reason, these fixed costs are better understood as sunk costs, which naturally create "stickiness" among participants in a GVC.

2. *Relationship-specific investments*. A source of lock-in for GVC relationships is that participants that often make many relationship-specific investments (such as purchasing specialized equipment or customizing products) would obtain a much-depressed return if GVC

links were broken. The need to customize inputs, coupled with quality sensitivity, makes matching buyers and sellers particularly important. If demand for a firm's goods suddenly increases, the firm cannot easily scale up by buying more foreign inputs from some centralized market. Typically, only a handful of suppliers worldwide can provide the additional customized inputs to scale up.

3. *Exchange of intangibles.* Furthermore, firms in GVCs do not trade only in tangible goods with other members of their value chains. GVCs often involve large flows of intangibles, such as technology, intellectual property, and credit. The exchange of these intangibles is much more complex than that of simple goods or services.

4. *Limited contractual security.* The lock-in effects and flows of intangibles within GVCs are particularly relevant given the limited contractual security governing transactions within these chains. GVCs often involve transactions that require a strong legal environment to bind producers together and preclude technological leakage. Yet they often lack this strong legal environment because cross-border exchanges of goods cannot generally be governed by the same contractual safeguards that typically accompany similar exchanges within borders. As a result, GVC participants have repeated interactions to provide implicit contract enforcement. As with matching frictions and relationship specificity, this force contributes to the "stickiness" of GVC relationships.

This concluding chapter explores some concrete questions to assist African policy makers in promoting regional and global value chains. First, what has been Sub-Saharan Africa's experience with GVC participation so far? For example, many Sub-Saharan African countries are producing and exporting agricultural products, but they are only marginally involved in food GVCs. Could NTMs be one of the reasons for such limited participation in food product GVCs? Furthermore, could restrictive services sectors explain the overall limited GVC participation of Sub-Saharan African firms in general? Finally, what will it take for Africa to create regional value chains? To that end, which regional policy options would complement the 2019 entry into force of the African Continental Free Trade Area (AfCFTA)?

What Is Africa's Experience in Global Value Chains?

As documented in *World Development Report 2020* on GVCs, Africa has joined GVCs in the apparel, food, and automotive industries and in some business services (World Bank 2020). But the region remains a small actor in the global economy, accounting for just 3 percent of global trade in intermediate goods.

Leading Sectors for GVC Participation

African countries' exports tend to enter at the beginning of GVCs, where a high share of their exports enter as inputs for other countries' exports, reflecting the still predominant role of agriculture and natural resources in the region's exports. Botswana, the Democratic Republic of Congo, and Nigeria have become integrated into GVCs through exports of oil and other natural resources. But Ethiopia, Kenya, and Tanzania have seen faster GVC integration, sourcing foreign inputs for their export-oriented businesses. Most of their integration has occurred in agribusiness and apparel, especially in Ethiopia and Kenya; in manufacturing in Tanzania; and also, although to a lesser extent, in transportation and tourism. Overall, GVC participation in some of these countries (Ethiopia, Kenya, South Africa, and Tanzania) grew by 10 percentage points or more between 1990 and 2015, close to what Poland and Vietnam—now success stories—experienced over the late 1990s and 2000s, respectively.[1]

Regarding overall participation in agriculture GVCs between 1990 and 2015, countries such as Ethiopia, Ghana, Kenya, and Rwanda stand out, with increases in GVC participation close to 10 percentage points or more. In contrast, Madagascar and resource-rich economies like Sudan have seen their integration in agriculture value chains drop by 5–30 percentage points.

African countries integrated in food value chains include Ethiopia, Kenya, and Tanzania, suggesting that those countries have been successfully developing food processing industries. Importantly, for most low- and middle-income countries (LMICs) involved in agriculture and food GVCs, their participation is largely forward looking, being limited to the supply of a specific product such as coffee in Ethiopia and Uganda and cocoa in Côte d'Ivoire and Ghana.

Challenges to GVC Participation

The automotive sector is more challenging for African countries because it relies strongly on fairly short regional value chains, which makes efficient regional logistics all the more important. Automotive components like car seats or engines can be heavy, bulky, and easily damaged, increasing transportation costs. Just-in-time production and high product variety often require the assembly of subcomponents to be close to final assembly. And final assembly often happens in large end markets with local content requirements in return for market access, as in Brazil, China, India, and South Africa. Morocco has taken advantage of its geographical proximity to the European Union (EU) market and in 2017 became Africa's largest producer of passenger vehicles, surpassing South Africa. Moroccan efforts to attract major manufacturers in the automotive industries over the past decade have continued to pay off, as with the 2019 arrival of a new

Peugeot facility, following in the footsteps of another French automaker, Renault-Nissan.

Similarly, slow and unpredictable land transportation keeps most Sub-Saharan African countries out of the electronics value chain. And, although air transportation could help bridge slow land transportation or long geographical distances, its high cost limits LMICs' exports to goods of very high unit value (such as gold and silver), time-sensitive goods (such as fast-fashion clothing), and perishable goods (such as cut flowers). *World Development Report 2020* estimates that a day's delay in transit due to a different transportation mode choice has a tariff equivalent of 0.6–2.1 percent, and the most sensitive trade flows are those involving parts and components (World Bank 2020).

Moreover, high logistics costs inhibit landlocked countries from participating in GVCs for electronics and fruits and vegetables. *World Development Report 2020* estimates that the average number of days from an origin country's warehouse to a destination country's warehouse in 2006–15 varied greatly by the type of GVC participation (World Bank 2020). Imports by countries engaged in innovative GVC activities (with relatively higher intensity in intellectual property and research and development) such as the Czech Republic, the Republic of Korea, and Singapore need fewer than 9 days on average to reach the importing firm's warehouse, but one additional week is needed by countries specialized in GVCs with high manufacturing and services links, such as the Philippines, Portugal, and Thailand. By contrast, the average time to import exceeds one month in countries specializing in commodity-linked GVCs (those with relatively higher intensity in raw materials and other minerals)—for example, 42 days in Ghana and 92 days in Iraq. A large portion of the long transportation times in Sub-Saharan Africa is attributed to relatively lengthy cargo dwell times at the port.

Some Initial Approaches to GVC Advancement

Relational GVCs—those that facilitate the flows of investments, technology, and know-how, particularly within a single multinational firm across multiple countries—may be a particularly powerful vehicle for technology transfer along the value chain for African countries to consider. It is well understood that real income grows when episodes of trade liberalization boost the diffusion of new technology. But relational GVC trade can multiply the positive effects. Interdependent firms may share know-how and technology with suppliers because this boosts their own productivity and sales, leading to faster catch-up growth across countries. This occurs because, unlike traditional trade formulations in which firms of different countries compete with each other, GVCs constitute networks of firms with common goals—such as minimizing the production costs or maximizing profits along the entire production chain of which the firms are part.

Surely, the incentives of agents (firms) in GVCs are not always aligned. However, although the division of the gains generated by GVCs may naturally be unequal, there is no doubt that downstream firms typically benefit when their suppliers become more productive and vice versa. A direct implication of this simple observation is that firms from high-income countries that import or export goods to less-developed economies might find it beneficial to share process and product innovations with their GVC coparticipants. Furthermore, the stickiness of relational GVCs makes firms particularly prone to benefit from learning by importing and exporting through repeated interactions with highly productive firms at the global frontier of knowledge.

Promoting regional value chains at the regional economic community level could be a second-best approach (after GVC participation) while conditions are being put in place at the continental level to foster Africa's full involvement in GVCs through the AfCFTA. The last section of this chapter explores ways to foster these regional value chains.

Are Nontariff Measures Limiting the GVC Participation of Firms in Sub-Saharan Africa?

Examining the impact of food standards on bilateral trade flows, Ehrich, Brümmer, and Martínez-Zarzoso (2015) hint at an answer. The study finds that specific standards are excluding farmers in LMICs from high-value chains because of the high investment costs to implement them. At the same time, standards reduce information asymmetries and reveal the changing preferences of consumers, which somehow levels the playing field for firms in the LMICs that can produce at scale. For Sub-Saharan African firms to participate in these GVCs, they must be productive, operate in a country that can credibly enforce contracts to fulfill stringent quality expectations, and operate in a sector with inelastic demand for the final product. Given the weak institutions in Sub-Saharan Africa and the generally low productivity of firms in the region, participation in such GVCs is constrained.

It is therefore relevant to assess what it will take for Sub-Saharan African firms to enter GVCs and access at scale the distribution networks in leading world markets in Asia, Europe, and North America.[2] More specifically, are NTMs a catalyst or a barrier to Sub-Saharan African firms' access to distribution networks in leading markets? This section provides a first attempt to answer this question, by examining the NTM structure of Sub-Saharan African countries using a newly collected NTM database provided by the United Nations Conference on Trade and Development (UNCTAD) and the World Bank. We analyze the import coverage of NTMs for the Sub-Saharan African countries in our database, highlighting the most-used measures, most-affected products, and most-targeted trading partners.

The trade impacts of NTMs are quantified using the estimated ad valorem equivalent (AVE) from Kee and Nicita (2016). We compare the restrictiveness of NTMs with that of tariffs across countries, regions, and markets and infer some policy implications on how to strategically diversify Sub-Saharan African market access through GVC participation.

Data on NTMs and Their Coverage in Sub-Saharan Africa

We use data on NTMs from UNCTAD's Trade Analysis Information System (TRAINS). Most of the NTM data were collected between 2011 and 2015. The database covers 15 African countries[3] and is complemented with tariff and trade product-level data (covering all 15 countries except Liberia), collected using the World Bank's World Integrated Trade Solution (WITS) tool. NTMs are classified according to the UNCTAD *Classification of Non-Tariff Measures* (UNCTAD 2015), which includes sanitary and phytosanitary measures (SPS) and technical barriers to trade (TBTs) covered under World Trade Organization (WTO) agreements. We group both types of measures as "SPS/TBT." Other types of NTMs are preshipment inspections and formalities; contingent trade-protective measures; licensing, quotas, and prohibitions; and price controls—all of which we group as "non-SPS/TBT" measures. We use the quantification of NTMs into AVEs from Kee and Nicita (2016). AVEs are available for Benin, Ethiopia, Ghana, Mali, Niger, Nigeria, and Togo.

Coverage of SPS/TBT measures in Sub-Saharan African countries' imports is partial, because the observations cover only 20 percent of the product-partner pairs, representing 31 percent of the import value (figure 7.1). It is also highly heterogeneous, with low coverage in Côte d'Ivoire, Senegal, and Togo, and high coverage in Benin and Ethiopia. In some countries, like Benin, Burkina Faso, and Cabo Verde, the frequency and value coverages are very different, with the value coverage generally being larger. This is explained by higher coverage of large products and partners. Conversely, coverage of the non-SPS/TBT measures is comprehensive, with an average coverage higher than 60 percent and little variation across countries. Additionally, non-SPS/TBT measures are not partner- or product-specific, so the value and frequency of coverage are very similar.

The average number of measures applied to an imported product varies by country, being very high in Cabo Verde, Ethiopia, Ghana, Mali, and Niger (figure 7.2). The average number of non-SPS/TBT measures is more than three times the number of SPS/TBT measures, with even higher ratios in Mali (12:1) and Ethiopia (5:1). The most common SPS/TBT measures used by Sub-Saharan African countries are conformity assessments, prohibitions, and labeling requirements for each SPS and TBT variant, accounting for 81 percent of total SPS/TBT measures (figure 7.3). Other common measures are tolerance limits for residues and restricted substances (4 percent) and hygienic requirements (3 percent), both for SPS reasons.

Different subtypes of measures have varied coverage. Preshipment inspection is the measure with the highest coverage, required for almost

Figure 7.1   NTM Coverage of Imports in Selected Sub-Saharan African Countries, by Type of Measure

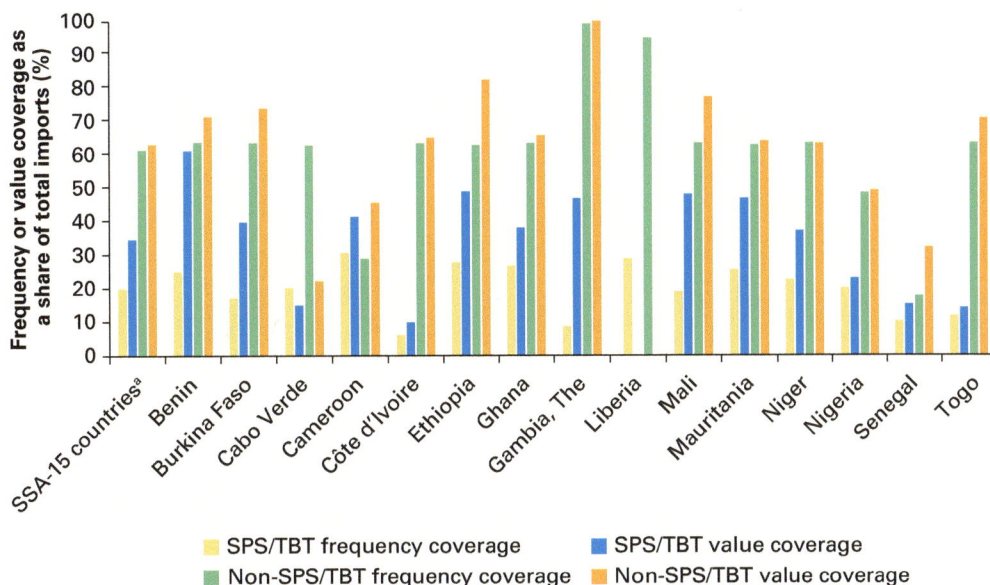

Source: Kee and Nicita 2016.
Note: SPS/TBT coverage data are partial, covering only 20 percent of the product-partner pairs observed, representing 31 percent of total import value. Data are the latest available between 2011 and 2015, varying by country. NTM = nontariff measure; SPS = sanitary and phytosanitary measures; SSA = Sub-Saharan Africa; TBT = technical barriers to trade.
a. The "SSA-15" countries are Benin, Burkina Faso, Cabo Verde, Cameroon, Côte d'Ivoire, Ethiopia, The Gambia, Ghana, Liberia, Mali, Mauritania, Niger, Nigeria, Senegal, and Togo. However, these data exclude Liberia for both SPS/TBT and non-SPS/TBT value coverage because the data were unavailable for Liberia.

18 percent of Sub-Saharan African imports; consumption taxes are the second most used, covering almost 12 percent of imports (figure 7.4).

Coverage of SPS/TBT measures varies significantly across sectors, whereas coverage of the non-SPS/TBT measures is more homogeneous. SPS/TBT measures mainly affect the agriculture and agroindustry sectors, with almost 60 percent coverage (figure 7.5). Oher sectors (like metals or stone and cement) have expectedly lower coverage of SPS/TBT measures. The average number of SPS/TBT measures per product is highest in agriculture and agroindustry, with more than three measures per imported product, and lower in sectors like stone and cement or textiles and apparel (figure 7.6). The average number of non-SPS/TBT measures is much more uniform because of the non-sector-specific coverage of these types of measures.

NTMs can be either nondiscriminatory or targeted at specific countries. More than 85 percent of the measures are nondiscriminatory in the 15 Sub-Saharan African countries in the sample (figure 7.7). Use of

Figure 7.2   Prevalence of NTMs in Selected Sub-Saharan African Countries, by Type

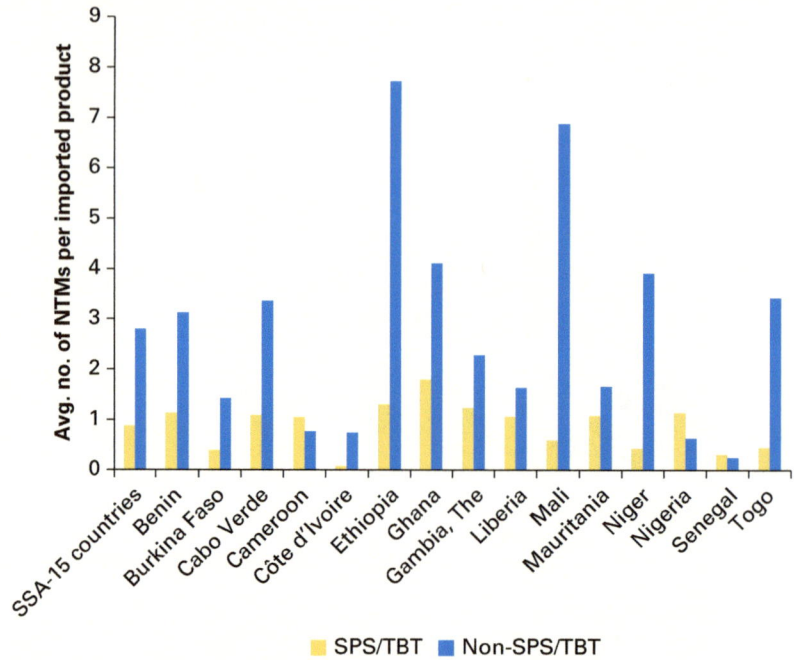

Source: Kee and Nicita 2016.
Note: Data are the latest available between 2011 and 2015, varying by country. The "SSA-15" countries are Benin, Burkina Faso, Cabo Verde, Cameroon, Côte d'Ivoire, Ethiopia, The Gambia, Ghana, Liberia, Mali, Mauritania, Niger, Nigeria, Senegal, and Togo. NTM = nontariff measure; SPS = sanitary and phytosanitary measures; SSA = Sub-Saharan Africa; TBT = technical barriers to trade.

nondiscriminatory measures is highly homogeneous across countries, with the lowest use—that is, the highest use of partner-specific measures (exceeding 20 percent)—being in Côte d'Ivoire. Many other countries (like Cabo Verde, Ghana, Mali, Nigeria, and Togo) have almost no partner-specific measures. Although most NTMs in Sub-Saharan Africa are nondiscriminatory, partner-specific measures affect some countries more than others.

The most frequently targeted country is China, followed by the United States and Thailand (figure 7.8). Other countries' targeting rates are more homogeneous, reflecting that many measures, although partner-specific, have multiple targets.

Restrictiveness of NTMs and Market Access

Because the coverage and prevalence of NTMs vary by type of measure, sector, and partner country, their impacts need not be homogeneous. We use the AVE to measure their restrictiveness against tariffs as the benchmark.

Figure 7.3   Most Common SPS/TBT Measures Imposed on Imports in Sub-Saharan African Countries

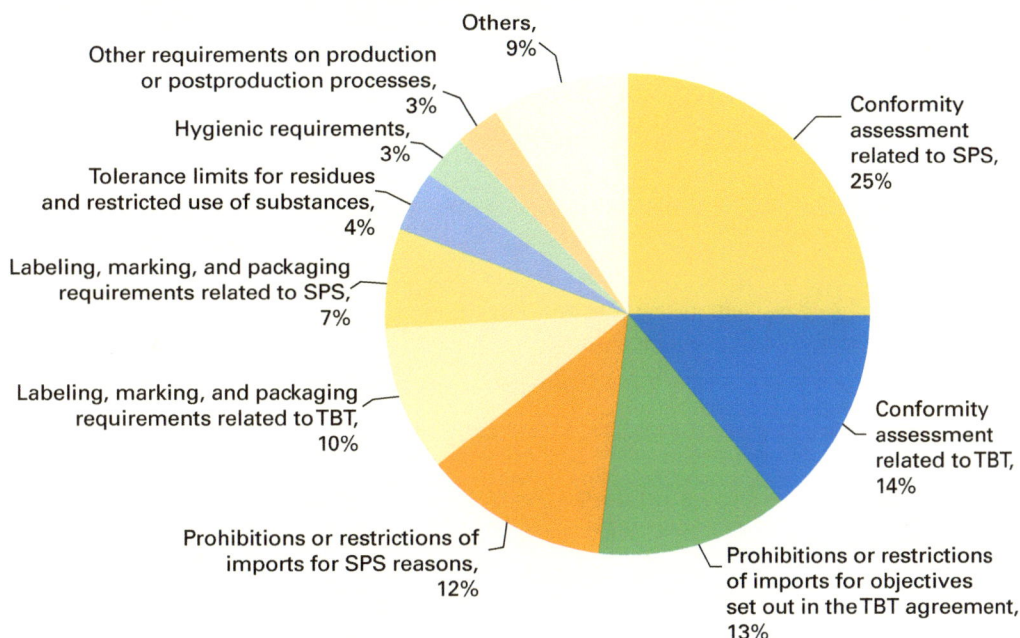

Source: Kee and Nicita 2016.
Note: The percentages are of the total measures and products in UNCTAD's Trade Analysis Information System (TRAINS), covering 15 Sub-Saharan African countries for which full nontariff measure data were available (Benin, Burkina Faso, Cabo Verde, Cameroon, Côte d'Ivoire, Ethiopia, The Gambia, Ghana, Liberia, Mali, Mauritania, Niger, Nigeria, Senegal, and Togo). Data are the latest available between 2011 and 2015, varying by country. SPS = sanitary and phytosanitary measures; TBT = technical barriers to trade.

Restrictiveness of African NTMs, by Type and Sector

We find that, for African imports from all countries, the average tariff is higher than the average AVE of the SPS/TBT or non-SPS/TBT measures. The average AVE of SPS/TBT NTMs in the sample ranges from 0 percent in Togo, to 2 percent in Mali and Niger, to about 4 percent in Ghana (figure 7.9). The range for non-SPS/TBT measures is larger, being close to 0 percent in Nigeria and greater than 6 percent in Niger.

An important distinction is that the AVE for agriculture imports is much lower on all importing partners than on African importing partners, which captures the high cost of SPS/TBT measures like labeling, certification, and special treatment in African countries (figures 7.10 and 7.13). Non-SPS/TBT measures are more common and more restrictive in other sectors, especially in precious stones and metals (figure 7.10).

Figure 7.4   Import Coverage of Top 10 NTMs in Sub-Saharan African Countries

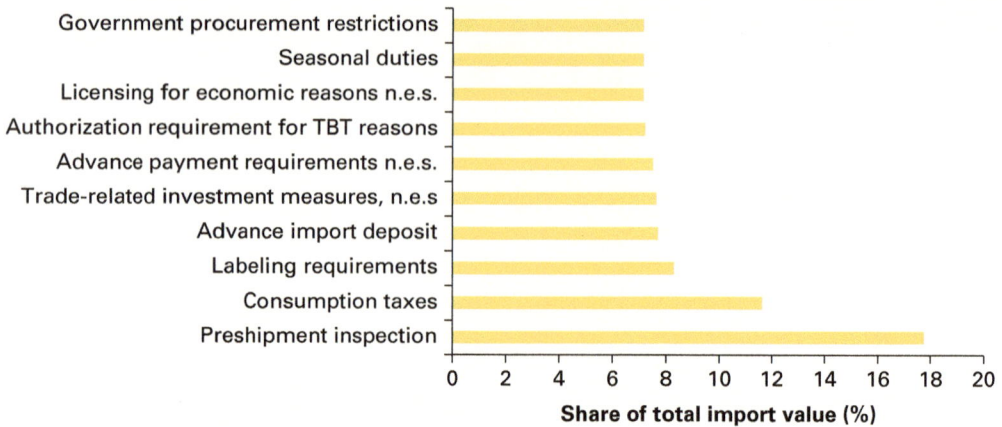

Source: Kee and Nicita 2016.
Note: The data cover 14 Sub-Saharan countries for which nontariff measure (NTM) data were available: Benin, Burkina Faso, Cabo Verde, Cameroon, Côte d'Ivoire, Ethiopia, The Gambia, Ghana, Mali, Mauritania, Niger, Nigeria, Senegal, and Togo. Data are the latest available between 2011 and 2015, varying by country. percentages are shares of the aggregate value of the 14 countries' imports. n.e.s. = not elsewhere specified; TBT = technical barriers to trade.

Restrictiveness of African NTMs, by Trade Partner Region

Compared with other regions, African restrictiveness is the world's highest in terms of tariffs but less restrictive than other regions regarding SPS/TBT NTMs (figure 7.11). By contrast, Sub-Saharan Africa is the second most restrictive region, after South Asia, in non-SPS/TBT measures.

Because most NTMs in Africa are nondiscriminatory, and not many free trade areas were in force in the region during the period of the data (2011–15),[4] it is not surprising that the Sub-Saharan African countries' tariffs and NTM AVEs on imports from other African trade partners are similar to those on imports from the rest of the world (figure 7.11). Nevertheless, the NTM AVEs of some of the region's countries, such as Ethiopia and Niger, are higher on African partners (figures 7.9 and 7.12). This is because some measures, like certification requirements, can be costlier to fulfill for African countries than for other, more-developed partners.

At the sectoral level, the patterns of NTM restrictiveness on African trade partners (figure 7.13) are similar to those on all partners (figure 7.10). Nevertheless, some important differences exist. For example, NTM restrictiveness is higher on African partners in agriculture (where the SPS/TBT AVEs double the tariffs) and in agroindustry (which match the tariffs) (figure 7.13). Non-SPS/TBT measures also affect those two sectors particularly.

Compared with the barriers that African exports face in other regions, tariffs are particularly high, whereas NTMs are lower than in other

Figure 7.5   Import Coverage of NTMs in Sub-Saharan Africa, by Sector

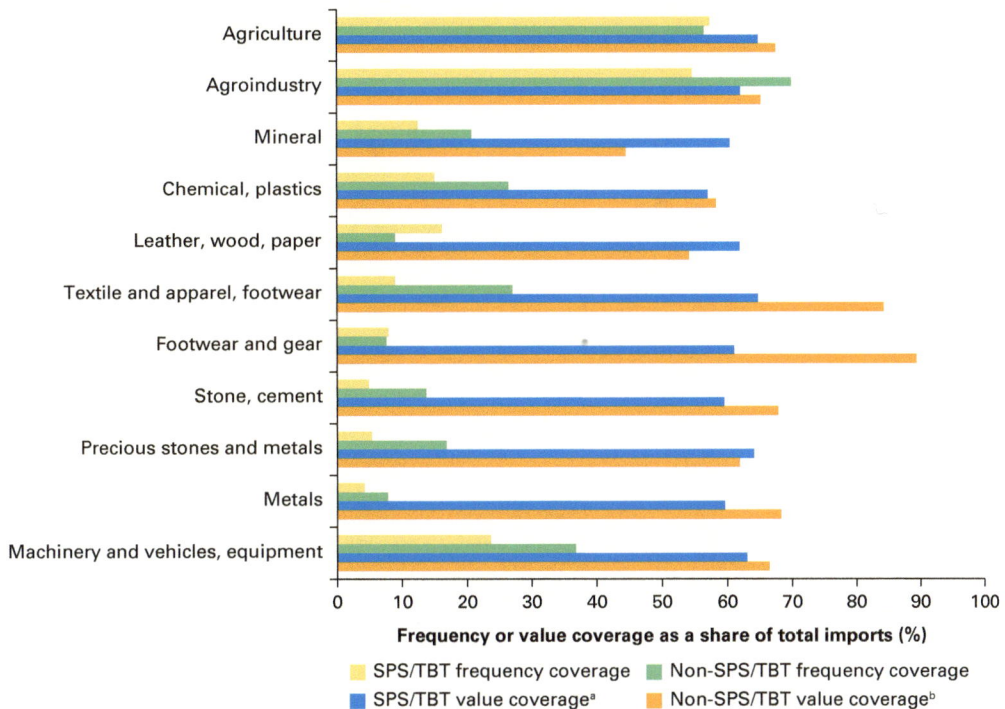

Frequency or value coverage as a share of total imports (%)

- SPS/TBT frequency coverage
- Non-SPS/TBT frequency coverage
- SPS/TBT value coverage[a]
- Non-SPS/TBT value coverage[b]

Source: Kee and Nicita 2016.
Note: SPS/TBT coverage data are partial, covering only 20 percent of the product-partner pairs observed, representing 31 percent of the total import value. The data, from 15 Sub-Saharan African countries, are the latest available between 2011 and 2015, varying by country. The 15 countries are Benin, Burkina Faso, Cabo Verde, Cameroon, Côte d'Ivoire, Ethiopia, The Gambia, Ghana, Liberia, Mali, Mauritania, Niger, Nigeria, Senegal, and Togo. NTM = nontariff measure; SPS = sanitary and phytosanitary measures; TBT = technical barriers to trade.
a. The average SPS/TBT and non-SPS/TBT value coverage data exclude Liberia because the data were unavailable.

regions. Sub-Saharan Africa's average tariff (14 percent) is higher than those of other regions known for imposing high tariffs, like South Asia (11 percent) and Latin America and the Caribbean (8 percent). However, Africa's NTMs are not as restrictive as in other regions, particularly Europe and North America (figure 7.14).

Restrictiveness of Market Access to High-Income Countries

Market access for African exports to high-income countries is more restricted by NTMs than by tariffs. Although tariffs are lower than 3 percent in Canada, the EU, and the US, and higher but still below 6 percent in Japan, the average AVE of SPS/TBT measures is 10 percent in Canada, 7 percent in the EU, 6 percent in the US, and almost 4 percent in Japan (figure 7.15). The impact of non-SPS/TBT measures on market access for African countries is also high in Canada—almost twice the impact of tariffs—but it is lower in other high-income countries.

Figure 7.6 Prevalence of NTMs Covering Imports in Sub-Saharan Africa, by Sector

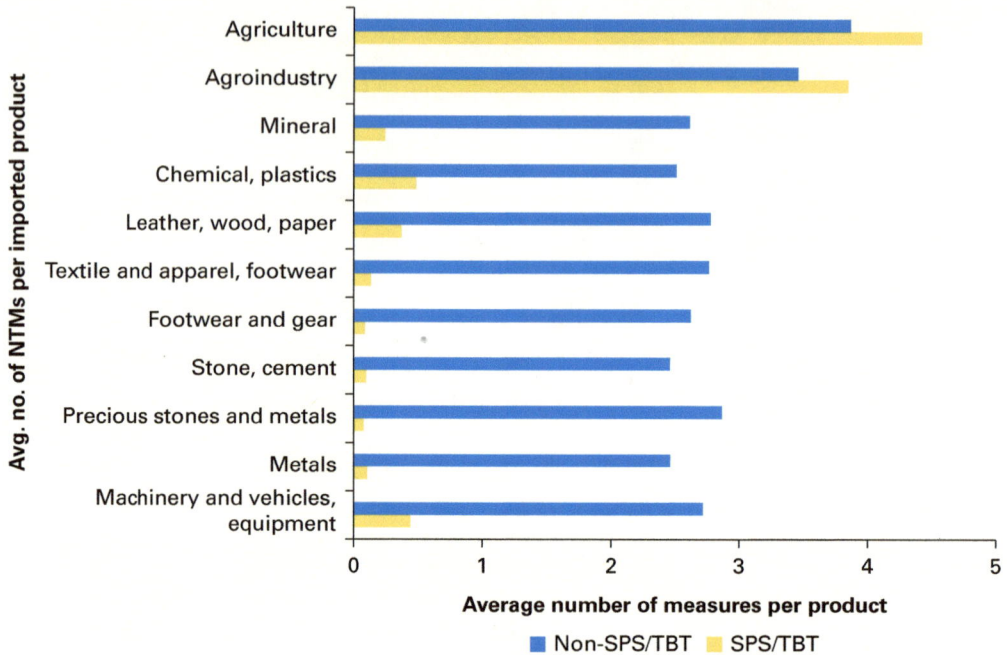

Source: Kee and Nicita 2016.
Note: The NTM data, covering 15 Sub-Saharan African countries, are the latest available between 2011 and 2015, varying by country. The 15 countries are Benin, Burkina Faso, Cabo Verde, Cameroon, Côte d'Ivoire, Ethiopia, The Gambia, Ghana, Liberia, Mali, Mauritania, Niger, Nigeria, Senegal, and Togo. NTM = nontariff measure; SPS = sanitary and phytosanitary measures; TBT = technical barriers to trade.

Considered by sector, market access to high-income countries is most restricted by NTMs in agriculture and agroindustry, followed by apparel and textiles. SPS/TBT measures are the most restrictive, and tariffs are very low except in agriculture, agroindustry, and textiles. Overall, restrictiveness for natural resources, like minerals and precious stones, is very low, whereas it is higher for manufactures such as agroindustry, apparel, and metals (figure 7.16).

Policy Implications

African countries have restrictive tariffs and NTMs relative to the rest of the world. This section has shown that the most-used NTMs "against" Sub-Saharan Africa's exports in high-income country markets are SPS- and TBT-related—mostly conformity assessments; prohibitions or restrictions; and labeling, marking, or packaging requirements. The coverage of SPS/TBT measures is particularly high in agriculture and agroindustry. Furthermore, there are significant tariff barriers to trade within Africa in manufactured products and very restrictive NTMs in agriculture. For those reasons, among others, the AfCFTA is a welcome initiative to promote more trade

Figure 7.7 **Percentage of Nondiscriminatory NTMs in Selected Sub-Saharan African Countries**

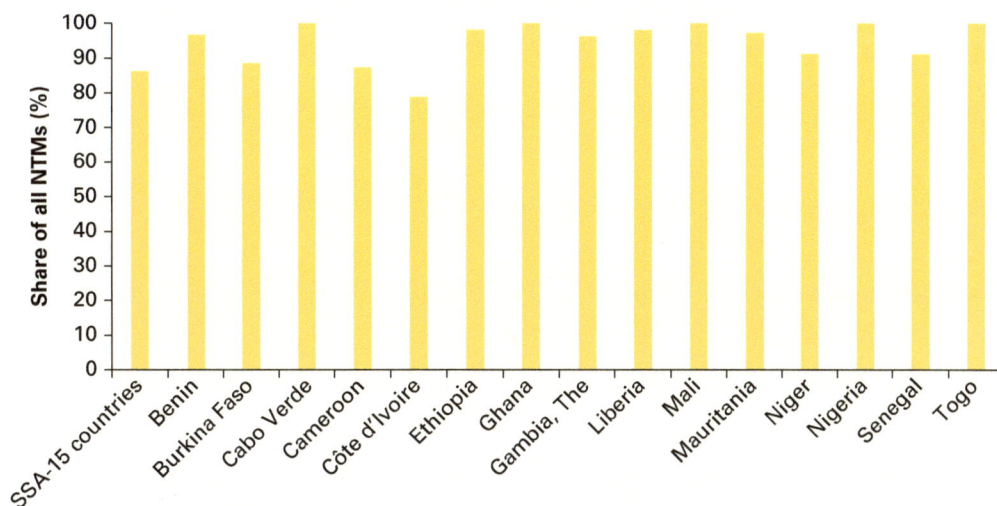

Source: Kee and Nicita 2016.
Note: A "nondiscriminatory" NTM is one that is not targeted at specific countries. Data are the latest available between 2011 and 2015, varying by country. The "SSA-15" countries are Benin, Burkina Faso, Cabo Verde, Cameroon, Côte d'Ivoire, Ethiopia, The Gambia, Ghana, Liberia, Mali, Mauritania, Niger, Nigeria, Senegal, and Togo. NTMs = nontariff measures; SSA = Sub-Saharan Africa.

within Sub-Saharan Africa and beyond. Efficient regional sourcing of intermediate goods and services can foster more participation of African firms in GVCs.

NTMs and tariffs that restrict trade between African countries are a self-imposed barrier. They make diversifying Sub-Saharan African economies no easy task. Hidalgo et al. (2007) show that a country's current export structure determines how easy it will be to diversify its production base to higher-value products. They use the metaphor of a forest representing the product space (the same for all countries in the world). Each tree is a product, and firms are monkeys that can climb higher on a tree to improve their value added (intensive diversification) or jump to another tree with higher value (extensive diversification). Firms in LMICs find it easiest to grow through intensive diversification, building on capabilities they already possess. But they need inducements to diversify through the extensive margin (as these countries become middle-income and upper-middle-income countries or simply in response to even lower-cost competitors), given that jumping to higher-value trees is a costly and risky business.

Diversification at the extensive margin may indeed require physical infrastructure, specific know-how, knowledge of the tastes and standards in the targeted markets, and accessible and affordable intermediate goods and services. Hausmann and Rodrik (2003) call these initial investment

Figure 7.8　Countries Whose Imports Are Most Frequently Targeted by Partner-Specific NTMs of Sub-Saharan African Countries

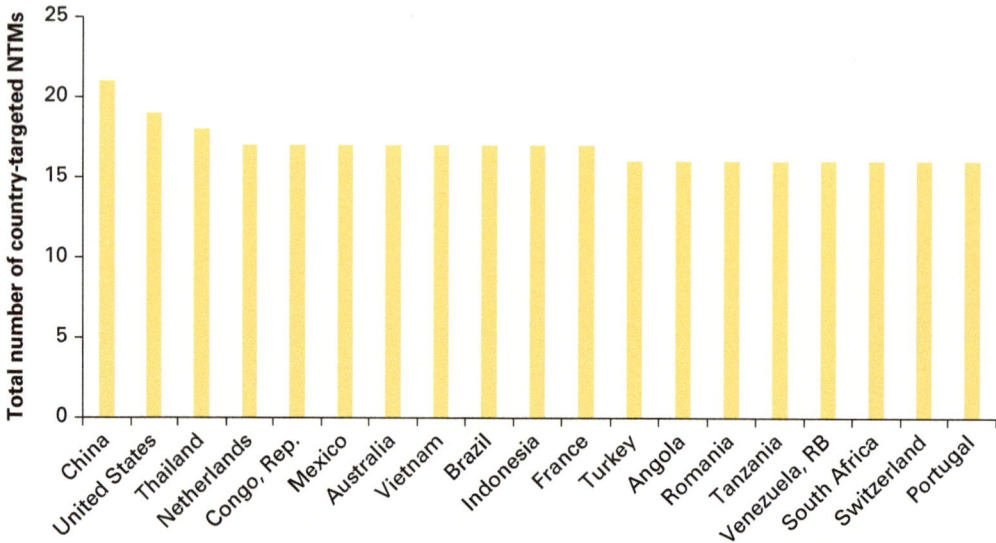

Source: Kee and Nicita 2016.
Note: The number of partner-specific nontariff measures (NTMs) is the aggregate number used by the study's sample of 15 Sub-Saharan African countries: Benin, Burkina Faso, Cabo Verde, Cameroo, Côte d'Ivoire, Ethiopia, The Gambia, Ghana, Liberia, Mali, Mauritania, Niger, Nigeria, Senegal, and Togo. Data are the latest available between 2011 and 2015, varying by country.

needs "cost discovery"—a search by the first firms to explore new opportunities.

Cost discovery can be facilitated in several ways. Foreign direct investment (FDI) can provide much of the required information and know-how as well as learning from neighbors. Cooperation between neighboring countries can therefore help, ensuring that the market size is attractive for foreign investors and securing access to critical intermediate goods to make the leap to a new product less costly and risky. For instance, nearly all members of the West African Economic and Monetary Union (WAEMU) can benefit from cooperation in at least six product clusters (fruits and vegetables and their products, wood and its manufactures, cotton, low-tech manufactures, chemicals, and minerals) to reduce their overdependence on traditional agricultural exports such as coffee and cocoa (World Bank 2009).

By determining which sector offers the most promise for further development, countries in a neighborhood can then focus cooperation on

Figure 7.9 Comparison of Tariffs and NTM Ad Valorem Equivalents on All Importing Partners, Selected Sub-Saharan African Countries

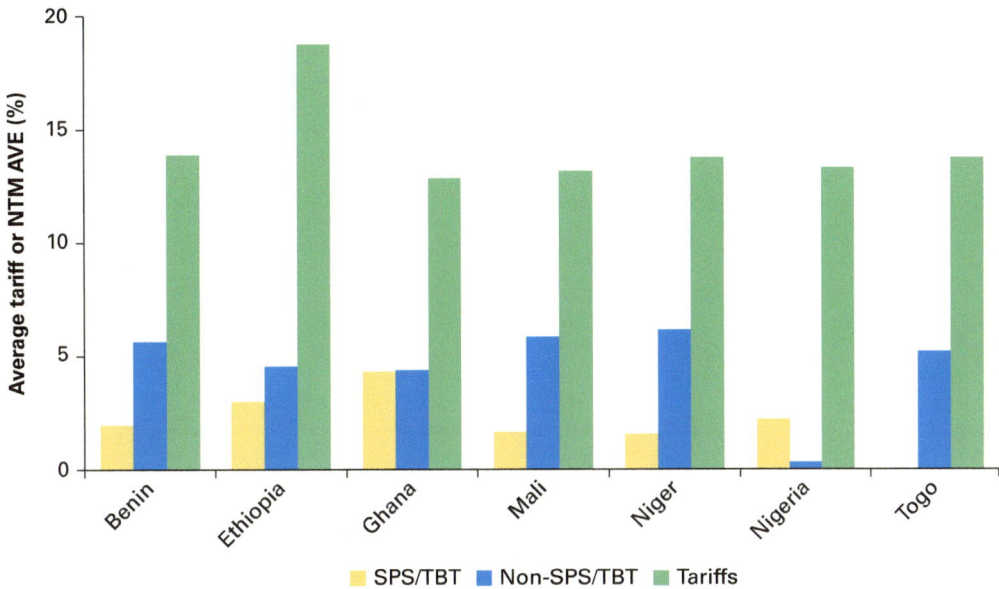

Source: Kee and Nicita 2016.
Note: The trade impacts of nontariff measures (NTMs) are quantified using the estimated ad valorem equivalent (AVE) to measure their restrictiveness against tariffs as the benchmark. Data are the latest available between 2011 and 2015, varying by country. SPS = sanitary and phytosanitary measures; TBT = technical barriers to trade.

sector-specific infrastructure (such as common standards, compliance, and metrology systems) and specific curricula to build a skilled labor force and adapt new technologies. By deepening their regional collaborations, including through timely and effective implementation of the AfCFTA, Sub-Saharan African countries can minimize the distortion of tariffs and NTMs and provide more opportunities for their firms to participate in regional and global value chains.

Are Restrictive Services Sectors Limiting Sub-Saharan African Firms' GVC Participation?

Many services are inputs into the production of other services and goods; hence, they are central to GVCs. Their cost and quality affect the economy's growth performance (Francois and Hoekman 2010), particularly in several sectors, as follows:

- *Financial services* that are efficient and competitive are critical for ensuring that capital is deployed where it has the highest returns.
- *Telecommunications*, at lower cost and higher quality, will generate economywide benefits, because this service is an intermediate input and a "transport" mechanism for information services and other products that can be digitalized.
- *Transportation services* similarly contribute to the efficient distribution of goods within and between countries and are the means through which services providers move to clients' locations (and vice versa).
- *Business services*, such as accounting and legal services, reduce the transaction costs associated with the operation of financial markets and enforcement of contracts.
- *Retail and wholesale distribution services* are a vital link between producers and consumers, with the margins that apply in the provision of such services influencing the competitiveness of firms on the local and international markets.

Figure 7.10   Comparison of Tariffs and NTM Ad Valorem Equivalents on All Importing Partners, by Sector, Selected Sub-Saharan African Countries

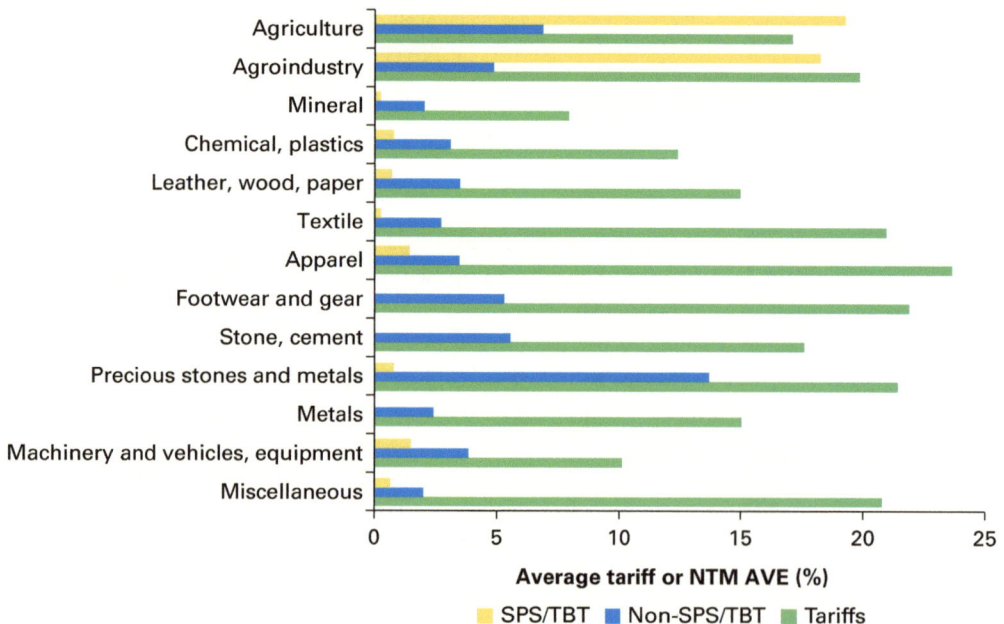

Source: Kee and Nicita 2016.
Note: Nontariff measures (NTMs) are quantified using the estimated ad valorem equivalent (AVE) to measure their restrictiveness against tariffs as the benchmark. The AVEs are calculated for seven Sub-Saharan African countries: Benin, Ethiopia, Ghana, Mali, Niger, Nigeria, and Togo. Data are the latest available between 2011 and 2015, varying by country. SPS = sanitary and phytosanitary measures; TBT = technical barriers to trade.

Figure 7.11 Comparison of Tariffs and NTM Ad Valorem Equivalents in Selected Sub-Saharan African Countries on All Importing Partners, by World Region

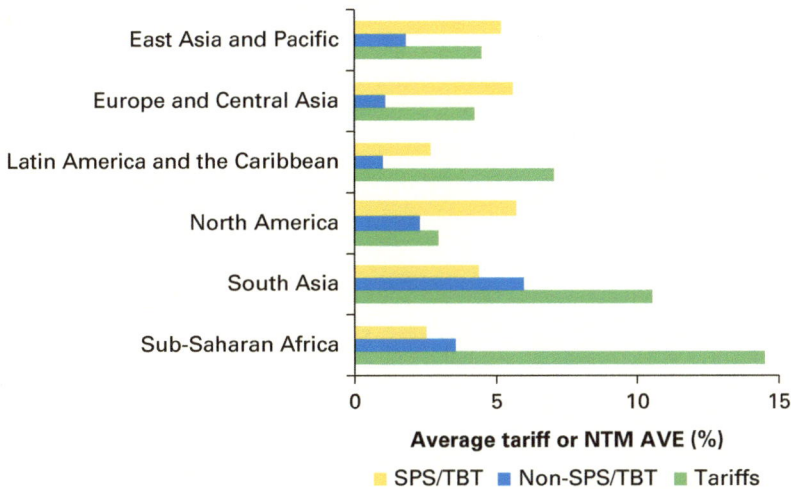

Source: Kee and Nicita 2016.
Note: The trade impacts of nontariff measures (NTMs) are quantified using the estimated ad valorem equivalent (AVE) to measure their restrictiveness against tariffs as the benchmark. The AVEs are calculated for seven Sub-Saharan African countries: Benin, Ethiopia, Ghana, Mali, Niger, Nigeria, and Togo. Data are the latest available between 2011 and 2015, varying by country. "North America" includes Bermuda, Canada, and the United States. The Middle East and North Africa region is excluded for lack of complete data. SPS = sanitary and phytosanitary measures; TBT = technical barriers to trade.

The ability of firms to compete and grow depends on their access to telecommunications, transportation, financial services, and other business services such as accounting and legal services. High-cost or low-quality services act as a tax on exporters. Services are thus a vital input into manufactured goods trade.

Links between services liberalization and manufacturing productivity. Using plant-level data, Arnold, Javorcik, and Mattoo (2011) find that reducing barriers to services trade increased the productivity of manufacturing firms in the Czech Republic. Their analysis shows that allowing foreign entry into services industries was the key channel through which services liberalization contributed to improved performance of the manufacturing sectors.

In addition, Arnold et al. (2016) examine the link between India's reforms in the services sectors and the productivity of manufacturing firms, using panel data for about 4,000 Indian firms from 1993 to 2005.

Figure 7.12   Comparison of Tariffs and NTM Ad Valorem Equivalents of Selected Sub-Saharan African Countries on Other African Importing Partners

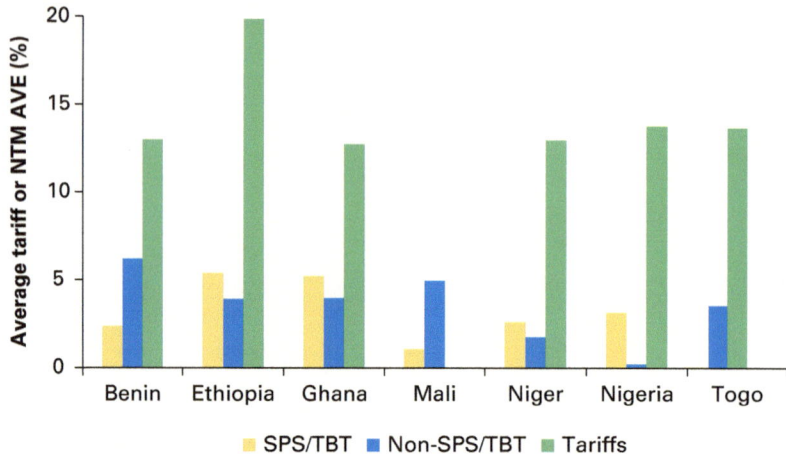

Source: Kee and Nicita 2016.
Note: The trade impacts of nontariff measures (NTMs) are quantified using the estimated ad valorem equivalent (AVE) to measure their restrictiveness against tariffs as the benchmark. Data are the latest available between 2011 and 2015, varying by country. SPS = sanitary and phytosanitary measures; TBT = technical barriers to trade.

They find that banking, telecommunications, insurance, and transportation reforms had significant, positive effects on the productivity of manufacturing firms. Services reforms benefited both foreign and locally owned manufacturing firms, but the effects on foreign firms tended to be somewhat stronger. An increase by 1 standard deviation in the aggregate index of services liberalization resulted in a productivity increase of 11.7 percent for domestic firms and 13.2 percent for foreign enterprises. Analogous results were established for Indonesia (Duggan, Rahardja, and Varela 2013).

A boosted effect from high institutional quality. Beverelli, Fiorini, and Hoekman (2017) examine whether this effect is observed more generally across countries, and how it is affected by differences in economic governance, by looking at the effect of services trade restrictions on manufacturing productivity for a broad cross-section of countries at different stages of economic development. They find that decreasing services trade restrictiveness had a positive impact on the productivity of manufacturing sectors that used services as intermediate inputs in production. They also find that countries with high institutional quality benefited the most from lower services trade restrictions in terms of increased productivity in downstream industries. Echoing previous studies, their analysis shows that the conditioning

Figure 7.13   Average Tariffs and NTM Ad Valorem Equivalents of Selected Sub-Saharan African Countries on African Importing Partners, by Sector

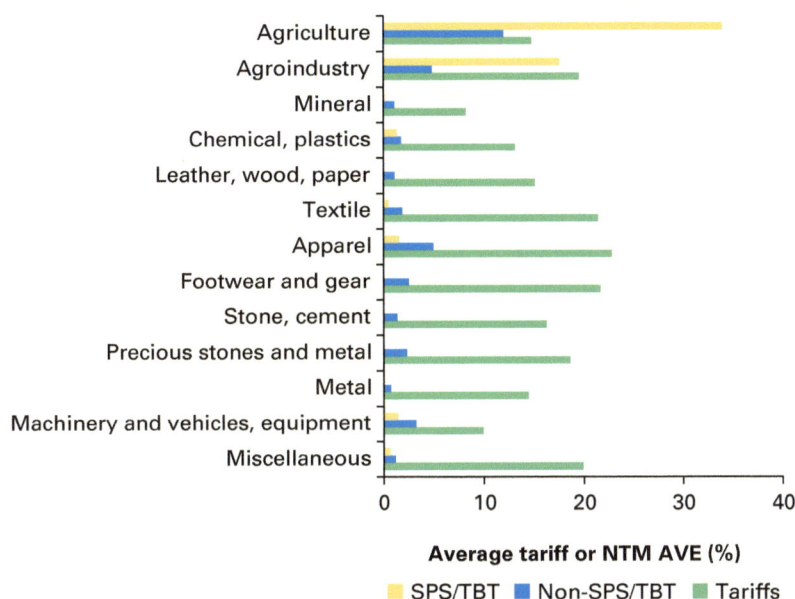

Source: Kee and Nicita 2016.
Note: The trade impacts of nontariff measures (NTMs) are quantified using the estimated ad valorem equivalent (AVE) to measure their restrictiveness against tariffs as the benchmark. AVEs are calculated for seven Sub-Saharan African countries: Benin, Ethiopia, Ghana, Mali, Niger, Nigeria, and Togo. Data are the latest available between 2011 and 2015, varying by country. SPS = sanitary and phytosanitary measures; TBT = technical barriers to trade.

effect of institutions operates through services trade that involves foreign establishments (FDI) as opposed to cross-border, arms-length trade in services.

From services trade liberalization to productivity to export performance. Trade is an important channel through which firms can improve their access to services inputs, resulting in lower prices, greater input variety, or both. The extent to which policies restrict access to foreign services inputs is therefore likely to be relevant for downstream productivity performance. Yet barriers to trade in services are rather substantial, even for high-income countries (Borchert, Gootiiz, and Mattoo 2014; OECD 2021).

Hoekman and Shepherd (2015) use data from the World Bank Enterprise Surveys to analyze how services productivity affects manufacturing productivity and the relationship between the latter and firm-level export performance. They find a strong link between services and manufacturing

Figure 7.14   Average Tariffs and NTM Ad Valorem Equivalents of All World Regions on Exports of Selected Sub-Saharan African Countries

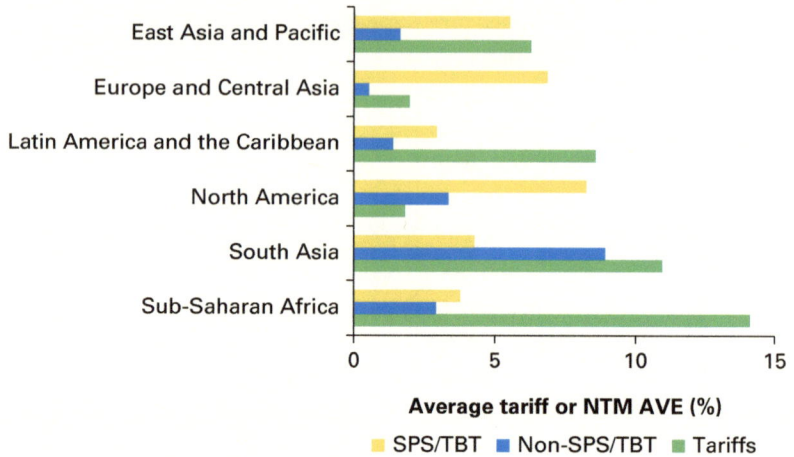

Source: Kee and Nicita 2016.
Note: The trade impacts of nontariff measures (NTMs) are quantified using the estimated ad valorem equivalent (AVE) to measure their restrictiveness against tariffs as the benchmark. The Sub-Saharan African sample includes seven countries: Benin, Ethiopia, Ghana, Mali, Niger, Nigeria, and Togo. Data are the latest available between 2011 and 2015, varying by country. SPS = sanitary and phytosanitary measures; TBT = technical barriers to trade.

performance, with an even stronger link between services productivity and manufacturing productivity for firms that use services inputs more intensively. At the average rate of services input intensity, they estimate that a 10 percent improvement in services productivity is associated with a 0.3 percent increase in manufacturing productivity and a resulting 0.2 percent increase in exports. At the sectoral level, they find that restrictions on transportation and retail distribution services have the largest negative impact on goods export performance.

This section explores the link between liberalization of services that are directly related to infrastructure (core services) and the competitiveness of African countries in manufactured goods, by focusing on the presence of foreign affiliates in these core services sectors. "Core services" are the most basic services needed to run a business, produce, and export—such as energy supplies, construction, transportation, communication, and banking services.

Services Restrictiveness in Four African Countries

This subsection provides a series of facts from the World Bank's Services Trade Restrictions Database. The data, which were compiled by administering questionnaires to key informants in 2008–10, give a first idea about the

Figure 7.15   Average Tariffs and NTM Ad Valorem Equivalents of High-Income Countries on Sub-Saharan African Exports

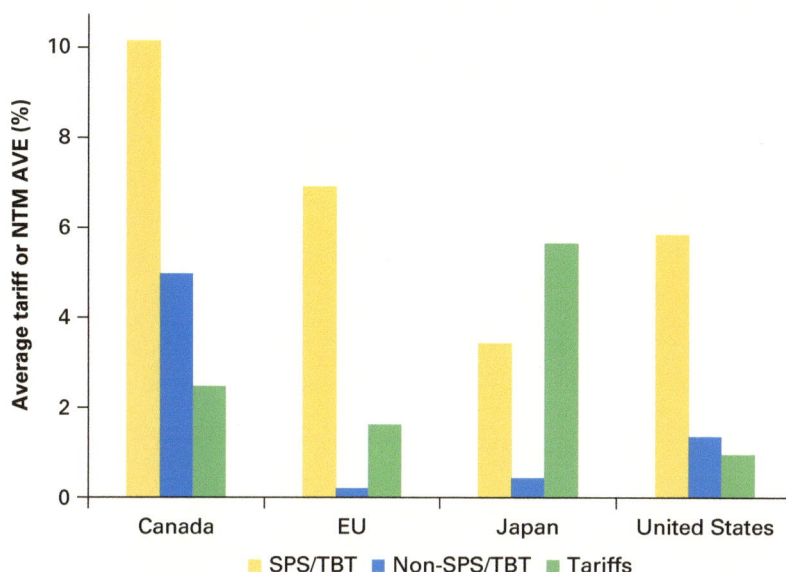

Source: Kee and Nicita 2016.
Note: The trade impacts of nontariff measures (NTMs) are quantified using the estimated ad valorem equivalent (AVE) to measure their restrictiveness against tariffs as the benchmark. Data are the latest available between 2011 and 2015, varying by country. The Sub-Saharan Africa sample includes seven countries: Benin, Ethiopia, Ghana, Mali, Niger, Nigeria, and Togo. EU = European Union; SPS = sanitary and phytosanitary measures; TBT = technical barriers to trade.

extent of regulations across countries in different services sectors and for different modes of supply.

The database reports the Services Trade Restrictiveness Index (STRI), which takes a value from 0 (open without restrictions) to 100 (completely closed), at the sector and mode of service levels for each country. It is based on a simple and transparent procedure that aggregates the scores given by qualified respondents in each country (that is, specialized law firms) on the degree of openness related to each of the policy measures proposed in the questionnaires, in each subsector. Different policy measures are assessed, mainly related to the entry and ongoing operations of foreign entities. At the end, the database provides for each country and each service sector an STRI value by mode of services delivery (mode 1, mode 3, and mode 4), together with an all-mode aggregate (or overall) STRI.[5]

Relative Restrictiveness, by Country, Region, and Income Group

Based on the overall STRI, the most services-restrictive country among the four selected African countries (the "Africa-4": the Arab Republic of Egypt, Morocco, Nigeria, and South Africa) is Egypt, with a score of 52.1, followed by South Africa (34.5) and Nigeria (27.1). Morocco is the least restrictive,

Figure 7.16 Comparison of Average Tariffs and NTM Ad Valorem Equivalents of High-Income Countries on African Exports, by Sector

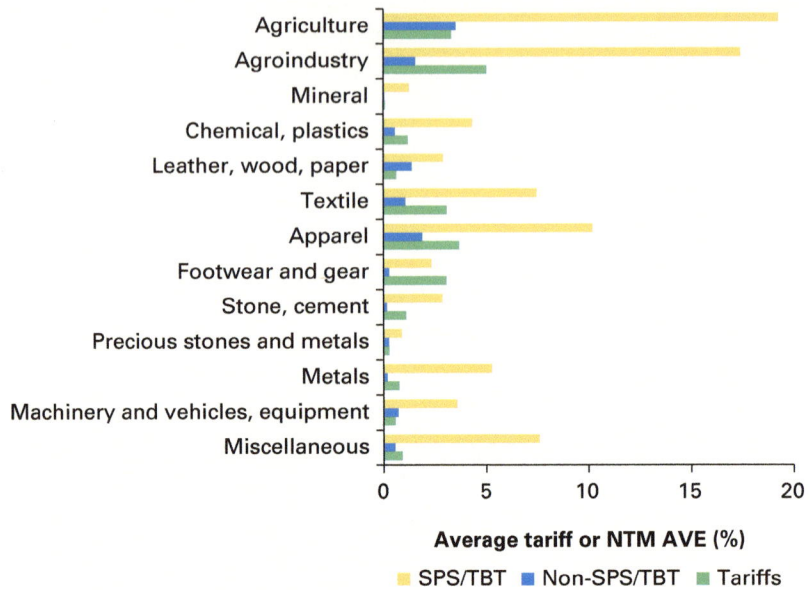

Source: Kee and Nicita 2016.
Note: The trade impacts of nontariff measures (NTMs) are quantified using their estimated ad valorem equivalents (AVEs) to measure their restrictiveness against tariffs as the benchmark. Data are the latest available between 2011 and 2015, varying by country. The Sub-Saharan Africa sample includes seven countries: Benin, Ethiopia, Ghana, Mali, Niger, Nigeria, and Togo. SPS = sanitary and phytosanitary measures; TBT = technical barriers to trade.

with a score of 21 (table 7.1). Morocco and Nigeria also appear to be less restrictive than the sample average (which is 33.1), whereas Egypt and South Africa are more restrictive than this average. Morocco's restrictiveness is comparable to that of the Americas (20.9) and slightly more than Europe's (19.3), whereas South Africa compares favorably to the level of Asia (37.2).

Relative to the country income groups to which the Africa-4 countries belong, Egypt is more closed than other lower-middle-income countries to foreign services and service suppliers—as is South Africa, compared with other upper-middle income countries. Nigeria, although more open than Africa overall, has an STRI score comparable to its own group of lower-middle-income countries. Morocco, in contrast, is significantly more open to foreign services entities than both Africa as a whole and its lower-middle-income peers.

Restrictiveness within Core Services Sectors, by Service Delivery Mode

Are the overall STRI scores good predictors of services trade regulation at a more disaggregated sectoral level? An analysis of the scores from 103 countries shows that, indeed, there is a positive relation between a given country's overall services restrictiveness and its restrictiveness in each

Table 7.1 **Aggregate Services Trade Restrictiveness Index Scores of Selected African Countries and Global Country Groups, 2008–10**

Country or group	Overall STRI
Africa-4[a]	
Egypt, Arab Rep.	52.1
Morocco	21.0
Nigeria	27.1
South Africa	34.5
Region[b]	
Africa	33.1
Americas	20.9
Asia	37.2
Europe	19.3
Oceania	15.6
Income group[c]	
High income	23.9
Low income	35.8
Lower-middle income	28.5
Upper-middle income	27.1

Source: World Bank's Services Trade Restrictions Database.
Note: The Services Trade Restrictiveness Index (STRI) score ranges from 0 to 100, where 0 is completely open and 100 is completely closed to foreign services and service suppliers. The aggregate scores for groups of countries are simple averages. Data were collected between 2008 and 2010 for all countries.
a. The Africa-4 countries are the only African countries also covered by the Foreign Affiliates Trade in Services (FATS) database of the Organisation for Economic Co-operation and Development (OECD), enabling a thorough assessment of the services sectors in overall country export performance.
b. For the complete list of countries included in each region, see the Supplementary Data annex in Borchert, Gootiiz, and Mattoo (2014).
c. Country income groups are defined according to World Bank classifications on the basis of gross national income per capita in current US dollars using Atlas method exchange rates.

of the three core services sectors considered here: financial and banking, transportation and telecommunications, and professional services.

Although the Africa-4 countries behave like the average country in the sample when looking at financial services (figure 7.17, panel a) or transportation and telecommunications (figure 7.17, panel b)—the link between the overall STRI and sector-specific STRI being very close to the one predicted by the whole sample—this is not the case for the professional services sector (figure 7.17, panel c). Compared with all countries in the sample that have similar overall regulation levels, Egypt and South Africa appear to be rather more regulated than the other countries in professional services, whereas Nigeria appears to be less regulated in that sector.

Figure 7.18 focuses on the restrictiveness service delivery mode 3 (foreign "commercial presence" in each of the service sectors at hand) for two

Figure 7.17   Correlation between Overall and Services-Specific Restrictions, 2008–10

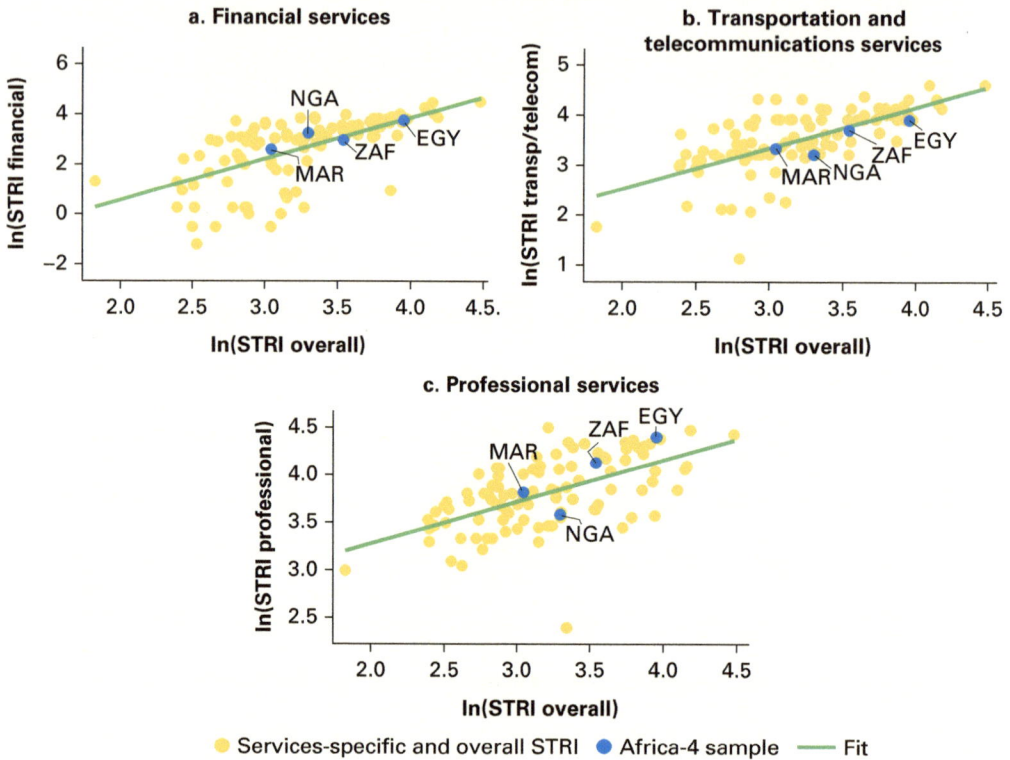

a. Financial services

b. Transportation and telecommunications services

c. Professional services

● Services-specific and overall STRI   ● Africa-4 sample   —— Fit

Source: Services Trade Restrictiveness Index (STRI) database, World Bank.
Note: The STRI score ranges from 0 to 100, where 0 is completely open and 100 is completely closed to foreign services and service suppliers. The full sample includes 103 countries across all regions worldwide. Data were collected between 2008 and 2010 for all countries. The "Africa-4" countries (labeled in the scatterplots by ISO alpha-3 code) are the Arab Republic of Egypt (EGY), Morocco (MAR), Nigeria (NGA), and South Africa (ZAF). ln = natural logarithm.

reasons: First, most of the trade in services is known to be linked to mode 3 (Francois and Hoekman 2010). Second, because we are mostly interested in investment- and infrastructure-related services (access to finance, transportation, telecommunications, and so forth), we expect even more that those services will be delivered through foreign presence (mode 3) rather than through cross-border provisions (mode 1).

The bisecting lines in the graphs show that there is high similitude between the STRI in mode 3 and the overall STRI (that is, aggregating modes 1, 3, and 4) in finance and banking services (figure 7.18, panel a) as well as in the transportation telecommunications sector (figure 7.18, panel b). There is less similitude in the case of professional services (figure 7.18, panel c).

Turning to the Africa-4 countries, Morocco appears to be the most liberalized in mode 3, and Egypt is the least liberalized. Further, for mode 3 in the financial sector, all but Morocco set more regulations against foreign presence than in the other modes. Morocco and Nigeria appear to be more open in mode 3 for professional services.

Figure 7.18   **Correlation between Overall and Foreign Presence Restrictions, 2008–10**

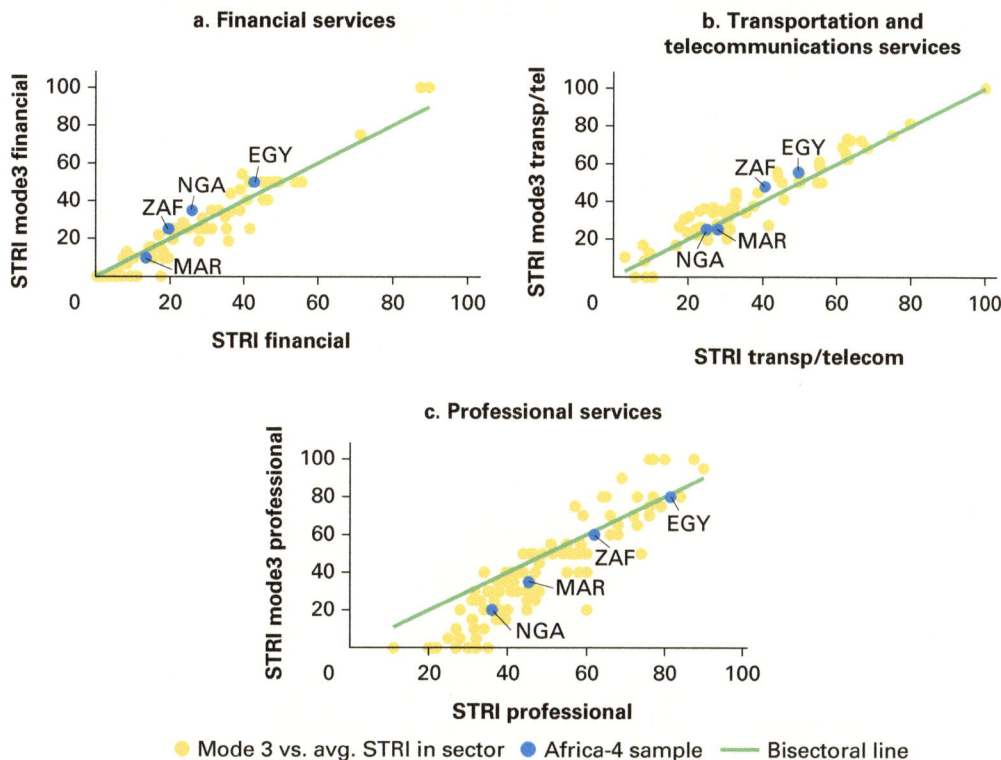

a. Financial services

b. Transportation and telecommunications services

c. Professional services

● Mode 3 vs. avg. STRI in sector   ● Africa-4 sample   ── Bisectoral line

Source: Services Trade Restrictiveness Index (STRI) database, World Bank.
Note: The STRI score ranges from 0 to 100, where 0 is completely open and 100 is completely closed to foreign services and service suppliers. The full sample includes 103 countries across all regions worldwide. Data were collected between 2008 and 2010 for all countries. The "Africa-4" countries (labeled in the scatterplots by ISO alpha-3 code) are the Arab Republic of Egypt (EGY), Morocco (MAR), Nigeria (NGA), and South Africa (ZAF). Under the General Agreement of Trade in Services (GATS) of the World Trade Organization (WTO), "mode 3" refers to services trade delivery through foreign commercial presence, such as through locally established subsidiaries or affiliates of foreign-owned companies.

To sum up, Morocco and, to a lesser extent, Nigeria appear to have "pro-openness" regulations in services provided from foreign entities, whereas Egypt is a rather closed country for services provisions. South Africa is between these two bounds.

Foreign Affiliates and Stringency of Services Regulations

This subsection uses the Foreign Affiliate Trade in Services (FATS) database, provided by the Organisation for Economic Co-operation and Development (OECD), to look at the involvement of affiliates from OECD origins in the services sectors of the Africa-4.[6] The data are mostly collected on majority-owned affiliates (affiliates in which foreign ownership exceeds 50 percent).

Activities of Foreign Affiliates in Services

Two variables are chosen from the data set to represent the activities of OECD-based affiliates in Africa: (a) the yearly number of employees, and

(b) the yearly sales turnover expressed in local currency, then converted into US dollars using yearly average exchange rates from the Penn World Table version 9.0. The data can be obtained for five broad sector aggregates observed for each of the four African countries' OECD affiliates: energy (grouping electricity, gas, and water supply); construction; finance and insurance; transportation and telecommunications; and other services (business, computer services, and research and development). Twenty-five OECD countries declare outward investments by partner. The figures have been aggregated over all the declarants for each of the Africa-4.

Unlike the World Bank's Services Trade Restrictions (STR) database, the data have the advantage of spanning 1995–2014. However, the data set has some drawbacks too, because it might be truncated. After checking with the OECD Statistics and Data Directorate, it appears that, in some sectors and for some pairs of countries (origin-destination), the data are not reported for confidentiality reasons. It is therefore important to keep in mind in what follows that the measures of employment and output of the foreign affiliates could be underestimated in some sectors. An indirect way to check the quality of the FATS data would be to assess the correlation of the regulations figures from the World Bank STR database with those of the FATS data in 2010 (common year of observation), which is what is pursued in the following after scanning the FATS data through some descriptive statistics.

Table 7.2 provides some descriptive statistics to give an idea about the share of foreign affiliates' activities in the Africa-4. The variables used are the share of foreign affiliates' employment in total services employment and

Table 7.2   Share of Foreign Affiliates in Total Employment and Total Value Added in the Services Sectors of Selected African Countries and Corresponding Income Groups, 1995–2014

Average annual share of foreign affiliates in total services employment and GDP (%)

Statistic	Egypt, Arab Rep.		Morocco		Nigeria		Lower-middle-income countries[a]		South Africa		Upper-middle-income countries[b]	
	Emp	Turn	Emp	Turn	Emp	Turn	Emp	Turn	Emp	Turn	Emp	Turn
Mean	0.03	0.39	0.24	2.19	0	0.79	0.02	0.72	0.30	4.75	0.14	1.55
SD	0.04	0.39	0.46	2.46	0	2.17	0.04	1.46	0.48	6.58	0.30	2.92
Min	0	0	0	0	0	0	0	0	0	0.02	0	0
Max	0.12	1.23	1.36	8.17	0.01	8.88	0.25	12.73	1.29	20.09	2.18	22.14

Sources: World Bank calculations using Foreign Affiliate Trade in Services (FATS) databases of the Organisation for Economic Co-operation and Development (OECD); the World Bank's World Development Indicators (WDI) database; and Penn World Table (PWT) 9.0 data from Feenstra, Inklaar, and Timmer 2015.

Note: For each country, the statistics are based on aggregate employment (Emp) and turnover shares (Turn) over 1995–2014 for OECD-based foreign affiliates doing business in five broad sector aggregates: energy (electricity, gas, and water supply); construction; finance and insurance; transportation and telecommunications; and other services (business, computer services, and research and development). SD = standard deviation.

a. Lower-middle-income economies (including the Arab Republic of Egypt, Morocco, and Nigeria) are those with gross national income (GNI) per capita of between $1,046 and $4,095 in 2020 (using World Bank classifications). They include all countries classified as such in the WDI database.

b. Upper-middle-income economies (including South Africa) are those with GNI per capita of between $4,096 and $12,695 in 2020 (using World Bank classifications). They include all countries classified as such in the WDI database.

the share of foreign affiliates' turnover in total services gross domestic product (GDP).[7]

The employment shares appear to be 10 times smaller than the turnover shares, which is quite surprising. This result could come from reporting biases that might be underestimating employment shares or overestimating turnover shares. The objective here is to provide insight about changes in these measures across countries and years, not to compare them per se. The analysis shows that there is a quite good correlation between employment shares and turnover shares, in logs. Both variables are considered in a systematic way to assess how they relate to the manufacturing exports of the Africa-4.

Morocco appears to outperform Egypt and Nigeria as well as all other lower-middle-income countries in the panel of recipient countries in the FATS database. South Africa also overperforms the panel's other upper-middle-income countries in its openness to foreign firms in services.

Here, a more detailed investigation is undertaken on foreign affiliates' activities over time and across sectors. Figure 7.19 begins by comparing Egypt, Morocco, Nigeria, and lower-middle-income countries, using measures based on turnover and employment. The foreign affiliates' employment at the sectoral level is not always reported for these countries or the income group; hence, there is possible underestimation.

First, we notice that Morocco outperforms lower-middle-income countries in the shares of foreign affiliates' turnover in all sectors (figure 7.19, panel a). More interestingly, Morocco appears to have the highest growth in foreign affiliate involvement over time. Second, the highest contribution to the aggregate figures for Egypt, Morocco, and lower-middle-income countries comes from the finance and insurance sector. In sharp contrast, foreign affiliates are not invested in finance in Nigeria.

Because of lack of data at the industry level for the employment figures, we can draw only sketchy conclusions. Nevertheless, where data on employment shares exist, the figures appear to be consistent with those based on turnover: we observe similar tendencies over time and across industries for Egypt and Morocco (figure 7.19, panel b).

Figure 7.20 presents the same data for South Africa and other upper-middle-income countries in the FATS database. The results are quite different across the two measures for South Africa. Although we observe a slight drop and then a dramatic increase by 2010 in foreign affiliates' involvement in terms of turnover (figure 7.20, panel a), the foreign affiliate share in employment increases at a relatively constant pace until 2010, and then it climbs by a factor of 3.5 by 2014 (figure 7.20, panel b). In both cases, the finance and insurance sector appears to be the leading force behind the increase in foreign affiliate involvement in South Africa.

Stringency of Services Regulation of Foreign Affiliates

Next, we investigate the link between regulations and the activity of foreign affiliates. More precisely, are countries with highly stringent regulations associated with limited involvement of foreign affiliates in local activities? Would the same tendencies be found for the Africa-4 countries? To conduct

Figure 7.19   Share of Foreign Affiliates' Turnover and Employment in Total Services in the Arab Republic of Egypt, Morocco, Nigeria, and Lower-Middle-Income Countries, by Broad Sector, 2002–14

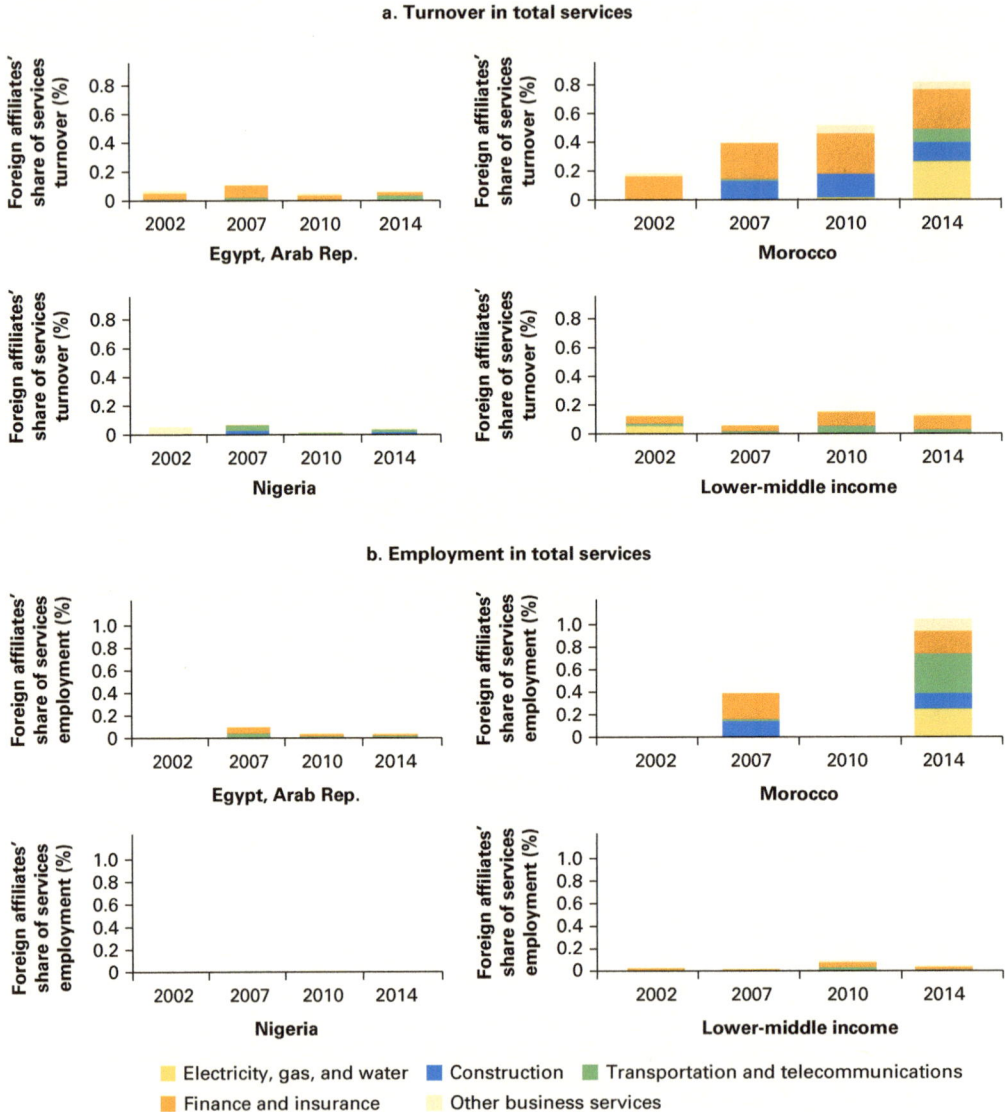

a. Turnover in total services

b. Employment in total services

Legend:
- Electricity, gas, and water
- Construction
- Transportation and telecommunications
- Finance and insurance
- Other business services

Sources: Activities of Multinational Enterprises (AMNE) and Foreign Affiliate Trade in Services (FATS) data from the Organisation for Economic Co-operation and Development (OECD); World Bank's World Development Indicators (WDI) database; Penn World Table (PWT) 9.0 data from Feenstra, Inklaar, and Timmer 2015.
Note: For each country and economy income group, the statistics are based on aggregate employment and turnover shares for OECD-based foreign affiliates doing business in five broad sector aggregates: energy (electricity, gas, and water supply); construction; finance and insurance; transportation and telecommunications; and other business services. Lower-middle-income economies (including the Arab Republic of Egypt, Morocco, and Nigeria) are those with 2017 gross national income (GNI) per capita of between $1,006 and $3,995 (using World Bank classifications). They include all countries classified as such in the WDI database.

Figure 7.20 **Share of Foreign Affiliates' Turnover and Employment in Total Services in South Africa and Upper-Middle-Income Countries, by Broad Sector, 2002–14**

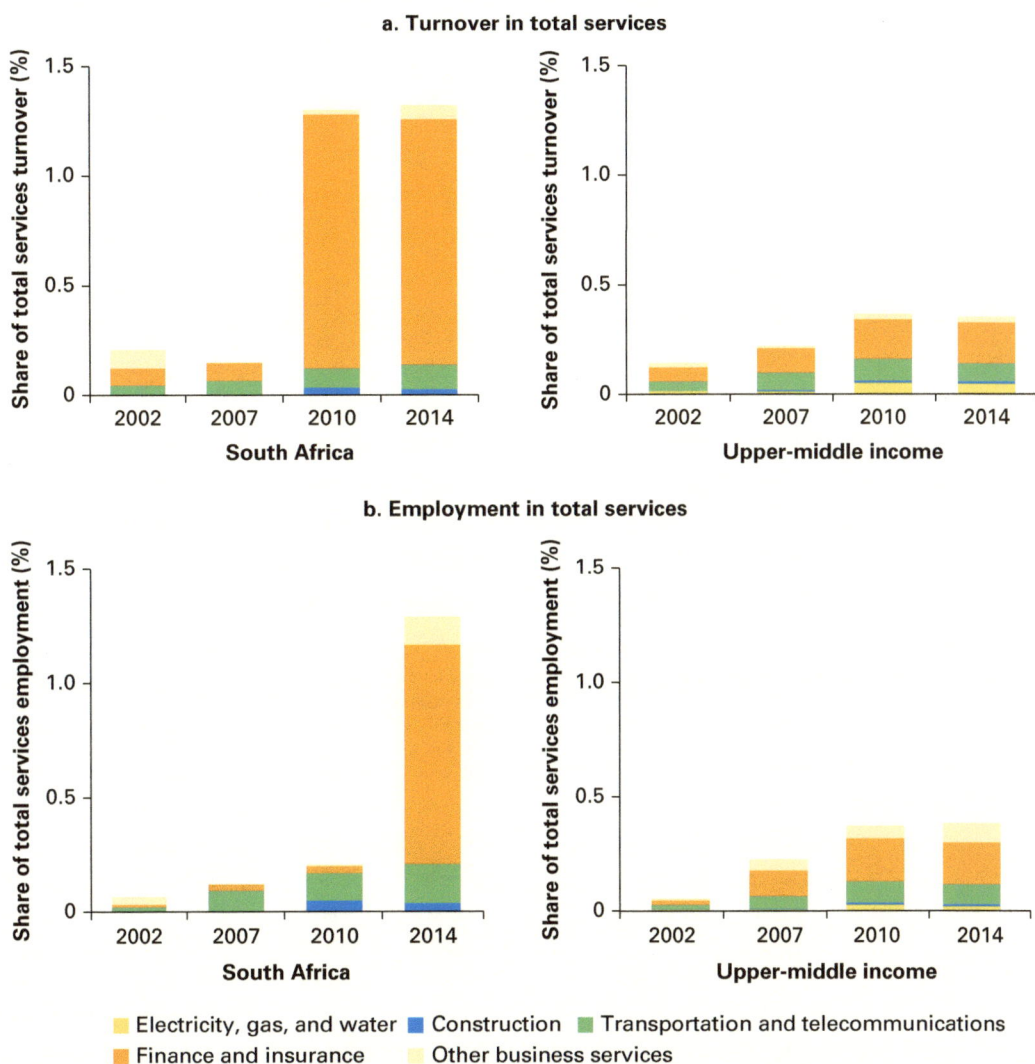

a. Turnover in total services

b. Employment in total services

Legend:
- Electricity, gas, and water
- Construction
- Transportation and telecommunications
- Finance and insurance
- Other business services

Sources: Activities of Multinational Enterprises (AMNE) and Foreign Affiliate Trade in Services (FATS) data from the Organisation for Economic Co-operation and Development (OECD); World Bank's World Development Indicators (WDI) database; Penn World Table (PWT) 9.0 data from Feenstra, Inklaar, and Timmer 2015.

Note: For each country and economy income group, the statistics are based on aggregate employment and turnover shares for OECD-based foreign affiliates doing business in five broad sector aggregates: energy (electricity, gas, and water supply); construction; finance and insurance; transportation and telecommunications; and other business services. Upper-middle-income economies (including South Africa) are those with 2017 gross national income (GNI) per capita of between $3,956 and $12,235 (using World Bank classifications). They include all countries classified as such in the WDI database.

such an analysis, we merged the STRI and FATS databases for 2010, the common year of observation.

As expected, figure 7.21 shows a quite clear and negative relationship between the foreign affiliate activities (employment and turnover) and the global measure of stringency provided by the STRI database. Morocco and,

Figure 7.21   Correlation between Services Restrictions Stringency and Foreign Affiliate Activities, 2010

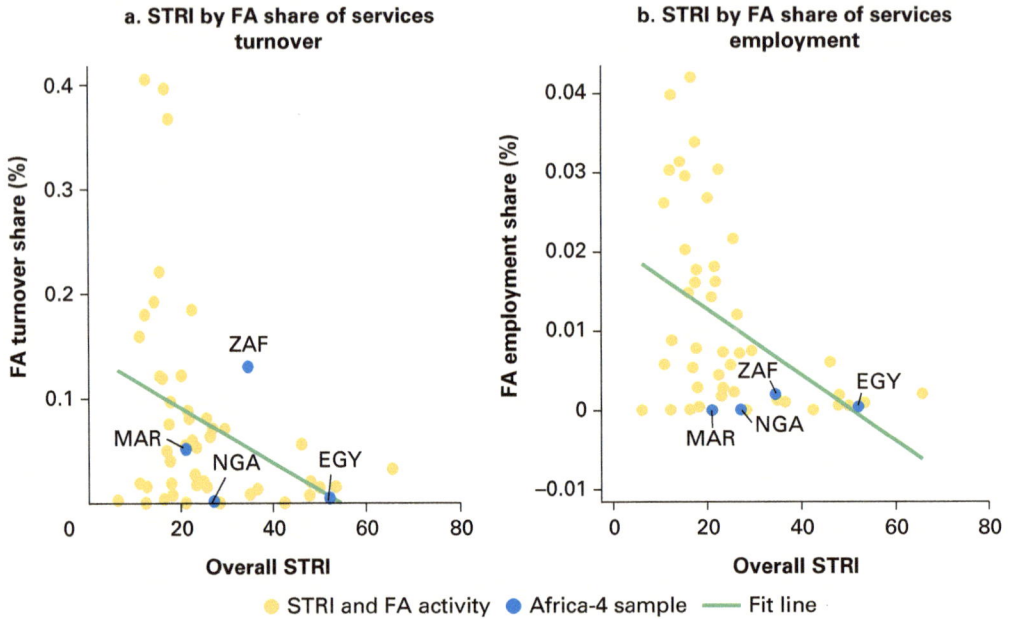

Sources: World Bank's Services Trade Restrictiveness Index (STRI) and World Development Indicators databases; Foreign Affiliate Trade in Services (FATS) database from the Organisation for Economic Co-operation and Development (OECD); Penn World Table (PWT) 9.0 data from Feenstra, Inklaar, and Timmer 2015.
Note: The STRI score ranges from 0 to 100, where 0 is completely open and 100 is completely closed to foreign services and service suppliers. The "Africa-4" countries (labeled in the scatterplots by ISO alpha-3 code) are the Arab Republic of Egypt (EGY), Morocco (MAR), Nigeria (NGA), and South Africa (ZAF). FA = foreign affiliates.

more so, Nigeria appear to have much less foreign affiliate activity than their average peers with an equal level of stringency (under the fitted line). Egypt has the most stringent regulations but turns out to be at its potential (on the fitted line) in terms of employment and turnover shares. The case of South Africa cannot be interpreted well, because the two measures (employment and turnover shares) are not consistent with each other.

Foreign Affiliates' Trade in Services and Overall Export Performance

The question here is whether foreign affiliate activities in services are associated with the patterns of exports of goods in the Africa-4 countries. To answer this question, it is important to see how changes in exports over time are associated with changes in foreign affiliate shares in services in each of the four countries. The results are shown in two ways: graphically and through regressions.

Graphical Assessment

Within-country variations in the period mean (in logs) have been computed for the foreign affiliate variables (employment shares and turnover shares in services) and linked graphically to within-country variations in the period

Figure 7.22 **Correlation between Foreign Affiliate Employment and Export Shares in Services Sectors of Four African Countries, 2001–14**

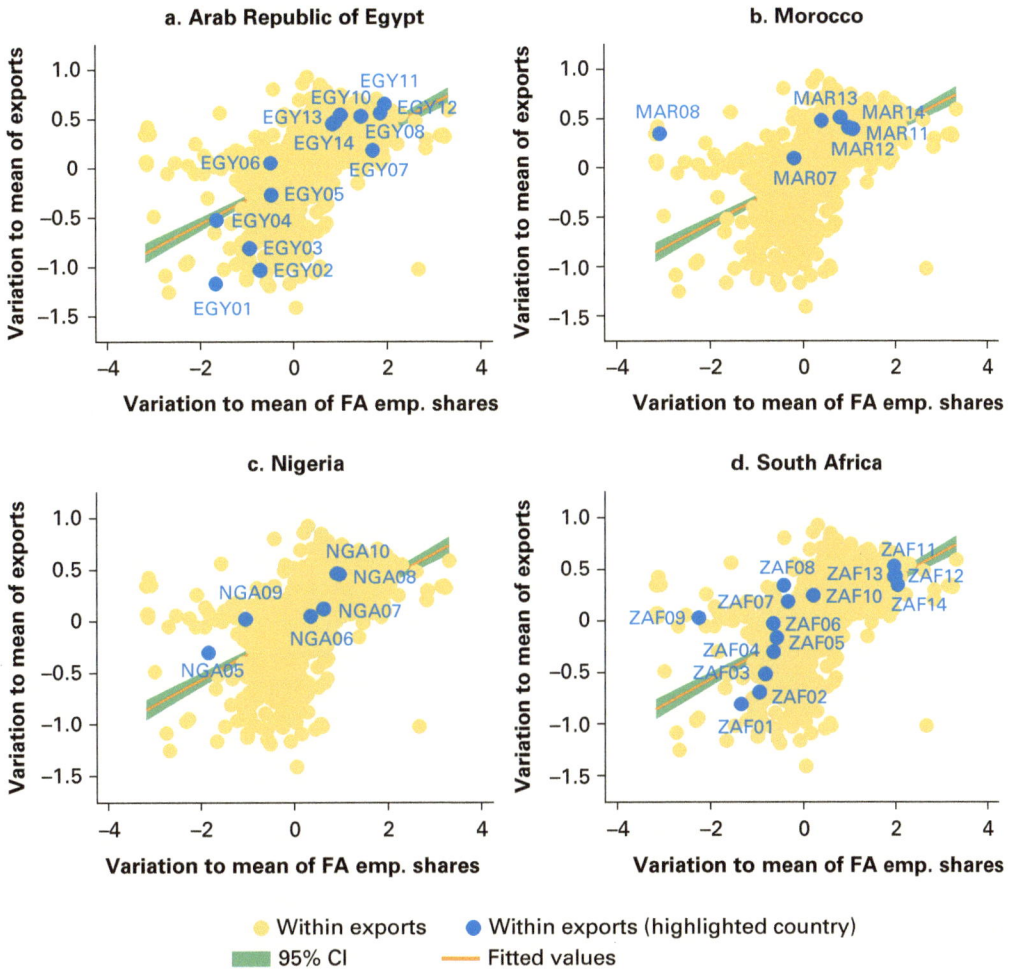

a. Arab Republic of Egypt

b. Morocco

c. Nigeria

d. South Africa

● Within exports   ● Within exports (highlighted country)
■ 95% CI   — Fitted values

Sources: Database for International Trade Analysis (BACI) of the Centre for Prospective Studies and International Information (CEPII); Foreign Affiliate Trade in Services (FATS) database of the Organisation for Economic Co-operation and Development.
Note: The "Africa-4" countries (labeled in the scatterplots by ISO alpha-3 code) are the Arab Republic of Egypt (EGY), Morocco (MAR), Nigeria (NGA), and South Africa (ZAF). CI = confidence interval; FA = foreign affiliates.

mean for exports in goods (in logs). All countries and years were considered. In figures 7.22 and 7.23, the dots for the four countries are highlighted to see whether they follow the general trend in the data set.

Figure 7.22 shows that there is an apparent positive relation between changes in foreign affiliate employment shares and changes in exports. Furthermore, at least three of the Africa-4 countries (Egypt, Nigeria, and South Africa) appear to be in line with such a tendency. The figures for Morocco are insufficiently reported for employment to make robust predictions.

Turning to the turnover indicator, figure 7.23 emphasizes a rather consistent link with figure 7.22: when considering the whole data set of countries,

Figure 7.23   Correlation between Foreign Affiliate Turnover Shares in Services and Exports of Four African Countries

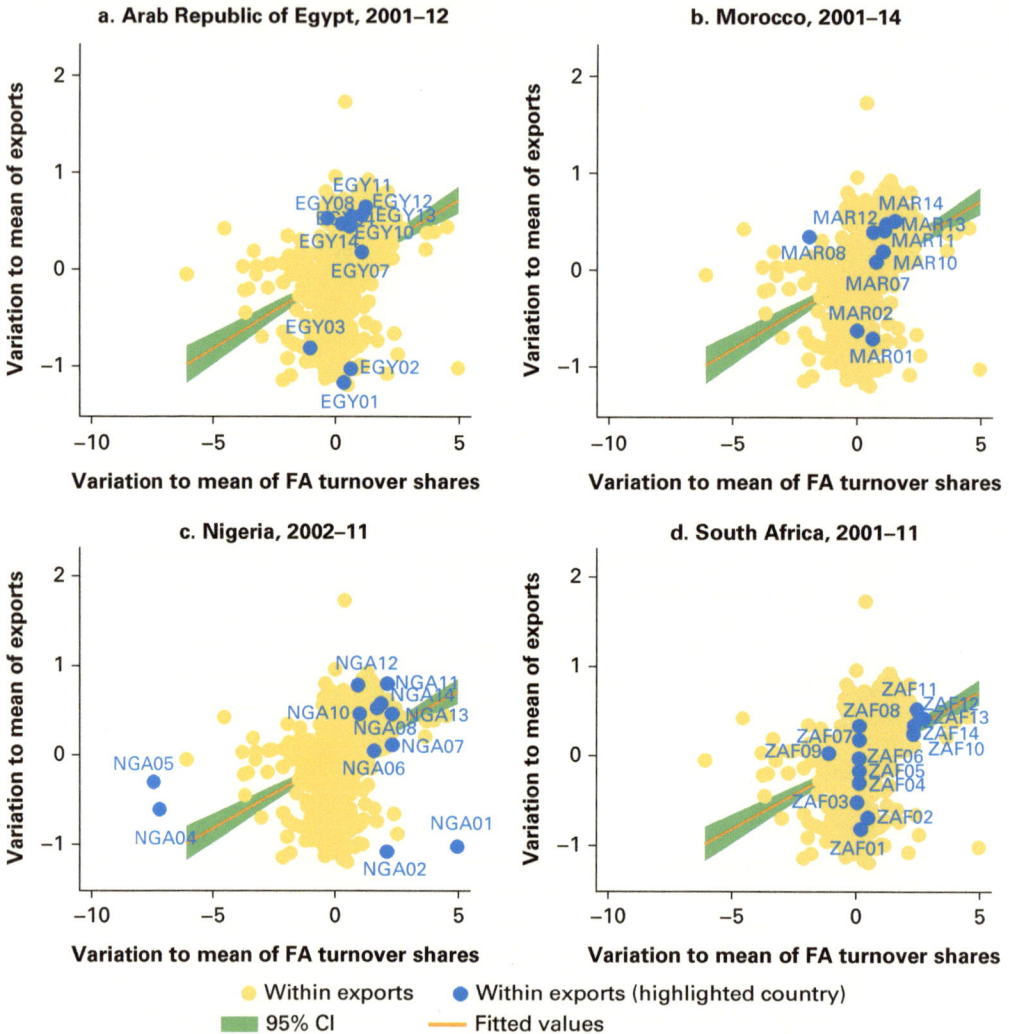

a. Arab Republic of Egypt, 2001–12

b. Morocco, 2001–14

c. Nigeria, 2002–11

d. South Africa, 2001–11

● Within exports   ● Within exports (highlighted country)
▬ 95% CI   ── Fitted values

Sources: Database for International Trade Analysis (BACI) of the Centre for Prospective Studies and International Information (CEPII); Foreign Affiliate Trade in Services (FATS) database of the Organisation for Economic Co-operation and Development.

Note: Panel values are the within-country variations to the period mean (in logs). The "Africa-4" countries (labeled in the scatterplots by ISO alpha-3 code) are the Arab Republic of Egypt (EGY), Morocco (MAR), Nigeria (NGA), and South Africa (ZAF). CI = confidence interval; FA = foreign affiliates.

higher involvement of foreign affiliates in services, as measured by their share of a country's total services turnover, results in higher exports. Nevertheless, when highlighting each of the four countries, the data are no longer as clear. The same conclusion prevails when looking at the link between changes in exports and changes in turnover shares by Broad Economic Categories of products.[8]

Econometric Assessment

Econometric regressions are undertaken to try to infer the link between exports of goods and foreign affiliate activities in core services, and to assess the intensity of the link, while controlling for other measures that affect exports. The link is expected to be more effective when the contribution of the core service infrastructure delivered by the foreign affiliates is more important in total inputs expenses.

Thus, the series of equations to be tested is represented by the following form:

$$\ln X_{ist} = a. \ln Market\_potential_{i,t} + b. \ln GDP_{i,t}$$
$$+ c. \ln(w_{i,s,t} . FA\ share_{i,t}) + \lambda_{i,s,t} + u_{ist}, \tag{7.1}$$

where X represents exports (obtained from the Database for International Trade Analysis [BACI] of the Centre for Prospective Studies and International Information [CEPII]) for each observed country i and aggregated at the level of the manufacturing sector provided by the International Standard Industrial Classification (ISIC) nomenclature (around 20 manufacturing sectors, indexed by s). The data are for 1995–2014. The variable $Market\_potential = \Sigma_j GDP_{jt}/dist_{ij}$ is the relevant demand addressed to country i. More important, the variable $FA\ share_{it}$ represents the foreign affiliates' share in total services in country i obtained from the OECD.

Alternatively, we use two measures of foreign affiliate importance in core services—the first computed in terms of employment and the second in terms of turnover. The *foreign share* alternative variables interact with the weight $w_{i,s,t}$, representing the share of expenses in core inputs with respect to total inputs used by the industry. These weights are derived from the input-output delivered by the OECD Database for STructural ANalysis (STAN) for each ISIC sector.[9] Finally, $\lambda_{[i,s,t]}$ designates the series of fixed effects capturing, alternatively, country, industry, and time unobservables or combinations of these.

Table 7.3 presents the results for the exports equation, using the first measure accounting for the importance of foreign affiliates (that is, based on employment).

In table 7.3, columns (1) to (6) are alternative specifications assessing the contribution of foreign affiliates in core services (based on their employment share) to manufacturing exports. Column (1) is the output of a basic equation linking the industrial exports of each of the four countries, over time, to market potential and the GDP of the observed country using a first series of fixed effects (industry effects, λ_s, and country fixed effects, λ_i). Market potential and GDP enter with the expected positive and statistically significant signs. But because these measures are in two dimensions (year and country) and because the country dimension is small (four countries in the data set), the values and signs of these effects do not hold up to the inclusion of different combinations of sets of fixed effects (compare the results in table 7.3, across columns [2] to [6]).

Table 7.3 Estimations of the Impact of Foreign Affiliates in Core Services on Exports of Goods in the Africa-4 Sample, Using the Employment-Related Definition of the Foreign Affiliates Services Linkage

Variable	(1)	(2)	(3)	(4)	(5)	(6)
ln(Market Potential i)	1.023***	−0.726	−1.719	−2.273	−2.299***	
	(0.295)	(1.429)	(2.173)	(2.178)	(0.789)	
ln(GDP i)	0.513***	0.569***	0.332	0.231	0.214*	
	(0.184)	(0.200)	(0.288)	(0.278)	(0.115)	
ln(foreign affiliates core services share in total employment)			0.161**			
			(0.073)			
Foreign affiliates services linkage measure (employment definition)				0.238**	0.145**	0.131
				(0.106)	(0.058)	(0.142)
Observations	952	952	663	663	663	663
R^2	0.703	0.706	0.726	0.727	0.956	0.784
Year FE		Yes	Yes	Yes	Yes	
Industry FE	Yes	Yes	Yes	Yes		
Exporter FE	Yes	Yes	Yes	Yes		
Exporter x Industry FE					Yes	Yes
Year x Industry FE					Yes	Yes

Source: World Bank calculations.
Note: Robust standard errors are in parentheses. The Africa-4 countries are the Arab Republic of Egypt, Morocco, Nigeria, and South Africa. FE = fixed effects; i = country *i*; ln = natural logarithm.
* $p < 0.10$; ** $p < 0.05$; *** $p < 0.01$.

The inclusion of alternative sets of fixed effects provokes some multicollinearity among these measures. For instance, it appears that, when allowing for additional year fixed effects (column [2]), the market potential becomes insignificant. This is because the market potential variable for these countries varies much more across the time dimension and much less across the country dimension. In column (3), the share of foreign affiliates in core services employment enters the equation without interacting it with the weight of the core services in total services. An increase in the share of foreign affiliates in core services happens to be positively associated with higher manufacturing exports. But, to identify this effect, this measure must be interacted with the relative use of those services in each industry, which is presented in column (4). Here, with the same set of fixed effects as in the prior specification, the point estimate on the foreign affiliate core services linkage measure (interaction measure) is higher and still statistically significant at the 5 percent level.

In table 7.3, column (5), we replace independent exporter and industry effects by (exporter × industry) pairs. The idea is to see whether we can still identify a positive association of foreign affiliate involvement in core services to exports through the input-output linkage, within pairs of industries and countries. Although the positive magnitude of the point estimate is smaller, it is still comparable to that of the specification in column (4) when accounting for confidence intervals, and it is still statistically significant. It is only when introducing exporter × industry effects together with time × industry effects that the statistical significance disappears, with a point estimate that is still comparable in magnitude, and when accounting for confidence intervals.

Table 7.4 reproduces the most important specifications in table 7.3 while using the alternative turnover measure of foreign affiliate core services linkages instead of the employment-related one. In table 7.4, column (1), the share of foreign affiliates in turnover terms is introduced without interacting

Table 7.4 Estimations of the Impact of Foreign Affiliates in Core Services on Exports of Goods in Africa-4 Sample, Using the Turnover-Related Definition of the Foreign Affiliates Services Linkage

Variable	(1)	(2)	(3)
ln(Market Potential i)	−1.415	−1.312	
	(1.915)	(1.906)	
ln(GDP i)	0.711***	0.704***	
	(0.223)	(0.222)	
ln(foreign affiliates core services share in total turnover)	0.048		
	(0.033)		
Foreign affiliates services linkage measure (turnover definition)		**0.357***	**0.415**
		(0.084)	**(0.162)**
Observations	765	765	748
R^2	0.714	0.720	0.751
Year FE	Yes	Yes	
Industry FE	Yes	Yes	
Exporter FE	Yes	Yes	
Exporter x Industry FE			Yes
Year x Industry FE			Yes

Source: World Bank calculations.
Note: Robust standard errors are in parentheses. The Africa-4 countries are the Arab Republic of Egypt, Morocco, Nigeria, and South Africa. FE = fixed effects; i = country *i*; ln = natural logarithm.
* $p < 0.10$; ** $p < 0.05$; *** $p < 0.01$.

it with the weight term. Table 7.4, column (1), should be compared with table 7.3, column (3). Here, although the point estimate is positive, it is small in magnitude (now closer to 0) and statistically insignificant. But, when interacting with the weights of core services in total inputs used (table 7.4, column [2]), the related point estimate appears to be much larger and statistically significant at the 1 percent level. Although it is a bit higher than what is shown in the counterpart (table 7.3, column [4]), this effect still compares to the latter in terms of order of magnitude, which is reassuring. Table 7.4, column (3), reproduces table 7.3, column (6), with a more demanding specification (that is, exporter × industry effects together with time × industry effects). The point estimate obtained is now about an average magnitude of 0.41, and it is still statistically significant at the 5 percent level.

All these results point to a reasonably probable positive effect of the contribution of foreign affiliates in core services to increased manufacturing exports for the four African countries that are studied.

However, it might be expected that freeing up services would affect some categories of goods differently from others, by making some goods that are more in need of those services relatively cheaper to produce. Or it might be that the availability of some core services incentivizes the establishment of businesses in some sectors more than others, or even incentivizes a switch from low-value-added sectors (where the efficiency of some of these services might not be so important) to some higher-value-added sectors (where the efficiency and quality are important enough). Thus, a series of regressions is run across different types of sector categories, where it is then left to the test to inform about whether the magnitudes of the effects on exports differ across categories (Coulibaly and Mirza 2017). We have split the industries into four categories: industries producing mostly primary products, labor-intensive industries, capital-intensive industries, and industries producing rather sophisticated products.

Beginning with the sectors producing mostly primary products and focusing on the variables of interest (foreign affiliates in core services employment share linkage and foreign affiliates in core services turnover share alternatively), it is interesting that the results are consistent, at least in sign and significance across the two variables. In particular, the average point estimate of foreign affiliate involvement appears to be positive for primary goods exports. A look at the interaction terms indicates that Egypt and Nigeria (estimates around 1.10) and, to lesser extent, South Africa (0.41) are gaining in terms of exports of primary goods that use services from foreign affiliates. In contrast, in Morocco, foreign affiliate involvement in services does not seem to increase exports of primary products.

Moving to the labor-intensive sectors sample, again the overall impact of foreign affiliate involvement in the sample is positive and statistically significant for the employment and turnover measures. Nevertheless, the point estimates across specifications and interaction terms are smaller in magnitude for this sample compared with the primary products sample. The estimated effects for the Africa-4 countries are consistent in sign but not always in significance across the two measures.

For instance, Egypt appears again with an estimate that is positive and statistically significant for the employment share in services, whereas South Africa has a negative and statistically significant coefficient (foreign affiliates' involvement reduces exports of labor-intensive industries). In the case of South Africa, the negative coefficient is consistent with a change in the specialization story away from labor-intensive industries and toward other industries. For Morocco, the effect is small and statistically insignificant across both measures (employment-related versus turnover-related). Finally, the point estimate measured for Nigeria is not robust across either measure (employment-related versus turnover-related).

Surprisingly, the results for the capital-intensive sectors seem to show that, by and large, capital-intensive industries do not appear to benefit from foreign affiliates in core services for three of the four countries. This is particularly clear for Morocco and South Africa. For Egypt, there appears to be a positive and statistically significant effect when using only one of the alternative measures. Nigeria is the only country that seems to benefit from foreign affiliates in core services, but the point estimates are only weakly statistically significant at the 10 percent level, across the two measures.

All these results seem to point to an important effect when measured on average for all the countries, but the point estimates by country are not robustly statistically significant across the two measures.

Policy Implications

This analysis is exploratory, given the poor coverage of African countries in the OECD FATS data as well as missing or truncated information, which most likely leads to underestimating the presence of foreign affiliates in core services sectors. However, to date, the analysis provides the most systematic estimations of the impacts of the presence of foreign affiliates in core services sectors such as finance, transportation, telecommunications, and professional services on the export performance of a few African countries. By focusing on the Broad Economic Categories of exports data for the African countries covered in the FATS data (Egypt, Morocco, Nigeria, and South Africa), the study rigorously estimates the impacts of foreign affiliate activities (measured as their shares of employment and turnover in total services) on the expansion, contraction, or shift of exports across different types of sectors.

The estimation results are summarized as follows:

- *Labor-intensive sectors* do not seem to benefit from the presence of foreign affiliates. For South Africa, the presence of foreign affiliates in these sectors even tends to have a negative effect on their performance in sales and employment.
- *Nigeria* appears to benefit significantly (in terms of sales and employment) from the presence of foreign affiliates in services in most sectors (primary, capital-intensive, and high-technology goods).
- *Egypt* also appears to benefit along the two dimensions (sales and employment) but to a lesser extent than Nigeria and mostly in primary and labor-intensive sectors.

- *South Africa* shows mixed results, with positive and significant effects obtained only for the employment measure, in primary and high-tech sectors.
- *Morocco* shows mostly statistically insignificant results, whichever measure is used and across the types of sectors considered.

Given Nigeria's relatively higher restrictions in these core services (according to the STRI scores), their full liberalization could attract more efficient, world-class foreign affiliates in these sectors and decisively boost the country's effort to diversify its economy. In Morocco, which is already at an advanced stage of liberalization, the presence of foreign affiliates in recent years does not seem to be bringing more benefits for the competitiveness of its manufacturing industries as a whole. More research is needed to understand the reasons behind this surprising result. In Egypt, foreign affiliates in core services appear to benefit manufacturing but not necessarily to switch to more sophisticated products. Instead, they have been increasing mostly exports of primary and labor-intensive sectors. In South Africa, foreign affiliate activities in these core services appear to have some impact on the exports of primary and high-value-added sectors, at the expense of labor-intensive sectors.

What Will It Take for Africa to Create Regional Value Chains?

The external context is currently extremely challenging, with growth slowing in major economies like China, the EU, and the US, which constrains global demand. This is happening in a context of increasing protectionism rhetoric between China and the United States and, to some extent, the EU. The lingering and intensifying trade tensions are disrupting regional and global value chains that have been the hallmark of the recent rapid global trade expansion. Because the rising protectionism rhetoric is mostly a China/EU/US affair, Sub-Saharan African countries have a unique opportunity to intensify and deepen their regional integration and diversify their global integration to take advantage of the trade and investment diversion opportunities created by the trade tensions.

World Development Report 2009: Reshaping Economic Geography concludes with a compelling message on how Sub-Saharan Africa should promote economic development: combine *regional integration* as a mechanism to increase local supply capacity with *global integration* to improve access to markets and suppliers (World Bank 2009). Regional integration can be rooted in the traditional economic and sociocultural interactions within natural neighborhoods, as building blocks for broader integration where trust can be built on common history and shared language and culture. Three Sub-Saharan African regional economic communities appear to be good candidates for natural neighborhoods: the Common Market for Eastern and Southern Africa (COMESA), the Economic Community of West African States (ECOWAS), and the Southern African Development Community (SADC).

However, the economic benefits of deepening regional integration in view of increasing access to global markets would accrue disproportionately to the leading countries in each of these regional economic communities. For regional integration to work best, these leading countries need to take the lead in the integration process. Ethiopia, Nigeria, and South Africa—being the natural leaders of COMESA, ECOWAS, and SADC, respectively, given their sizes (population and GDP)—might have a key role to play in fostering regional production networks throughout Sub-Saharan Africa (box 7.1).

The 2018 World Bank report, "Reinvigorating Growth in Resource-Rich Sub-Saharan Africa," expanded on this idea by suggesting that the region

---

Box 7.1   Diversifying Production through Regional Cooperation

Diversifying an economy is no easy task. Initial phases of diversification in lower-middle-income African economies should rely significantly on strengthening and upgrading existing production and export capabilities from which countries can continuously expand into related higher-value activities. Hence, there is a need for a policy of intensive diversification that builds on existing capabilities.

The alternative—required at higher incomes or in response to even lower-cost competitors—is to jump to higher-value production activities. Even if a country is lucky enough to have such activities close to its production base, the jump remains costly and risky. It may require an available pool of facilities and infrastructures, including physical infrastructure; specific human capital; particular expertise on the demand and tastes of destination markets; and easy, cheap access to specific inputs.

These initial investment needs can be facilitated by foreign direct investment (FDI) inflows. Regional cooperation by providing economies of scale in production and larger markets increases the region's attractiveness to FDI. In addition, cooperation can provide an outlet for intermediate goods producers who sell to innovating firms elsewhere in the neighborhood.

When Sub-Saharan African exports from 1980 to 2004 are mapped against a global product space of some 800 products (4-digit industries), the Central African Economic and Monetary Community (CEMAC) appears to have only a few options for diversification (wood and its manufactures). Members of the East African Community (EAC) have more options because their exports are more diversified (fruits and vegetables, prepared food, fish, wood and its manufactures, cotton, textiles, low-tech manufactures, metallic products, chemicals, and minerals). Other countries with similar production structures have diversified into such clusters as cotton, textiles, and garments, which currently enjoy preferences under the African Growth and Opportunity Act (AGOA) in the US market. Southern African Customs Union (SACU) members, except South Africa, can gain significantly more than countries in other unions from cooperation in natural resource–based and manufacturing clusters, because they have much easier diversification options driven by the logistics, finance, skills, and infrastructure that reflect their middle-income status.

The volume and diversity of exports grow when countries cooperate regionally in terms of economies of scale, greater factor mobility, and lower transportation costs. To achieve this, there is a need to identify industries or sectors of economic activity—and the associated sector-specific infrastructure—to integrate regional markets with improved access to inputs and markets as well as easier mobility of factors (including labor), enabling a more efficient allocation of resources. That effort can complement the general areas of cooperation in regional infrastructure, better business regulations, and a strong judicial system.

Source: World Bank 2009.

consider several lessons from the development experience of many East Asian countries (Izvorski, Coulibaly, and Doumbia 2018):

- Use the advantage of low labor costs and a large domestic labor force that is perhaps just moving out of agriculture in search of employment.
- Provide political and macroeconomic stability.
- Work closely with foreign investors to arrange for better local infrastructure and access to export routes.

These policy lessons are actionable recommendations for national governments in many areas—particularly in their emphasis on bolstering investment in infrastructure and human capital and improving market and government institutions. Reinvigorating growth in resource-rich Africa will depend crucially on countries' ability to integrate regionally and hence work in common to overcome the burdens of low density, thick borders, and long distances.

The parallel with the Tigers of East Asia and the next generation of Asian countries is important. The Republic of Korea and Taiwan, China, which have large populations and sizable domestic markets, integrated globally first. They took advantage of the unique international landscape after World War II and into the 1980s, which was characterized by segmentation of countries with endowments of low-cost and high-cost labor, gradual trade integration, fixed exchange rates, and managed capital flows; dedicated US investments that helped shift manufacturing to East Asia; and a robust US security umbrella that contained enmities and fostered trade. For the Asian Tigers, integrating regionally was not practical or politically feasible until the late 1970s. The next generation of East Asian countries to rise economically, such as Malaysia and Thailand, integrated regionally and globally on the basis of a consistent platform of WTO accession and joining the many production chains that started or ended in the Tigers and then shifted to China. East Asia also benefited from abundant, low-cost labor either moving out of agriculture or planning to make the transition.

The current rapid technological advances are producing skill- and capital-biased globalization that creates unique challenges for resource-rich Sub-Saharan Africa. Global integration of the region is a must, including through the WTO and by leveraging the AfCFTA. Regional integration must proceed even more forcefully because, except for Ethiopia, Nigeria, and South Africa, the countries in Sub-Saharan Africa have smaller populations, smaller markets, and a smaller middle class than countries in other regions, and they have few attractive investment options that often require scale. Opening the borders will allow positive spillovers from the sectors in which these countries have a competitive advantage. It will also allow the regional champions to intensify trade with their neighbors through the establishment of regional production networks, to build bigger markets, and to access regional and global production networks aside from those in commodities.

Some Regional Policy Options to Complement the AfCFTA

Compared with the rest of the world, African countries levy higher tariffs. But "traditional" NTMs, especially SPS/TBT restrictions, are often lower in Africa than in other regions. In general, low-income countries, including those in Africa, adopt traditional NTMs less often than high-income countries do. Still, a significant number of other barriers can be categorized as nontariff that restrict trade within the region. These include inadequate infrastructure, cumbersome customs procedures, higher transportation costs, high fragmentation, thick borders, poor coordination between and within country agencies, and a multiplicity of cross-border regulations.

More stringent NTMs restrict the growth of intraregional trade as well as imports of the essential intermediate and capital goods that are required for actively engaging in regional and global value chains. In exporting to the markets of high-income countries, African countries especially face restrictive NTMs, the most predominant of which are SPS/TBT. However, Africa's NTMs are not as restrictive as those in other regions like Europe and North America. Market access for African exports in high-income countries is restricted more by NTMs than by tariffs. Effectively, NTMs pose even higher barriers to exports because some measures, like certification and standards requirements, are costlier to fulfill for African countries than for other, more-developed partners. A joint UNCTAD–World Bank study (2018) finds that NTMs hurt low-income countries (including those in Africa) disproportionately because of the relatively higher prevalence of NTMs in sectors of export interest to these economies (such as agriculture and apparel) and the lower capacity of firms in low-income countries to comply with such requirements.

As for trade within the region, NTMs in agriculture are very restrictive, even compared with those in other sectors, including manufacturing, where tariff barriers are significantly higher. Although agriculture remains a key source for jump-starting growth and development by initiating and strengthening new and existing value chains, this sector has been restricted by the high trade costs associated with NTMs. The AfCFTA could provide the much-needed impetus to reinforce cooperation to address these challenges, but, for the AfCFTA to succeed, countries must reduce these barriers.

Among other actions, reduction of NTMs should be a prominent consideration in national and regional trade reforms because they pose the biggest barriers to trade, particularly for trade within the region. By minimizing the distortions of tariffs and NTMs, Sub-Saharan African countries can provide more opportunities for their farms and firms to participate in regional and global value chains through increased integration, as is well-articulated in the AfCFTA and existing regional economic communities.

Addressing these challenges also requires stronger cooperation between neighboring countries to enlarge markets so they attract foreign investors, to secure access to critical intermediate goods, and to make the leap to new products less costly and risky. By looking at which sector offers the most promise for further development, countries in a neighborhood can focus cooperation on sector-specific infrastructure (such as common standards, compliance and metrology systems) as well as specific curricula to build a skilled labor force and adapt new technologies. For example, given their comparative advantage, WAEMU countries can benefit from cooperation in specific production sectors—fruits and vegetables and their products, wood and its manufactures, cotton, low-tech manufactures, chemicals, and minerals—and reduce their overdependence on traditional agricultural exports such as coffee and cocoa.

What conditions would facilitate the fruitful participation of Sub-Saharan African firms in GVCs, and to what extent are these conditions under the influence of government policy? What must be done to reap the full benefits from GVCs? And how can we manage the negative consequences that may be associated with GVC activity? *World Development Report 2020: Trading for Development in the Age of Global Value Chains* examines in detail the drivers of GVC participation and lays out some key policy options that could complement the AfCFTA's entry into force (World Bank 2020):

- First, because market size matters, countries should liberalize trade to expand their markets and promote their participation in GVCs.
- Second, because geography matters, countries should overcome remoteness by improving their connectivity and lowering trade costs.
- Third, because institutional quality matters, countries should use deep preferential trade agreements to improve the rule of law and step up contract enforcement. GVCs thrive on the flexible formation of networks of firms.
- Fourth, because endowments matter, countries should promote foreign investment and upgrade capabilities.

Special economic zones could also be a successful addition when they address specific market failures. However, even in a restricted area, getting the conditions right requires careful planning and implementation to ensure that the needed resources—such as labor, land, water, electricity, and telecommunications—are readily available, regulatory barriers are minimized, and connectivity is seamless. Communication with businesses in the targeted sectors is critical to ensure that the zone meets their needs. However, special economic zones cannot address all investor concerns such as political or macroeconomic stability. For example, a volatile exchange rate will affect investors inside and outside the zone.

To succeed, African countries must be integrated into world markets. Despite some progress in recent years, Sub-Saharan African countries still have heavy barriers around their borders, which exacerbates the fragmentation inherited from colonization and makes Africa the continent most prone to ethnic-based conflicts. What policies can help overcome the triple disadvantage of low economic density, long distance to world and regional markets, and thick borders? The development experience of East Asia and Pacific and recently South Asia makes the answer clear: use the advantage of low labor costs and a large domestic labor force, perhaps just moving out of agriculture in search of employment; provide political and macroeconomic stability; and work closely with foreign investors to arrange for better local infrastructure and access to export routes. These policy lessons are actionable recommendations for national governments in many areas, such as the emphasis on bolstering investment in infrastructure and human capital and improving market and government institutions.

Finally, an initiative that can complement the AfCFTA to speed the integration of the countries in Sub-Saharan Africa would be to make Africa's leading regional economic communities more vibrant. This could be done by granting all the countries in regional groupings such as ECOWAS, COMESA, and the SADC preferential access to leading world markets with attractive rules of origin, conditional on their taking the lead in promoting regional production networks in competitive sectors in West, Southern, Central, and East Africa. This effort might require revisiting the US African Growth and Opportunity Act and the EU's Everything but Arms program—two preferential agreements that have been available to some LMICs since 2001. In the spirit of the G-20 Compact with Africa, a complementary aid-for-trade initiative could help bolster investment in sectors other than natural resources, to build up non-resource exports from African countries.

Notes

1. GVC participation is measured by the share of trade that crosses at least two borders (Borin and Mancini 2019). It is composed of two key indicators: *backward GVC participation* (the share of foreign value-added content of exports in the economy's total gross exports) and *forward GVC participation* (the share of domestic value added sent to third economies in the economy's total gross exports). "Foreign value-added content of exports" refers to the value added of inputs that were imported to produce intermediate or final goods or services to be exported. "Domestic value added" is contained in intermediate goods or services exported to a partner economy that reexports them to a third economy as embodied in other products.
2. "North America" follows the World Bank's regional definition, comprising Bermuda, Canada, and the United States.
3. The 15 Sub-Saharan African countries covered are Benin, Burkina Faso, Cabo Verde, Cameroon, Côte d'Ivoire, Ethiopia, The Gambia, Ghana, Liberia, Mali, Mauritania, Niger, Nigeria, Senegal, and Togo.
4. This discussion excludes the AfCFTA, which came into operation in 2021 and is not reflected in the data, which are for 2011–15 in this study.
5. Trade in services is defined as the supply of a service through four modes, only three of which are discussed here, numbered by the General Agreement of Trade in Services (GATS) of the World Trade

Organization (WTO) as follows: (1) cross-border supply of services (that is, from one economy's territory to another's); (3) commercial presence (by a service supplier of one economy that establishes business in the territory of another economy); and (4) presence of natural persons (that is, when a service supplier sends an individual abroad to provide the service).

6. The FATS database has been replaced since 2008 by the Activity of Multinational Enterprises (AMNE) database, which groups together statistics on foreign affiliates in services and manufacturing. Here, only the data on services from AMNE are used, which is why the data are still called FATS in this study.

7. The denominators, total services employment and total services GDP, are calculated by the authors through the help of two sources, the World Bank's World Development Indicators (WDI) and the Penn World Table (PWT). The WDI data provide the percentage share of services in total GDP and percentage share of services employment in total employment. Multiplying by the total GDP of a country from WDI yields the services GDP value. And multiplying the share of employment in services by total employment from PWT yields the number of employees in the services sectors. Ideally, it would have been preferable to have the same data but only for the services in which we are interested. But, to our knowledge, the data are not readily available for these countries.

8. The figures for changes in exports and in turnover shares by Broad Economic Category are available upon request.

9. The United Nations delivers data on the input-output matrix for Morocco and South Africa from 1995 to 2011. Because we do not have access to input-output data for Egypt and Nigeria, we applied Morocco's input-output matrix to the two countries. We also applied 2011 w figures to the 2012–14 period.

References

Arnold, J. M., B. S. Javorcik, and A. Mattoo. 2011. "Does Services Liberalization Benefit Manufacturing Firms? Evidence from the Czech Republic." *Journal of International Economics* 85 (1): 136–46.

Arnold, J. M., B. Javorcik, M. Lipscomb, and A. Mattoo. 2016. "Services Reform and Manufacturing Performance: Evidence from India." *Economic Journal* 126 (590): 1–39.

Beverelli, C., M. Fiorini, and B. Hoekman. 2017. "Services Trade Policy and Manufacturing Productivity: The Role of Institutions." *Journal of International Economics* 104: 166–82.

Borchert, I., S. Gootiiz, and A. Mattoo. 2014. "Policy Barriers to International Trade in Services: Evidence from a New Database." *World Bank Economic Review* 28 (1): 162–88.

Borin, A., and M. Mancini. 2019. "Measuring What Matters in Global Value Chains and Value-Added Trade." Policy Research Working Paper 8804, World Bank, Washington, DC.

Coulibaly, Souleymane, and Daniel Mirza. 2017. "Liberalization of Infrastructure Services and Export Goods: A Focus on Four African Countries Using FATS Data." Unpublished working paper, World Bank, Washington, DC.

Duggan, V., S. Rahardja, and G. Varela. 2013. "Service Sector Reform and Manufacturing Productivity: Evidence from Indonesia." Policy Research Working Paper 6349, World Bank, Washington, DC.

Ehrich, M., B. Brümmer, and I. Martínez-Zarzoso. 2015. "Do Food Standards Enhance the Concentration of Food Export Markets? A Quantile Regression Approach." Paper presented at the European Trade Study Group 17th Annual Conference, Paris, September 10–12.

Feenstra, R. C., R. Inklaar, and M. P. Timmer. 2015. "The Next Generation of the Penn World Table." *American Economic Review* 105 (10): 3150–82.

Francois, J., and B. Hoekman. 2010. "Services Trade and Policy." *Journal of Economic Literature* 48 (3): 642–92.

Hausmann, R., and D. Rodrik. 2003. "Economic Development as Self-Discovery." *Journal of Development Economics* 72 (2): 603–33.

Hidalgo, C. A., B. Klinger, A. L. Barabási, and R. Hausmann. 2007. "The Product Space Conditions for the Development of Nations." *Science* 317 (5837): 482–87.

Hoekman, B., and B. Shepherd. 2015. "Services Productivity, Trade Policy and Manufacturing Exports." *World Economy* 40 (3): 499–516.

Izvorski, I., S. Coulibaly, and D. Doumbia. 2018. "Reinvigorating Growth in Resource-Rich Sub-Saharan Africa." Report No. 129775, World Bank, Washington, DC.

Kee, H. L., and A. Nicita. 2016. "Trade Frauds, Trade Elasticities and Non-Tariff Measures." Unpublished manuscript, World Bank, Washington, DC.

OECD (Organisation for Economic Co-operation and Development). 2021. "OECD Services Trade Restrictiveness Index." Trade Policy Brief, February 2021, OECD, Paris.

UNCTAD (United Nations Conference on Trade and Development). 2015. *International Classification of Non-Tariff Measures, 2012 Version.* Geneva: UNCTAD.

UNCTAD (United Nations Conference on Trade and Development) and World Bank. 2018. "The Unseen Impact of Non-Tariff Measures: Insights from a New Database." Report, UNCTAD and World Bank, Geneva.

World Bank. 2009. *World Development Report 2009: Reshaping Economic Geography.* Washington, DC: World Bank.

World Bank. 2020. *World Development Report 2020: Trading for Development in the Age of Global Value Chains.* Washington, DC: World Bank.

www.ingramcontent.com/pod-product-compliance
Lightning Source LLC
Chambersburg PA
CBHW050519240326
41598CB00086B/118